Radial Basis Function Networks 2

Studies in Fuzziness and Soft Computing

Editor-in-chief
Prof. Janusz Kacprzyk
Systems Research Institute
Polish Academy of Sciences
ul. Newelska 6
01-447 Warsaw, Poland
E-mail: kacprzyk@ibspan.waw.pl
http://www.springer.de/cgi-bin/search_book.pl?series=2941

Further volumes of this series can be found at our homepage.

Vol. 45. N. Kasabov (Ed.)
Future Directions for Intelligent Information Systems on Information Sciences, 2000
ISBN 3-7908-1276-5

Vol. 46. J.N. Mordeson and P.S. Nair
Fuzzy Graphs and Fuzzy Hypergraphs, 2000
ISBN 3-7908-1286-2

Vol. 47. E. Czogała† and J. Łęski
Fuzzy and Neuro-Fuzzy Intelligent Systems, 2000
ISBN 3-7908-1289-7

Vol. 48. M. Sakawa
Large Scale Interactive Fuzzy Multiobjective Programming, 2000
ISBN 3-7908-1293-5

Vol. 49. L.I. Kuncheva
Fuzzy Classifier Design, 2000
ISBN 3-7908-1298-6

Vol. 50. F. Crestani and G. Pasi (Eds.)
Soft Computing in Information Retrieval, 2000
ISBN 3-7908-1299-4

Vol. 51. J. Fodor, B. De Baets and P. Perny (Eds.)
Preferences and Decisions under Incomplete Knowledge, 2000
ISBN 3-7908-1303-6

Vol. 52. E.E. Kerre and M. Nachtegael (Eds.)
Fuzzy Techniques in Image Processing, 2000
ISBN 3-7908-1304-4

Vol. 53. G. Bordogna and G. Pasi (Eds.)
Recent Issues on Fuzzy Databases, 2000
ISBN 3-7908-1319-2

Vol. 54. P. Sinčák and J. Vaščák (Eds.)
Quo Vadis Computational Intelligence?, 2000
ISBN 3-7908-1324-9

Vol. 55. J.N. Mordeson, D.S. Malik and S.-C. Cheng
Fuzzy Mathematics in Medicine, 2000
ISBN 3-7908-1325-7

Vol. 56. L. Polkowski, S. Tsumoto and T.Y. Lin (Eds.)
Rough Set Methods and Applications, 2000
ISBN 3-7908-1328-1

Vol. 57. V. Novák and I. Perfilieva (Eds.)
Discovering the World with Fuzzy Logic, 2001
ISBN 3-7908-1330-3

Vol. 58. D.S. Malik and J.N. Mordeson
Fuzzy Discrete Structures, 2000
ISBN 3-7908-1335-4

Vol. 59. T. Furuhashi, S. Tano and H.-A. Jacobsen (Eds.)
Deep Fusion of Computational and Symbolic Processing, 2001
ISBN 3-7908-1339-7

Vol. 60. K.J. Cios (Ed.)
Medical Data Mining and Knowledge Discovery, 2001
ISBN 3-7908-1340-0

Vol. 61. D. Driankov and A. Saffiotti (Eds.)
Fuzzy Logic Techniques for Autonomous Vehicle Navigation, 2001
ISBN 3-7908-1341-9

Vol. 62. N. Baba and L.C. Jain (Eds.)
Computational Intelligence in Games, 2001
ISBN 3-7908-1348-6

Vol. 63. O. Castillo and P. Melin
Soft Computing for Control of Non-Linear Dynamical Systems, 2001
ISBN 3-7908-1349-4

Vol. 64. I. Nishizaki and M. Sakawa
Fuzzy and Multiobjective Games for Conflict Resolution, 2001
ISBN 3-7908-1341-9

Vol. 65. E. Orłowska and A. Szalas (Eds.)
Relational Methods for Computer Science Applications, 2001
ISBN 3-7908-1365-6

Vol. 66. R.J. Howlett and L.C. Jain
Radial Basis Function Networks 1, 2001
ISBN 3-7908-1367-2

Robert J. Howlett
Lakhmi C. Jain
Editors

Radial Basis Function Networks 2

New Advances in Design

With 109 Figures
and 28 Tables

Springer-Verlag Berlin Heidelberg GmbH

Dr. Robert J. Howlett
University of Brighton
School of Engineering
Intelligent Signal Processing Laboratories (ISP)
Moulsecoomb, Brighton BN2 4GJ
United Kingdom
r.j.howlett@brighton.ac.uk

Professor Lakhmi C. Jain
Knowledge-Based Intelligent
Engineering Systems Centre
University of South Australia
Adelaide, Mawson Lakes
South Australia 5095
Lakhmi.Jain@unisa.edu.au

ISSN 1434-9922

DOI 10.1007/978-3-7908-1826-0

Cataloging-in-Publication Data applied for
Die Deutsche Bibliothek – CIP-Einheitsaufnahme
Radial basis function networks 2 / Robert J. Howlett; Lakhmi C. Jain, ed. – Heidelberg; New York: Physica-Verl., 2001
New advances in design; with 28 tables. – 2001
(Studies in fuzziness and soft computing; Vol. 67)

Originally published by Physica-Verlag Heidelberg New York in 2001
MyCopy version of the original edition 2001

Hardcover Design: Erich Kirchner, Heidelberg
www.springer.com/mycopy

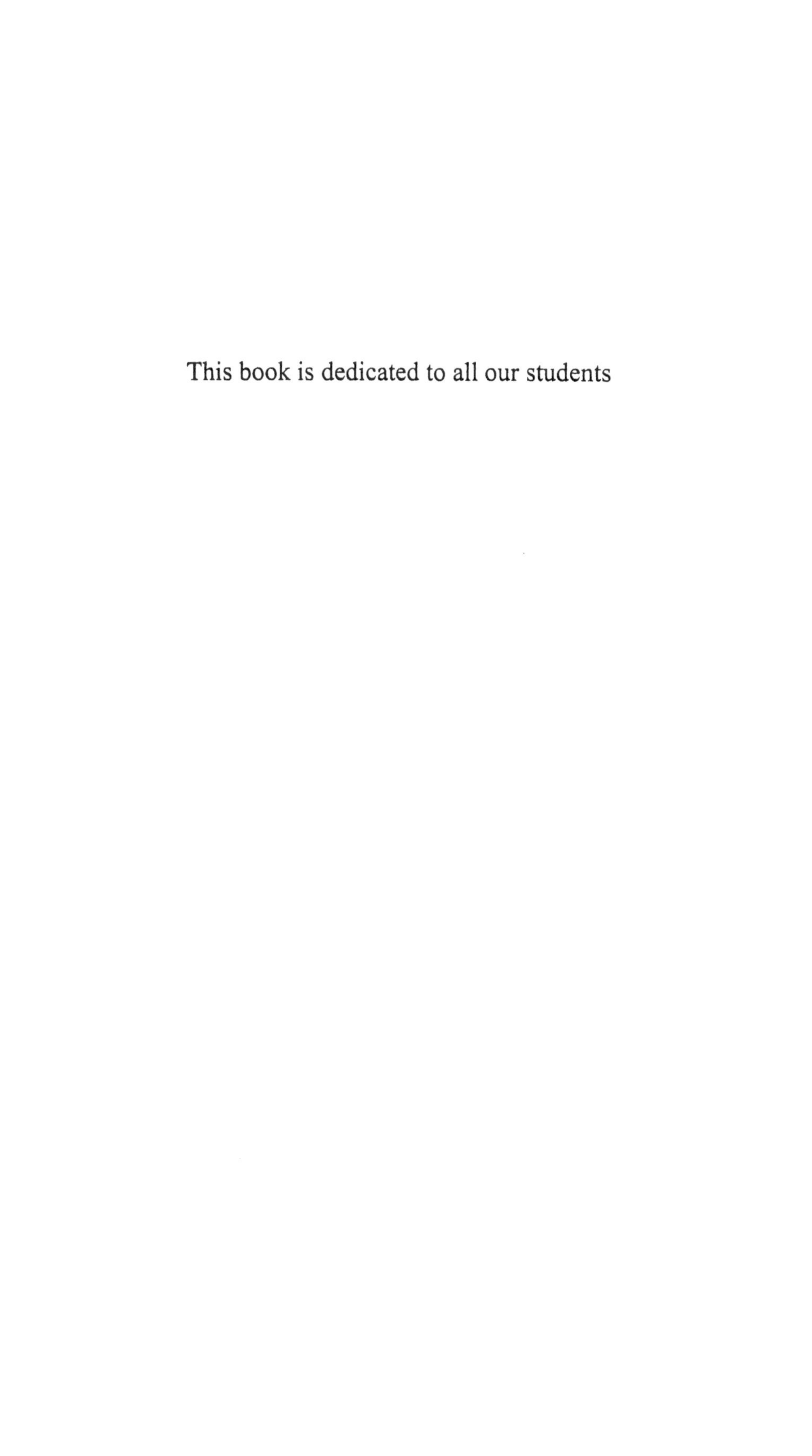

This book is dedicated to all our students

Preface

The Radial Basis Function (RBF) network has gained in popularity in recent years. This is due to its desirable properties in classification and functional approximation applications, accompanied by training that is more rapid than that of many other neural-network techniques. RBF network research has focused on enhanced training algorithms and variations on the basic architecture to improve the performance of the network. In addition, the RBF network is proving to be a valuable tool in a diverse range of applications areas, for example, robotics, biomedical engineering, and the financial sector.

The two-title series ***Theory and Applications of Radial Basis Function Networks*** provides a comprehensive survey of recent RBF network research. This volume, ***New Advances in Design***, contains a wide range of applications in the laboratory and case-studies describing current use. The sister volume to this one, ***Recent Developments in Theory and Applications***, covers advances in training algorithms, variations on the architecture and function of the basis neurons, and hybrid paradigms. The combination of the two volumes will prove extremely useful to practitioners in the field, engineers, researchers, students and technically accomplished managers.

There has been debate over whether the RBF network is truly a "neural" network, and thus whether it is correct to use the term "RBF neural network." Whether the operation of the RBF network is more or less biologically plausible than that of the Multi-Layer Perceptron using back-propagation training can be debated. However, this is something of a sterile discussion. Of greater importance is that the RBF network represents a useful tool with increasingly widespread application. For this reason we have not prevailed on authors to be consistent about the use of the term "RBF network" or "RBF neural network."

This book contains 11 chapters, each contributed by a researcher who has practical experience of applying RBF networks to solve practical problems.

Chapter 1, by Ghosh and Nag, is a general introduction to RBF networks which forms a good foundation for the applications described in subsequent chapters. Readers requiring a treatment which considers RBF algorithms and architectures in greater depth will find it in the sister volume to this one.

In Chapter 2, Salomon and Weissmann describe a data-glove system that forms a powerful input device for virtual-reality and multi-media applications. The performance of various RBF networks for recognition of the gestures is described. Evolutionary algorithms are proposed as a method of fine-tuning the networks. Chapter 3, by Fels, continues and extends the data-glove theme. The author describes Glove-Talk II, a system that translates hand gestures into speech. Normalized RBF units are used to map hand gestures to consonant sounds. Comparisons are made between this and a number of other neural network paradigms in this application.

Two chapters then follow that consider the use of RBF networks for the interpretation of visual data relating to the human face. In Chapter 4, Howell presents an example-based approach to a number of recognition tasks using pose-varying face data. It is claimed that the approach is flexible and computationally efficient. In Chapter 5, Hogan, Norris, and Diederich examine the problem of categorization of facial expressions through the use of a receptive field neural network model. This is based on novel domain Gaussian units trained using a back-propagation algorithm. The approach is evaluated and practical results are presented.

The next two chapters are on the subject of advances using RBF networks in the medical field. Chapter 6, by Kestler and Schwenker, describes two approaches to stratification of risk of sudden cardiac death using an RBF network interpretation of electrocardiogram (ECG) recordings. In Chapter 7, Saastamoinen, Lehtokangas, Värri, and Saarinen discuss the use of RBF networks in biomedical engineering. The chapter begins with a review of biomedical applications of RBF networks and follows by considering some general design principles based on experiences in the field. Finally, the chapter describes the automated interpretation of electroencephalograph (EEG) waveforms using an RBF network.

The volume contains two chapters with robotics as the application domain. In Chapter 8, by Schwenker and Kestler, a 3-dimensional object recognition system is described for use in conjunction with an autonomous mobile robot. The visual system performs a number of tasks, for example, localization, feature extraction and classification. Results are presented for a number of different RBF paradigms used in this application. Chapter 9, by Takahashi, describes methods of designing an RBF network-based controller and implementing it for servo-control of mechanical systems. The approach is illustrated using the control of a micro-actuator and a robot manipulator as examples.

In the final chapter of the volume, Chapter 10, Gan and Danai present a model-based recurrent neural network, the activation functions of which consist of contours of Gaussian RBF nodes. The use of this network for modeling and fault diagnosis of dynamic systems is discussed.

We would like to express our sincere thanks to Berend-Jan van der Zwaag for his efficient help in preparing the manuscript. We are grateful to the authors for their high-quality contributions and to the publishers for their editorial assistance.

R.J. Howlett, University of Brighton, U.K.
L.C. Jain, University of South Australia

Biographical Notes

Dr Robert J. Howlett has a PhD from the University of Brighton, an MPhil from the University of Sussex, and a BSc(Hons) from Portsmouth Polytechnic. He is a member of the British Computer Society and a Chartered Engineer. Dr Howlett is the Director of the University of Brighton TCS Centre, which currently has over 15 technology and knowledge transfer programmes in partnership with UK companies. He is also Head of the Intelligent Signal Processing Laboratories at the University.

Dr Howlett has a number of years experience of applying neural-networks and other intelligent techniques to industrial problems. He is leader of a research team in this area, has published widely on the subject, and has presented invited talks, keynote addresses, etc. He is currently Editor-in-Chief of the International Journal of Knowledge-Based Intelligent Engineering Systems. He is a past and current member of the International Scientific Committees of a number of conferences, and was the General Chair of the Fourth International Conference in Knowledge-Based Intelligent Engineering Systems and Allied Technologies (KES 2000) at the University of Brighton, UK, and is Executive Chair of KES 2001. He is the UK head of two Anglo-French projects funded by the European Union Interreg Programme, and a multi-national Framework V project. He is an Expert Evaluator for European Framework 5 projects.

L.C. Jain is a Director/Founder of the Knowledge-Based Intelligent Engineering Systems (KES) Centre, located in the University of South Australia. He is a fellow of the Institution of Engineers Australia. He has initiated a postgraduate stream by research in the Knowledge-based Intelligent Engineering Systems area. He has presented a number of Keynote addresses in International Conferences on Knowledge-Based Systems, Neural Networks, Fuzzy Systems and Hybrid Systems.

He is the Founding Editor-in-Chief of the International Journal of Knowledge-Based Intelligent Engineering Systems and served as an Associate Editor of the IEEE Transactions on Industrial Electronics. Dr Jain was the Technical chair of the ETD2000 International Conference in 1995, and Publications Chair of the Australian and New Zealand Conference on Intelligent Information Systems in 1996. He also initiated the First International Conference on Knowledge-based Intelligent Electronic Systems in 1997. This is now an annual event. He served as the Vice President of the Electronics Association of South Australia in 1997. He is the Editor-in-Chief of the International Book Series on Computational Intelligence, CRC Press U.S.A. His interests focus on the applications of novel techniques such as knowledge-based systems, artificial neural networks, fuzzy systems and genetic algorithms and the application of these techniques

Contents

Chapter 1.
An overview of radial basis function networks
J. Ghosh and A. Nag

Chapter 2.
Using radial basis function networks for hand gesture recognition
R. Salomon and J. Weissmann

Chapter 3.
Using normalized RBF networks to map hand gestures to speech
S.S. Fels

Chapter 4.
Face recognition using RBF networks
A.J. Howell

Chapter 5.
Classification of facial expressions with domain Gaussian RBF networks
J.M. Hogan, M. Norris, and J. Diederich

Chapter 6.
RBF network classification of ECGs as a potential marker for sudden cardiac death
H.A. Kestler and F. Schwenker

Chapter 7.
Biomedical applications of radial basis function networks

A. Saastamoinen, M. Lehtokangas, A. Värri, and J. Saarinen

Chapter 10.

Model-based recurrent neural network for fault diagnosis of nonlinear dynamic systems

C. Gan and K. Danai

Chapter 1

An Overview of Radial Basis Function Networks

J. Ghosh and A. Nag

This chapter presents a broad overview of Radial Basis Function Networks (RBFNs), and facilitates an understanding of their properties by using concepts from approximation theory, catastrophy theory and statistical pattern recognition. While this chapter is aimed to provide an adequate theoretical background for the subsequent application oriented chapters in this book, it also covers several aspects with immediate practical implications: alternative ways of training RBFNs, how to obtain an appropriate network size for a given problem, and the impact of the resolution (width) of the radial basis functions on the solution obtained. Some prominent applications of RBFNs are also outlined.

1 Introduction

A Radial Basis Function (RBF), ϕ, is one whose output is symmetric around an associated *center*, $\boldsymbol{\mu}_c$. That is, $\phi_c(\mathbf{x}) = \phi(||\mathbf{x} - \boldsymbol{\mu}_c||)$, where $|| \cdot ||$ is a vector norm. For example, selecting the Euclidean norm and letting $\phi(r) = e^{-r^2/\sigma^2}$, one sees that the Gaussian function is an RBF. Note that Gaussian functions are also characterized by a *width* or scale parameter, σ, and this is true for many other popular RBF classes as well. So such classes can be represented as:

$$\phi_c(\mathbf{x}) = \phi(||\mathbf{x} - \boldsymbol{\mu}_c||; \sigma). \tag{1}$$

A set of RBFs can serve as a basis for representing a wide class of functions that are expressible as linear combinations of the chosen RBFs:

$$y(\mathbf{x}) = \sum_{j=1}^{M} w_j \phi(||\mathbf{x} - \boldsymbol{\mu}_j||). \tag{2}$$

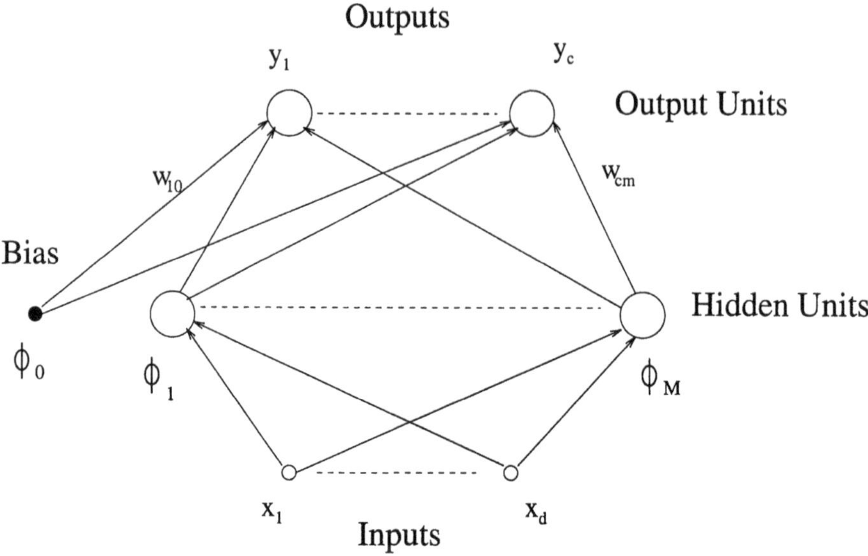

Figure 1. Radial basis function network.

A Radial Basis Function Network (RBFN) (Figure 1), is nothing but an embodiment of Equation 2 as a feedforward network with three layers: the inputs, the hidden/kernel layer and the output node(s). Each hidden unit represents a single radial basis function, with associated center position and width. Such hidden units are sometimes referred to as centroids or kernels. Each output unit performs a weighted summation of the hidden units, using the w_js as weights.

The issue of finding the individual components given a superposition of Gaussians was explored in the early 1960s [35]. Subsequently, the use of RBFs for numerical interpolation and function approximation was demonstrated [5], [48]. Neural network formulations of this approach led to renewed interest in these functional forms [30], [34], [45]. Part of the excitement was due to analogies with *localized receptive fields* found in several biological structures including the visual cortex and the ganglion cells. This further motivated the study of bell-shaped functions which take on high values only in the neighborhood of a specific input. Powerful *universal* approximation properties of Equation 2 were demonstrated for various settings [24], [49], [50], and convergence rates were established [41], [66]. By decoupling the estimation of the center locations and widths ($\boldsymbol{\mu}_j$s and σ_js) from the weights (w_js) to the output layer, fast and practical training algorithms were developed to realize suitable networks given a set of possibly noisy training data. At the same time, useful ties were shown between RBFNs and regularization theory, kernel regression, Bayesian classification etc. At present, RBFNs are perhaps second in popularity only to multilayered perceptrons as the neural network of choice for realizing static maps for a variety of function approximation and classification problems. Many of the advantages of RBFNs will be evident in the following sections.

2 Exact Interpolation

Consider the exact interpolation problem: given a set of N different d-dimensional input vectors $\mathbf{x}^n$ and a corresponding set of one-dimensional targets t^n, find a continuous function $h(\mathbf{x})$ such that

$$h(\mathbf{x}^n) = t^n, \quad n = 1, \ldots, N. \tag{3}$$

The solution to this problem by adopting the radial basis function approach consists of choosing a set of N *basis functions*, centered at the N data points, and using the functional form of Equation 1 giving:

$$h(\mathbf{x}) = \sum_{n=1}^{N} w_i \phi(||\mathbf{x} - \mathbf{x}^n||). \tag{4}$$

An exact solution is possible if one can solve the following set of N simultaneous linear equations to find the unknown coefficients (weights) of the expansion:

$$\begin{bmatrix} \phi_{11} & \phi_{12} & \cdots & \phi_{1N} \\ \phi_{21} & \phi_{22} & \cdots & \phi_{2N} \\ \vdots & \vdots & \vdots & \vdots \\ \phi_{N1} & \phi_{N2} & \cdots & \phi_{NN} \end{bmatrix} \begin{bmatrix} w_1 \\ w_2 \\ \vdots \\ w_N \end{bmatrix} = \begin{bmatrix} t_1 \\ t_2 \\ \vdots \\ t_N \end{bmatrix} \tag{5}$$

where

$$\phi_{ij} = \phi(||\mathbf{x}^i - \mathbf{x}^j||), \quad i, j = 1, 2, \ldots, N. \tag{6}$$

The compact matrix form of Equation 5 is

$$\mathbf{\Phi w} = \mathbf{t}. \tag{7}$$

It has been shown by Michelli [36] and more recently by Light [28] that there exists a large class of functions $\phi(\cdot)$, including Gaussians, inverse multiquadrics and thin-plate splines, for which the interpolation matrix $\mathbf{\Phi}$ is non-singular provided the data points are distinct. Hence, we may solve Equation 7 to give

$$\mathbf{w} = \mathbf{\Phi}^{-1}\mathbf{t}, \tag{8}$$

and achieve exact interpolation. This is because, when the weights obtained by Equation 8 are substituted in Equation 4, the function $h(\mathbf{x})$ represents a continuous differentiable surface passing through each data point.

Both theoretical studies and empirical results show that many characteristics of the interpolating function are relatively insensitive to the precise type of the nonlinearity, ϕ. Relatively non-intuitive functions such as thin plate splines, which have a global response, have been used successfully for interpolation. In fact, the form of ϕ can itself be adapted during training, though this typically does not yield extra power unless the number of kernels is small [65]. Gaussian RBFs are the most popular choices for ϕ [30]. Their localized response helps in the decoupling of the learning process as will be discussed later and is also more biologically plausible. Gaussian RBFs have a number of other useful analytical properties, as will be apparent later on.

Generalization to multidimensional target space is straightforward. The mapping from d-dimensional input space $\mathbf{x}$ to k-dimensional target space $\mathbf{t}$ is given by

$$h_k(\mathbf{x}^n) = t_k^n, \quad n = 1, \ldots, N, \tag{9}$$

where t_k^n are components of the output vector $\mathbf{t}^n$ and $h_k(\mathbf{x})$ are obtained by linear superposition of the same N basis functions as used for the one-dimensional output case:

$$h_k(\mathbf{x}) = \sum_n w_{kn}\phi(||\mathbf{x} - \mathbf{x}^n||). \tag{10}$$

The weight parameters are obtained in the form

$$w_{kn} = \sum_j (\mathbf{\Phi}^{-1})_{nj} t_k^j \tag{11}$$

where the same matrix $\mathbf{\Phi}^{-1}$ is used for each of the output functions.

3 Function Approximation

In practice, one is typically not interested in exact interpolation. Firstly, data is usually noisy, and an interpolating function passing through every data point will lead to overfitting and thereby poor generalization. Better generalization will be achieved using a smoother fit that averages out the noise in the data. Secondly, to guarantee exact interpolation, the number of basis functions required is equal to the number of patterns in the learning data set. Thus, it is apparent that for a large data set the mapping function can become very costly to evaluate.

A radial basis function model for function approximation and generalization is obtained by modifying the exact interpolation procedure [5], [34]. This model gives a smoother fit to the data using a reduced number of basis functions which depends on the complexity of the mapping function rather than the size of the data set. The modifications are as follows:

1. Number of basis functions: The number of basis functions M is typically less than N.
2. Centers of basis functions: The centers of the basis functions are determined as a part of the training process, rather than being constrained to be located at each input data point.
3. Width of the basis functions: The training process may adapt the width parameter σ_j for each of the basis functions, instead of assigning the same width parameter σ to all the basis functions.
4. Addition of bias parameters: Bias in the form of a constant may be added to Equation 2 to compensate for the difference between the average value over the data set of the basis function activations and the corresponding values of the targets.

By applying these modifications to the exact interpolation formula, the form of the radial basis function network mapping obtained is

$$y_k(\mathbf{x}) = \sum_{j=1}^{M} w_{kj}\phi_j(\mathbf{x}) + w_{k0}. \tag{12}$$

The biases w_{k0} can be incorporated into the summation by introducing an extra basis function ϕ_0 and setting its activation to unity, so that one can write:

$$y_k(\mathbf{x}) = \sum_{j=0}^{M} w_{kj}\phi_j(\mathbf{x}) \tag{13}$$

or, in matrix form,

$$\mathbf{y}(\mathbf{x}) = \boldsymbol{W}\boldsymbol{\phi}. \tag{14}$$

The equation of a Gaussian basis function is

$$\phi_j(\mathbf{x}) = e^{\left(-\frac{\|\mathbf{x}-\boldsymbol{\mu}_j\|^2}{2\sigma_j^2}\right)} \tag{15}$$

where $\mathbf{x}$ is the d-dimensional input vector with elements x_i and $\boldsymbol{\mu}_j$ is the center of the basis function ϕ_j and has elements μ_{ji}.

The property of *universal approximation* by linear superposition of Gaussian basis functions, in which the widths of the Gaussians are treated as adjustable parameters was proved by Hartman *et al.* (1990). More general results were obtained by Park and Sandberg (1991, 1993) who show that, with only mild restrictions on the form of the kernel functions, the universal approximation property still holds. These proofs are existence proofs relying on the availability of arbitrarily large number of hidden units, and do not offer practical procedures for the construction of networks. Nevertheless, these theorems are crucial in providing a theoretical foundation on which practical applications can be based with confidence. Any parametric model used for function approximation, defines a space of approximating functions. A model having a unique set of parameters which best approximates the underlying function is said to possess the property of *best approximation*. Radial basis function networks exhibit this property [45], which is not shown by multilayered perceptrons.

For arbitrary covariance matrices $\boldsymbol{\Sigma}_j$, Gaussian radial basis functions, or more appropriately, "elliptical" basis functions, have the form

$$\phi_j(\mathbf{x}) = e^{\left\{-\frac{1}{2}(\mathbf{x}-\boldsymbol{\mu}_j)^T\boldsymbol{\Sigma}_j^{-1}(\mathbf{x}-\boldsymbol{\mu}_j)\right\}} \tag{16}$$

The number of independent adjustable parameters for each basis function is $d(d+3)/2$ for symmetric covariance matrices $\boldsymbol{\Sigma}_j$, where d is the dimensionality of the input space. This is in comparison with the $(d+1)$

independent parameters for the basis functions. If σ_j is also adapted during training, the resultant network is less susceptible to noise, as less important dimensions can be tuned out [3]. However, more fine-tuning of the learning rates needs to be done for better results. Thus, one of the design issues is the consideration of the tradeoff involved between the use of smaller number of basis functions with many adjustable parameters versus a larger number of less flexible functions.

3.1 Convergence Rates

Given that RBFNs can uniformly approximate any continuous function to an arbitrary precision if enough hidden units are provided, a natural question arises regarding the convergence rate, i.e., how does the accuracy of approximation improve with the number of hidden units, M. Clearly, the answer depends on the class of functions being considered for approximation, as well as the type of basis functions used. One can show that the kernel regression estimator - an extension of the Parzen window estimator for statistical regression problems - is expressible as a *normalized* RBFN (see Section 7) using Gaussian basis functions. By using the theoretical results already known about kernel regression estimators, one readily obtains a number of interesting convergence results for (normalized) RBFNs [66]. For example, an upper bound on the L_2 convergence rate for approximating a function in the function class that satisfies a Lipschitz condition of order α, $0 < \alpha \leq 1$ is $O(M^{-2\alpha/(2\alpha+d)})$, where d is the input dimension. Similarly, for the class of functions that have order q ($q \geq 1$) derivatives that are square integrable, the corresponding bound is $O(M^{-2q/(2q+d)})$. As expected, the more smooth the functions are (the larger the α or q), the faster is the rate. In particular, if the ratio d/q is held constant, the convergence rate does not depend on the input dimensionality. Thus, for this class of functions, the curse of dimensionality can be avoided. Furthermore, if $q >> d$, the rate approaches O(M).

In the results stated above, the number of training samples does not figure, since estimation error is not accounted for. In other words, the results are for the best possible choice of the parameters. In practice, given a finite training set and a heuristic learning rule, the parameters obtained may not be optimal. Recognizing that the total generalization error is the sum of estimation and approximation errors, Niyogi and Girosi [41] provide bounds that incorporate the number of training samples available.

A powerful approach to balancing estimation and approximation errors is complexity regularization. When applied to a nested family of functions of adequate power (including RBFs with increasing number of kernel units), complexity regularization aims to automatically choose a suitable network size depending on the number of training samples and the VC dimension of the problem, and then directly minimize the empirical risk. Using this framework and several reasonable constraints, strong consistency results [26] and $O(\sqrt{\frac{\log n}{n}})$ convergence rates have been proved for RBF networks [25].

4 Radial Basis Function Network Training

From Equation 2, one can see that designing an RBFN involves selecting the type of basis functions, ϕ with associated widths, σ, the number of functions, M, the center locations $\boldsymbol{\mu}_j$ and the weights w_j. Typically Gaussians or other *bell-shaped* functions with compact support are used, though thin-plate splines have performed better for some function approximation problems. The choice of M is related to the important problem of model order selection, and is treated in detail in Section 5. Given that the number of basis functions and their type have been selected, training an RBFN involves determining the values of three sets of parameters: the centers, the widths and the weights, in order to minimize a suitable cost function. In general, this is a non-convex optimization problem.[1]

4.1 Supervised Training

One can perform stochastic gradient descent on the cost function to iteratively update the parameters, once per training sample presentation. As

[1]In certain special cases, such as classification problems in which the patterns are separable by hyperspheres, a cost function that is local minima free with respect to all the weights, can be obtained [2].

an illustration, consider the sum-of-squares cost function given by

$$E = \sum_n E_n \tag{17}$$

such that:

$$E_n = \frac{1}{2} \sum_k \{t_k^n - y_k(\mathbf{x}^n)\}^2, \tag{18}$$

where t_k^n is the target value of output unit k when the network is presented with input vector $\mathbf{x}^n$. If Gaussian basis functions are used to minimize this cost function, one readily obtains the update equations [15]:

$$\Delta w_{kj} = \eta_1 (t_k^n - y_k(\mathbf{x}^n))\phi_j(\mathbf{x}^n) \tag{19}$$

$$\Delta \boldsymbol{\mu}_j = \eta_2 \phi_j(\mathbf{x}^n) \frac{||\mathbf{x}^n - \boldsymbol{\mu}_j||}{\sigma_j^2} \sum_k \{y_k(t_k^n) - \mathbf{x}^n\} w_{kj} \tag{20}$$

$$\Delta \sigma_j = \eta_3 \phi_j(\mathbf{x}^n) \frac{||\mathbf{x}^n - \boldsymbol{\mu}_j||^2}{\sigma_j^3} \sum_k \{y_k(t_k^n) - \mathbf{x}^n\} w_{kj} \tag{21}$$

where η_1, η_2, η_3 are the learning rates.

4.2 Two-Stage Training

The simultaneous update of all three sets of parameters using Equations 19, 20, and 21 may be suitable for non-stationary environments or on-line settings. But for static maps, RBFNs with localized basis functions offer a very attractive alternative, namely that in practice, the estimation of parameters can be decoupled into a *two-stage procedure*:
(i) determine the $\boldsymbol{\mu}_j$s and σ_js, and
(ii) for the centers and widths obtained in step (i), determine the weights to the output units.
Both sub-problems allow for very efficient batch mode solutions. Moreover, for many situations, this decoupling leads to little loss in the quality of the final solution as compared to the optimal solution. In fact, given finite training data and computational resources, they often provide better solutions than those obtained by attempting to simultaneously determine all three sets of parameters.

In the first stage only the input values $\{\mathbf{x}^n\}$ are used for determining the centers $\boldsymbol{\mu}_j$ and the widths σ_j of the basis functions. Thus, learning is unsupervised and can even use unlabeled data. Once the basis function parameters are fixed, supervised training (i.e., training using target information) can be employed for determining the second layer weights. We shall now consider the two stages in more detail.

4.2.1 Unsupervised Training of Basis Function Centers and Widths

The key to determining the location and widths of the *localized* basis functions is to view them as representing the input data density. Since one would like at least one hidden unit to be active in regions of the input space where data is present, basis functions with localized responses should be placed in regions of data concentration, and the widths should be related to the local spread of data and the distance to nearby centroids. This viewpoint suggests the following alternatives:

(i) **Random subset selection**: The simplest way of choosing the radial basis function centers $\boldsymbol{\mu}_j$ is to locate the centers at a subset of the data points, chosen randomly from the training data set. This choice is sensitive to how representative are the selected data points of the overall population. However, it provides an initial starting point from which various adaptive techniques can be used to tune the center locations and, optionally, to change the number of centers used.

(ii) **Clustering algorithms**: A better approach is to cluster the input vectors and then locate the basis functions at the cluster centers. A variety of clustering techniques can be used. Suppose we need to partition N data points $\mathbf{x}^n$ into K clusters and find the corresponding cluster centers. The K-means algorithm seeks to partition the data points into K subsets S_j by minimizing the sum of squares clustering function:

$$J = \sum_{j=1}^{K} \sum_{n \epsilon S_j} ||\mathbf{x}^n - \boldsymbol{\mu}_j||^2 \tag{22}$$

where $\boldsymbol{\mu}_j$ is the geometric mean of the data points in the subset S_j and is given by

$$\boldsymbol{\mu}_j = \frac{1}{N_j} \sum_{n \epsilon S_j} \mathbf{x}^n. \tag{23}$$

One method of finding these clusters is by using the batch version. First the data points are randomly assigned to K subsets. The centers for each of the subsets is then computed. The data points are then reassigned to the cluster whose center is nearest. The procedure is repeated till there are no further changes in the grouping. Alternatively one can use a stochastic online process, where initial centers are randomly chosen from the training data, and are then updated as each data is presented sequentially, using the rule

$$\Delta \boldsymbol{\mu}_j = \eta(\mathbf{x}^n - \boldsymbol{\mu}_j) \tag{24}$$

where η is the learning rate parameter. Other unsupervised techniques such as Kohonen's self organizing feature map can also be used for determining the basis function centers.

(iii) **Mixture models**: A probability density function $p(\mathbf{x})$ can be modeled as a superposition of component densities as

$$p(\mathbf{x}) = \sum_{j=1}^{M} P(j)\psi_j(\mathbf{x}) \tag{25}$$

where P is the prior probability of the component density ψ_j. The parameters of such a mixture model can be obtained using maximum likelihood [4]. If the component densities are bell-shaped, they indicate local peaks in density and suggest placement of basis functions at their locations.

(iv) **Width determination**: The basis function widths can either be chosen to be the same for all the units or can be chosen differently for each unit depending on the part of the input space they represent. In the first case, the common width can be set as some multiple of the average distance between the basis centers. This multiple governs the amount of smoothing; small widths lead to less smooth functions. In the second case each center's width is set to a multiple typically 1.5 to 2 times of the average distance to L nearest neighbors. While the widths can be adjusted during subsequent training using Equation 21 or other techniques, many researchers do not do so and prefer the simplicity resulting from a smaller (though sub-optimal) search space.

The widths play an important part in the nature of the function realized by an RBFN, and leads to qualitatively different behaviors when varied over a large space. This issue is further considered in Section 6.

4.2.2 Batch Training of Output Layer Weights

Once the basis parameters are determined, the transformation between the inputs and the corresponding outputs of the hidden units is fixed. The network can thus be viewed as an equivalent single-layer network with linear output units. Minimization of the sum-squared error function (Equation 17) yields the well-known least-squares solution for the weights:

$$\mathbf{W}^T = \mathbf{\Phi}^{\dagger}\mathbf{T} \tag{26}$$

where $(\mathbf{T})_{nk} = t_k^n$, $(\mathbf{\Phi})_{nj} = \phi_j(\mathbf{x}^n)$, and $\mathbf{\Phi}^{\dagger} = (\mathbf{\Phi}^T\mathbf{\Phi})^{-1}\mathbf{\Phi}^T$ denotes the pseudo-inverse of $\mathbf{\Phi}$. $\mathbf{\Phi}$ is referred to as the *design matrix* and $\mathbf{A} = \mathbf{\Phi}^T\mathbf{\Phi}$ is called the *variance matrix*. Thus, the weights can be obtained by direct batch-moded matrix inversion techniques. In practice, to avoid the possible problems due to ill-conditioning of the matrix $\mathbf{\Phi}$, singular value decomposition is usually used to solve the equation.

4.3 Comparison of Two-Stage Training with Supervised Training

Neglecting the output data, while determining the basis function centers and widths using the above mentioned unsupervised training techniques leads to sub-optimal choices of these parameters. Supervised training may lead to optimal estimation of the centers and widths. However, there are a number of disadvantages with the latter scheme. Firstly, the gradient descent method discussed earlier is a non-linear optimization technique and is computationally expensive. However, if the basis functions are well localized then only few basis functions will generate significant activation. Efforts to determine these units and only using them in the subsequent computation can reduce the training time. Another disadvantage of this kind of training is that there is no guarantee that the basis functions will remain localized. Finally the main attraction of radial basis function network is its two stage learning, which is lost while using supervised training.

4.4 Variants

For classification problems, each local basis function is typically preferentially responsive to a certain class. Based on this observation, an iterative hybrid learning algorithm was proposed in which the center locations are updated by LVQ while the output weights are updated in the usual way [6], [14]. Another possibility is to select the kernel(s) to be updated in a probabilistic rather than deterministic manner [42]. In [6], ideas from robust statistics were leveraged to determine the center locations and widths using the marginal median and absolution deviations of the (windowed) data points assigned to each kernel. Finally, a subtle link between unsupervised and supervised learning has been shown in [14]. If the output weights are held constant and a fake (constant) output target is provided for all samples, the kernel locations adapt in a manner very similar to Kohonen's self-organizing feature map.

5 Model Selection

The primary goal of network training is not to find an exact fit to the training data but to model the statistical process responsible for generating the data. Thus, the emphasis is on generalization or performance on data outside the training set. The key to valid generalization is to select a generalizer whose inductive bias is suited to the data, and then to match the model complexity with the complexity of the underlying map generating the data.

The problem of model selection can be understood as a trade-off between bias and variance [13]. The generalization error can be decomposed into the sum of bias squared and variance. A typical trade-off between these two components of generalization error is a function of the model complexity [13]. Too simple a model will have a high bias in the sense that the model, on the average will differ considerably from the desired one, even though specific instances of the model, obtained by changing the training data, initialization conditions etc., may hardly differ from one another. On the other hand, too complex a model may have a low bias but will have high variance and be prone to the specific features of the finite training set.

The balancing of bias and variance can be viewed as a problem of finding the right number of free parameters. For RBFNs, this involves trying to determine the optimal number of hidden units. Hence, the analysis of the effect of adding a new hidden unit or removing an existing unit is an important one. A brute-force approach is to train several networks using different numbers of hidden units and/or different number of training samples. Then, one of the networks can be chosen based on cross-validation or some other criteria such as AIC or generalized cross-validation (GCV) [38].

Fortunately, the localized nature of RBFs and the decoupled training methods suggest superior alternatives to brute-force model selection. Two main approaches to model selection have been taken for RBFNs: one may choose an adequate number of basis functions, but then add a regularization term to the cost function to enforce smoothness or some other desirable characteristic of the function to be realized. Similar effects can be achieved through early stopping of the training process. The second approach is to either add or delete hidden units as training proceeds, leading to growing or pruning algorithms [19], [51]. These two approaches are examined in the next two sections.

5.1 Regularization of RBFNs

Regularization is a powerful technique to favor certain solutions over others by adding a penalty functional to the original cost function. The penalty embodies *Occam's Razor* in some form by penalizing more complex solutions (ridge regression, subset selection) or solutions that are less smooth (non-parametric penalty functionals using a differential operator). A variety of penalties are studied in [12]. Regularization can be linked to *weight decay* [8], [23] and to the use of model priors in the Bayesian framework [33]. Complexity regularization followed by empirical risk minimization has been studied because of nice convergence properties, as mentioned in Section 3.1.

Below, we outline how the linear nature of the second-stage training allows one to apply well known solutions to ridge regression in linear systems, for determining the weights of an RBFN with regularization. For details and a very readable exposition, see [43] and [44].

5.1.1 Projection Matrix

Consider an RBFN with M hidden units, 1 output unit and $N > M$ training samples. For each of the hidden units, one can associate a N dimensional vector whose i^{th} component is the unit's response to the ith training sample. Since the network output is a linear combination of the hidden unit outputs, the possible output vector lies in a M dimensional space spanned by the M N-dimensional hidden unit vectors. However, the training set output vector $\mathbf{t}$ lives in an N-dimensional space. The closest output vector to $\mathbf{t}$ (in L_2 norm) is nothing but the projection of $\mathbf{t}$ onto the M dimensional subspace. The sum squared error for this solution is

$$E = \mathbf{t}^T \mathbf{P}^2 \mathbf{t} \tag{27}$$

with the projection matrix

$$\mathbf{P} = \mathbf{I}_N - \mathbf{\Phi} \mathbf{A}^{-1} \mathbf{\Phi}^T \tag{28}$$

where $\mathbf{I}_N$ is an identity matrix of dimension N, $\mathbf{\Phi}$ is the matrix of basis functions and $\mathbf{A} = \mathbf{\Phi}^T \mathbf{\Phi}$. The projection matrix will prove useful in methods such as ridge regression and forward selection described later.

5.1.2 Cross-Validation

The cross-validation technique divides the available data measurements into two sets, the training set and the test set. The training set is used for determining the network parameters and the test set is used to compute the prediction error. However, this may introduce a bias since we are relying on one particular division of the data into training and test samples. A better way is to partition the original data in several different ways, each time training the network on training samples and computing the prediction error. We could then obtain an unbiased estimate of the prediction error by averaging over all the prediction errors. An extreme form of this type of cross-validation technique is one in which all but one data point is used as the training set and the last one is used as the test data, i.e., given N patterns, $N-1$ are used for training and 1 for testing. This leads to N such partitions and is called the Leave one out method (LOO). Leave one out is attractive since it uses all the data available for training. Also for linear models like RBFNs, LOO has a closed form equation for variance of the prediction error estimate

$$\hat{\sigma}^2_{LOO} = \frac{\mathbf{t}^T\mathbf{P}(diag(\mathbf{P}))^{-2}\mathbf{P}\mathbf{t}}{\mathbf{P}} \tag{29}$$

where $\mathbf{P}$ is the projection matrix.

5.1.3 Ridge Regression

Regularization involves adding a penalty functional to the cost so as to bias the solution towards more desirable solutions. For RBFNs, a popular choice for the modified cost function is the summed squared error,

$$SSE = \sum_{n=1}^{N}\{t^n - y(\mathbf{x}^n)\}^2 + \lambda\sum_{j=1}^{M} w_j^2. \tag{30}$$

The above expression is associated with ridge regression where λ is the regularization parameter and models with large weights at the output layer are penalized. As λ increases the network function becomes smoother. Due to the change in the error function, the variance matrix now becomes

$$\mathbf{A} = \mathbf{\Phi}^T\mathbf{\Phi} + \lambda\mathbf{I}_M. \tag{31}$$

This matrix is better conditioned than $\mathbf{\Phi}^T\mathbf{\Phi}$, a useful property since the optimal weight vector is now

$$\mathbf{W}^T = (\mathbf{\Phi}^T\mathbf{\Phi} + \lambda\mathbf{I}_M)^{-1}\mathbf{\Phi}^T\mathbf{T}. \tag{32}$$

The projection matrix is still given by Equation 28, but using Equation 31 for $\mathbf{A}$.

The regularization parameter λ can be chosen by minimizing the prediction error as estimated by using K-fold cross validation, generalized cross validation or some other criterion. However, one of the most convenient methods is to use the generalized cross-validation (GCV) since it leads to the following reasonably simple iterative formula for the estimate of regularization parameter [44]:

$$\hat{\lambda} = \frac{\mathbf{T}^T\mathbf{P}^2\mathbf{T}trace(\mathbf{A}^{-1} - \hat{\lambda}\mathbf{A}^{-2})}{\mathbf{W}\mathbf{A}^{-1}\mathbf{W}^T trace(\mathbf{P})}. \tag{33}$$

5.1.4 Local Ridge Regression

This is a variation of ridge regression where each weight term is penalized differently thereby associating a different regularization parameter with each basis function. The error function is given by:

$$E = \sum_{n=1}^{N} \{t^n - y(\mathbf{x}^n)\}^2 + \sum_{j=1}^{M} \lambda_j w_j^2. \tag{34}$$

This is called local ridge regression because the basis functions used have localized responses. Hence, the effect of each regularization parameter is to allow the smoothness to be adapted to local conditions. This is especially useful when the underlying function has different smoothness properties in different parts of the input space. The effect of the change in the error function affects the form of the variance matrix as:

$$\mathbf{A}^{-1} = (\mathbf{\Phi}^T \mathbf{\Phi} + \mathbf{\Lambda}) \tag{35}$$

where $\mathbf{\Lambda}$ is a diagonal matrix containing the regularization parameters $\{\lambda\}_{j=1}^{M}$ along its diagonal.

5.2 Pruning and Growing RBFNs

The concept of projection matrix and the associated geometrical interpretation of SSE provides an appealing way of growing an RBFN using forward selection.

5.2.1 Forward Selection

One is given an initial network configuration and a candidate pool of basis functions, typically Gaussians centered at the training data points. At each step, the hidden unit (basis function) which decreases the error (such as sum squared error) most, is removed from the candidate pool and added to the network. This process of adding hidden units and increasing the model complexity is continued till some criterion such as GCV stops decreasing. Though forward selection is a nonlinear optimization technique, it has the advantage of not having to fix the number of units in advance and also a tractable model order selection criterion. Besides, it is computationally efficient. The projection matrix for the case where an extra hidden unit has been added is given by

$$\mathbf{P}_{M+1} = \mathbf{P}_M - \frac{\mathbf{P}_M \mathbf{f}_{M+1} \mathbf{f}_{M+1}^T \mathbf{P}_M}{\mathbf{f}_{M+1}^T \mathbf{P}_M \mathbf{f}_{M+1}} \tag{36}$$

where $\mathbf{f}_{M+1}$ is the column of the design matrix $\mathbf{\Phi}$ corresponding to the most recently recruited hidden unit. The reduction in the sum squared error due to the addition of the unit is given by

$$E_M - E_{M+1} = \frac{(\mathbf{t}\mathbf{P}_M \mathbf{f}_{M+1})^2}{\mathbf{f}_{M+1}^T \mathbf{P}_M \mathbf{f}_{M+1}} \tag{37}$$

The unit which reduces the sum squared error most is the chosen candidate. Geometrically this will be the unit whose corresponding basis vector is most closely aligned to the perpendicular from $\mathbf{t}$ to the current M-dimensional space. Though the sum squared error reduces as more hidden units are added, the model selection criterion will reach a minima before it starts increasing again. This is the point where the process is stopped. Forward selection and ridge regression can be combined to yield further improvement in the choice of model complexity. A sophisticated variant of forward selection based on *orthogonal least squares* has been proposed [44].

5.2.2 Backward Elimination

In backward elimination, a network is constructed with all the basis functions in the candidate pool. At each step, the unit which least increases the error, is eliminated from the network. Again, this procedure is continued till some model selection criterion stops decreasing. At this point, the complexity of the model is assumed to be sufficient to represent the underlying function complexity.

5.3 Hierarchical Growing

As discussed in the next section, σ directly relates to the notion of scale in RBFNs. This was exploited by Moody (1989) who proposed a multi-resolution approach to training and growing an RBFN. The network would be first trained using large but fixed values of σ, to form a coarse approximation. The residual error would then be modeled by additional kernels with smaller values of σ. Moody showed that such a hierarchical, coarse-to-fine training is efficient and suited to real-time applications. He used B-splines as activation functions, but also noted that they are not convenient for high-dimensional spaces. Subsequently, the use of wavelet based kernels, recast in the RBFN framework, was advocated as a powerful, multi-resolution approach to function approximation [7].

Another interesting approach to network growing for classification problems is presented in [31]. With each Gaussian hidden unit is associated a region of influence as well as a class label. As training samples are examined, parameters are adjusted in the usual way unless a sample does not fall in the region of influence of any hidden unit with the same class label. In the latter case, a new hidden unit, positioned on top of that sample, is created with the same class label. Also, if the MSE flattens out at an unacceptable level, the width of each Gaussian is decreased, so that additional kernel units are more likely to be created in the next iteration.

5.3.1 Online Approaches: the Resource Allocating Network

The resource allocating network [46] is similar in spirit to the hierarchical technique mentioned above, but works for function approximation problems also and is tailored for on-line learning. Again, the motivation of such an approach is to match the model complexity with that of the data. The resource allocating network uses a sequential learning technique. As new data elements are presented, based on two thresholds viz. a prediction error threshold and a data novelty threshold, it either adapts the existing network parameters or grows the network. Kadirkamanathan and Niranjan [27] provide a theoretical foundation for RANs using a sequential function estimation approach based on the principle of F projection. The principle states that the posterior estimate of an unknown function $f^{(n)}$ can be obtained from its prior estimate $f^{(n-1)}$ and a new observation $I^{(n)}$ such that the function has the least L_2 norm $||f_{(n)} - f_{(n-1)}||$. Using the same approach Molina and Niranjan [37] provide a pruning with replacement rule for RAN architectures with limited number of units. Such a rule is useful in an online setting where the network is implemented in hardware. A relevance criteria is associated with each hidden unit. When a new observation arrives, based on the two thresholds mentioned above, it is determined whether a new unit needs to be added. If no more hidden units are available, then the relevance of the new unit is compared with the existing ones. If any unit is found which has a lower relevance, then it is replaced with the new unit. Thus, we obtain a pruning rule which helps in increasing the information contained in the network having limited resources. More recently, a pruning algorithm for RAN, that removes units showing little activation over a windowed period, has been presented along with strong comparative experimental results [67].

6 The Role of Scale in RBFNs

The width parameter, σ, invokes the notion of scale in families of functions, including wavelets. Previously we saw that the chosen scale impacted the degree of smoothness of the function realized by an RBFN. Also, a popular way of obtaining center locations is through clustering. Now clustering naturally involves the *scale* idea since at a sufficiently small scale every sample point becomes a cluster, and at some large scale the entire data set may be viewed as a single cluster. The question then arises, can the clustering procedure and the choice of σ be viewed in a unifying framework, and does this provide added insight into what type of function an RBFN realizes? This question is addressed in [11], and the answers are multi-faceted and very positive.

6.1 Training Centroids Using Scale-Based Clustering

First, it is observed that a Gaussian RBFN can by itself cluster data in a *scale-based* manner. In a scale-space approach to clustering, clusters are determined by analyzing the data over a range of scales, and clusters that are stable over a considerable scale interval are accepted as *true* clusters [63], [64]. Suppose we assign w_{kj}, t_k^n and σ_j constant values, w, t and σ respectively, with $t > 0$ and $w/t << 1$, thus we are training an RBFN with a constant output value, and the only variables to be estimated are the center locations. In this setting, Equation 20 can be approximated by:

$$\Delta \boldsymbol{\mu}_j = (\eta_4) \frac{||\mathbf{x}^n - \boldsymbol{\mu}_j||}{\sigma_j^2} e^{\left(-\frac{||\mathbf{x}^n - \boldsymbol{\mu}_j||^2}{2\sigma_j^2}\right)}, \tag{38}$$

where $\eta_4 = \eta_2 w$. At equilibrium one obtains:

$$\nabla(\phi_j(\mathbf{x};\sigma) * p(\mathbf{x})) = 0. \tag{39}$$

where $p(\mathbf{x})$ is the input probability density and '*' is the convolution operator. Centroids obtained by iterating Equation (38) are the extrema of the input density $p(\mathbf{x})$, smoothed by a Gaussian of width σ. Therefore, the width acts as a scale parameter for clustering; the number of clusters obtained is a function of the width, and decreases as width is increased.

Equation 38 can be used for clustering problems. On the well-known Iris classification data, the above method outcompeted standard clustering algorithms like FORGY and CLUSTER even though it did not use class information [9].

The right set or number of clusters, in other words the right width value, can be picked by computing cluster centers for a range of width values. Clusters that hardly change over a long range of width values (using a logarithmic scale), are natural clusters for the given data, and the centers of these clusters are the solutions to Equation 39. Thus, this procedure, in one shot, provides center locations, width values as well as model selection in terms of the number of centers needed.

6.2 Weight Training and Network Complexity

An important problem that is encountered in training of a feedforward network is: how to match the network complexity (size, number of trainable parameters etc.) with the problem complexity.

We addressed some aspects of this issue while studying model selection for RBFNs. On contrasting the localized fitting of RBFNs with spline models which generate piece-wise, smooth fit to observational data [60], one can identify cases where the localized receptive field approach places increased demands on the network complexity for fitting even simple problems. For example, consider the task of learning a low-order polynomial relation, $y = \sum_{i=0}^{n-1} a_i x^i$, using a RBFN over a finite domain. Although the target function complexity is described by the number of parameters (n), in a local approximation approach, the required RBFN size increases with the size of the input domain. The desired network complexity is unrelated to target complexity. This problem can be mended by getting rid of local approximation approach to training RBFN.

The usual path (of centroid clustering followed by weight matrix inversion) for RBFN training is meaningful only for small width values. When widths are allowed to be large, the localized receptive field concept becomes inapplicable. In that new regime, the width parameter controls the network complexity independent of network size. To take an extreme situation, consider what happens when widths of an RBFN are very large compared to spread of the sample data. The network output stays close to a constant value independent of the input vector and the number of hidden units. That is, width determines complexity independent of the network size.

More generally, width can be used to control the nonlinearity of network function. For simplicity, consider the output of a single-input, single-output RBFN given by

$$y(x) = \sum_{j=0}^{N} w_j \phi_j(x; \sigma_j) \tag{40}$$

Assuming uniform width ($\sigma_j = \sigma, \forall j$), and Gaussian RBFs the output can be expressed as,

$$y(x) = \sum_{j=0}^{n} w_j \left(1 - \frac{(x - \mu_j)^2}{\sigma^2} + \ldots\right)$$

or,

$$y(x) = L_m(x; w_j; \sigma) + H_m(x; w_j; \sigma) \tag{41}$$

where, L_m comprises of the m lower-order terms in x, and H_m includes the remaining higher-order terms. Note that a higher value of σ, the network output $y(x)$ approximates a polynomial of degree $m - 1$ with error,

$$\|y(x) - L_m(x; w_j; \sigma)\| \leq O(\sigma^{-2m}). \tag{42}$$

Further, it can be easily verified that coefficients of the polynomial L_m linearly depend on network weights, w_j. Therefore, in principle, by proper choice of σ and weights, w, the RBFN can approximate a mth degree polynomial with only $m + 1$ RBF nodes. In this way the target complexity could be matched with network complexity, with the width parameter playing a crucial role in this process [21].

The procedure to train RBFN so as to approximate polynomials is distinct from the usual training procedures since it does not create a local approximation of the target. The steps in the training process are given below [10]:

- Step 1: Choose a RBFN with $m+1$ RBF nodes to fit a univariate mth degree target polynomial. (The case of multi-variate targets is much more complicated. Some special results are derived using the tools of Catastrophe Theory in [10]). Also choose a uniform width value ($\sigma_j = \sigma, \forall j$).
- Step 2: Train the centroids using a standard clustering procedure, or using Equation 38 of the previous section.
- Step 3: The weights are calculated by minimizing squared output error. This must be done by a pseudoinversion procedure like the Singular Value Decomposition [18].
- Step 4: Calculate the squared output error, E, obtained after training the network.
- Step 5: Update σ as: $\sigma \leftarrow \beta\sigma$, where $\beta > 1$. If $\sigma > \sigma_{max}$ terminate, else go back to Step 3.

The desired polynomial approximation is obtained at a value of σ that globally minimizes $E(\sigma)$.

The above polynomial approximation scheme has been used to calculate a local fit to a smooth target function depending on the local "shape" of the target. According to Catastrophe theory (CT) ([16], [58]), the shape of a smooth function, $f(\mathbf{x})$, is determined by its Critical Points (CP) ($\mathbf{x}_0$s), defined as points where $\nabla f(\mathbf{x}) = 0$. Depending on the Hessian at $\mathbf{x}_0$, CT puts each CP into one of several distinct types. The complexity of $f(\mathbf{x})$ near a CP is described by a parameter known as the *codimension*. In [10], it has been shown how a smooth target of a known "shape" can be locally approximated using a RBFN, such that the desired network complexity is related to codimension, i.e. the target complexity.

In summary, we note that the goal of matching target complexity to network complexity is frustrated by the traditional local approach to approximation using RBFN. This difficulty is overcome by allowing very large width values. This takes us into a new regime of RBFN parameter space where the network can be made to approximate polynomial targets accurately. It is then possible to design a training scheme where the desired network size is closely related to the target complexity. The design of RBFNs where different basis functions may have widely varying width values promises to be an exciting area of investigation.

7 Normalized RBFNs

By adding a normalizing factor to the equation of the basis function, one obtains normalized radial basis functions:

$$\phi_i(\mathbf{x}) = \frac{\phi(||\mathbf{x} - \boldsymbol{\mu}_i||)}{\sum_{j=1}^{M} \phi(||\mathbf{x} - \boldsymbol{\mu}_j||)} \tag{43}$$

where M is the total number of kernels. A network obtained using the above form for the basis functions is called a normalized RBFN and has several interesting properties. Firstly this is the natural form of the function obtained in various settings such as noisy data interpolation and regression [4]. Also since the basis function activations are bounded between 0 and 1, they can be interpreted as probability values, especially in classification applications as will be seen below.

7.1 Classification Using Radial Basis Function Networks

Radial basis function networks can be effectively used for classification purposes. We will look at two ways of interpreting the classification capabilities of RBFNs. Both interpretations can be obtained by comparing the approach to a Bayesian classification strategy. Consider the data set as shown in Figure 2. The data points belonging to the different classes can either be separated using hyperplanes (as in multilayered perceptrons) or alternatively by placing localized kernels around each group. The latter approach is associated with RBFNs. One could first model the class conditional densities for each class. Using these densities and appropriate class priors, Bayes theorem could be applied to obtain the posterior probabilities of each class. The classification rule then consists of choosing the class with the highest posterior probability. One can model this

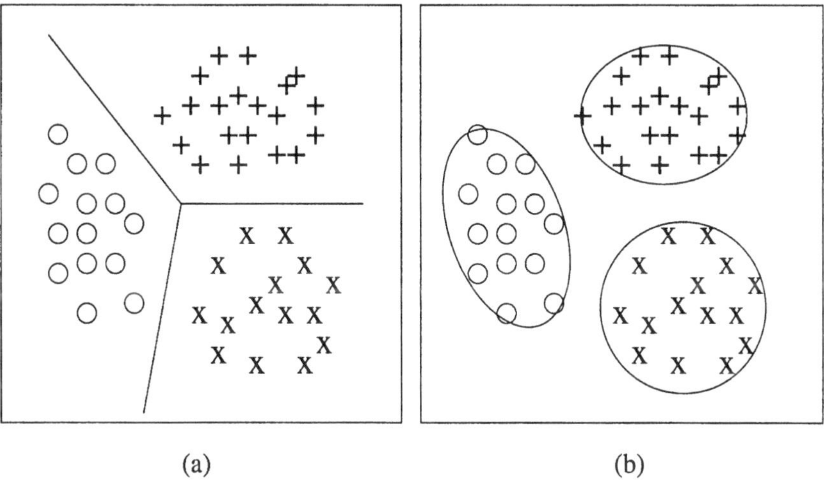

Figure 2. Classification. The 3 different kinds of symbols represent elements of three distinct classes. (a) Classes separated using hyperplanes. (b) Classes separated using localized kernels.

with an RBFN in which, each basis function models the class conditional density for each class. The kth hidden unit is only connected to the kth output unit to represent the corresponding prior. Thus, the kth output of the overall network can be viewed as the posterior probability $P(C_k|\mathbf{x})$ of the pattern $\mathbf{x}$ belonging to class C_k:

$$P(C_k|\mathbf{x}) = P(C_k)\phi_k(\mathbf{x}) \tag{44}$$

where

$$\phi_k(\mathbf{x}) = \frac{p(\mathbf{x}|C_k)}{\sum_i p(\mathbf{x}|C_i)P(C_i)} \tag{45}$$

and $p(\mathbf{x}|C_k)$ is the class conditional density.

Instead of assigning a separate basis function for each class conditional density, a mixture model could be used for modeling the densities. An efficient method involves the use of a common set of M basis functions to represent all class conditional distributions. This leads to a normalized RBFN:

$$P(C_k|\mathbf{x}) = \sum_{j=1}^{M} w_{kj}\phi_j(\mathbf{x}). \tag{46}$$

where

$$\phi_j(\mathbf{x}) = \frac{p(\mathbf{x}|j)P(j)}{\sum_{i=1}^{M} p(\mathbf{x}|i)P(i)} = P(j|\mathbf{x}) \tag{47}$$

and the hidden to output unit weights are given by

$$w_{kj} = \frac{P(j|C_k)P(C_k)}{P(j)} = P(C_k|j) \tag{48}$$

In this scenario, the hidden unit centers can be considered as representative feature vectors and hidden unit activations can be interpreted as the posterior probabilities of the presence of corresponding features in the input space. Thus, the overall output of the network represents the posterior probability of a class membership, given these features. The weights provide the prior probability of each feature.

7.2 Noisy Data Interpolation Theory

Consider a mapping from a one-dimensional input x to a one-dimensional output y such that the output data is obtained from a smooth noise-free function $h(x)$. However, assume that the input has been corrupted by additive noise. Then the sum-of-squares error will be given by

$$E = \frac{1}{2} \int \int \{y(x+\zeta) - h(x)\}^2 q(\zeta) p(x) d\zeta dx \tag{49}$$

where $p(x)$ and $q(\zeta)$ are the probability density functions of the input data and noise respectively. If we assume the distribution of noise to be normal i.e. $q(\zeta) \propto exp(-\zeta^2/2\sigma^2)$, then minimization of the error term for a finite training data set $\{x^n, t^n\}$ gives:

$$y_k(x) = \frac{\Sigma_n h_k(x^n) exp\{-(x-x^n)^2/2\sigma^2\}}{\Sigma_n exp\{-(x-x^n)^2/2\sigma^2\}}. \tag{50}$$

This expression can be looked upon as an expansion in normalized radial basis functions with the weights given by $h(x^n)$ and the basis functions given by

$$\phi(x-x^n) = \frac{exp\{-(x-x^n)^2/2\sigma^2\}}{\Sigma_n exp\{-(x-x^n)^2/2\sigma^2\}}. \tag{51}$$

The weights $h(x^n)$ are unknown and have to be determined from the training data points. However, we know that the function $h(x)$ is noise-free and hence we have $h(x^n) = t^n$. Thus, noisy data interpolation theory provides another insight into the origin of radial basis function expansions.

7.3 Kernel Regression

The theory of kernel regression provides another viewpoint to the use of radial basis functions for function approximation. It provides a framework for estimating regression functions for noisy data using kernel density estimation techniques. Let us reconsider the problem of mapping a d-dimensional input vector $\mathbf{x}$ to an output vector $\mathbf{y}$ of dimensionality c. Suppose we are given a set of training data of N data samples $\{\mathbf{x}^n, \mathbf{t}^n\}$. The joint probability density $p(\mathbf{x}, \mathbf{t})$ can be modeled using a Parzen kernel estimator. If we use Gaussian kernel functions, then the estimator will have the form

$$\hat{p}(\mathbf{x}, \mathbf{t}) = \frac{1}{N} \sum_{n=1}^{N} \frac{1}{(2\pi h^2)^{(d+c)/2}} e^{\left(-\frac{\|\mathbf{x}-\mathbf{x}^n\|^2}{2h^2} - \frac{\|\mathbf{t}-\mathbf{t}^n\|^2}{2h^2}\right)}. \tag{52}$$

The objective of function approximation is to find a mapping from the input space to the output space. Under many circumstances, it can be shown that the mapping is provided by forming the regression, or conditional average of the target data, conditioned on the input variables. The conditional average can be expressed in terms of the conditional density which in turn can be derived from Equation 52. The regression function is known as the Nadaraya-Watson estimator [40], [61] and is given by:

$$\mathbf{y}(\mathbf{x}) = \frac{\sum_n \mathbf{t}^n e^{\left(-\frac{\|\mathbf{x}-\mathbf{x}^n\|^2}{2h^2}\right)}}{\sum_n e^{\left(-\frac{\|\mathbf{x}-\mathbf{x}^n\|^2}{2h^2}\right)}} \tag{53}$$

It has been rediscovered in the context of neural networks [55], [54]. The above expression can be looked upon as an expansion in normalized radial basis functions with the expansion functions once again being provided by the target data $\mathbf{t}_n$. As discussed earlier, assigning a kernel for each data point greatly increases the cost of computing. Thus, the joint probability distribution could be modeled using an adaptive mixture model instead of the kernel estimator. Algorithms such as the EM (expectation-maximization) algorithm could then be used for determining the parameters of the model.

7.4 Solution for Missing Variables

Many real world applications need to deal with data having incomplete feature vectors or missing variables. Image occlusion and sensor failure are examples of cases which present the need to find efficient methods of training and prediction in the presence of incomplete data. The use of heuristic methods, such as substituting the mean value for the unknown feature, lead to sub-optimal solutions and in some cases may be worse than neglecting the sample. It has been shown [1], [56], [59] that the optimal solution involves integrating the network output over the missing dimensions weighted by local probability densities. Efficient closed form solutions exist for Gaussian basis function networks. [56] showed that the use of Parzen windows with Gaussian kernels for estimating probability densities leads to a solution in the form of an RBF network of normalized Gaussians centered at the known components of data points. Assume $NN(\cdot)$ is a neural network which has been trained to predict $E(y|\mathbf{x})$ where $\mathbf{x}$ is a d-dimensional vector and y is a 1-dimensional scalar. If such a network is presented with an incomplete input vector $\mathbf{x} = (\mathbf{x}^c, \mathbf{x}^u)$ where $\mathbf{x}^c$ denotes the known inputs and $\mathbf{x}^u$ denotes the unknown inputs, the optimal prediction for $E(y|\mathbf{x}^c)$ would be given by:

$$E(y|\mathbf{x}^c) \approx \frac{\sum_{k=1}^{N} \alpha_k G(\mathbf{x}^c; \mathbf{x}^{c,k}, \sigma)}{\sum_{k=1}^{N} G(\mathbf{x}^c; \mathbf{x}^{c,k}, \sigma)}, \quad \alpha_k = NN(\mathbf{x}^c, \mathbf{x}^{u,k}) \tag{54}$$

under the condition that the input probability density is estimated using Parzen windows with Gaussian kernels. Here k iterates over N training points, $NN(\mathbf{x}^c, \mathbf{x}^{u,k})$ is the neural network prediction obtained by substituting the corresponding components of the training data points for the unknown input and $G(\mathbf{x}^c; \mathbf{x}^{c,k}, \sigma)$ is a Gaussian kernel whose center $\mathbf{x}^{c,k}$ is obtained by considering only those components which correspond to the known input. Ghahramani and Jordan [17] provide an EM approach to supervised learning using incomplete data where the joint probability density of the data is modeled using a mixture of Gaussian basis functions.

8 Applications

Since RBFNs have powerful function approximation capabilities, good local structure and efficient training algorithms, they have been used for a wide variety of applications such as chaotic time series prediction, speech pattern classification, image processing, medical diagnosis, nonlinear system identification, adaptive equalization in communication systems, and nonlinear feature extraction [20], [39], [62]. The various applications described in this book, including hand gesture recognition, face recognition, classification of ECGs, mapping hand gestures to speech, object recognition and minefield detection, all involve an underlying mapping problem that exploits the universal and smooth function approximation capabilities of RBFNs.

Since in many of these applications, the RBF is used as a static function approximator, the question arises, why not use an MLP instead? The suitability of course depends on the nature of the problem. For several applications, the two types of networks, if chosen and trained carefully, are seen to attain similar levels of performance [29]. Often an RBF is quicker to train but is more memory intensive as compared to an MLP. Also, as with any kernel based approach, it is more susceptible to the curse of dimensionality [12].

But for many applications, the RBFN is a natural choice, and adds extra capabilities. For example, the error observed for a training sample can be apportioned among the localized hidden units depending on their proximity. Then, for a new sample, the output can be supplemented by a weighted average of the "errors" or uncertainty associated with each kernel unit that contributed to that output. In this way, input-dependent confidence intervals can be obtained for the output estimate [32].

The link between Bayesian classifiers and the normalized RBFN has been shown in Section 7.1. This relationship is specifically exploited in applications such as design of adaptive equalizers [39]. Some other applications are based on relating RBFNs to fuzzy inference systems [22], [47], [53]. Here the kernels are viewed as providing membership functions, whose outputs pass through one or more layers of nodes for fuzzy inferencing. Moreover, the backpropagation algorithm can be extended to modify the kernel location and widths, and thereby the membership functions [53], [57].

Like the MLP, the RBF network can be readily extended for dealing with dynamic maps. In signal processing applications such as speech processing and forecasting, a tapped delay line has been used to feed the current and past input values into an RBF network [39]. Recurrent connections reminiscent of the IIR filter have also been proposed. A nice application to face and gesture recognition incorporates past information into the input vector by using attenuated feedback from the previous state of the input vector [52]. RBFNs are expected to continue to enjoy popularity as a versatile and practical nonlinear function approximator for a variety of engineering applications.

Acknowledgments

This research was supported in part by the NSF under Grant ECS-9900353, and ARO under contract DAAG55-98-1-0230.

References

[1] Ahmad, S. and Tresp, V. (1993), "Some solutions to missing feature problem in vision," in Cowan, J.D., Hanson, S.J., and Giles, C.L. (Eds.), *Advances in Neural Information Processing Systems*, vol. 5, pp. 393-400. The MIT Press.

[2] Bianchini, M., Frasconi, P., and Gori, M. (1995), "Learning without local minima in radial basis function networks," *IEEE Transactions on Neural Networks*, vol. 6, no. 3, pp. 749-756.

[3] Beck, S. and Ghosh, J. (1992), "Noise sensitivity of static neural classifiers," *SPIE Conf. on Applications of Artificial Neural Networks, SPIE Proc. Vol. 1709*, pp. 770-779, Orlando, Fl., April.

[4] Bishop, C.M. (1995), *Neural Networks for Pattern Recognition*, Oxford University Press, New York.

[5] Broomhead, D.S. and Lowe, D. (1988), "Multivariable functional interpolation and adaptive networks," *Complex Systems*, vol. 2, pp. 321-355.

[6] Borş, A.G. and Pitas, I. (1996), "Median radial basis function neural network," *IEEE Transactions on Neural Networks*, vol. 7, no. 6, pp. 1351-1364, November.

[7] Bakshi, B.R. and Stephanopoulos, G. (1993), "Wave-net: a multiresolution, hierarchical neural network with localized learning," *AIChE Journal*, vol. 39, no. 1, pp. 57-81, January.

[8] Le Cun, Y., Denker, J.S., and Solla, S.A. (1990), "Optimal brain damage," *Advances in Neural Information Processing Systems-2*, pp. 598-605.

[9] Chakaravathy, S.V. and Ghosh, J. (1996), "Scale based clustering using a radial basis function network," *IEEE Transactions on Neural Networks*, vol. 5, no. 2, pp. 1250-61, Sept.

[10] Chakaravathy, S.V. and Ghosh, J. (1997), "Function emulation using radial basis function networks," *Neural Networks*, vol. 10, pp. 459-478, May.

[11] Chakravarthy, S.V. (1996), *On the role of singularities in neural networks*, PhD thesis, Dept. of Elect. Comp. Eng., Univ of Texas, Austin, May.

[12] Friedman, J.H. (1994), "An overview of predictive learning and function approximation," in Cherkassky, V., Friedman, J.H., and Wechsler, H. (Eds.), *From Statistics to Neural Networks, Proc. NATO/ASI Workshop*, pp. 1-61. Springer Verlag.

[13] Geman, S., Bienenstock, E., and Doursat, R. (1992), "Neural networks and the bias/variance dilemma," *Neural Computation*, vol. 4, no. 1, pp. 1-58.

[14] Ghosh, J. and Chakravarthy, S.V. (1994), "The rapid kernel classifier: a link between the self-organizing feature map and the radial basis function network," *Jl. of Intelligent Material Systems and Structures*, vol. 5, pp. 211-219, 2.

[15] Ghosh, J., Deuser, L., and Beck, S. (1992), "A neural network based hybrid system for detection, characterization and classification of short-duration oceanic signals," *IEEE Jl. of Ocean Engineering*, vol. 17, no. 4, pp. 351-363, October.

[16] Gilmore, R. (1981), *Catastrophe Theory for Scientists and Engineers*, Wiley Interscience, New York.

[17] Ghahramani, Z. and Jordan, M. (1994), "Supervised learning from incomplete data via an em approach," in Tesauro, G., Cowan, J.D., and Alspector, J. (Eds.), *Advances in Neural Information Processing Systems*, vol. 6, pp. 120-127. The MIT Press.

[18] Golub, G. and Van Loan, C. (1989), *Matrix Computations*, John Hopkins University Press, Baltimore, MD.

[19] Ghosh, J. and Tumer, K. (1994), "Structural adaptation and generalization in supervised feedforward networks," *Jl. of Artificial Neural Networks*, vol. 1, no. 4, pp. 431-458.

[20] Haykin, S. (1994), *Neural Networks: a Comprehensive Foundation*, Macmillan, New York.

[21] Hoskins, J.C., Lee, P., and Chakravarthy, S.V. (1993), "Polynomial modelling behavior in radial basis function networks," *Proc. of World Congress on Neural Networks*, pp. 693-699, Portland, OR, July.

[22] Jang, J.S.R. and Sun, C.T. (1993), "Functional equivalence between radial basis function networks and fuzzy inference systems," *IEEE Transactions on Neural Networks*, vol. 4, no. 1, pp. 156-159, January.

[23] Krogh, A. and Hertz, J.A. (1992), "A simple weight decay can improve generalization," in Hanson, S.J., Moody, J.E., and Lippmann, R.P. (Eds.), *Advances in Neural Information Processing Systems-4*, pp. 950-957. Morgan Kaufmann, San Mateo, CA.

[24] Kowalski, J., Hartman, E., and Keeler, J. (1990), "Layered neural networks with gaussian hidden units as universal approximators," *Neural Computation*, vol. 2, pp. 210-215.

[25] Krzyżak, A. and Linder, T. (1997), "Radial basis function networks and complexity regularization in function learning," in Mozer, M.C., Jordan, M.I., and Petsche, T. (Eds.), *Advances in Neural Information Processing Systems*, vol. 9, p. 197.

[26] Krzyzak, A., Linder, T., and Lugosi, G. (1996), "Nonparametric estimation and classification using radial basis function nets and empirical risk minimization," *IEEE Transactions on Neural Networks*, vol. 7, no. 2, pp. 475-487, March.

[27] Kadirkamanathan, V. and Niranjan, M. (1993), "A function estimation approach to sequential learning with neural networks," *Neural Computation*, vol. 5, pp. 954-975.

[28] Light, W.A. (1992), "Some aspects of radial basis function approximation," in Singh, S.P. (Ed.), *Approximation Theory, Spline Functions and Applications*, pp. 163-90. NATO ASI Series Vol. 256, Kluwer Acad., Boston.

[29] Lippmann, R.P. (1991), "A critical overview of neural network pattern classifiers," *IEEE Workshop on Neural Networks for Signal Processing*.

[30] Lee, S. and Kil, R.M. (1988), "Multilayer feedforward potential function network," *Proceedings of the Second International Conference on Neural Networks*, pp. 161-171.

[31] Lee, S. and Kil, R.M. (1991), "A Gaussian potential function network with hierarchical self-organizing learning," *Neural Networks*, vol. 4, pp. 207-224.

[32] Leonard, J.A., Kramer, M.A., and Ungar, L.H. (1992), "Using radial basis functions to approximate a function and its error bounds," *IEEE Transactions on Neural Networks*, vol. 3, no. 4, pp. 624-627, July.

[33] Mackay, D.J.C. (1995), "Probable networks and plausible predictions - a review of practical Bayesian methods for supervised neural networks," *Network: Computation in Neural Systems*, vol. 6, no. 3, pp. 469-505.

[34] Moody, J. and Darken, C.J. (1989), "Fast learning in networks of locally-tuned processing units," *Neural Computation*, vol. 1, no. 2, pp. 281-294.

[35] Megdassy, P. (1961), *Decomposition of superposition of distributed functions*, Hungarian Academy of Sciences, Budapest.

[36] Micchelli, C.A. (1986), "Interpolation of scattered data: distance matrices and conditionally positive definite functions," *Constructive Approximation*, vol. 2, pp. 11-22.

[37] Molina, C. and Niranjan, M. (1996), "Pruning with replacement on limited resource allocating networks by F-projections," *Neural Computation*, vol. 8, pp. 855-868.

[38] Moody, J.E. (1994), "Prediction risk and architecture selection for neural networks," in Cherkassky, V., Friedman, J.H., and Wechsler, H. (Eds.), *From Statistics to Neural Networks, Proc. NATO/ASI Workshop*, pp. 143-156. Springer Verlag.

[39] Mulgrew, B. (1996), "Applying radial basis functions," *IEEE Signal Processing Magazine*, pp. 50-65, March.

[40] Nadaraya, E.A. (1964), "On estimating regression," *Theory of Probability and its Applications*, vol. 9, no. 1, pp. 141-142,.

[41] Niyogi, P. and Girosi, F. (1996), "On the relationship between generalization error, hypothesis complexity and sample complexity for radial basis functions," *Neural Computation*, vol. 8, pp. 819-842.

[42] Osman, H. and Fahmy, M.M. (1994), "Probabilistic winner-take-all learning algorithm for radial-basis-function neural classifiers," *Neural Computation*, vol. 6, no. 5, pp. 927-943.

[43] Orr, M.J.L. (1995), "Regularization in the selection of radial basis function centers," *Neural Computation*, vol. 7, pp. 606-623.

[44] Orr, M.J.L. (1996), "Introduction to radial basis function networks," Technical Report April, Center for Cognitive Science, Univ. of Edinburgh.

[45] Poggio, T. and Girosi, F. (1990), "Networks for approximation and learning," *Proc. IEEE*, vol. 78, no. 9, pp. 1481-97, Sept.

[46] Platt, J.C. (1991), "A resource allocation network for function interpolation," *Neural Computation*, vol. 3, no. 2, pp. 213-225.

[47] Pal, S.K. and Mitra, S. (1992), "Multilayer perceptron, fuzzy sets, and classification," *IEEE Transactions on Neural Networks*, vol. 3, no. 5, pp. 683-697, September.

[48] Powell, M.J.D. (1985), "Radial basis functions for multivariable interpolation: a review," *IMA Conf. on Algorithms for the approximation of functions and data*, pp. 143-167.

[49] Park, J. and Sandberg, I.W. (1991), "Universal approximation using radial basis function networks," *Neural Computation*, vol. 3, no. 2, pp. 246-257, Summer.

[50] Park, J. and Sandberg, I.W. (1993), "Universal approximation and radial basis function networks," *Neural Computation*, vol. 5, no. ??, pp. 305-316.

[51] Reed, R. (1993), "Pruning algorithms – a survey," *IEEE Transactions on Neural Networks*, vol. 4, no. 5, pp. 740-747, September.

[52] Rosenblum, M., Yacoob, Y., and Davis, L.S. (1996), "Human expression recognition from motion using a radial basis function network architecture," *IEEE Transactions on Neural Networks*, vol. 7, no. 5, pp. 1121-1138, September.

[53] Shim, C. and Cheung, J.Y. (1995), "Pattern classification using RBF based fuzzy neural network," *Intelligent Engineering Systems Through Artificial Neural Networks*, vol. 5, pp. 485-90. ASME Press, November.

[54] Schioler, H. and Hartmann, U. (1992), "Mapping neural network derived from the parzen window estimator," *Neural Networks*, vol. 5, pp. 903-909.

[55] Specht, J. (1990), "Probabilistic neural networks," *Neural Networks*, vol. 3, pp. 45-74.

[56] Tresp, R., Neuneier, V., and Ahmad, S. (1995), "Efficient methods for dealing with missing data in supervised learning," in Touretzky, D.S., Tesauro, G., and Leen, T.K. (Eds.), *Advances in Neural Information Processing Systems*, vol. 7, pp. 687-696. The MIT Press.

[57] Taha, I. and Ghosh, J. (1997), "Hybrid intelligent architecture and its application to water reservoir control," *International Journal of Smart Engineering Systems*, vol. 1, pp. 59-75, 1.

[58] Thom, R. (1975), *Structural Stability and Morphogenesis*, Reading:Benjamin.

[59] Tresp, S., Ahmad, V., and Neuneier, R. (1994), "Training neural networks with deficient data," in Tesauro, G., Cowan, J.D., and Alspector, J. (Eds.), *Advances in Neural Information Processing Systems*, vol. 6, pp. 128-135. The MIT Press.

[60] Wahba, G. (1990), *Spline Models for Observational Data*, vol. 59. Society for Industrial and Applied Mathematics, Philadephia.

[61] Watson, G.S. (1964), "Smooth regression analysis," *Sankhya: the Indian Journal of Statistics*, Series A 26, pp. 359-372.

[62] Webb, A.R. (1996), "An approach to non-linear principal component analysis using radially symmetric kernel functions," *Statistics and Computing*, vol. 9, pp. 159-68.

[63] Witkin, A.P. (1983), "Scale-space filtering," *8th Int. Joint Conf. Art. Intell.*, pp. 1019-1022, Karlsruhe, Germany, August.

[64] Wong, Y.F. (1993), "Clustering data by melting," *Neural Computation*, vol. 5, no. 1, pp. 89-104.

[65] Webb, A.R. and Shannon, S.M. (1996), "Spherically-symmetric basis functions for discrimination and regression: determining the nonlinearity," Technical Report 651/2/JP95/22, DRA/CIS, Malvern, England.

[66] Xu, L., Krzyzak, A., and Yuille, A. (1994), "On radial basis function nets and kernel regression: statistical consistency, convergence rates and receptive field size," *Neural Networks*, vol. 7, no. 4, pp. 609-628.

[67] Yingwei, L., Sundererararajan, N., and Saratchandran, P. (1997), "A sequential learning scheme for function approximation using minimal radial basis function networks," *Neural Computation*, vol. 9, pp. 461-78.

Chapter 2

Using Radial Basis Function Networks for Hand Gesture Recognition

R. Salomon and J. Weissmann

This chapter is about a data-glove/neural network system as a powerful input device for virtual reality and multi media applications. In contrast to conventional keyboards, space balls, and two-dimensional mice, which allow for only rudimental inputs, the data-glove system allows the user to present the system with a rich set of intuitive commands. Previous research has employed different neural networks to recognize various hand gestures. Due to their on-line adaptation capabilities, radial basis function networks are preferable to backpropagation. Unfortunately, the latter have shown better recognition rates. This chapter describes the application and discusses the performance of various radial basis function networks for hand gesture recognition. This chapter furthermore applies evolutionary algorithms to fine tune pre-learned radial basis function networks. After optimization, the network achieves a recognition rate of up to 100%, and is therefore comparable or even better than that of backpropagation networks.

1 Introduction

Most of the currently-available interfaces for virtual reality (and multimedia even though not explicitly mentioned) applications offer only relatively simple user-system interactions. Even sophisticated devices, such as space balls, three-dimensional mice, and data-gloves, do not go beyond the simple point-and-grab I/O-paradigm, fundamental to the conventional two-dimensional mice. Furthermore, research in the context of word processing systems has shown [20], for example, that experienced users prefer keyboard shortcuts over mouse clicks for efficiency reasons. These observations suggest that their shortcomings prevent simple standard point-and-click devices from being adequate control tools for virtual

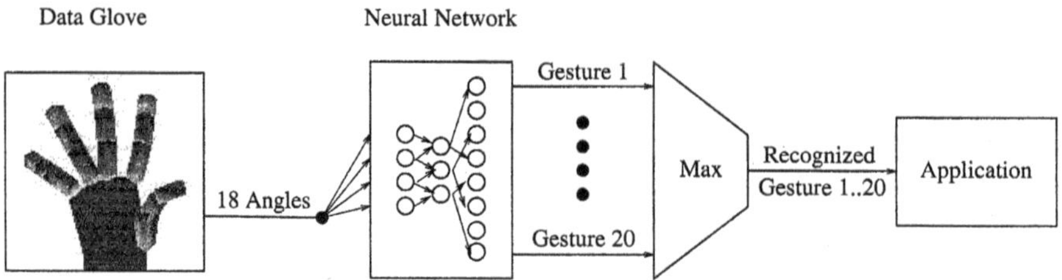

Figure 1. This recognition system utilizes a data-glove to measure various finger and hand angles. In a subsequent stage, a neural network maps these angular measurements onto a set of predefined hand gestures. Finally, the application executes commands associated to each hand gesture.

reality applications.

For interacting with virtual reality applications, hand gesture recognition systems are a quite powerful and compact alternative. Such systems (see, for example, [9]), normally employ a camera to present a pixel image to a recognition system, which in turn classifies each hand gesture with respect to a predefined set of prototypes. Unfortunately, image processing in such camera-based systems is computationally very expensive and also sensitive to exogenous factors, such as illumination, hand position, hand size, and hand orientation.

In order to avoid the problems of previous approaches, this chapter considers a quite different system as is illustrated in Figure 1. The recognition system consists of three main components, a data-glove, a neural network, and a simple classifier. The data-glove measures the current angles of various finger and hand joints. These measurements are then sensed by a neural network, which maps them onto a set of predefined hand gestures. For this purpose, the neural network features one output neuron for each gesture and signals the "degree" of similarity by the neuron's activity. Finally, a simple maximum estimation module signals the recognized gesture to the application, which in turn executes the commands associated with each hand gesture.

For interacting with the application, the user is provided with a set of 20 different hand gestures eight of which are illustrated in Figure 2. All hand gestures serve different purposes and are called, for example, "claw", "co-ord", "three", "victory", "devil", "devil-gun", "finger", and "finger-

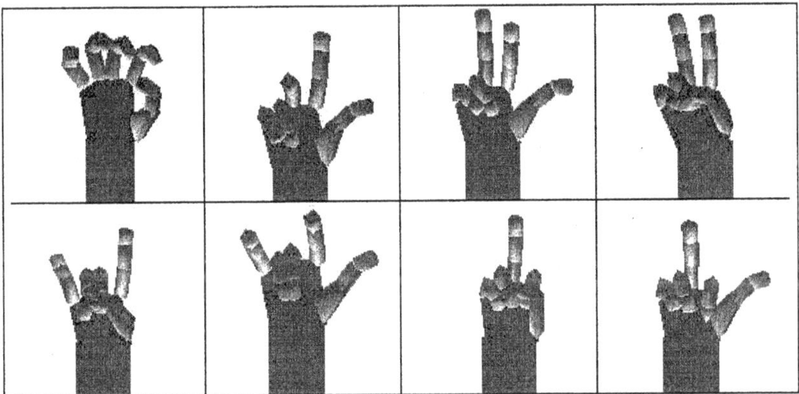

Figure 2. For the application, 20 defined hand gestures have been defined. The eight illustrated examples are called "claw", "co-ord", "three", "victory", "devil", "devil-gun", "finger", and "finger-plus".

plus". For the design process, it should be kept in mind that these gestures should be natural, easy to present, and – for the recognition process – highly distinct.

Figure 3 shows the system in operation. The virtual reality application consists of a gripper (close to the screen's center) and several objects two of which are drawn on the screen. In this screen shot, the gripper is about to grab an object. With the gestures, the user is able to manipulate the gripper in complete three dimensions. The "devil" gesture, for instance, is being used to rotate the gripper clock-wise around the x-axis, whereas the "devil-plus" gesture rotates the gripper counter clock-wise. The figure also shows the data-glove itself. Modern data-gloves are very thin and almost comparable to regular gloves. The user therefore does not notice this device after a short initial phase.

As has already been mentioned, the neural network's purpose is to map the angular measurements onto a set of predefined hand gestures. For the actual implementation, the literature [7], [16] provides various options. In a preliminary study [19], backpropagation has been used. As Section 2 summarizes, backpropagation networks yield (surprisingly) high recognition rates but lack online adaptation, a highly-desirable option; even for fine tuning, backpropagation requires the presentation of *all* training patterns and not just a few. If presenting merely some misclassified pat-

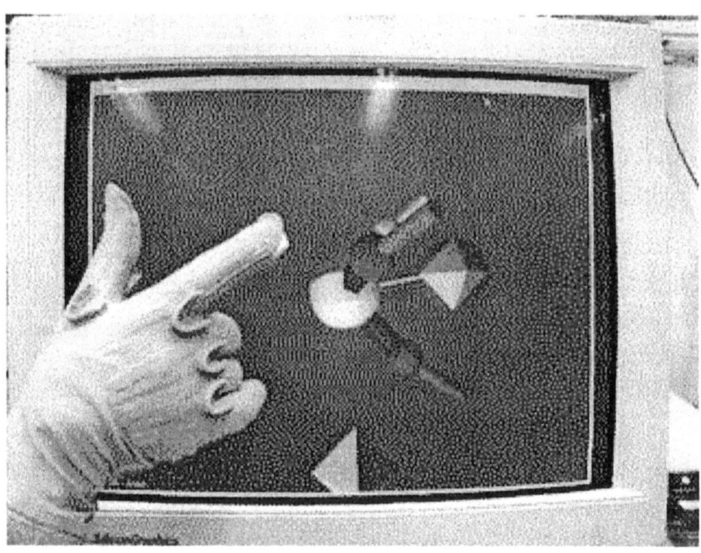

Figure 3. The virtual reality application consists of a gripper and some boxes two of which are drawn. The gestures are provided by to the system by a data-glove, which provides 18 angular measurements. A neural network maps these measurements onto predefined gestures.

terns, a backpropagation network normally forgets everything else. Since online fine tuning might be a highly desirable feature, if the system be used by a wide selection of different persons with significantly varying hand properties, this chapter explores the implementation of the classification network by radial basis function networks. Section 3 summarizes just some basic properties of radial basis function networks, since further details (practical as well as theoretical), can be found elsewhere in this book.

Generally, the network's connections evolve during a learning process. It turns out, as Section 4 shows, that these learning procedures evolve networks that exhibit inferior performance as compared to backpropagation, especially for "advanced" network architectures. Since such a compromise, i.e., trading better online adaptation capabilities for worse recognition rates, does not seem the optimal performance theoretically achievable, Section 5 analyzes the underlying problems and indicates that radial basis function networks misclassify some gestures due to some parameter mismatches. Consequently, this chapter explores to which extent and at which computational cost evolutionary algorithms may alleviate this problem. The algorithms used as well as all parameter settings are summarized in Section 6. Section 7 presents some results, which indicate that recognition rates of up to a 100% can be obtained when using particular algorithms. These results also show that standard algorithms cannot be used in a straight forward manner; some special tailoring is required. Section 8 concludes this chapter with a discussion and an outlook for further research.

2 Background

In general, neural networks consist of individual nodes, called units u_i, which are labeled with an index i and often grouped into different layers, such as input, hidden, and output. Hidden layers comprise units that are not directly visible from outside, but interact with the environment only indirectly via input and/or output units. Most mathematical descriptions indicate the particular layer in which a unit is situated by a subscript, e.g., u_i^O, or by defining different sets, such as $u_{i \in O}$ with $O = \{1, 2, 3, \ldots, k\}$, as far as necessary for clarity.

Two different units i and $j \neq i$ may communicate with each other by means of directed connections w_{ij}, where in most cases, the indices j and i refer to source and destination, respectively. Depending on the types of layers, connections, and direction of communication, different network models are distinguished in the literature. A good overview including various examples as well as theoretical discussions can be found in [16] and [7].

Except for the input units, which are set by external quantities, all hidden and output units calculate their summed input net_i and activation u_i as follows:

$$\begin{aligned} \text{net}_i &= \sum_j w_{ij} u_j \\ u_i &= f(\text{net}_i) = \frac{1}{1 + e^{-\text{net}_i}}, \end{aligned} \tag{1}$$

where $f(\text{net}_i)$ denotes the transfer function, often called logistic function.

To apply learning, the procedure defines an error function

$$E(w_{ij}) = \sum_{p} \sum_{i \in O} (t_i^p - u_i)^2 , \tag{2}$$

which calculates for each pattern and each output unit the difference between the expected t_i^p and obtained output u_i and sums up their squares over all output units and all training patterns. Backpropagation then calculates the gradient $\nabla E(\vec{w})$ with respect to each connection and then does an update $w_{ij} \leftarrow w_{ij} - \eta(\partial E/\partial w_{ij})$ either after each step or after a whole sweep through all patterns. Backpropagation calculates the gradient in a recursive manner. But since the actual learning procedure is not in the focus of this chapter, the rather cumbersome equations are omitted here, and for further details, the interested reader is referred to [7] and [16]. It should be noted though that the complete update of the network requires a whole sweep through all training patterns.

For "regular" backpropagation networks with one simple hidden layer and all hidden units being connected to all input and output units, previous research [19] reports rather medium performance. However, when connecting all hidden units to only those input units that receive angular measurements only from neighboring fingers, the performance was significantly improved; the recognition rates on various test sets varied between 88% and a 100%.

Even though the literature offers a large number of quite efficient enhancements [8] and modifications of the learning procedure, backpropagation lacks reasonable online adaptation capabilities; it is required to always present *all* and not just a few training patterns. Since online adaptation seems a very desirable capability for this kind of application, further research considered radial basis function networks.

3 Summary of Radial Basis Function Networks

Even though similar to multi-layer perceptrons, radial basis function networks have some distinct features. First, a radial basis function network normally consists only of an input and an output layer, i.e., no hidden layers are present. Second, rather than propagating and modifying the activation from one layer to the next, each output unit of a radial basis function network stores a set of features w_{ij} (like connections) and compares these features with the activation of the input units. The output unit's activation then reflects the similarity between its stored feature vector and the current input pattern. More formally, activation G_i of output unit i is given by

$$G_i = \exp\left(\frac{1}{\beta}\sum_j(\varphi_j - w_{ij})^2\right) , \tag{3}$$

with β denoting a scaling factor and φ_j denoting the jth angle seen via input unit j. For convenience, the inputs are sometimes collected into $\vec{\varphi}$ and the features of the ith output unit into $\vec{w}_i$. With this vector representation, Equation (3) can also be formulated as

$$G_i = \exp\left(\frac{1}{\beta}||\vec{\varphi} - \vec{w}_i||^2\right) . \tag{4}$$

Due to this representation, each output unit is often thought of calculating the "distance" of its particular features as stored in its weights w_{ij} and the current input pattern $\vec{\varphi}$ representing current features.

Figure 4 shows some basic properties of the radial basis functions as defined by Equation (4). The activation of each output unit is described as a "bump" centered at the (spatial) location of the stored feature vector, which is just a simple number in the one-dimensional case. The upper part of Figure 4 shows three such bumps at x=2, x=4, and x=9 with the decision boundaries at x=3 and x=5.5. The upper part also shows that the value of β determines the width of a bump. The absolute value of β is not of most importance, but rather its relative value with respect of the other bumps' β's, as the lower part of Figure 4 shows. It can be seen, for example, that a uniform modification $\beta \leftarrow 5\beta$ of all β's changes the bumps' shape but not the location of the decision boundaries.

In the simple vectorial form (Equation (4)), each feature dimension has the same significance, since the differences are summed up in the exponent and the scaling factor β equally affects each dimension. This is sometimes considered a shortcoming, since the objects of constant activation G_i=const are n-dimensional hyperspheres and might not adequately represent the problem at hand.

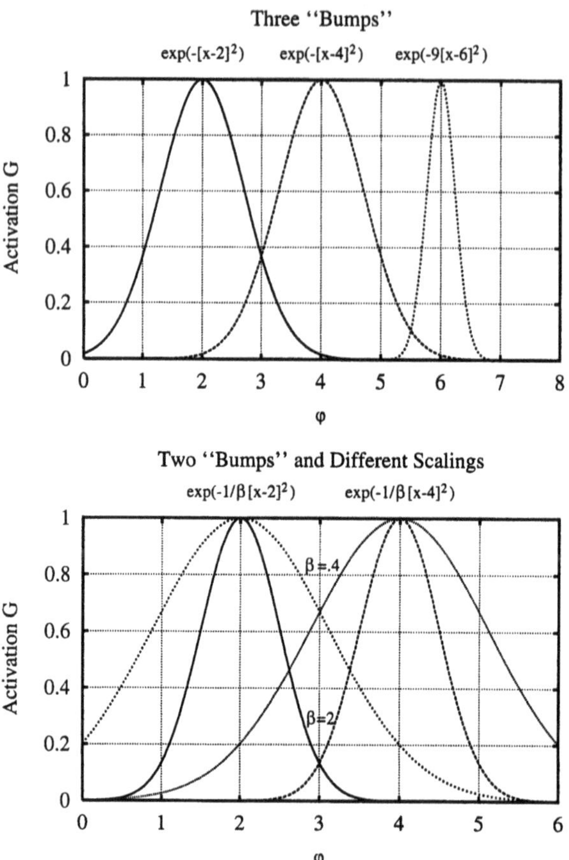

Figure 4. The upper figure show three different "bumps" with the decision boundaries being at x=3 and x=5.5. The figure also illustrates that a smaller scaling factor ($\beta = 1/9$ as compared to $\beta = 1$) leads to a smaller bump (but still with the same height). The lower figure illustrates that a uniform rescaling of all scaling factors β involved does change the bump's shape but does not change the location of the decision boundaries.

Therefore, more elaborate forms of radial basis function networks enhance the differences $(\varphi_j - w_{ij})$ by individual scaling factors $\alpha_{ij}(\varphi_j - w_{ij})^2$, one for each feature j. The individual scaling factors represent – in a sense – the variance of feature j in the neighborhood of neuron's i center $\vec{w}_i$.

For some applications, even this enhanced radial basis function network is considered not sufficient; the objects of constant activation G_i=const appear as n-dimensional ellipses, which are *always* aligned with the coordinate axes. This is generally satisfactory, but for applications with significant dependencies between different parameters, arbitrary orientations of the ellipses are required. This can be achieved by utilizing a two-dimensional transformation matrix $(\boldsymbol{M}_i\varphi - \vec{w}_i)^2$, with $\vec{w}_i$ consisting of all w_{ij}.

With n features to consider, each output unit G_i, which might represent a particular gesture i, has n, $2 \times n$, or $0.5 \times n \times (n+1)$ free parameters, respectively, that have to be determined by a learning or optimization procedure.

4 Gesture Recognition Using Radial Basis Functions

Traditionally, most neural network training procedures utilize some sort of gradient descent algorithm to minimize a problem-dependent error or energy functions. Backpropagation is a well-known example for such approaches.

The same is normally done for radial basis function networks, since one primary goal is to determine both the number and the particular locations of all "bumps". The gesture recognition task at hand, however, allows for some important short cuts, since first of all, the number of centers is already known; each gesture might be represented by one output unit. Furthermore, the classification of each training pattern is also known in advance, since the test persons are asked to present particular gestures. Therefore, the centers w_{ij} for each gesture i can be directly calculated by averaging the angular measurements φ_j^i that belong to gesture i, i.e.,

$$w_{ij} = \frac{1}{N^i} \sum_{k=1}^{N^i} \varphi_j^i(k) , \tag{5}$$

where k denotes the pattern's number and N^i the total number of patterns of gesture i.

Preliminary experiments have shown that some variations of Equation (5), such as calculating the modal value of all features, only slightly influences the final performance. With this simple training procedure, recognition rates of previously unseen patterns (i.e., generalization) of 72-99% [19] can be achieved.

The more advanced form, described as the second form in Section 3, requires the calculation of n scaling factors α_{ij} for each gesture i. Possible options are to set each α_{ij} to the standard deviation of the jth feature φ_{ij} that belong to gesture i, or to simply use their differences $\alpha_{ij} = \max_k(\varphi_{ij}(k)) - \min_k(\varphi_{ij}(k))$ of their minimal and maximal values. With this form, however, the application at hand did not yield any significant improvement and is therefore not discussed any further in this chapter.

The transformation matrix $\boldsymbol{M}_i$ of the third form can be determined by applying a principal component analysis (PCA) [12], [16]. A principal analysis first determines the direction in n-dimensional search space with the largest variance, i.e., the most significant one. From the remaining $n-1$ dimensions, the principal component analysis then determines the direction that is both perpendicular to the first one and exhibits the most variation. The algorithm proceeds in this form until all n directions, also called eigendirections, are determined. In other words, a principal component analysis constructs a matrix $\boldsymbol{M}$ that performs a rotation into a new coordinate system in which the coordinate axes equal the system's principal axes. Unfortunately, this form of radial basis function network did not yield any improvement; it rather exhibits significantly worse performance, which is quite contra-intuitive.

Before proceeding with discussing further enhancements, an important note should be made on principal component analyses. Since this algorithm has to determine n directions in the n-dimensional search space, at least n data points must be known for each matrix $\boldsymbol{M}$; otherwise the algorithms fails, since the matrix is not fully determined.

5 Problem Description

Section 4 has already indicated that a principal component considers the data points as n-dimensional "clouds" and accounts for the uneven data point distribution by generating two-dimensional transformation matri-

Figure 5. Three different ellipses for $||\boldsymbol{M}_i\vec{\varphi}||$ = const for three matrices with very different eigendirections and eigenvalues.

ces $\boldsymbol{M}_i$. With such matrices, each radial basis function network unit calculates its activation by (refer also to Equation (4)):

$$G_i = \exp\left(\frac{1}{\beta}\sum_j ||\boldsymbol{M}_i\varphi - \vec{w}_i||^2\right) . \tag{6}$$

Performance problems, as briefly described in Section 4, can occur due to some parameter mismatches, and can be best discussed by calculating the points of constant activation G_i=const, which is equivalent to looking at $||\boldsymbol{M}_i\vec{\varphi}||^2 =$ const. Figure 5 illustrates that these points appear as n-dimensional ellipses. After performing the principal component analysis for a particular gesture, the eigenvalues may vary considerably and might degenerate the "spheres" (upper left) to "disks" (bottom left) or even "cigars" (middle right).

In case degenerated ellipses are involved, gestures can be easily misclassified, if they are slightly off a "disk" or "cigar". To better understand this point, Figure 6 illustrated an extreme case. Here, the test point t is

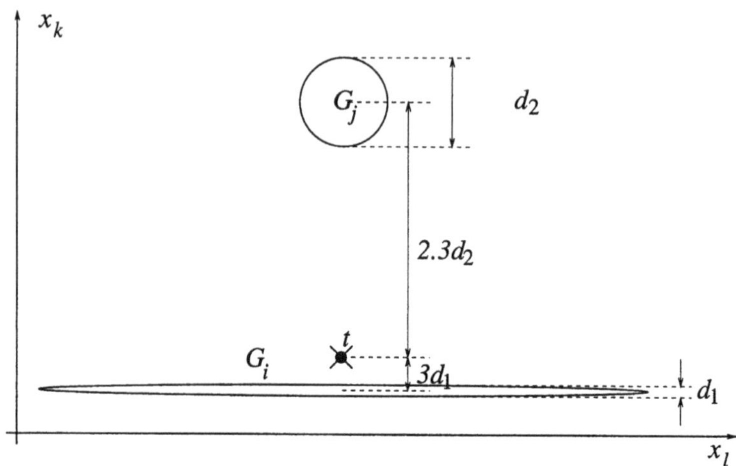

Figure 6. In this constellation, the test point t is considered as gesture G_j as opposed to gesture G_i, which would be done by most humans. This misclassification is due to the very different widths $d_1 \ll d_2$ of the ellipses, which leads to a small distance to gesture j in terms of d_1 and d_2.

"slightly" off gesture i and quite far from gesture j. Most humans would probably classify the test point t as gesture i. The radial basis function network, however, yields gesture j, since the test point's distance to gesture j is only $2.3d_2$ as compared to $3d_1$. Obviously, this misclassification is mainly due to the huge differences of the widths of the gestures' ellipses.

The degree of each gesture's degeneration can be measured by the quotient $\epsilon_i = \lambda^i_{\text{min}}/\lambda^i_{\text{max}}$ of smallest and the largest eigenvalue λ^i_{min} and λ^i_{max}, respectively. The goal of the remainder of this chapter is to apply an evolutionary algorithm to evolve a set minimal quotients $\{\epsilon_i\}$. To this end, the system first determines the largest eigenvalue λ^i_{max} for each matrix $\boldsymbol{M}_i$. It then sets all eigenvalues such that all quotients are above ϵ_i, i.e., the following statement is executed for all eigenvalues λ^i_j:

```
if ( λ^i_j / λ^i_max < ε_i )
then λ^i_j ← λ^i_max * ε_i;
```

In summary, a set of eigenvalues $\{\epsilon_i\}$ has to be evolved such that training and generalization performance is maximal.

6 Methods

This section summarizes the various algorithms and parameter setting, and is organized in a sequence of subsections each discussing a particular point.

6.1 Data-Glove and Gestures

The current system is equipped with the CyberGlove distributed by Virtual Technologies Inc. [13]. This data-glove measures 18 joint angles, two for each finger, one between each pair of neighboring fingers, as well as one for thumb rotation, palm arch, wrist pitch, and wrist yaw.

For the application, 20 different hand gestures were defined. Eight of these gestures have already been illustrated in Figure 2. This setup implies that any neural network must have 18 input units (one for each angle) and 20 output units (one for each hand gesture to be recognized).

6.2 The Neural Network

The gesture recognition is done by means of radial basis function networks as already described in Section 5, and all calculations were done according to Equation (6). In all experiments, the scaling factor was set to $\beta = 0.01$. The actual value of β is without any practical consequence, since β merely scales the width of all "bumps". Even though rescaling would change the absolute activation of all output units, it would not influence the classification result at all.

During initialization (training), the parameters w_{ij} were set to the average value of angle j of gesture i. The 20 matrices $\boldsymbol{M}_i$, i.e., the eigendirections as well as eigenvalues, were calculated by employing a principal component algorithm [12]. The quotients were all initialized to $\epsilon_i = 0.06$ at the beginning of each experiment.

6.3 Training and Test Patterns

For the experiments, ten prototypes per hand gesture were collected from five different persons with a total of 1000 patterns. From these 1000 patterns, 140 patterns (seven from each gesture) were randomly drawn from only four different persons. This total of 140×4=560 patterns were used to initialize the weights w_{ij} and matrices $\boldsymbol{M}_i$. For the overall testing, i.e., the fitness of a particular set of eigenvalues, P=700 patterns were randomly drawn anew from all five persons.

6.4 The Evolutionary Algorithms

The term evolutionary algorithms refers to a class of heuristic population-based search procedures that incorporate random variation and selection, and provide a framework that mainly consists of genetic algorithms [6], evolutionary programming [4], [5], and evolution strategies [14], [15], [18].

All evolutionary algorithms maintain a population of μ individuals, also called parents. In each generation g, an evolutionary algorithm generates λ offspring by copying randomly selected parents and applying variation operators, such as mutation and recombination. It then assigns a fitness value (defined by a fitness or objective function) to each offspring. Depending on their fitness, each offspring is given a specific survival probability. For a good overview of these algorithms, the interested reader is referred to [2] and [3].

Since all quotients ϵ_i are real-valued parameters, it is straight forward to resort to evolution strategies and the breeder genetic algorithm [10]. In their simplest form, evolution strategies maintain one global step size σ for each individual, and they typically apply mutations to all n parameters, i.e., $p_m = 1$, as follows

$$x_i \leftarrow x_i + \sigma N(0,1)\ , \tag{7}$$

with $N(0,1)$ denoting normally-distributed random numbers with expectation value 0 and standard deviation 1. Each offspring inherits the step size from its parent, and prior to mutation, the inherited step size is modified by log-normally-distributed random numbers[1] $\exp(N(0,1))$. This simple evolution strategy is denoted as (μ,λ)-ES or (μ+λ)-ES for short; the first notation indicates that the new parents are selected only from the

[1]Constant factors, such as 1.5, 1.0, and 1/1.5, might work as well; see also [14].

offspring (i.e., no elitism), whereas the latter also considers *all* parents from the previous generation (i.e., μ-fold elitism). In addition, some evolution strategies also feature various recombination operators (see [2] and [3] for further details), such as discrete and intermediate recombination. For similarity reasons, it can be expected that evolutionary programming yield nearly equivalent results and is thus not further considered in this chapter.

The breeder genetic algorithm [10] is the second algorithm considered here, since it is a genetic algorithm variant that is especially tailored to continuous parameter optimization. The breeder genetic also encodes each parameter x_i as a floating-point number, and implements mutation by adding or subtracting small random numbers. It normally applies a mutation to each parameter with probability $p_m = 1/n$. In addition, it features different crossover operators, such as discrete recombination, extended intermediate recombination, and extended line recombination (see [10] for further details). It is recommended [10] to use discrete recombination with $p_r = 0.5$. The current breeder genetic algorithm's mutation operator [17] is typically defined as

$$x_i \leftarrow x_i \pm A2^{-ku} , \quad u \in [0, 1) , \tag{8}$$

where "+" and "-" are selected with equal probability, A denotes the mutation range, k denotes a precision constant, and u is a uniformly-distributed random number. Unless otherwise stated, $A = 0.1$ and $k = 16$ were used in all experiments. Previously, discrete mutations were used [10].

6.5 The Fitness Function

The optimization goal is to minimize the number of misclassifications. In order to avoid discrete "plateaus" of the fitness values, the fitness function consists of several parts. Therefore, it first counts the number of misclassifications. It then calculates the n-dimensional distance to a target vector t_p that consists of "0"s except a "1" for the desired gesture. The fitness function can be formally expressed as

$$f = \sum_{p=1}^{P} \text{mis}(p) + \text{error}(p)/(P * N)$$

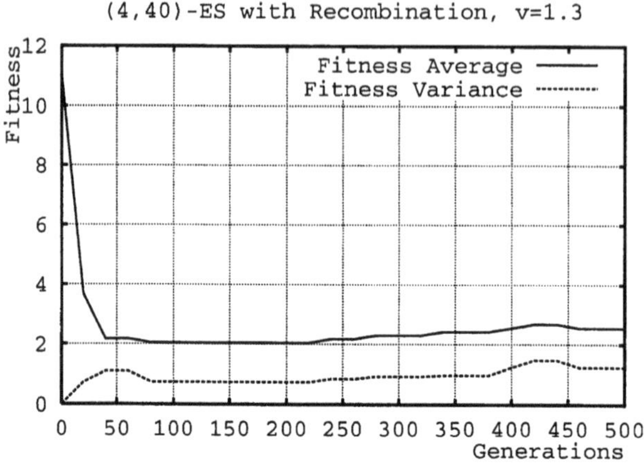

Figure 7. Performance of the (4,40)-evolution strategy (ES) with recombination and step size adaptation (with variance v=1.3).

$$\begin{aligned} \text{mis}(p) &= \begin{cases} 0 & \text{if } p = i, \forall k : u_i \geq u_k \\ 1 & \text{otherwise} \end{cases} \\ \text{error}(p) &= \sum_{j=1}^{N} \begin{cases} u_i^2 & \text{if } p \neq i \\ 1 - u_i^2 & \text{if } p = i \end{cases} \end{aligned} \tag{9}$$

where N=18 denotes the number of input features φ_i, P=700 denotes the number of test patterns, and u_i denotes the unit with the highest activation, i.e., the winner of the classification process. As can be seen, the error term is bounded by $0 \leq \text{error}(p) \leq 1$ and is required to avoid plateaus.

7 Results

A small sample of our results are presented in Figures 7 to 12. Each of these figures shows both the population's average fitness as well as its fitness variance. All figures are averages over eight independent runs. Figure 7 shows the performance of the (4,40)-evolution strategy with recombination and self-adaptation of step size (with variance v=1.3). It can be clearly seen that after approximately 50 generations, the systems had only two remaining misclassifications on average. Unfortunately, the fitness value did not dropped any further within the next 450 generations. The evolution strategy could not escape from these (local) minima, since

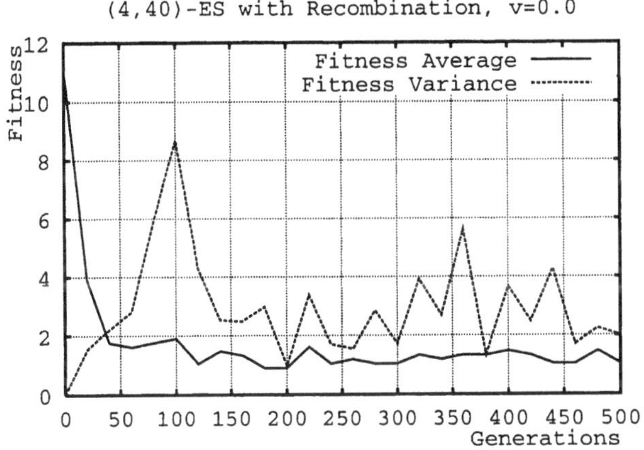

Figure 8. Performance of the (4,40)-evolution strategy (ES) with recombination but with constant step size (variance v=0.0), i.e., without any self-adaptation.

the step size approached very small values. In order to verify the possible existence of local minima, Figure 8 shows the same experiment but without any self-adaptation of the step size. It can be clearly seen that in this case, the procedure often reaches a 100% recognition rate, i.e., no misclassifications; the fitness variance is quite high though.

In comparison, Figure 9 shows the performance of the (4+40)-evolution

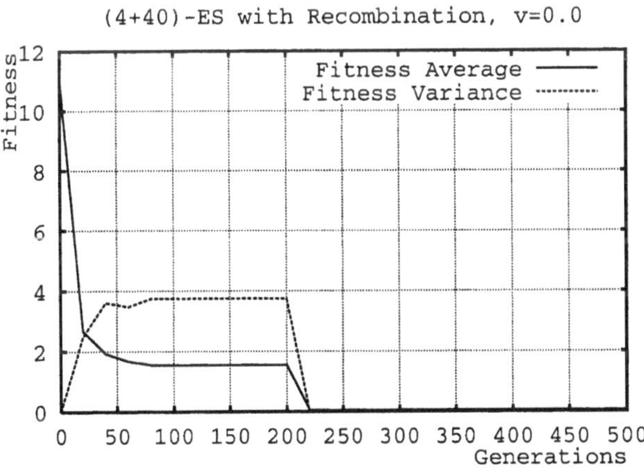

Figure 9. Performance of the (4+40)-evolution strategy (ES) with recombination and with constant step size (variance v=0.0), i.e., without any self-adaptation.

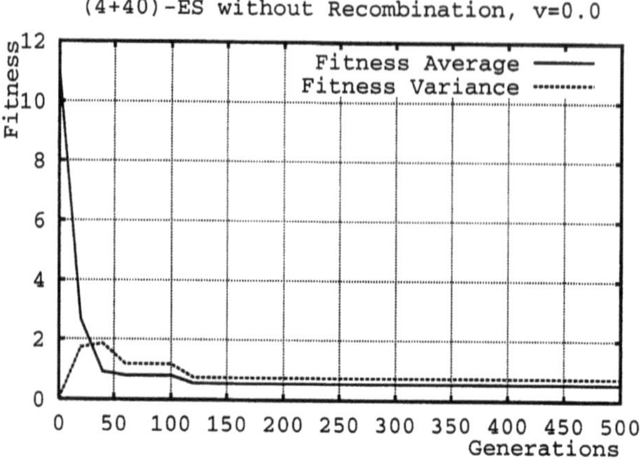

Figure 10. Performance of the (4+40)-evolution strategy (ES) without recombination and with constant step size (variance v=0.0), i.e., without any self-adaptation.

strategy with recombination and with constant step size (variance v=0.0). It can be clearly seen, that due to the μ-fold elitism, the procedure *reliably* finds the optimal case with a 100% recognition rate; after approximately 220 generations, the fitness values approach zero with vanishing variance.

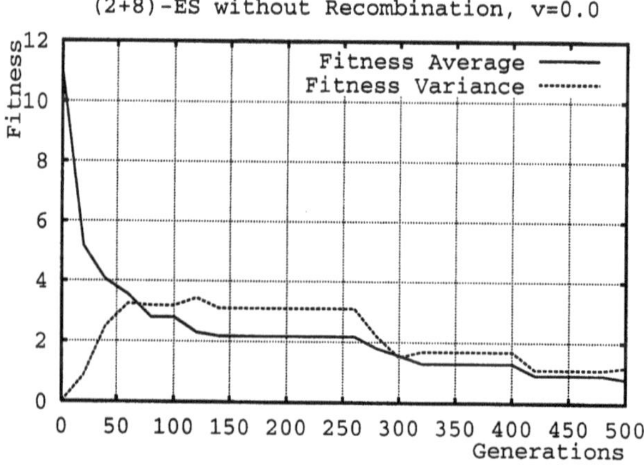

Figure 11. Performance of the (2+8)-evolution strategy (ES) with recombination and without step size adaptation (variance v=0.0), i.e., without any self-adaptation.

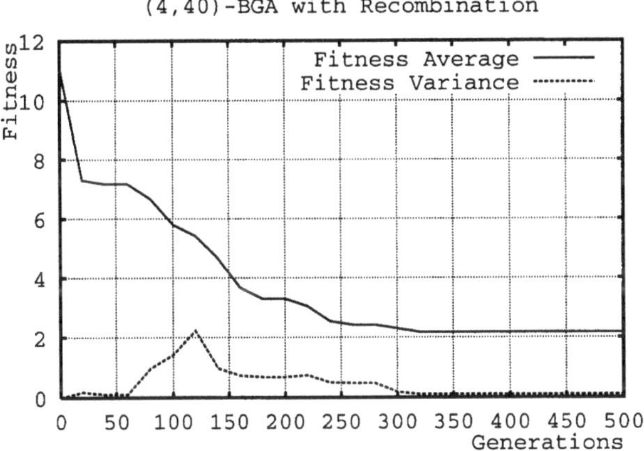

Figure 12. Performance of the (4,40)-breeder genetic algorithm (BGA) with recombination.

The performance effect of recombination can be seen by comparing Figure 9 with Figure 10. This comparison indicates that recombination yields some performance advantage; not using recombination (Figure 10) slightly slows down the evolutionary process.

Figure 11 shows the effect of the population size on the performance. As can be expected, a smaller population size leads to a significant increase of the number of generations. However, when focusing on the number of function evaluations, the (2+8)-evolution strategy is actually significantly faster. Finally, Figure 12 shows the performance of the (4,40)-breeder genetic algorithm with recombination. The figure indicates that this procedure stagnates at two misclassifications with vanishing variance. This experiment suggests that applying mutations with only a small probability $p_m = 1/n$ has some disadvantages and is not suitable to escape from local optima. Moreover, the application of recombination did not solve this problem.

8 Discussion

This chapter has shown that it is feasible to utilize a data-glove and neural network classifier as a control system for a simple virtual reality application. The experiments have demonstrated that evolutionary algorithms can tune a previously trained radial basis function network, such that it yields recognition rates comparable to backpropagation networks.

In addition, radial basis function networks allow for an efficient online tuning. In order to exploit this capability, an online-tuning module is currently under development. A situation in which all output units are below a certain threshold or in which at least two units have almost the same activation indicates that the system is used by a new user who may have hand characteristics too different from the training persons. In this case, the online-tuning module may ask the user to provide a set of some typical prototypes with which the radial basis function can easily be tuned.

Future research will be devoted to the following topics:

- Recognition of dynamic gestures, such as waving or wagging a finger, which can make a sign language much more intuitive. In order to correctly recognize dynamic gestures, the data-glove must be equipped with a tracking device, such as the Ascension Flock of Birds [1] or the Polhemus Fastrak [11], in order to provide the system with positional and orientational information.

- Using both hands may also be considerable improvement. In a virtual reality application, where a particular gesture of the right hand, such as "extended index finger", for instance, is assigned to the command "move forward", gestures of the left hand could be used as modifiers to regulate the speed.

- The recognition of gesture sequences imposes the problem of detecting and eliminating unwanted intermediate gestures. If, for example, the gesture "thumb up" is followed by an "extended index finger", the gesture "gun" (extended index finger plus thumb) might unintentionally be formed during the transition.

The application of a gesture recognition system as described in this chapter must not necessarily be restricted to virtual reality applications. Once the problems mentioned above have been solved, it is also conceivable, for example, to use such systems to help translate the American Sign Language (ASL) into spoken English.

Acknowledgments

The authors gratefully thank Peter Stucki and Rolf Pfeifer for their continuous support. This research was supported in part by the Swiss National Foundation, grant number 21-50684.97.

References

[1] Ascension Technology Corporation, P.O. Box 527, Burlington, VT 05402, ascension@ascension-tech.com, http://www.ascension-tech.com.

[2] Bäck, T., Hammel, U., and Schwefel, H.-P. (1997), "Evolutionary computation: comments on the history and current state," *IEEE Transactions on Evolutionary Computation*, vol. 1, no. 1, pp. 3-17.

[3] Bäck, T. and Schwefel, H.-P. (1993), "An overview of evolutionary algorithms for parameter optimization," *Evolutionary Computation*, vol. 1, no. 1, pp. 1-23.

[4] Fogel, L.J. (1962), "Autonomous automata," *Industrial Research*, vol. 4, pp. 14-19.

[5] Fogel, D.B. (1995), *Evolutionary Computation: Toward a New Philosophy of Machine Learning Intelligence*, IEEE Press, Jersy, NJ.

[6] Goldberg, D.E. (1989), *Genetic Algorithms in Search, Optimization and Machine Learning*, Addison-Wesley, Reading, MA.

[7] Hertz, J., Krogh, A., and Palmer, R. (1991), *Introduction to the Theory of Neural Computation*, Addison-Wesley Publishing Company, Redwood City, CA.

[8] Kamarthi, S.V. and Pittner, S. (1999), "Accelerating neural network training using weight extrapolations," *Neural Networks*, vol. 12, pp. 1285-1299.

[9] Kieldsen, R. and Kender, J. (1996), "Toward the use of gesture in traditional user interfaces," *Proceedings of the Second International Conference on Automatic Face and Gesture Recognition*, IEEE, pp. 151-156.

[10] Mühlenbein, H. and Schlierkamp-Voosen, D. (1993), "Predictive models for the breeder genetic algorithm I," *Evolutionary Computation*, vol. 1, no. 1, pp. 25-50.

[11] Polhemus Inc., 1 Hercules Drive, P.O. Box 560, Colchester, VT 05446, `sales@polhemus.com`, `http://www.polhemus.com`.

[12] Press, W.H., Flannery, B.P., Teukolsky, S.A., and Vetterling, W.T. (1987), *Numerical Recipes in C: the Art of Scientific Computing*, Cambridge University Press.

[13] Production and distribution of data gloves and related devices. Virtual Technologies, Inc., 2175 Park Boulevard, Palo Alto, CA 94306, `http://www.virtex.com`.

[14] Rechenberg, I. (1973), *Evolutionsstrategie*, Frommann-Holzboog, Stuttgart. Also printed in [15]. (In German.)

[15] Rechenberg, I. (1994), *Evolutionsstrategie*, Frommann-Holzboog, Stuttgart. (In German.)

[16] Rojas, R. (1996), *Neural Networks: a Systematic Introduction*, Springer-Verlag, Berlin, Germany.

[17] Schlierkamp-Voosen, D. and Mühlenbein, H. (1994), "Strategy adaptation by competing subpopulations," in Davidor, Y., Schwefel, H.-P., and Männer, R. (Eds.), *Parallel Problem Solving from Nature (PPSN III)*, Springer-Verlag Berlin, pp. 199-208.

[18] Schwefel, H.-P. (1995), *Evolution and Optimum Seeking*, John Wiley and Sons, NY.

[19] Weissmann, J. and Salomon, R. (1999), "Gesture recognition for virtual reality applications using data gloves and neural networks," *Proceedings of the 1999 International Joint Conference on Neural Networks*, IEEE.

[20] d'Ydewalle, G. *et al.* (1995), "Graphical versus character-based word processors: an analysis of user performance," *Behaviour and Information Technology*, vol. 14, no. 4, pp. 208-214.

Chapter 3

Using Normalized RBF Networks to Map Hand Gestures to Speech

S.S. Fels

Glove-TalkII is a system that translates hand gestures to speech through an adaptive interface. Hand gestures are mapped continuously to 10 control parameters of a parallel formant speech synthesizer. The mapping allows the hand to act as an artificial vocal tract that produces speech in real time. This gives an unlimited vocabulary in addition to direct control of fundamental frequency and volume. Currently, the best version of Glove-TalkII uses several input devices (including a Cyberglove, a 3-space tracker, a keyboard and a foot-pedal), a parallel formant speech synthesizer and 3 neural networks. The gesture-to-speech task is divided into vowel and consonant production by using a mixture of experts architecture where the gating network weights the outputs of a vowel and a consonant neural network. The gating network and the consonant network are trained with examples from the user. The vowel network implements a fixed, user-defined relationship between hand-position and vowel sound and does not require any training examples from the user. Volume, fundamental frequency and stop consonants are produced with a fixed mapping from the input devices. One subject has trained to speak intelligibly with Glove-TalkII. He speaks slowly with speech quality similar to a text-to-speech synthesizer but with far more natural sounding pitch variations.

In the final Glove-TalkII system [8], one of the main networks is the consonant network comprised of a input layer of 12 units corresponding to twelve hand sensors, a hidden layer of fifteen *normalized* RBF units connected to nine sigmoid output units. Normalized RBF units provide a much better topology for mapping hand gestures to consonant sounds than either unnormalized RBF units or sigmoid units. The RBFs were trained in two passes. First, an approximation of the RBF centers was obtained in a single quick pass through the training data. The centers were clamped while the output layer was trained iteratively using conjugate gradient descent on the training data. After this first stage of training was complete, the RBF centers were unclamped and all the network parameters were optimized. The vowel network also used a hidden layer with normalized RBF activation functions which proved to be critical in the performance of the final Glove-TalkII system. The V/C gating network used sigmoid activation units. In this discussion of Glove-TalkII, the implementation, training, implications, and interpretation of normalized RBF units are covered. The normalized RBF architecture is compared to architectures having linear, sigmoid, sigmoid plus softmax, and unnormalized RBF activation functions in both gesture-to-vowel and gesture-to-consonant mapping . In addition, using a normalized RBF network in the context of a mixture-of-experts framework in a soft real-time environment is also discussed.

1 Introduction

Adaptive interfaces are a natural and important class of applications for neural networks. When a person must provide high bandwidth control of a complex physical device, a compatible mapping between the person's movements and the behavior of the device becomes crucial. With many devices the mapping is fixed and if a poor mapping is used, the device is difficult to control. Using adaptive neural networks, it is possible to build device interfaces where the mapping adapts automatically during a training phase. Such adaptive interfaces would simplify the process of designing a compatible mapping and would also allow the mapping to be tailored to each individual user. The key features of neural networks in the context of adaptive interfaces are the following:

- Neural networks learn input/output functions from examples provided by the user who demonstrates the input that should lead to a specified output. This "extensional" programming requires no computer expertise.

- Adapting the interface to the peculiarities of a new user is simple. The new user has only to create example data to retrain the network.

- Once trained, the networks run very quickly, even on a serial machine. Also, neural networks are inherently suitable for parallel computation.

In this chapter, neural networks are used to implement an adaptive interface, called Glove-TalkII, which maps hand gestures to control parameters of a parallel formant speech synthesizer to allow a user to speak.

There are many different possible schemes for converting hand gestures to speech. The choice of scheme depends on the granularity of the speech that you want to produce. Figure 1 identifies a spectrum defined by possible divisions of speech based on the duration of the sound for each granularity. What is interesting is that in general, the coarser the division of speech, the smaller the bandwidth necessary for the user. In contrast, where the granularity of speech is on the order of articulatory muscle movements (i.e. the artificial vocal tract [AVT]) high bandwidth control is necessary for good speech. Devices which implement this model of speech production are like musical instruments which produce speech sounds. The user must control the timing of sounds to produce speech much as a musician plays notes to produce music. The AVT allows unlimited vocabulary, control of pitch and non-verbal sounds. Glove-TalkII is an adaptive interface that implements an AVT.

Translating gestures to speech using an AVT model has a long history beginning in the late 1700's. Systems developed include a bellows-driven hand-varied resonator tube with auxiliary controls (1790's [16]), a rubber-moulded skull with actuators for manipulating tongue and jaw position (1880's [1]) and a keyboard-footpedal interface controlling a set of linearly spaced bandpass frequency generators called the Voder (1940 [5]). The Voder was demonstrated at the World's Fair in 1939 by operators who had trained continuously for one year to learn to speak with the system. This suggests that the task of speaking with a gestural interface is very difficult and the training times could be significantly decreased with a better interface. Glove-TalkII is implemented with neural networks which allows the system to learn the user's interpretation of an articulatory model of speaking.

This chapter begins with an overview of the whole Glove-TalkII system. Then, each neural network is described along with its training and test results. Finally, a qualitative analysis is provided of the speech produced by

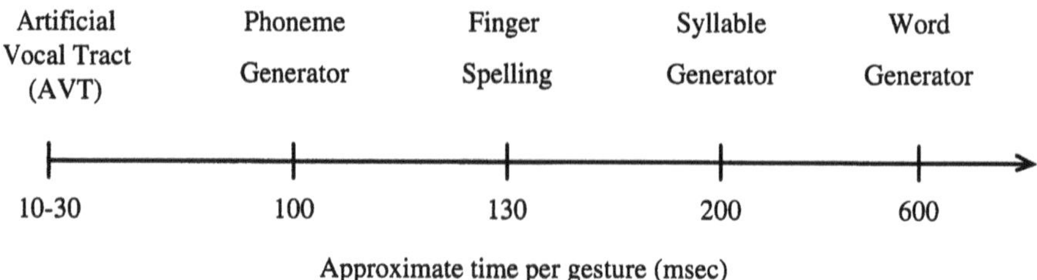

Figure 1. Spectrum of gesture-to-speech mappings based on the granularity of speech.

a single subject after 100 hours of speaking with Glove-TalkII followed by a summary.

2 Overview of Glove-TalkII

The Glove-TalkII system converts hand gestures to speech, based on a gesture-to-formant model. The gesture vocabulary is based on a vocal-articulator model of the hand. By dividing the mapping tasks into independent subtasks, a substantial reduction in network size and training time is possible (see [7]).

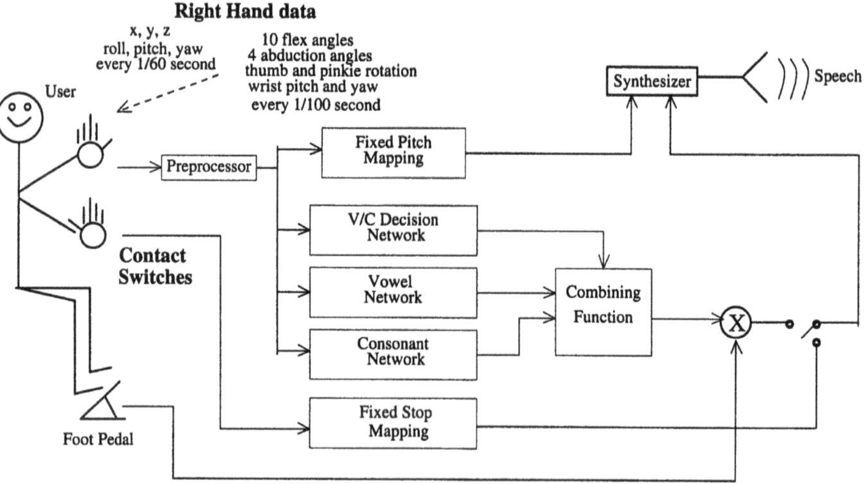

Figure 2. Block diagram of Glove-TalkII: input from the user is measured by the Cyberglove, polhemus, ContactGlove and foot pedal, then mapped using neural networks and fixed functions to formant parameters which drive the parallel formant synthesizer [15].

Figure 2 illustrates the whole Glove-TalkII system. Important features include the input devices, the three neural networks labeled vowel/consonant decision (V/C), vowel, and consonant, and the speech output device. Input to the system is measured with a Cyberglove, polhemus sensor, keyboard and footpedal. The Cyberglove measures 18 angles of the user's hand every 10 msec including two flex angles for each finger (metacarpophalangeal and proximal interphalangeal joints) and abduction angles. The polhemus sensor measures 6 degrees of freedom of the hand including the X,Y,Z, roll, pitch, and yaw of the user's hand relative to a fixed source. The ContactGlove measures nine contact points between the fingers and thumb on the left hand. The footpedal measures the depression angle of the pedal. These inputs are mapped to speech using three neural networks and other fixed mappings. In the results reported, the analyzed networks differ slightly from the *final* Glove-TalkII system. The number of input and hidden units were tailored to the one user trained to use Glove-TalkII. The types of units and overall architecture were determined from the analysis presented here.

The V/C network is trained on data collected from the user to decide whether he wants to produce a vowel or a consonant sound. Likewise, the consonant network is trained to produce consonant sounds based on user-generated examples of phoneme sounds defined in an initial gesture vocabulary. In contrast, the vowel network implements a fixed mapping between hand-positions and vowel phonemes defined by the user. Nine contact points on the ContactGlove designate the stop consonants (B, D, G, J, P, T, K, CH, NG)[1], because the dynamics of such sounds proved too fast to be controlled by the user. The foot pedal provides a volume control by adjusting the speech amplitude and this mapping is fixed. The fundamental frequency, which is related to the pitch of the speech, is determined by a fixed mapping from the user's hand height.

100 times a second the system sends 10 control parameters to a Loughborough Sound Images parallel formant speech synthesizer [15]. The 10 parameters are: nasal formant amplitude (ALF), first, second and third formant frequency and amplitude (F1, A1, F2, A2, F3, A3), high fre-

[1]Capital letters are used to indicate phonemes available from the text-to-speech synthesizer to differentiate them from phoneme representations like the International Phonetic Alphabet (IPA).

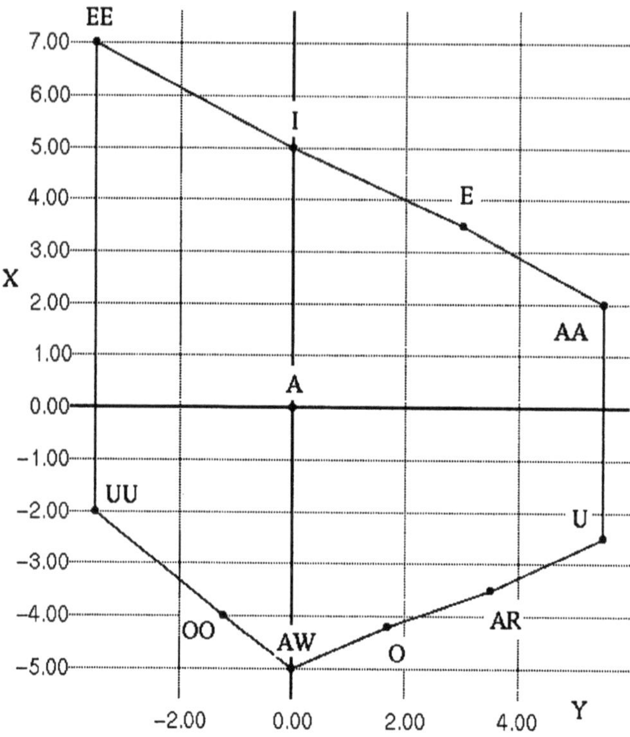

Figure 3. Hand-position to Vowel Sound Mapping. The coordinates are specified relative to the origin at the sound A. The X and Y coordinates form a horizontal plane when the user is sitting. The X coordinate increases away from the user and the Y coordinate increases to the user's right. The text-to-speech synthesizer uses 11 cardinal phonemes which are used as targets for the vowel network.

quency amplitude (AHF), degree of voicing (V) and fundamental frequency (F0). Each of the control parameters is quantized to 6 bits.

Once trained, Glove-TalkII can be used as follows: to initiate speech, the user forms the hand shape of the first sound she intends to produce. She depresses the foot pedal and the sound comes out of the synthesizer. Vowels and consonants of various qualities are produced in a continuous fashion through the appropriate co-ordination of hand and foot motions. Words are formed by making the correct motions; for example, to say "hello" the user forms the "h" sound, depresses the foot pedal and quickly moves her hand to produce the "e" sound, then the "l" sound and finally the "o" sound. The user has complete control of the timing and quality of the individual sounds. The articulatory mapping between ges-

Table 1. Static Gesture-to-Consonant Mapping for all phonemes. Note, each gesture corresponds to a static *non-stop* consonant phoneme generated by the text-to-speech synthesizer.

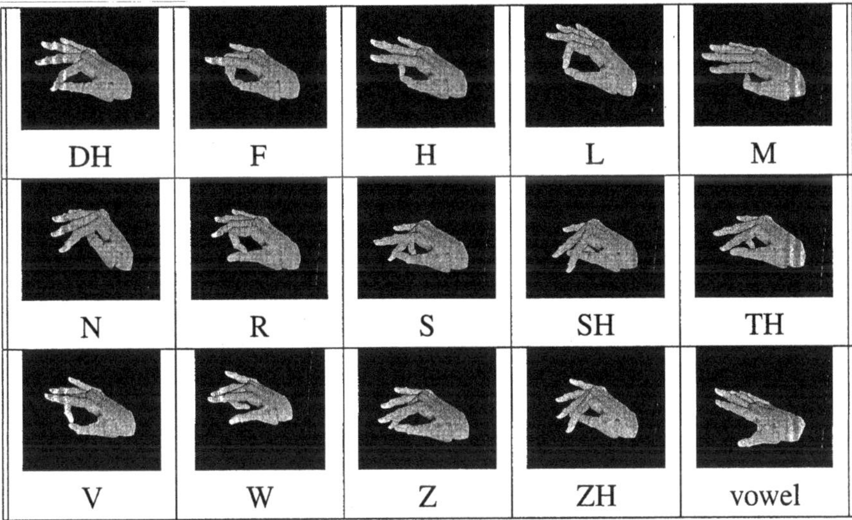

DH	F	H	L	M
N	R	S	SH	TH
V	W	Z	ZH	vowel

tures and speech is decided *a priori*. The mapping is based on a simplistic articulatory phonetic description of speech [11]. The X,Y coordinates (measured by the polhemus) are mapped to something like tongue position and height[2] producing vowels when the user's hand is in an open configuration (see Figure 3 for the correspondence and Table 1 for a typical vowel configuration). Manner and place of articulation for non-stop consonants are determined by opposition of the thumb with the index and middle fingers as described in Table 1. The ring finger controls voicing. Only *static* articulatory configurations are used as training points for the neural networks, and the interpolation between them is a result of the learning but is not explicitly trained. Ideally, the transitions should also be learned, but in the text-to-speech formant data we use for training [12] these transitions are poor, and it is very hard to extract accurate formant trajectories from real speech to use for training. The next sections describe the structure and training of each of the three different neural networks.

[2] In reality, the XY coordinates map more closely to changes in the first two formants, F1 and F2 of vowels. From the user's perspective though, the link to tongue movement is useful.

3 Glove-TalkII's Neural Networks

3.1 The Vowel/Consonant Decision Network (V/C Net)

The vowel/consonant network (V/C network) is responsible for figuring out whether the user wants to say a vowel sound or a consonant sound based on the current configuration of his hand. It uses 10 hand parameters from the Cyberglove to measure hand configuration: 8 flex angles (metacarpophalangeal and metacarpocarpal joints (knuckle and middle joints) of the thumb, index, middle and ring fingers), thumb abduction angle and thumb rotation angle. The output is a single number representing the probability that the hand configuration indicates a vowel. As described in Section 2, vowels are produced when the user's hand makes an open configuration illustrated for the vowel hand shape in Table 1. Whenever the user has a closed hand configuration he produces a consonant; for example, when he produces an "l" sound (see Table 1).

The output of the V/C network is used to weight the outputs of the vowel and consonant networks, which then produce a mixture of vowel and consonant formant parameters. The only training data available will include user-produced vowel or consonant sounds, no intermediate data is available[3]. The network should interpolate between the intermediate hand configurations to create a monotonic transition between vowels and consonants. A fairly sharp transition enables the user to move quickly from a vowel sound to a consonant sound in a reliable manner.

The V/C network should also produce reasonable outputs for unexpected hand configurations. For example, if the user hyperextends his hand, the network should continue to produce a vowel sound, since the hand remains in an open configuration. Similarly, if he exaggerates a consonant hand configuration, some type of consonant sound should be produced since the hand forms a virtual constriction. Such configurations are unusual and not expected in the training corpus, but may occur while the user is speaking.

---

[3]Intermediate training data is difficult to produce since the text-to-speech synthesizer only produces formant data which is categorized as vowels or phonemes.

Two different network configurations are considered. The first network is a 10-5-1 network with sigmoid activations. The inputs are the 10 scaled hand angles specified above. The output is the probability of a vowel sound. The important feature of this configuration is that only the current hand configuration influences whether a vowel or consonant is produced. The second network is a 30-15-1 network which uses 3 banks of 10 shift units of the 10 hand parameters. The current value of the 10 hand parameters (i.e. the values of the hand parameters at time t) constitute the values for the first bank of units. The second shift unit bank is the mean of the next two time steps of the hand angles (i.e. average hand parameters from time $t-1$ and $t-2$). The final shift unit bank is the mean of the next four time steps (i.e. from hand parameters averaged at times $t-3$, $t-4$, $t-5$ and $t-6$). Figure 4 illustrates this V/C network architecture. A reliable V/C decision may depend on the history of hand configurations, for example, a history of noisy hand data. In such case, if the network only considers the current (noisy) time step of hand data, it may oscillate between a vowel and consonant decision even though the user's hand is relatively still. This is not desirable behaviour perceptually since the speech outputs from the vowel and consonant networks are usually very different, causing the speech to switch back and forth between two very different sounds. Conversely, it is desirable to have the V/C network respond quickly when the user changes from a vowel configuration to a consonant configuration and vice-versa. The averaging scheme used provides a compromise between sensitivity to current hand configurations and averaging over past values to reduce the effects of noise.

A trade-off typically exists with averaging schemes between the relative importance of current hand parameters and past ones. In terms of the vowel/consonant decision, it is important that the user hear any difference immediately during transitions between consonants and vowels so that he can quickly adjust his speech. Clearly, current hand parameters are very important. Conversely, his hand may potentially produce noisy hand parameters (due to shaking for example), thus some averaging seems worthwhile. The compromise made here is to use a total of 7 time steps of hand parameters. The current time step is not averaged at all so that the network has access to the most recent hand configuration. The remaining time steps are averaged as specified above, allowing different amounts of averaging, depending on the relative temporal distance from

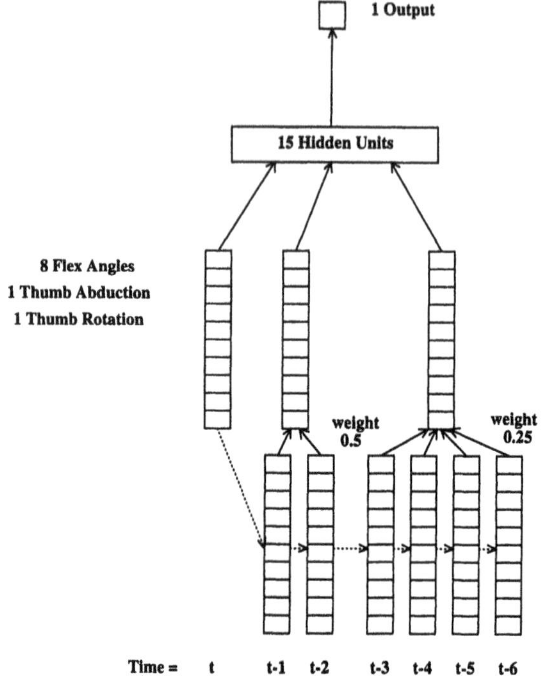

Figure 4. Proposed architecture for V/C network. This network uses three banks of shifted values of hand parameters. The first bank uses the current time step of hand parameters. Subsequent banks average previous hand parameter values as shown in the figure.

the current time.

3.1.1 Performance of the V/C Network

The two V/C networks are compared perceptually and in terms of mean squared error. The training data consists of 2600 examples of consonant configurations (350 approximants, 1510 fricatives [and aspirant], and 740 nasals) and 700 examples of vowel configurations obtained from an expert user. The test set consists of 1614 examples (1380 consonants and 234 vowels). Section 3.4.2 describes training and testing data collection. Table 2 shows the results from both networks.

As is clear from Table 2, both networks perform very well in terms of mean squared error. Both networks performed well when used with the whole system. During normal speaking neither network made perceptual

Table 2. Training and testing results for the two V/C networks. In the training set there were 2600 consonants and 700 vowels. In the test set there were 1380 consonants and 234 vowels.

Net	V/C	epochs	Train mean squared	Test mean squared	weights
1	vowels	47	0.00000	0.00000	61
	consonants		0.00000	0.00000	
2	vowels	61	0.00000	0.00135	481
	consonants		0.00000	0.00000	

errors. For the user that these networks were trained for, the decision boundary feels quite sharp, and provides very predictable, quick transitions from vowels to consonants and back. Also, vowel sounds are produced when the user hyperextends his hand. Any unusual consonant configurations which intuitively should be consonants produced consonant-like sounds. As the smaller of the two, network one appears to be the most obvious choice for the final Glove-TalkII system. However, since network two's averaging allows greater noise levels in the user's movements, it should be considered, especially if the user has difficulty making reliable hand gestures. Such difficulties arise when a user first learns to speak with Glove-TalkII. As the user progresses, network one can be trained on the more robust data and used subsequently.

3.2 The Vowel Network

In Glove-TalkII, the user's hand position in the x-y plane determines vowel sounds. Eight different neural network architectures are considered in this section to map the x and y values of the hand into the 8 relevant formant parameters (ALF, F1, A1, F2, A2, F3, A3 and AHF; V is fixed at 63 since all vowels are fully voiced). For the initial hand position to vowel mapping the absolute x and y positions of the hand for each static vowel sound are determined *a priori* (see Figure 3). From this predefined mapping, artificial training and test data are generated. This mapping is loosely based on a simple model of tongue position and height mapped to hand position. For all the networks considered, the x and y values and formant values were roughly scaled between 0 and 1.

Eight different networks are considered:

1. 2-8 linear network
2. 2-8-8 feed forward network with sigmoid activations
3. 2-8-8-11 feed forward network with sigmoid activations and an extra 11 unit softmax layer (see below)
4. eight 2-3-1 feed forward networks with sigmoid activation functions
5. (eight 2-3-1)-11 feed forward network with sigmoid activation functions and an extra softmax layer (see below)
6. 2-11-8 network with radial basis function hidden units with no normalization and sigmoid output units
7. 2-11-8 network with normalized radial basis function hidden units and sigmoid output units
8. 2-11-8-8 network with normalized radial basis function hidden units and sigmoid output units

Preliminary testing showed that the linear network and the feed forward sigmoid activation networks had difficulty separating some of the sounds (this was especially true for similar consonant network architectures, see Section 3.3). Therefore, some networks were tried with an extra layer of softmax units [2] (see appendix A) connected to the outputs of the networks. These networks can be thought of as performing "soft" categorization of the formant outputs (in addition to minimizing the formant error) into one of the 11 known vowel categories during training. This process should help the network disambiguate conflicting sounds (in the sum-square error and perceptual domain). For example consider network 3, a 2-8-8-11 network. Figure 5 shows it schematically. Notice the formant outputs are fully connected to the 11 softmax units. The softmax units categorize the outputs into one of the 11 target vowels. Note that the softmax units are used only to help train the networks, and only the formant outputs are needed when the system speaks. The softmax units' errors were scaled by 0.01 during training to limit their contributions during error backpropagation. Requiring the network to categorize the formant outputs causes it to learn to minimize the mean squared error

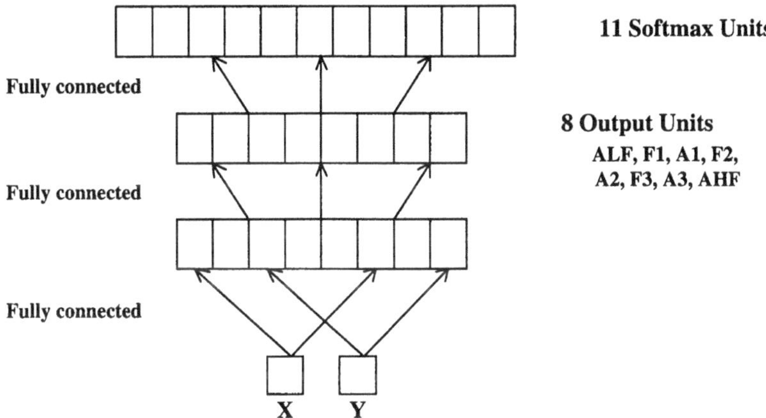

Figure 5. Network 3 - the formant output units are fully connected to the layer of softmax units.

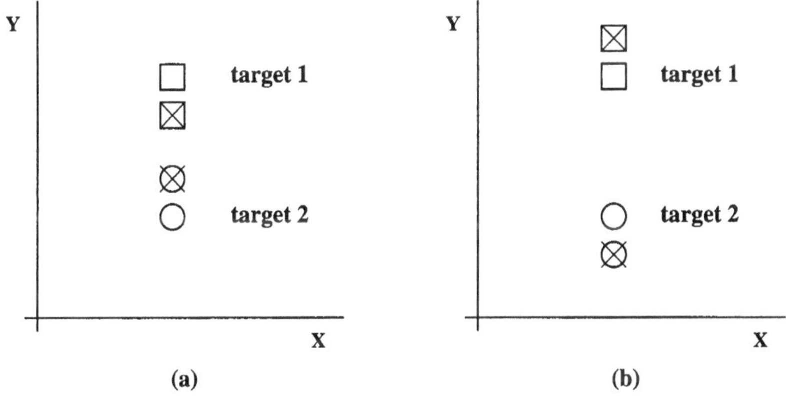

Figure 6. Example of more separate equivalent squared error. In Figure (a) the outputs are between the two target values. In Figure (b), the outputs are outside the target values making them easier to separate; yet, the mean squared error is the same in both cases.

and to maximize its ability to discriminate. Figure 6 illustrates how this process works. Here the target values are shown by t_1 and t_2. The output of a network for two cases of each class are marked x_1 and x_2. In both cases, the squared error remains the same, but in case b the outputs separate more easily. The analogue in the formant space makes the outputs in case b perceptually more distinct than in case a. The extra layer of softmax units at the outputs should pressure the network to behave as in case b.

The second architecture considered uses *normalized* radial basis function (RBF) units [4]. The radial basis function units used are described by the following equation:

$$o_j = e^{-\frac{\sum(w_{ji}-o_i)^2}{\sigma_j{}^2}} \tag{1}$$

where o_j is the (un-normalized) output of the RBF unit, w_{ji} is the weight from unit i to unit j and σ_j is the width of the RBF. The summation is performed over all units connected to unit j. The RBF can be considered as a Gaussian bump centered at the incoming weights (w_{ji}'s) with variance $\sigma_j{}^2$ (or width of σ_j). The normalization (as described in appendix A) is this:

$$n_j = \frac{o_j}{\sum\limits_{\omega \in \Omega} o_\omega} \tag{2}$$

where n_j is the normalized output of unit j and the summation lies over all the units in the group, Ω, of normalized RBF units. The X and Y values of each of the 11 vowels in the predefined mapping (see Figure 3) determine the centers of the RBFs.

Normalization should provide the required interpolation properties for the task. In particular, the user has a wider dynamic range in the x-y space than the training data. This occurs because the training data was determined from typical values in the x-y plane instead of considering every possible value. Hence, many values in the x-y plane are never seen by the network during training but are seen during running of the network. The network should respond in a reasonable way to these novel observed values. To illustrate, consider the vowel mapping in Figure 3. Here the (x,y) coordinates are the abscissa and the ordinate axis. The 11 cardinal vowels are positioned on the page according to the hand position that should produce them. The corresponding cardinal-vowel formants should be produced at these 11 positions. This can be accomplished relatively easily by an RBF network. But, what should be produced at places far away from the cardinal vowels? Consider for example, what sound should be produced if the user's hand is in the upper left corner? One answer to these questions is that once the user's hand extends past the cardinal sound, only the cardinal sound can be heard; that is, if the user passes the EE sound the sound produced continues to sound like an EE. Normalizing the RBF units provides this type of extrapolation. To understand why, imagine 11 RBFs centered at the cardinal vowel sounds with some small but reasonable width. Next, consider a point left and above the RBF centered at the EE sound. The EE-RBF will have a greater response (though the response will likely be very small) than all the other 10 RBF's since it is closest. After normalization this difference magnifies so that only the normalized EE-RBF responds, producing an EE sound.

The next section discusses and compares the training and test results for each network architecture.

3.2.1 Performance of the Vowel Network

The different vowel networks are compared in four different ways. First, the mean squared error is compared for the training set and a test set. Second, a range of X and Y values which span the user's movement space are input to the networks and the F1 and F2 output values are plotted and compared. Third, a perceptual comparison is made by actually attempting to speak with the networks. Fourth, the sizes of the network are considered since significant computing constraints exist when using the system to speak.

Mean Squared Error (MSE) Performance

Table 3 shows the training and test results from the different networks. The training set consists of 100 examples of each vowel sound with random noise added to the x and y centre values. The added noise was picked from the rangc [-0.025, 0.025] for x and y with uniform distribution (this corresponds to a range of [-0.5,0.5] cm in the x range and [-0.26,0.26] cm in the y range after scaling). Fifty examples of each cardinal vowel with different ranges of noise added to the centers provide test results; for example, the test results under the right sub-column of Test MSE derive from a test set with uniformly distributed noise in the range [-0.1,0.1] added to the x and y coordinates of fifty examples of each cardinal vowel. The number of run weights is the number of weights in each network when the network is used in the final system. For most of the networks there are the same number of weights when training and running. The only networks where the number is different are the softmax networks since the softmax units are not required once the networks are trained.

Two variations were tried with networks 7 and 8. In both networks, vari-

Table 3. Training and test results for 8 different vowel networks. There are 1100 training cases and 550 test examples. The mean cross-entropy error is scaled by 0.01 during training. Three different noise levels are used in the testing data. For networks 7 and 8, case 'a' has the RBF variance fixed at 0.025 and for case 'b' it optimizes from an initial value of 0.025.

Net	epochs	Training Error		Testing MSE			run weights	total weights
		mean squared	mean X-entropy	0.05	0.1	0.2		
1	6	0.0069		0.0070	0.0087	0.0154	24	24
2	1000	0.0023		0.0025	0.0052	0.0168	96	96
3	1000	0.0027	0.0056	0.0028	0.0060	0.0197	99	99
4	1000	0.0022		0.0024	0.0050	0.0162	104	104
5	1000	0.0027	0.0032	0.0028	0.0057	0.0181	104	104
6a	200	0.0010		0.0013	0.0030	0.0112	118	129
6b	126	0.0010		0.0012	0.0031	0.0124	129	129
7a	150	0.0016		0.0018	0.0038	0.0120	118	129
7b	50	0.0007		0.0008	0.0020	0.0107	129	129
8a	150	0.0019		0.0021	0.0039	0.0112	190	201
8b	150	0.0006		0.0007	0.0019	0.0103	201	201

ation 'a' uses fixed RBF widths of $\sqrt{0.025}$ (half of the range of random noise added to the training data). In variation 'b' the widths were nominally set to $\sqrt{0.025}$ and then optimized with the rest of the parameters.

All the networks were trained with conjugate gradient descent and a line search [9]. Weight decay was investigated with some of the networks, but offered no significant improvement in results (and in many cases caused poorer performance). Training stopped after 1000 epochs unless the error appeared to stabilize earlier. With networks 1 and 6b the line search failed [9] after 6 and 126 epochs respectively.

For networks using the extra layer of softmax units (networks 3 and 5), errors from the softmax units had to be weighted with respect to the mean squared error. If the errors were weighted equally, the cross entropy error from the softmax would dominate the mean squared error, causing very poor performance. After a number of different weightings were tried, a relative weighting of 0.01 was found to give good results.

Network 8b is the best network (on the most difficult test set) in terms of mean squared error with an expected formant error of $\pm$ 5%[4]. It is

[4]The expected formant error for the vowel net is found by the following equation:

$$fe = \sqrt{\frac{2 \cdot \text{total error}}{(\#\ \text{examples}) \cdot (\#\ \text{formants})}}.$$

also the largest network to use with 201 run weights. However, if just the mean squared error is considered, all the networks appear to have generalized reasonably well; at least for noise levels up to 0.2. The worst network in terms of generalization is network 3 with an error of 0.0197 which leads to an expected error for each formant of $\pm$ 7%. Network 7a is emphasized in the table since it is the one used in the final version of Glove-TalkII for reasons described below. Further comparison is still possible before actually trying to speak with each network to determine which networks are suitable.

Mapping Topology Comparison

Vowels can be identified approximately by the first two formants, F1 and F2. Thus, one technique for comparing the different networks involves graphing the F1 and F2 outputs with respect to a large range of x and y values. To this end, a test set was created which tesselated the x-y plane in the interval [0,1] on each axis by 400 evenly distributed points. The F1 and F2 outputs of the networks were plotted together on one graph. These graphs show for each network which vowel sound is produced depending on the position of the user's hand. F1 is plotted as the height of the cross and F2 is plotted as its width at each of the test points. For example, as shown in Figure 7, a medium length horizontal line represents the EE sound, a shorter vertical line represents a U sound and a small cross represents the AA sound. The 11 cardinal vowel sounds used to train the networks are shown on the graph as reference points. Remember, the networks were trained on X and Y coordinates of these canonical vowels with added noise ($\pm$ 0.025). The range of X and Y values plotted shows almost the full range of motion the user will ever make while speaking, therefore, the graphs give a good indication of the vowel sounds the user will say.

Consider the graph in Figure 7 which is produced using network 1. This graph shows that at each of the reference points the network produces sounds reasonably close to those desired. However, outside the reference points the formants are extrapolated linearly. That is, the changes in each of the parameters continues changing the formant parameters which in turn makes the sounds less vowel-like. For instance, the horizontal lines gradually get longer and the vertical ones get shorter for points to the left

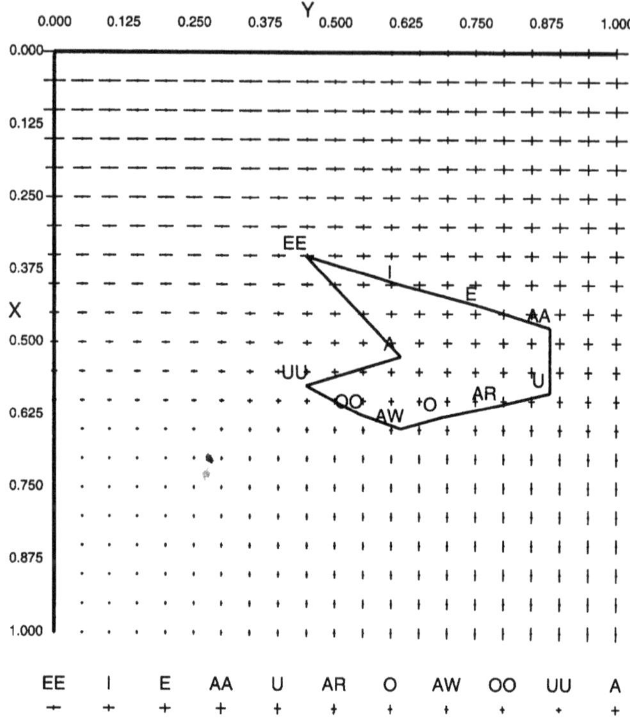

Figure 7. Vowel space for network 1. The height of the cross represents the F1 value and the width represents the F2 value.

and above the EE sound. The speech therefore begins at the EE sound but as the user's hand moves to the left and above, it changes to an extreme EE sound, and finally to a non-vowel like sound. Therefore, if the user overshoots the EE sound he will get unintelligible speech using network 1. Networks 1-5 all exhibit this type of behaviour.

The unnormalized RBF network suffers a different problem. The vowel space for network 6a in Figure 8 shows that the values inside its reference points are all very reasonable; however, outside the reference points the vowel sound becomes similar to the A sound. This is not surprising since none of the RBF units are active outside the reference range, thus, the RBF layer has no activity and the output is determined by the output units' bias. After the training session the biases produce an A sound like the average of all the vowels.

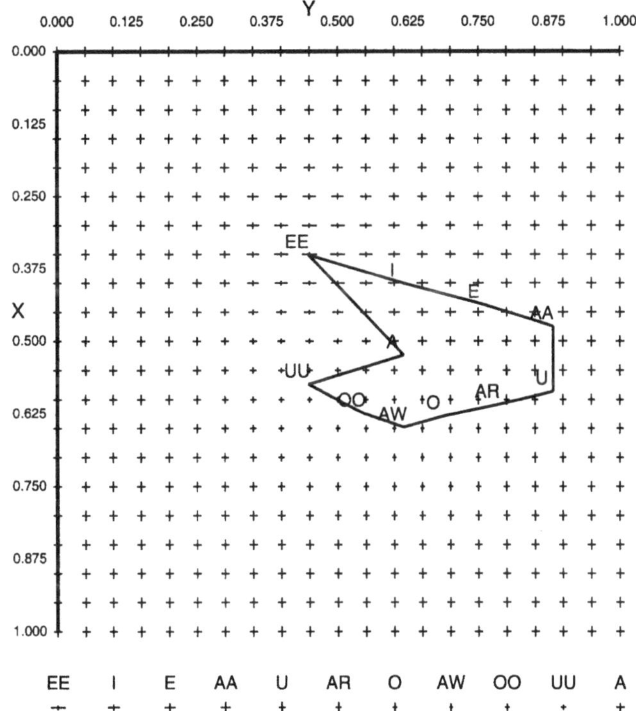

Figure 8. Vowel space for network 6a. The height of the cross represents the F1 value and the width represents the F2 value.

The normalized RBF networks (networks 7 and 8) are the most interesting. In the cases with fixed RBF widths, the extrapolation appears sensible as shown in Figure 9 which is obtained from network 7a. Consider the area to the left and above EE. For a large part of the area, the EE sound is produced (though it is slightly closer to the cardinal value using network 8a). For each cardinal vowel a corresponding patch outside the reference area extends to the border. This is desirable behaviour since overshoots will continue to produce the same vowel sounds as the nearest cardinal vowel. The RBF networks which allow their widths to vary also have this desirable quality as shown in Figure 10 obtained from network 7b. However, it only extends so far. At the extreme values (i.e., the unmapped section in the upper left and right parts in the figure), the RBF units underflow, causing the normalization to be ill-defined.

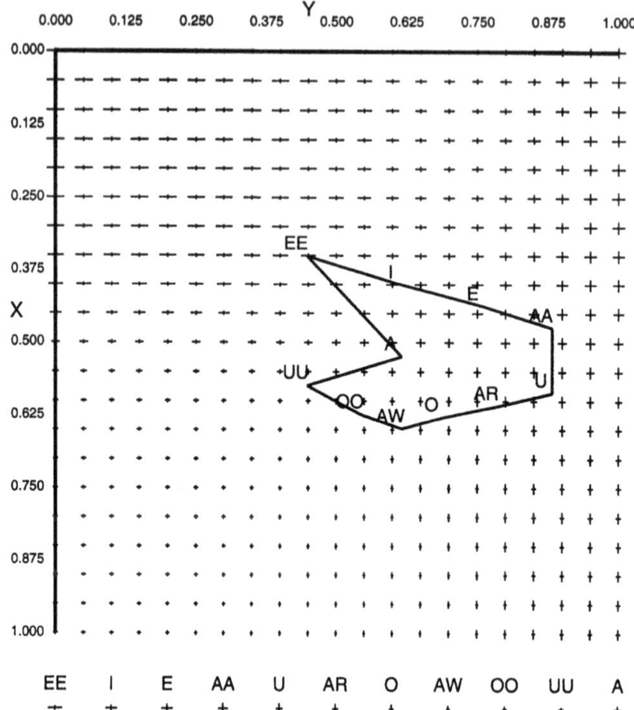

Figure 9. Vowel space for network 7a. The height of the cross represents the F1 value and the width represents the F2 value.

Perceptual Testing and Size Comparison

The analysis of the vowel space suggests that either network 7 or 8 would be best. At this point one must try speaking with each of the different networks to determine the best choice. Networks 1, 3, 7a and 8a were all tried. As expected, both networks 1 and 3 caused problems whenever diphthongs like IE and AE were spoken. In these cases, the user often overshot the EE sound and produced a nonsensical sound. Network 7a and 8a sounded very similar. With both networks all vowel sounds were easy to produce. The smaller of the two, network 7a, is chosen as the best network to use in the final version of Glove-TalkII.

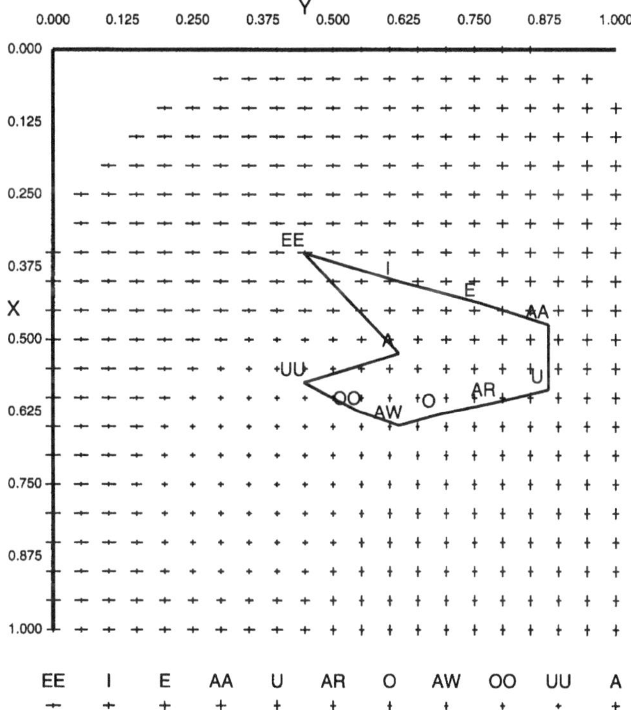

Figure 10. Vowel space for network 7b. The height of the cross represents the F1 value and the width represents the F2 value.

3.3 The Consonant Network

The consonant net translates hand configurations to consonant sounds. Section 2 describes the mapping. There are 14 static hand configurations mapped to static formant parameters, corresponding to available phonemes from the text-to-speech synthesizer. The input requires only 10 parameters to measure the hand configuration. Angles measured include the inner and outer flex angles of the thumb, index, middle and ring fingers, the thumb abduction angle and the thumb rotation angle. The output space has 9 formant parameters consisting of ALF, F1, A1, F2, A2, F3, A3, AHF, and V. Notice the voicing parameter is required since consonants have different degrees of voicing. This space has considerably more dimensions than the vowel space, thus, training data obtained from the user may not cover the entire space. One feature that makes consonant space different from vowel space is the relatively well-defined ranges of the input parameters.

Several performance criteria are relevant when considering the design of the consonant network. First, the training data from the text-to-speech synthesizer has 14 distinct static phonemes (that are not stop consonants). Each of these phonemes corresponds to a static hand configuration (see the definition of the initial consonant vocabulary in Section 2). The consonant network must map these hand configurations so that each phoneme sounds clear. Second, interpolation between static phonemes should be reasonable. When the user moves his hand between different static phonemes (i.e. from an “l” to an “r”) the intermediate sounds produced should not pass through any other phonemes. The hand configurations have been carefully designed to minimize overlap; however, the inductive bias of the network remains responsible for sensibly interpolating the formant space between hand configurations not in the training set. Third, another desirable feature, similar to the vowel space property, is that small errors in achieving targets in formant space should make the sounds more distinctive rather than less distinctive.

Four different consonant network architectures are compared:

1. 10-9 linear network,
2. 10-14-9 feed forward network with sigmoid activations,
3. 10-14-9-14 feed forward network with sigmoid activations and an extra layer of softmax units,
4. 10-14-9 network with normalized radial basis function (RBF) hidden units with sigmoid output units.

Networks 1 and 2 are self-explanatory. Network 3 is a feed forward network with an additional layer of softmax units to assist training (see appendix A). As discussed in Section 3.2, softmax units are added to make formant space squared errors sound more distinctive. This becomes particularly important in consonant space since some of the consonants are easily confused (i.e. M and N). In network 3, the softmax units are fully connected to the formant output units. The softmax units are not used during speaking. The normalized RBF network (network 4) is similar to the one used in the vowel network (Section 3.2).

The next section compares the performance of each of the networks. The networks are compared using mean squared error, subjective listening tests and size. Unfortunately, consonants depend critically on all 9 formant parameters, so it is difficult to compare the networks graphically as done with the vowel networks.

3.3.1 Performance of the Consonant Network

The four different networks are compared in three different ways. First, the mean squared error is compared on a training set and a test set. Second, speech produced while using each of the four networks gets compared. Third, the sizes of the networks are compared.

Mean Squared Error (MSE) Performance

Table 4 shows the training and test results from the different networks. The training data consists of 2600 examples. The static consonant phonemes can be broken down into approximants (R, L, and W), fricatives (F, V, S, Z, SH, ZH, TH, DH and the aspirant H) and nasals (M and N). There were 350 approximants (approximately 115 examples of each), 1510 fricatives (170 examples per fricative) and 740 nasals (370 examples per nasal). The 1380 example test set consisted of these:

- 255 approximants
- 960 fricatives
- 165 nasals

The consonants are divided into different categories since it is important to see if the networks perform better on some types of phonemes than others. Section 3.4.1 describes collection of the training and test data.

The number of hidden units in networks 2 and 3 are chosen so that they are comparable in size to network 4. As in the case of the vowel network using softmax units, consonant network 3 weights softmax errors by 0.01. For network 4, the centers of the RBF units were determined by averaging the hand parameter values for each of the 14 consonant phonemes. After experimenting with different values, the RBF widths were fixed at a value of $\sqrt{0.05}$.

All the networks were trained with conjugate gradient descent and a line search. The training stopped when the error did not decrease significantly.

Table 4. Training and test results for 4 different consonant networks. Network 3 used an extra layer of softmax units connected to the outputs with the cross-entropy errors weighted by 0.01; only the sum squared error on the formant outputs are reported.

Net	consonant	epochs	Training MSE	Testing MSE	run size
1	approximant	142	0.048	0.105	99
	fricative		0.036	0.097	
	nasal		0.035	0.044	
	total		0.037	0.091	
2	approximant	499	0.004	0.022	289
	fricative		0.004	0.084	
	nasal		0.001	0.002	
	total		0.003	0.063	
3	approximant	700	0.003	0.003	289
	fricative		0.004	0.051	
	nasal		0.001	0.001	
	total		0.003	0.056	
4	approximant	172	0.001	0.001	289
	fricative		0.007	0.014	
	nasal		0.001	0.002	
	total		0.005	0.010	

Clearly, network 4 scores best in terms of mean squared error on the test set. The second best network is network 3. Most of the errors of these two networks come from fricatives. This is not surprising since the hand configurations for fricatives are very similar.

Perceptual Testing and Size Comparisons

Informal listening tests are performed using each network in order to compare them. The main trials consist of trying to produce static consonant phonemes. Network 1 produced very poor speech. Most of the consonant phonemes are difficult to produce if not impossible. With network 2 all the phonemes are easy to produce except for W, M and N. The W phoneme is impossible to make. The M and N phonemes are indistinguishable; sounding something like a cross between M and N most of the time. With network 3 the M and N phonemes are more distinctive as expected, however, the W and SH phonemes are difficult to produce. All the other consonants sound good. Network 4 produces all the consonants well. The only difficulty is that the R and L phonemes are very sensitive to motion of the index finger.

The speech produced with network 4 sounds best. Further, all the networks that produce reasonable speech require the same amount of computation at run time; hence, network 4 is selected for the final version of Glove-TalkII.

3.4 Generating Training Data and Test Data for Glove-TalkII

This section describes the procedures used to collect training and test data for all the networks in Glove-TalkII. The data for the consonant networks and vowel/consonant decision network are obtained from the user. The data for the vowel network are created from a user-defined mapping and does not require data from the user.

Initially, before any data are collected from the Cyberglove, the sensors are calibrated with a gain and offset and angles compared to a graphical hand model displayed in real-time. After this, the typical ranges of motion of each sensor are determined to produce a scale file. The scale file values are used to scale the sensor values to between approximately 0 and 1 for use as inputs to the neural networks.

The data collection for the consonant network is described first. Data for the V/C network is collected in the same manner as for the consonant network, as described in the next section. The vowel data, created artificially, is described last.

3.4.1 Consonant Network Data Collection

The text-to-speech synthesizer produces 14 different static consonant phonemes (not including stop consonants). The initial mapping described in Section 2 provides the static hand configurations for each phoneme. To train the consonant network the user must provide real example hand configurations for each of the 14 different phonemes.

The first step in the data collection procedure is creating target data for each of the 14 consonant phonemes using the text-to-speech synthesizer. The typical data collection scheme for a single phoneme is as follows:

1. A target consonant plays for 100 msec through the speech synthesizer.

2. The user forms a hand configuration corresponding to the phoneme.
3. The user depresses the foot pedal to begin recording; the start of the recording is indicated by a green square appearing on the monitor.
4. 10-15 time steps of hand data are collected and stored with the corresponding formant targets and phoneme identifier; the end of data collection indicated by the green square turning red.
5. The user chooses whether to save data to a file and whether to redo the current target or move to the next one.

The targets are presented in a fixed order grouped into blocks. The three blocks are approximants (L, R, and W), fricatives (F, V, S, SH, Z, ZH, TH, DH and the aspirant H), and nasals (M and N). All 24 input parameters of the hand are recorded during the training sessions and coupled to the appropriate targets. These are scaled by the minimum and maximum values in the scale file.

Typically, the user performs about 5 trials per consonant before continuing on to the next target in the group. While the training data is being recorded, the user is encouraged to move his hand simulating the motions he might make while saying the sound. The more representative the training data the better the system will work once trained. For the results reported the data collection scheme was repeated at different times until 350 approximants, 1510 fricatives and 700 nasals were collected and scaled for the training data. A disproportionate number of nasals were collected since the consonant network had a difficult time finding suitable decision regions for the M and N phonemes. By providing more training data it was hoped that the networks would produce a better mapping for nasals. For the test data, 255 approximants, 960 fricatives and 165 nasals were collected and scaled.

The use of the foot pedal to begin recording data represents an important development. The foot pedal makes data collection very quick and easy. Before the addition of the foot pedal several methods were tried which proved difficult to use. One technique which worked poorly required the user to move his hand past an imaginary plane (using the polhemus to measure his hand position) to begin the recording. Another unusable technique required the user to press a key to begin recording.

A further useful feature gives the user the ability to choose immediately what to do with each example. When the user makes obvious errors she can immediately delete the examples. This feature eliminates much of the data that would cause problems for the learning algorithms. This becomes particularly important for novice users since their error rates are very high. Deleting poor examples after all the data has been generated is cumbersome and error prone.

3.4.2 V/C Network Data Collection

The V/C network requires hand configurations labeled as consonants or vowels. The hand data collected for the consonant network corresponds exactly to the data needed to indicate that a consonant should be produced. Thus, no further data collection is necessary for consonant-decision data. Unfortunately, for vowels, the hand configurations go unspecified in training data for the vowel network, since only the X and Y coordinates are used for inputs and the data are not collected from the user.

To get vowel targets for the V/C network the same procedure used for collecting consonant data is used (see Section 3.4.1). Instead of producing consonants though, the user must make hand configurations that produce vowels (i.e. she makes an open configuration of her hand according to the mapping defined in Section 2 and illustrated in Table 1). Typically, the training session is set up to record 100-200 time steps (1-2 seconds) of data from the user, rather than only the 10-15 time steps recorded during the consonant network training session. During the recording stage, the user moves his hand around as much as possible creating many different hand positions that produce vowels. For example, the user hyperextends his fingers as well as moving towards consonant configurations without actually making a consonant shape to simulate vowel-consonant transitions and vice-versa. Each data vector is labeled with a target of 1.0 indicating a vowel.

700 vowel decision examples were collected in this manner. As stated above, the training data for the consonant network was relabeled providing 2600 examples of consonant decisions.

3.4.3 Vowel Network Data Collection

The training and test data for the vowel network is artificially generated based on an initial vowel mapping (see Section 2). Obtaining reliable vowel data from the user for vowels is very difficult since there is poor feedback to provide absolute position of the user's hand relative to the source. This makes it difficult for users to repeat hand positions reliably for vowels as specified in the initial mapping. Absolute positioning is not as much of a problem while speaking since the sounds, once produced, provide feedback indicating the user's location in vowel space. The example data generated is described in Section 3.2.

3.5 Summary of Glove-TalkII's Neural Networks

The above analysis illustrates the process of selecting the final network architectures for the Glove-TalkII system. The recommended architecture has two parts for the V/C network. The novice user should use the larger, noise resistant network. As the user begins to make more reliable hand gestures, the smaller, single time-step network becomes sufficient. Clearly, for the vowel and consonant networks the normalized RBF hidden units are preferred.

Training the vowel network on artificial data from the initial mapping provides an easily navigated vowel space. The size of the vowel space can be easily adjusted to suit individual tastes by creating new training data from a user-defined mapping. An easy to use interface helps obtain the training data for the consonant network. To fine tune the consonant mapping the user only has to provide new training data for the phonemes she wants altered. The training data from the consonant network is exactly the data needed to train the V/C network to output a consonant decision. For vowel decision data, the user makes as many different vowel hand configurations as anticipated during speaking.

The main problem with using RBF units for the hidden layer is that if additional sounds/phonemes are required (i.e. to allow for a different language) additional RBF units must be added. This increases the size of the network, and, the whole network has to be retrained. The other network architectures need only be retrained with each new sound/phoneme added to the rest of the training set.

It is important to stress that the mean squared error criterion is only a guide to selecting the best vowel and consonant network. Subjective listening tests must be performed before the final architecture can be decided upon.

4 Qualitative Performance of Glove-TalkII

One subject, who is an accomplished pianist, has been trained extensively to speak with Glove-TalkII. We expected that his pre-existing skill in forming finger patterns and his musical training would help him learn to speak with Glove-TalkII. After 100 hours of training, his speech with Glove-TalkII is intelligible and somewhat natural-sounding. He still finds it difficult to speak quickly, pronounce polysyllabic words, and speak spontaneously. While learning to speak with Glove-TalkII the user progressed through 8 distinct stages:

1. familiarize user with system
2. initial training of the V/C and consonant networks with user-supplied training data
3. individual phoneme formation within simple words and CV/VC pairings
4. word formation and interword pitch control
5. short segment formation with suprasegmental pitch control and singing
6. passage reading
7. fine tuning; movement control and phrasing
8. spontaneous speech

Of course, his progression through the stages is not as linear as suggested by the above list. Some aspects of speaking were more difficult than others, so a substantial amount of mixing of the different levels occurred. Practice at the higher levels facilitated perfecting more difficult sounds that were still being practiced at the lower levels. Also, the stages are iterative, that is, at regular intervals the subject returns to lower levels to further refine his speech.

During his training, Glove-TalkII also adapted to suit changes required by the subject. Initially, good performance of the V/C network is critical for the user to learn to speak. If the V/C network performs poorly the user hears a mixture of vowel and consonant sounds making it difficult to adjust his hand configurations to say different utterances. For this reason, it is important to have the user comfortable with the initial mapping so that the training data collected leads to the V/C network performing well. In the 100 hours of practice, Glove-TalkII was retrained about 15 times[5]. Four significant changes were made for the new user from the original system analyzed in Sections 3.1, 3.2 and 3.3. First, the NG sound was added to the non-stop consonant list by adding an additional hand shape. For the NG sound the user touches his pinkie to his thumb on his *right* hand. To accommodate this change, the consonant and V/C network had two inputs added to represent the two flex angles of the pinkie. Also, the consonant network has an extra hidden unit for the NG sound. Second, the consonant network was trained to allow the RBF centers to change. This was done by first training the hidden-to-output weights until little improvement was seen. Then both the input-to-hidden weights (i.e. the RBF centers) and the hidden-to-output weights were allowed to adapt. This noticeably improved performance for the user. Third, the vowel mapping was altered so that the I was moved closer to the EE sound and the entire mapping was reduced to 75% of its size. Fourth, for this subject, the V/C network needed was a 12-10-1 feed-forward sigmoid unit network. It is anticipated that this network will be sufficient for most users. Understanding the interaction between the user's adaptation and Glove-TalkII's adaptation remains an interesting research pursuit.

When learning to speak with Glove-TalkII it may be useful for the user to have a teacher signal to help learn hand trajectories for particular utterances. For this, an inverse mapping of the forward hand-to-gesture mapping is needed. Using the inverse mapping, a target utterance can be mapped to the required hand trajectory (including the foot pedal depression). In the final Glove-TalkII system, an iterative inverse was investi-

[5]Far fewer retrainings would be required for future users.

gated to obtain an inverse mapping of target utterances. This inverse allowed the user to specify an utterance and have the Glove-TalkII demonstrate the hand gesture necessary to say the utterance. Several techniques were investigated to iteratively determine the inverse through the normalized RBF units. These results are reported in [6].

5 Summary of Glove-TalkII

The initial mapping for Glove-TalkII is loosely based on an articulatory model of speech. An open configuration of the hand corresponds to an unobstructed vocal tract, which in turn generates vowel sounds. Different vowel sounds are produced by movements of the hand in a horizontal X-Y plane that corresponds to movements of the first two formants which are roughly related to tongue position. Consonants other than stops are produced by closing the index, middle, or ring fingers or flexing the thumb, representing constrictions in the vocal tract. Stop consonants are produced by contact switches worn on the left hand. F0 is controlled by hand height and speaking intensity by foot pedal depression.

Glove-TalkII learns the user's interpretation of this initial mapping. The V/C network and the consonant network learn the mapping from examples generated by the user during phases of training. The vowel network is trained on examples computed from the user-defined mapping between hand-position and vowels. The F0 and volume mappings are non-adaptive. In many interface applications it is necessary to map from a user's gesture space to control a complex device. The methods used to build Glove-TalkII can be applied to these interfaces.

One of the key developments in the Glove-TalkII work is the investigation of the properties of normalized RBF networks in comparison to networks with linear, sigmoid, sigmoid plus softmax and unnormalized RBF activation units. For the task of mapping the topology of hand gestures to formant space the normalized RBF units were much better. The reason for this is that the normalization provides zones of activation where the output of the network is relatively stable over a large range of input values beyond the distribution in the training set. This is important as the user often moves in a much larger range than the original training data.

These active zones provide a stable output sound even in the presence of large overshoots in the users' gesture space.

One subject was trained to use Glove-TalkII. After 100 hours of practice he is able to speak intelligibly. His speech is fairly slow (1.5 to 3 times slower than normal speech). It sounds similar to speech produced with a text-to-speech synthesizer but has a far more natural intonation contour which greatly improves the intelligibility and expressiveness of the speech. Reading novel passages intelligibly usually requires several attempts, especially with polysyllabic words. Intelligible spontaneous speech such as found in conversation is possible but difficult. It is anticipated that training on formant trajectories estimated from real-speech will significantly improve the quality of the user's speech. Currently, it is an open research issue to extract accurate formant trajectories for this synthesizer automatically [13].

Glove-TalkII could be used by speech-impaired people. To make it useful for this community it must be made portable and inexpensive. The current implementation requires a machine capable of approximately 200K floating point operation per second that has 3 serial ports and a parallel port. Inexpensive embedded computers could be used to fit these requirements. The glove and footpedal devices are tethered to the machine which limits mobility of the user. To solve this limitation it is necessary for the input devices to have a system of wireless transmission of the data to the host computer or to mount the host computer on the user. Finally, the foot pedal would be cumbersome in a completely portable system but it should be possible to design an alternative method of controlling the single volume parameter. Once these technical issues are resolved, Glove-TalkII could provide a portable, inexpensive, adaptive, Artificial Vocal Tract device to assist speech-impaired people.

Acknowledgments

Many thanks to John Bridle, Drew van Camp, Peter Dayan, Geoff Hinton, David Mackay, Sageev Oore, Mike Revow, Mike Ruicci and members of the Neuron Group at the University of Toronto for their contributions.

Appendix

A Normalized Units and Weights

In this appendix, the partial derivatives necessary for backpropagation through networks which use units (or weights) that are normalized with respect to some group of units (weights) are derived. The activity functions of the units and the normalization function are arbitrary. Softmax units at the output and hidden layers are a special case of normalized units and are used to illustrate the derivations. The important point to notice is that the derivative of the error with respect to a normalized unit is a function of the derivative of the error with respect to all of the units in the normalized group. The equations derived can also be applied analogously to normalized weights.

Often, when designing neural networks one has occasion to use normalized units (see for example [10]). Typically, the performed normalization divides all the outputs of a group of units by their sum. Softmax units are the most common example of normalized units (see [3] and [17]). Here, the units have an exponential activation function and the outputs are normalized with respect to all the units in the softmax group. Softmax units are typically used as output units to model a probability distribution such that all the activities sum to one. Usually, a cross-entropy error function is used in a 1-of-N classification task, where the correct class' target is set to one and the other classes set to zero. Three different variations of the normalization paradigm are often desired:

- different activation functions for each of the units before normalization is performed; i.e. exponential activation in softmax units or negative exponential activation in the case of radial-basis functions.
- different error functions if the units are output units
- different types of normalization, i.e. dividing the activation of each unit by the sum of the activations of the units in the normalized group, dividing a unit's activation by the L_2 norm of the group of units.

Further, the group may be either at the output layer or a hidden layer. The following discussion describes the necessary equations for implementing normalized units with arbitrary activation functions, arbitrary error functions and arbitrary normalization functions[6]. Further, the well known equations for softmax output

[6]"Arbitrary" in the sense that the first derivative is well defined.

units will be derived using this formulation. The equations for softmax units in the hidden layers will also be derived.

Consider the following notation (similar to [14]). First, the activation function for unit j in the normalized group is

$$o_j = f(x_j) \tag{3}$$

where o_j is the unnormalized activation of the unit and x_j is the total input of the unit (typically formed from the dot product of weights and outputs of units in the layer below)[7].

For illustration purposes, consider the normalized output of the unit as

$$n_j = \frac{o_j}{\sum_{m=1}^{N} o_m} \tag{4}$$

where N is the number of units in the group. Any differentiable function of the group of units' activations suffices.

The implementation for the forward propagation through these normalized units is straight forward. Backpropagation of the error signal through these units is less simple. It is necessary to calculate the term $\frac{\partial E_p}{\partial x_{pj}}$ where E_p is the error on a particular example p, to implement the backpropagation procedure[8]. Complications arise due to error propagated back to one unit in the group will affect the others. Thus, extra care is needed to ensure the correct influence is calculated.

Consider unit j in the group of normalized units on some example p. If we consider the effect of the total input of unit j on the error, the expression is

$$\frac{\partial E}{\partial x_j} = \frac{\partial o_j}{\partial x_j}\frac{\partial n_j}{\partial o_j}\frac{\partial E}{\partial n_j} + \sum_{k=1;k\neq j}^{N} \frac{\partial o_j}{\partial x_j}\frac{\partial n_k}{\partial o_j}\frac{\partial E}{\partial n_k} \tag{5}$$

This expression is much easier to understand if we only consider the error that is backpropagated to unit j (which is referred to here as E^j) first and see how that error is propagated to all the other units in the group. In this case, we exclude

[7] In the case of radial basis function the term x_j is calculated using a distance measure like $x_j = \frac{1}{\sigma_j}\sum(w_{ji} - o_i)^2$. Of course, the outputs from the lower layer could be normalized as well.

[8] From $\frac{\partial E_p}{\partial x_j}$ we can easily get $\frac{\partial E_p}{\partial w_{ji}}$ in the manner described in [14].

the effects errors distributed from the other units in the group have on unit j. For unit j the equation is

$$\frac{\partial E^j}{\partial x_j} = \frac{\partial o_j}{\partial x_j}\frac{\partial n_j}{\partial o_j}\frac{\partial E^j}{\partial n_j} \tag{6}$$

The first term from equation 3 is simply:

$$\frac{\partial o_j}{\partial x_j} = f'(x_j) \tag{7}$$

The second term is obtained from equation 4:

$$\frac{\partial n_j}{\partial o_j} = \frac{1}{\sum_{m=1}^{N} o_m} + \frac{-o_j}{\left(\sum_{m=1}^{N} o_m\right)^2} \tag{8}$$

$$= \frac{\sum_{m=1}^{N} o_m - o_j}{\left(\sum_{m=1}^{N} o_m\right)^2} \tag{9}$$

$$= \frac{\sum_{m=1;m\neq j}^{N} o_m}{\left(\sum_{m=1}^{N} o_m\right)^2} \tag{10}$$

The third term has two different forms depending upon whether the unit is an output unit or a hidden unit. The first case shows an error function in terms of n_j and the derivative is calculated. In the latter case, the derivative is calculated by backpropagating the error through the weights from the layer above unit j. Refer to [14] for an example using a Euclidean error function and sigmoid hidden units. Softmax units are used below to illustrate how these equations are calculated in a specific case.

Now consider unit k in the normalized group where k is some other unit besides j. What is the effect on the error by unit k? The equation is derived as follows:

$$\frac{\partial E^j}{\partial x_k} = \frac{\partial o_k}{\partial x_k}\frac{\partial n_j}{\partial o_k}\frac{\partial E^j}{\partial n_j} \tag{11}$$

The important point to notice in this equation is that **the change in the error with respect to $\mathbf{x_k}$ is a function of the change in error with respect to $\mathbf{n_j}$.**

Remember, we are only considering the error localized at unit j; that is, the error signal propagated back to unit j, which we can see must be distributed as above to all the other units too. Completing equation 11, the first term is (from equation 3):

$$\frac{\partial o_k}{\partial x_k} = f'(x_k) \tag{12}$$

The second term follows from equation 4:

$$\frac{\partial n_j}{\partial o_k} = \frac{-o_j}{\left(\sum_{m=1}^{N} o_m\right)^2} \tag{13}$$

The third term is discussed above.

The above equations are general in the sense that they do not differentiate between hidden units and output units. The only change necessary for the different types of units, as described above, is that the partial derivative of the error should be either obtained from the error function or the backpropagated error function. Each unit in the group of normalized units is considered as unit j, one at a time, and its error gets distributed to all the other units. In this way the total expression in equation 5 is calculated. Using this method, the complexity to calculate the required partial derivatives for the group of normalized units is $O(N^2)$, where N is the number of units in the group, since at each unit the error is distributed to the other $N - 1$ members in the group. Normally, the number of units in the group is small, therefore, this is not much of a computational penalty. On the positive side, with respect to implementation, the above method requires a single procedure to compute the derivatives for each unit. Further, the form is general enough to work with any type of normalization function.

If we consider the normalization function used in the example above (equation 4) we can write equation 5 as

$$\frac{\partial E}{\partial x_j} = f'(x_j)\left[\left[\frac{\sum_{m=1}^{N} o_m - o_j}{\left(\sum_{m=1}^{N} o_m\right)^2}\right]\frac{\partial E}{\partial n_j} + \sum_{k=1;k\neq j} \frac{-o_j}{\left(\sum_{m=1}^{N} o_m\right)^2}\frac{\partial E}{\partial n_k}\right] \tag{14}$$

which reduces[9] after simple algebraic manipulation to

$$\frac{\partial E}{\partial x_j} = f'(x_j)\left[\frac{1}{\sum_{m=1}^{N} o_m}\frac{\partial E}{\partial n_j} - o_j\sum_{k=1}^{N} \frac{1}{\left(\sum_{m=1}^{N} o_m\right)^2}\frac{\partial E}{\partial n_k}\right] \tag{15}$$

[9]This reduction was pointed out by S. Becker and T. Plate, personal communication.

In this form the calculation can be done in two stages: first, for the whole group calculate the term

$$\sum_{k=1}^{N} \frac{1}{\left(\sum_{m=1}^{N} o_m\right)^2} \frac{\partial E}{\partial n_k} \tag{16}$$

which can be done in $O(N)$ calculations. Second, for each unit in the group, calculate the required partial derivative using equation 15 and the term from equation 16 calculated for the whole group. This reduces the complexity to $O(N)$ to compute the required partial derivatives (as compared to $O(N^2)$ for the general case). Notice, this reduction depends on the normalization function which means it is not completely general, however, in most cases this type of normalization is used[10].

A.1 Normalized Weights

The above discussion can be directly applied to normalized weights[11]. In particular, consider the normalizing weight equation[12]:

$$\eta_{ij} = \frac{w_{ij}}{\sum_{k=1}^{M} w_{ik}} \tag{17}$$

where η_{ij} is the normalized weight connecting unit i to unit j, w_{ij} is the unnormalized weight connecting unit i to unit j, and M is the number of weights being normalized. A typical combining function for unit j is

$$x_j = \sum_{i=1}^{P} \eta_{ij} o_i \tag{18}$$

where P is the fan in to unit j and o_i is the output of unit i that connects to unit j. The derivative of the error (E) with respect to each of the weights is analogous to equation 5. The equation is

$$\frac{\partial E}{\partial w_{ij}} = \frac{\partial \eta_{ij}}{\partial w_{ij}} \frac{\partial x_j}{\partial \eta_{ij}} \frac{\partial E}{\partial x_j} + \sum_{k=1;k\neq j}^{M} \frac{\partial \eta_{ik}}{\partial w_{ij}} \frac{\partial x_k}{\partial \eta_{ik}} \frac{\partial E}{\partial x_k} \tag{19}$$

For the usual case given in equations 17 and 18, equation 19 simplifies to

$$\frac{\partial E}{\partial w_{ij}} = \left[\frac{\sum_{k=1}^{M} w_{ik} - w_{ij}}{\left(\sum_{k=1}^{M} w_{ik}\right)^2}\right] o_i \frac{\partial E}{\partial x_j} - \sum_{k=1;k\neq j}^{M} \frac{w_{ik}}{\left(\sum_{k=1}^{M} w_{ik}\right)^2} o_i \frac{\partial E}{\partial x_k} \tag{20}$$

[10] L_2 normalization reduces to a similar form.

[11] Thanks to Peter Dayan for pointing this out, personal communication.

[12] Note that another normalizing function may be used.

which may be further simplified as suggested for normalized units. The next sections provide examples of normalized units using softmax units at the output layer and the hidden layer.

A.2 Example: Softmax Units

The above formulation can be used to obtain the necessary equations for back-propagating through softmax units. Consider the following notation for softmax units:

The activation function is

$$o_j = f(x_j) = e^{x_j} \tag{21}$$

and the normalized output of unit j is (equation 4)

$$n_j = \frac{o_j}{\sum_{m=1}^{N} o_m} \tag{22}$$

The derivative of the activation function is

$$\frac{\partial o_j}{\partial x_j} = f'(x_j) = e^{x_j} = o_j \tag{23}$$

The error function is usually chosen to be the cross entropy function:

$$E = -log(n_j) \tag{24}$$

where j is the output unit with target = 1.

The partial derivative of the error function is:

$$\frac{\partial E}{\partial n_j} = \frac{-1}{n_j} \tag{25}$$

The partial derivative of the error function with respect to other units besides the target unit is 0, thus, in our notation above $E^j = E$. The partial of the error with respect to n_j is the backpropagated error from preceding layers, if the units are not in the output layer[13].

[13] In [14] this backpropagated derivative is the negative of the δ_{pj} term for example p.

A.2.1 Softmax Output Units

Consider the equations derived for softmax units that are output units. There are two different cases to discuss; target output and non-target output. First consider the target output unit j (i.e. its target output is 1). If we substitute equations 23, 10 and 25 into 6 we get the following:

$$\frac{\partial E}{\partial x_j} = \frac{\partial o_j}{\partial x_j}\frac{\partial n_j}{\partial o_j}\frac{\partial E}{\partial n_j} \tag{26}$$

$$= o_j \left[\sum_{m=1;m\neq j}^{N} \frac{o_m}{\left(\sum_{m=1}^{N} o_m\right)^2} \right] \frac{-1}{n_j} \tag{27}$$

$$= o_j \left[\frac{\sum_{m=1}^{N} o_m - o_j}{\left(\sum_{m=1}^{N} o_m\right)^2} \right] \frac{-1}{n_j} \tag{28}$$

$$= \frac{o_j}{\sum_{m=1}^{N} o_m} \left[\frac{\sum_{m=1}^{N} o_m - o_j}{\sum_{m=1}^{N} o_m} \right] \frac{-1}{n_j} \tag{29}$$

$$= n_j - 1 \tag{30}$$

Second, consider the non-target output unit k (i.e. its target output is 0). The effect of the error is transmitted to this unit by the effect of the normalization. Remember, the derivative of the error function with respect to the output of non-target units is 0; thus, only the redistribution from the target unit derivative effects the partial derivative of the error with respect to the non-target units' total inputs. The equation is derived from equation 11 with equations 23, 13 and 25 substituted. Particular attention should be paid to the second term as it differs from the second term in equation 27:

$$\frac{\partial E}{\partial x_k} = \frac{\partial o_k}{\partial x_k}\frac{\partial n_j}{\partial o_k}\frac{\partial E}{\partial n_j} \tag{31}$$

$$= o_k \frac{-o_j}{\left(\sum_{m=1}^{N} o_m\right)^2} \frac{-1}{n_j} \tag{32}$$

$$= \frac{o_k}{\sum_{m=1}^{N} o_m} \frac{-o_j}{\sum_{m=1}^{N} o_m} \frac{-1}{n_j} \tag{33}$$

$$= n_k \tag{34}$$

Clearly, these are the equations for the partial derivatives of the error with respect to the input of a unit for softmax output units, that is: $\frac{\partial E}{\partial x_j} = n_j - target_j$ (compare to [7]).

The next subsection shows that the same equations are used to derive the error derivatives necessary for softmax units that are not output units.

A.2.2 Softmax Hidden Units

The equations for softmax hidden units are basically identical to the ones for softmax output units, except that the third term in equation 30 is the back-propagated error from the above layer. Briefly, if we consider the jth unit from equation 6 we get the following:

$$\frac{\partial E^j}{\partial x_j} = \frac{\partial o_j}{\partial x_j} \frac{\partial n_j}{\partial o_j} \frac{\partial E^j}{\partial n_j} \tag{35}$$

$$= o_j \left[\frac{\sum_{m=1;m\neq j}^{N} o_m}{\left(\sum_{m=1}^{N} o_m \right)^2} \right] \frac{\partial E^j}{\partial n_j} \tag{36}$$

$$= n_j(1 - n_j) \frac{\partial E^j}{\partial n_j} \tag{37}$$

Once we calculate this term we also have to consider how the other units in the group are affected. From equation 11 we get this:

$$\frac{\partial E^j}{\partial x_k} = \frac{\partial o_k}{\partial x_k} \frac{\partial n_j}{\partial o_k} \frac{\partial E^j}{\partial n_j} \tag{38}$$

$$= o_k \frac{-o_j}{\left(\sum_{m=1}^{N} o_m \right)^2} \frac{\partial E^k}{\partial n_j} \tag{39}$$

$$= -n_k n_j \frac{\partial E^j}{\partial n_j} \tag{40}$$

From the view point of implementation, when unit j is encountered its error has to be propagated through itself, using equation 37 as well as all the other units in the group using equation 40. Each unit in turn considers itself as unit j, and distributes its error to all the other units in the group, implementing equation 5 in the process. Softmax units are particularly pleasant when used with the cross entropy error function at the outputs, since the derivatives simplify down to a local form. Unfortunately, this is not true of the softmax units at the hidden layers.

It is interesting to note that the equations above can be used for training softmax units to learn a probability distribution using a cross-entropy error function. The only necessary modification involves the $\frac{\partial E^j}{\partial n_j}$ term being non-zero for each unit in the group, since these are target values for each of the output units.

A.3 Summary of Normalization

The equations presented in appendix A describe the necessary relationships to backpropagate error through normalized units. The important point to remember is that the error backpropagated through a unit j must also be distributed to all the other units. This must be repeated for each unit in the group that has any error backpropagated to it. The equations described are general in the sense that any activation function (with a first derivative) can be used as well as any error function (with a first derivative). Additionally, a similar formulation for normalized weights is derived in Section A.1.

References

[1] Bell, A.G. (1909), "Making a talking-machine," *Beinn Bhreagh Recorder*, pp. 61-72, November.

[2] Bridle, J.S. (1990), "Probabilistic interpretation of feedforward classification network outputs, with relationships to statistical pattern recognition," in Fougelman-Soulie, F. and Herault, J. (Eds.), *NATO ASI Series on Systems and Computer Science*, Springer-Verlag.

[3] Bridle, J.S. (1990), "Training stochastic model recognition algorithms as networks can lead to maximum mutual information estimation of parameters," in Touretzky, D.S. (Ed.), *Neural Information Processing Systems*, vol. 2, pp. 111-217, San Mateo, CA, Morgan Kaufmann.

[4] Broomhead, D. and Lowe, D. (1988), "Multivariable functional interpolation and adaptive networks," *Complex Systems*, vol. 2, pp. 321-355.

[5] Dudley, H., Riesz, R.R., and Watkins, S.S.A. (1939), "A synthetic speaker," *Journal of the Franklin Institute*, vol. 227, no. 6, pp. 739-764, June.

[6] Fels, S.S. (1994), *Glove-TalkII: Mapping Hand Gestures to Speech Using Neural Networks*, Ph.D. thesis, University of Toronto, Toronto, ON, August.

[7] Fels, S.S. and Hinton, G. (1993), "Glove-Talk: a neural network interface between a data-glove and a speech synthesizer," *IEEE Transaction on Neural Networks*, vol. 4, pp. 2-8.

[8] Fels, S.S. and Hinton, G.E. (1998), "Glove-TalkII: a neural network interface which maps gestures to parallel formant speech synthesizer controls," *IEEE Transactions on Neural Networks*, vol. 9, pp. 205-212.

[9] Connectionist Research Group (1990), *Xerion Neural Network Simulator Libraries and Man Pages; version 3.183*, University of Toronto, Toronto, ON, CANADA.

[10] Jones, R.D., Lee, Y.C., Qian, S., Barnes, C.W., Bisset, K.R., Bruce, G.M., Flake, G.W., Lee, K., Lee, L.A., Mead, W.C., O'Rourke, M.K., Poli, I.J., and Thodes, L.E. (1990), "Nonlinear adaptive networks: a little theory, a few applications," Technical Report LA–UR–91–273, Los Alamos National Laboratory.

[11] Ladefoged, P. (1982), *A Course in Phonetics (2 ed.)*, Harcourt Brace Javanovich, New York.

[12] Lewis, E. (1989), "A 'C' implementation of the JSRU text-to-speech system," Technical report, Computer Science Dept., University of Bristol.

[13] Lowry, A., Hall, M.C., and Hughes, P.M. (1989), "Iterative parameter optimization techniques for parallel-formant encoding of speech," *European Conference on Circuit Theory and Design*, pp. 537-541.

[14] Rumelhart, D.E., Hinton, G.E., and Williams, R.J. (1986), "Learning internal representations by back-propagating errors," *Nature*, vol. 323, pp. 533-536.

[15] Rye, J.M. and Holmes, J.N. (1982), "A versatile software parallel-formant speech synthesizer," Technical Report JSRU-RR-1016, Joint Speech Research Unit, Malvern, U.K.

[16] Von Kempelen, W. Ritter (1970), *Mechanismus der menschlichen Sprache nebst Beschreibung einer sprechenden Maschine. Mit einer Einleitung von Herbert E. Brekle und Wolfgang Wild*, Stuttgart-Bad Cannstatt F. Frommann, Stuttgart. (In German.)

[17] Yair, E. and Gersho, A. (1989), "The Boltzmann perceptron network: a multilayered feed-forward network equivalent to the Boltzmann machine," in Touretzky, D. (Ed.), *Advances in Neural Information Processing Systems 1 (NIPS*88)*, pp. 116-123, San Mateo, Morgan Kaufman Publishers.

Chapter 4

Face Recognition Using RBF Networks

A.J. Howell

We present an example-based approach to learning several recognition tasks using pose-varying face data. We show how computationally cheap radial basis function (RBF) classifiers can be developed for three separate, static recognition tasks, identity, expression and pose, with the same training data. The flexibility of such an approach means that, provided an appropriate representation is chosen for the data, re-learning for new tasks is both practical and computationally efficient.

1 Introduction

This chapter describes practical work using example-based learning on a pose-varying face recognition task. The particular task considered here is recognizing in real-time a known group of people in an indoor environment such as a domestic living-room. Within such a task, it cannot be assumed that there will be clear frontal views of faces at all times. It is important not to lose such vital information, which may only be present for a split-second if the subject is moving fast, and so our primary objective is to identify faces at a range of head poses.

Although one can implicitly model a view-based recognition task using linear combinations of 2-D views [33] to represent any 2-D view of an object, a simpler approach is for the system to use view interpolation techniques [7], [25] to learn the task explicitly. Radial basis function (RBF) neural networks have been identified as valuable adaptive learning model by a wide range of researchers [1], [3], [4], [21], [24], [27] for such tasks. Their main advantages are computational simplicity, supported by well-developed mathematical theory, and robust generalization, powerful enough for real-time real-life tasks [28], [30]. They are seen as ideal for practical vision applications by [11] as they are good at handling sparse, high-dimensional data and because they use approximation to handle noisy, real-life data. The nonlinear decision boundaries of the RBF network make it better in general for function approximation than the hyperplanes created by the multi-layer perceptron (MLP) with sigmoid units [27], and they provide a guaranteed, globally optimal solution via simple, linear optimization. In addition, the RBF network is a poor extrapolator (compared to the MLP) and this behaviour can give it useful low false-positive rates in classification problems. This is because its basis functions cover only small localized regions, unlike sigmoidal basis functions which are nonzero over an infinitely large region of the input space.

Throughout the chapter, we will be emphasizing the flexibility of the example-based RBF learning approach, which allows us to reformulate the training in terms of the specific classes we wish to distinguish. In this way, we can extract identity, head pose and expression information separately from the same face data.

Recognizing people in day-to-day life is generally effortless and unconscious. The ease with which humans manipulate such visual data makes it easy to underestimate the difficulty and complexity of such processing. Identifying a face poses several severe tests for any visual system, such as the high degree of similarity between different faces, the great extent to which lighting conditions and expressions can alter the face, and the large number of different views from which a face can be seen. Indeed, variations in facial appearance due to lighting, pose and expression can be greater than those due to identity [23]. In addition, there are many other, lesser influences on an individual's facial appearance from day to day, such as aging and makeup [16], which need to be acknowledged and handled in a robust real-life application.

To effectively tackle such a task requires the combination of three real-time processes: tracking of individuals as they move around the room, detection and localization of their faces, and recognition of the final, segmented face information. Each of these three processes currently occupies a large area of research within computer vision. It is very difficult to consider an overall solution, and, therefore, this chapter will be confined to the process of face recognition from pre-localized video images, with the assumption that other processes, e.g., [12], [19], [20], will provide suitable segmented face images and image sequences from our target environment.

In Section 2.1, we start by analyzing our face recognition task to determine the suitability of the RBF network. We do this by looking specifically at the separability of face and head pose classes using Euclidean distances between images. Since such distance comparisons are at the heart of the RBF network, it is essential to know if the desired classes (in this case, identity and head pose) are actually separable through such distance values.

Section 3 will present our RBF network model. Previous comparative tests [16, Section 6] with the standard ORL face database show that this approach has a sufficient level of performance for our target application, where it will have to deal with image sequences. In this case, training data is relatively sparse (compared to the large range of variation in real-life images, such as lighting and occlusion) and test data is abundant. Section 3.3 introduces our discard measure, where a level of confidence in output levels in the RBF network is used to remove ambiguous results. This has proved especially useful for improving generalization when dealing with real-life noisy data. Although discarding does reduce the number of useful classifications, a significant amount of data will remain when such techniques are used with image sequences [18].

Section 4 investigates the invariance properties of the RBF network. The issue of invariance has to be considered carefully for any task, though this rarely needs to be an absolute invariance. However closely in time two images of the same person are taken, there will always be some differences between them. The goal of any face recognition system, natural or artificial, is to associate some previously learned identity with a previously encountered appearance of that same identity. The representation and similarity metric chosen, therefore, must be sufficiently invariant to changes between two images of the same person that they look more 'similar' to each other than to one of another individual. Prior knowledge about image variations likely to be useful for a task allows these variations to be explicitly highlighted within the representation during preprocessing and those that are not useful to be suppressed. We first look at head pose invariance, then go on to assess invariance to localization error, both in position and scale. It is important to know how much invariance can be expected from the network, so that trade-offs between explicit processing stages for specific types of invariance can be made, and the bounds on localization accuracy determined.

Section 5 describes how RBF network learning can be reformulated in terms of the classes to be learned to produce a 'face unit RBF network.' This concentrates on learning to identify one identity class at a time, and allows a variety of modular learning schemes which could be applied to other tasks.

We finish in Section 6 by showing how our approach can be used to train computationally cheap and fast RBF classifiers from the same database for three particular static recognition tasks: identity, expression and pose. This will demonstrate the power and flexibility of the example-based approach to learning with the RBF network.

2 Class Separability of Pose-Varying Faces

Our approach to the main task of face recognition is to use computationally efficient RBF networks with receptive field-based preprocessing. Before we experiment with this specific configuration, we need to establish the learnability of the task. Because it is essential to be able to classify images of pose-varying faces in situations where people are free to move around, we start in this section by investigating how the image data varies over pose for each individual, specifically, in relation to Euclidean distance comparisons between images of the same and other identity classes. In this way, we can establish how distinct such face-classes are under pose change.

Apart from Section 6, our experiments will use the 'Sussex face database', which allows testing of face recognition techniques over moderate pose ranges. This database contains images of ten people in ten different pose positions from face-on to profile, 100 images in all, see Figure 1 ([14, Appendix A] contains full specifications).

Our face recognition task requires a tolerance of large pose variation,

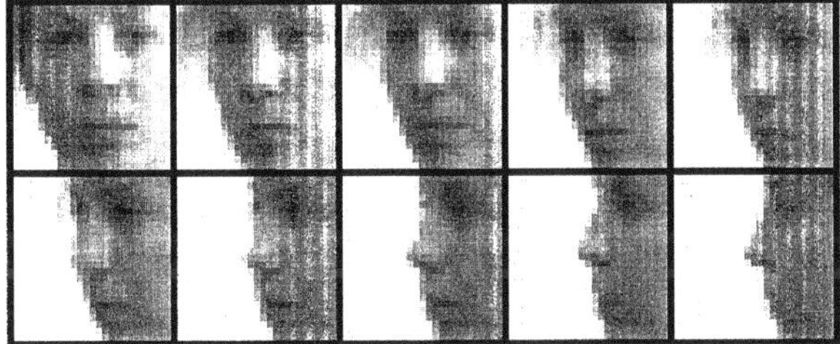

Figure 1. Examples of all ten images for one person from the Sussex database, nose-centered and subsampled to 25×25 before preprocessing, showing a y-axis rotation of 90°.

and it was necessary for us to create this specific database, as there is no other publicly available data that systematically varies pose over a useful range for all individuals. Generally, it is desirable to have more widely-tested data, such as the ORL database tests mentioned above, so that comparable results are available. Section 6 uses another standard face database, the Weizmann FaceBase.

2.1 Euclidean Distances for Faces

The fundamental similarity mechanism we will use for image-based face class discrimination is the Euclidean distance measure, as this is at the heart of the vector comparison mechanism of the RBF network. This is applied to vectors of our basic representational 'feature', the pixel or pixel-based coefficient. Using the Sussex database as a source of suitable data, we can now establish how difficult it is to distinguish the individuals over varying pose. To do this, we can compare the Euclidean distances to all other images in the database (the *test images*), distinguishing two types of class distance:

Intra-class Distance The Euclidean distance between the reference image and a test image, where both are of the *same* identity class.

Inter-class Distance The Euclidean distance between the reference image and a test image, where both are *different* identity classes.

Obviously, if the former are less than the latter in all cases, the classification problem is solved, as perfect discrimination between the identity classes will be possible based on simple comparison alone. We do not expect this to be the case in practice, as real-life images are noisy and faces vary enormously over pose, expression and lighting.

We consider that preprocessing will be an important part of any real-life application, where lighting variation will be expected, and therefore needs to be included even in initial studies of the recognition process. We used sparse-sampled Gabor filtering for these tests (details in Section 4.1).

2.1.1 Varying Head Pose

The pose view of the person is a factor that affects the inter-class distinction. This is illustrated by Figure 2(a–c), which shows all Euclidean distances for six individual images at the 25×25 resolution from the Sussex Database, using pose angles of 0° (frontal), 40° and 90° (profile). All 100 distances are shown on the graphs, connected by lines according to class, and the zero value can be seen where the image is compared to itself.

It can be seen that extreme profile view (90°) is less distinct than the center views, and this will add to the problem of lack of interpolative data when we come to use these images with the RBF network, which largely relies on data interpolation. Because of this, we can expect that performance for the RBF networks using profile information will be significantly lower than for the central views and also lower than for the frontal (0°) view, where the intra-class views remain distinct for a greater range of views.

Intra-class Euclidean distances have been shown to be less, for some specific images in the Sussex database at least, than for inter-class comparisons for small pose angle ranges. This shows the potential of using such comparisons for recognition, especially where training examples can be provided at regular pose intervals.

2.1.2 Pose Classes

Figure 2(d) shows that the intra- and inter-class Euclidean distances are much less well defined for pose than for identity. Specifying an exact 10° pose position will be harder than specifying an exact identity. However, since the poses are linked, we might be able to improve recognition by asking for a less exact pose estimation, such as ±15°, which would require the identification of the pose within a 3-step range.

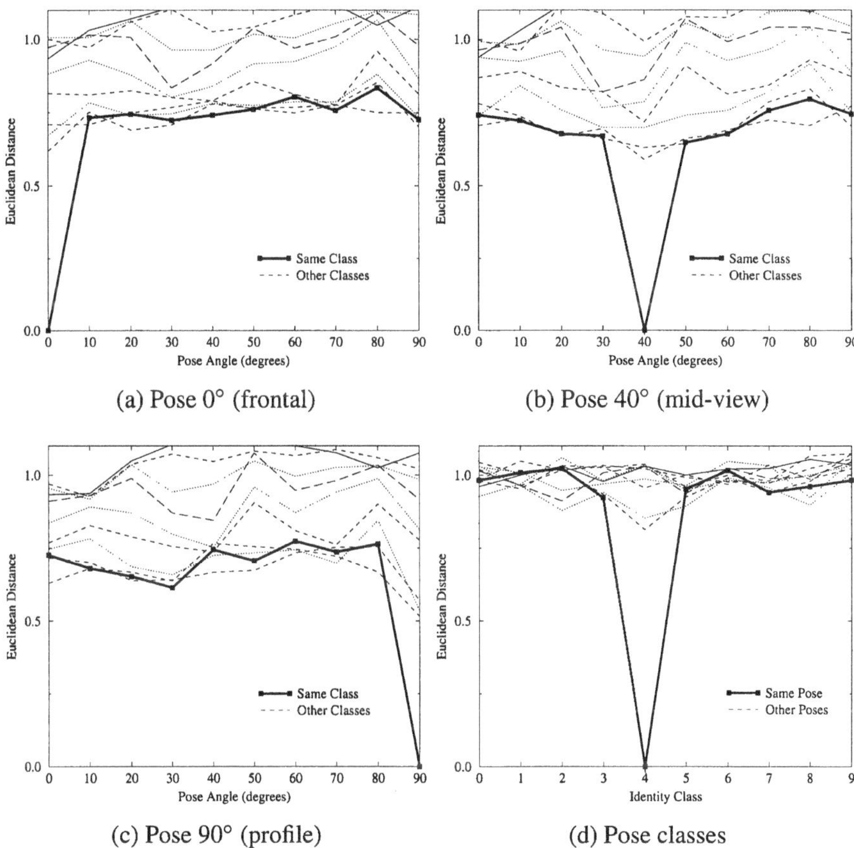

(a) Pose 0° (frontal)

(b) Pose 40° (mid-view)

(c) Pose 90° (profile)

(d) Pose classes

Figure 2. Euclidean distances from single 25×25 face images to all others from the Sussex database. Images are compared (a–c) at specific pose angles from one identity class to all others, each line denotes one class (person): the thin lines showing inter-class distances, the thick intra-class distances, (d) with classes based on pose, rather than identity, each line represents a pose class, each point on x-axis an identity class (person).

Test results [14] suggest that, for this database at least, images of different identity are further apart in Euclidean space than images of different pose. We can say that the use of learning by examples distinguished by Euclidean distances is therefore especially appropriate for face recognition in the presence of large pose changes, as the distances are affected more by identity than pose.

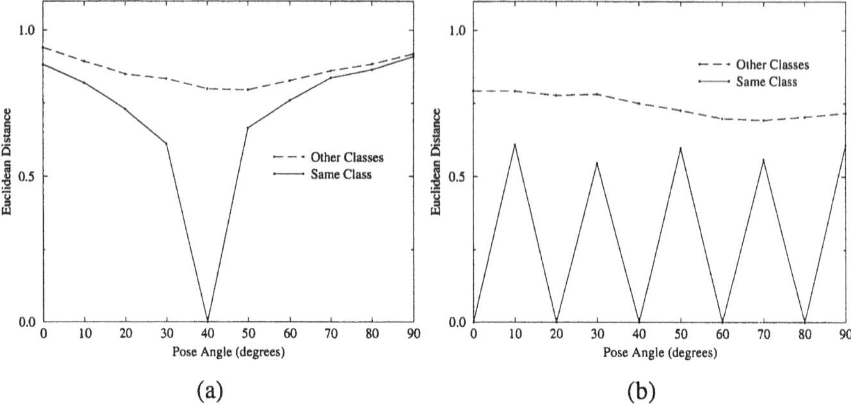

Figure 3. Average Euclidean distances for 25×25 face images from Sussex database, with Gabor preprocessing, between same and other classes while varying pose angle (a) compared to one pose angle, (b) compared to 5 pose angles (using the lowest distance over the five).

2.2 Discussion

This section has investigated how face pose variations affect the distinction between Euclidean distances for images compared with others within its class and with those from other identity classes. We have been able to show that Euclidean distance comparisons can be used to distinguish between images from same and other identity classes within the Sussex database, at least for a few pose steps (each step is roughly 10°) closest to the pose angle of the reference image. The divisions between pose classes, however, do not appear to be so distinct.

To see how different these distances are over the entire Sussex database, Figure 3 shows the overall average value for all intra- and inter-class distances, on a pose-by-pose basis. In (a), one image from a class (pose 40°) is compared to all others in the database. For clarity, the distances for the other classes are averaged for each pose position (examples of specific values for these classes can be seen in Figure 2(b)) to provide a single line on the graph. For Figure 3(b), the same process is carried out for five images from one class, and the lowest distance value to those five images for each class at each pose position is then used as before (inter-class distances averaged before plotting).

A clear division can be seen between the two lines in Figure 3(a), indicating that the two types of distances can, in principle, be distinguished for most pose angles with a single reference image. However, there are specific images where the distinction is unclear, and so contextual classification methods may be needed to disambiguate such data. The 5-example graphs (b), which use five examples of each class as reference images, show a wider gap between the two average distance lines, indicating that the increased class knowledge will improve classification.

3 The RBF Network Model

We employ a Gaussian radial basis function (RBF) neural network model as proposed by [21] and [22] (also proposed similarly by [4], [26], and [27]). This combines a supervised layer from the hidden to the output units with an unsupervised layer from the input to the hidden units. The network model is characterized by individual radial Gaussian functions for each hidden unit, which simulate the effect of overlapping and locally tuned receptive fields.

The size of our RBF network is determined by (1) the size of the face data, as the number of pixels gives the number of input units, (2) the number of training examples, which gives the number of hidden units, and (3) the number of individuals to be distinguished (the number of classes), which gives the number of output units.

The RBF network's success in approximating non-linear multidimensional functions is dependent on sufficient hidden units being used and the suitability of the centers' distribution over the input vector space [8]. Each training example is assigned a corresponding hidden unit, with the image vector used as its center, as is common with Regularization Networks [2]. This approach should not lead to over-fitting because each image in the dataset contains unique 3-D information. Normalization of hidden unit outputs means that a 'bias' hidden unit is not required [24].

3.1 Unsupervised Learning

The unsupervised part of the training procedure for the RBF network is concerned with determining center vectors and widths for the hidden units. For this implementation of the network, it is simple to find the center vectors, as we assign one hidden unit to each training example so that each training vector becomes the corresponding center vector. Therefore, our main discussion in this section is about methods for determining the width values for the hidden unit Gaussian functions.

3.1.1 Hidden Unit Widths

Each hidden unit (Gaussian basis function) is given an associated width or scale value, σ, which, signifying the standard deviation of the function, defines the nature and scope of the unit's receptive field response [31]. This gives an activation that is related to the relative proximity of test data to the center vector associated with the hidden unit, allowing a direct measure of confidence in the output of the network for a particular pattern. In addition, patterns more than slightly different to those trained will produce very low (or no) output.

An adaptive P-nearest neighbor heuristic to determine the center σ values is reported in [21]. We calculate individual σ values for each of the hidden units from the mean Euclidean distance between the center of each hidden unit and all others [32]. An alternative would be to use a fixed number P of closest distance values to determine the mean value, but this would require an extra parameter (which would require optimization). Although the values in our approach may become closer to the overall mean value for large numbers of hidden units, it was felt this was a better approach than to have such extra parameters, which can interrupt automatic operation.

Generalization performance for RBF networks is dependent on the appropriate choice of the σ center width values for the hidden units [24]. However, we have shown [14, Table B.2] that, in practice, the precise form of σ calculation was found not to affect generalization greatly (for our particular task, at least), particularly after discard, but the use of individual mean values did give the best results.

3.2 Supervised Learning

The supervised part of the training procedure for the RBF network is concerned with determining suitable values for the weight connections between the hidden and the output unit layers.

We use the matrix pseudo-inverse method [26], using Singular Value Decomposition (SVD) [29], which allows an exact solution in a single processing stage and almost instantaneous 'training' of the network, regardless of size.

3.3 RBF Discard Measure

A major advantage of the RBF network over other network models, such as the multi-layer perceptron (MLP), is that a direct level of confidence is reflected in the level of each output unit. This is because regions in input space that are far from training vectors are always mapped to low values due to the local nature of the hidden units receptive fields, so that 'novel' input will give a low activation. This is in contrast to the global function approximation of the sigmoidal hidden units in the MLP, which can have spurious high output in similar regions of input space, allowing high confidence output. In addition, the normalization of RBF hidden unit activities allow their output to represent probability values for the presence of their class [22]. In light of the probabilistic nature of the RBF network's output, we will be using a discard measure in our work to exclude low-confidence output and reduce false positives in ambiguous real-life data.

4 Invariance Properties of RBF Networks

This section explores the invariance characteristics of the RBF network, looking at how tolerant it is to particular forms of image variation, and how this is affected by the preprocessing of the input data. It is important to know how robust our system is to the variation anticipated for the main task, as this will determine the accuracy of face segmentation and preprocessing computational load required for data to be learned or recognized.

The experiments in the first half of the section are designed to show how well the RBF network can learn identity and generalize to novel images with data where the pose varies. For instance, can profile images, where eye information from the far side of the face is occluded, be generalized to front views? This will determine over how wide a pose range the system will be effective, and the optimal paving of pose examples in the face 'view sphere' (the 360° range along x-, y- and z-axes of views from which it can be seen). The second half of the section investigates how 2-D shift and scale variations in the image affect this process.

The property of 'invariance' can be seen at different processing stages. Not only can the data representation be thought of as being invariant to various forms of image variation, but the processing and reasoning performed on that representation can also give further invariance. For instance, a 'foveal' space-variant representation can give rotational and scale invariance simply by the nature of the representation. In addition, a preprocessing stage, such as the Gabor filtering stage, will give scale invariance, and a reasoning process, such as a weight-sharing or convolutional network, can give shift (translation) and deformation invariance. Each stage can be seen to be contributing different aspects of invariance, but it is not easy to isolate the characteristics of these stages, as they need to be considered together to give a coherent view of the entire scheme.

Two basic types of invariance to a particular parameter, such as illumination or head pose, can be distinguished: an *inherent invariance* which is present in any representation, processing or reasoning stage, and a *learned invariance* which can be obtained during the learning stage by the use of training with suitably varying example images. Inherent invariance can be observed if the network is trained with images which do not exhibit variation in the parameter, whereas learned invariance requires training images with examples of the variation.

The basic ability gained from the RBF network is that of interpolation between examples. Naturally, this technique will not be utilized in the inherent invariance tests that follow, as these use unvarying data (one example per class) and so there is nothing to interpolate. Therefore, we do not expect to see high performance from the network in these tests, as they will be extrapolating from the single training example to the test images. From the learned invariance tests, we will be determining what intervals through the varying data being tested provide optimal interpolation from the hidden units and therefore give the best invariance performance.

4.1 Test Details

All the experiments in this section use the 100 image, 10 person 'Sussex Database' described in Section 2.1. A pixel-based representation of the 2-D image, used as a 1-D vector for input to the network, will not provide any particular invariance to image variation by itself. It will be the preprocessing and reasoning stages that provide the necessary invariance. In this section, two main preprocessing techniques are used (further details on specific implementations can be found in [14]):

Single-scale Difference of Gaussians (DoG) filtering This filtering is performed as a convolution of the image with a 2-D DoG filter mask of a single scale factor (0.4), with thresholding to give binary zero-crossing information. Each processed image has 441 samples, corresponding to a 21×21 convolution of the original 25×25 image.

Gabor filtering This is 2-D Gabor wavelet analysis at four scales and three orientations (termed 'A3' in [16]). Each processed image has 510 coefficients, corresponding to the outputs of the different scaled and oriented filters at different positions.

4.2 Pose Invariance

Our target task requires an invariance to pose, and so it is important to test our system to determine what limits it has in this respect. In our potential environment, the subjects are allowed unrestricted movement around the room, and therefore will be visible at any pose angle towards the camera that is physiologically possible for the head around the vertical (y-) axis. Obviously, views such as the back of the head are not learnable, in terms of identity, especially if we specify an invariance to hair style, etc.

A useful system in an unrestricted environment should be expected to cope with the full range of views that contain facial information, which is roughly $\pm 120°$, where $0°$ is the frontal view. Such a wide pose range is in contrast to many face recognition systems which do not explicitly dealt with pose, preferring to restrict data to face images with very slight pose variation (typically $\pm 15°$), which can be approximated as linear. RBF networks, in view of their interpolation properties, should allow some pose invariance (given sufficiently close examples for effective interpolation), but the extent of this will need to be determined empirically.

In this section, we will be testing the RBF network for two types of pose invariance by training with two different arrangements of the data examples: the first searches for *inherent invariance* by training with unvaried images (in other words, one fixed pose for all classes) and testing with varied images only (all the other poses not seen during training), the second is looking for *learned invariance* by training with explicit examples of pose variation.

4.2.1 Inherent Pose Invariance

The pose invariance that we have termed 'inherent' in this section is the generalization obtained when the RBF network has been trained with images that have no pose variation (that is, they all come from one fixed pose position), and is then tested with images of different pose to that used for training.

When testing for inherent pose invariance with the Sussex database, where all images for each class have a different pose angle, there can only be one image per class available for training. This type of training will produce a 10/90 RBF network, with 10 training examples (one per class) and 90 test images.

Results

Figure 4(a) shows how the specific pose angle used to train the 10/90 network affects the test generalization, and it can be seen that network performance is rather poor whatever the pose angle used to train it. As discussed above, this network arrangement is effectively being tested for pose *extrapolation*, as only one example of each class is available for learning. This kind of extrapolation from data is not a particular strength of RBF networks, as they are much better suited to interpolation. We expect performance for the interpolating RBF networks in the next section

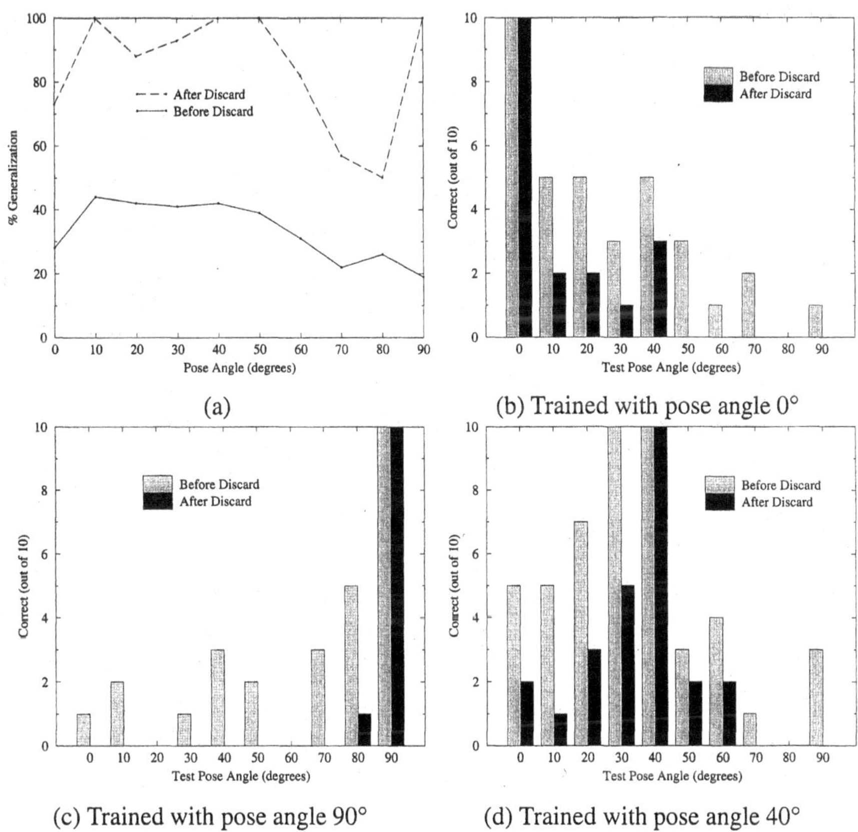

Figure 4. Inherent Pose Invariance: (a) Test generalization over face pose view with 10/90 (trained with one image per class) extrapolating RBF networks, the training view varying over pose. (b–d) Number of correct classifications (out of 10) of test images at specific training pose angles for 10/90 extrapolating RBF networks with DoG preprocessing.

to be significantly better than these extrapolating networks.

The chaotic nature of the graph line for the 'after discard' values in Figure 4(a) reflects how little information remains after extremely high discard levels. It is more informative here to compare the 'before discard' performance. The front to middle range of poses, around 15–45°, appear best for generalization. This corresponds to all the major facial features being visible on the face, without being flattened or foreshortened as they are at more oblique angles. This may have a similar basis to psychological findings on a 45° or '3/4 view advantage' in face recognition [5].

A different view of the RBF network's ability to extrapolate can be seen in Figure 4(b–d), which shows how the numbers of correct classifications vary by pose angle of the test images for varying pose angle in the images used to train the network. As could be expected, the 40° trained network (d), where the test images span a ±45° range relative to the trained image, does better than the 0° (b) and 90° (c) trained networks, which have to generalize to test images up to 90° from the trained image. The graphs clearly show how generalization tails off as the angular difference between the train and test image increases.

In addition, it can be seen in Figure 4(b–d) that the frontal views (0–40°) have an advantage, in terms of generalization, over the profile end of the pose range (50–90°) regardless of the training pose angle. As mentioned above, such an advantage may be due to images in the former pose range containing a greater area of facial information (more pixels representing part of the face) than those in the latter range.

Finally, Figure 4(b–d) also shows how the discard measure removes a large proportion of the correct classifications in order to eliminate false classifications, especially in (c) (compare these to the generalization rates after discard in Figure 4(a)). The lower the black bars are in comparison to the shaded bars, the less of the original correct output is being retained. Through the use of a variable confidence measure, the ratio of lost true positives to discarded false positives can be adjusted according to requirements. In general, we expect large amounts of data and can justify a fairly high discard rate, but in this case, it is not clear there is enough useful data remaining after discard.

Summary

Although there does seem to be some inherent pose invariance in the RBF network, it does not seem to be very controllable due to the low number of example training views. This means that the extrapolating RBF networks we used in this section are only usefully invariant over a pose range of about ±20°.

It should be noted that greater pose invariance is expected if interpolation between trained views is used. The next section will be testing this type of interpolating RBF network to confirm this expectation.

Table 1. The four different types of interpolating RBF networks, used to test learned pose invariance.

Network	Number of Training examples	Number per Class	Number of Test images
20/80	20	2	80
30/70	30	3	70
40/60	40	4	60
50/50	50	5	50

Table 2. Learned Pose Invariance: Effect on varying number of training examples on test generalization for interpolating RBF networks with Gabor preprocessing, both before and after discarding of low-confidence classifications.

Network	Training Examples	Training Pose Angles (°)	Initial %	% Discarded	% After Discard
20/80	2	20,70	71	51	95
30/70	3	20,50,70	80	39	98
40/60	4	10,30,60,80	88	35	97
50/50	5	10,30,50,70,90	96	20	98

4.2.2 Learned Pose Invariance

This section presents experiments where the RBF network learns face-class information from more than one example for each class. This will allow better generalization than for the extrapolating networks above, as these networks can interpolate between training views of the same person at different pose angles.

The network configuration allowed for this type of test is much less constrained than for the extrapolating networks in the previous section (they were confined to one network size due to the nature of the Sussex database), and we are able to perform experiments with four types of interpolating RBF networks, ranging from 2 to 5 training examples per class. The specific details for these are in Table 1.

Results

Table 2 shows the results for the four types of interpolating RBF networks with fixed selections of training pose angles. All configurations provided good levels of generalization performance, especially after discard. This confirmed the expectation that interpolation between training examples is crucial for effective use of the RBF hidden units for pose invariance.

This table also shows that the main advantage gained by adding more training examples per class was in the reduction in number of classifications discarded through low confidence, rather than an improvement in the generalization rate (although there were more correct classifications made).

Figure 5 shows how the number of correct classifications for specific 20/80 and 50/50 networks vary according to the pose angle of the test images. It can be seen that there is slightly better generalization performance for images from the frontal views (0–40°) than for the profile end of the pose range (50–90°).

This higher level of generalization for the interpolating RBF networks with the frontal, rather than profile, views is a similar response to that seen above (see Figure 4) with the extrapolating RBF networks. However, the interpolating networks here are different in that they were able to maintain some generalization performance over all pose angles for test images, while the extrapolating networks completely failed to recognize test images at some pose angles, for instance 80° in Figures 4(b) and (d).

Influence of Training Selection in Learning Pose

To compare the interpolating RBF networks with the earlier extrapolating networks in a more direct way, a range of two-example per class 20/80 and three-example 30/70 networks were tested, having been trained with differing pose selections, similar to the tests done in Section 4.2.1 for inherent pose invariance, from very widely spaced intervals to very close intervals between the training examples.

It was immediately clear that the behaviour of these two networks, in Figure 6, with two and three examples per class, was less erratic than the 10/90 (see Figure 4(a)), which only had one per class. In addition, these networks were able to give a more useful level of generalization, especially after discard.

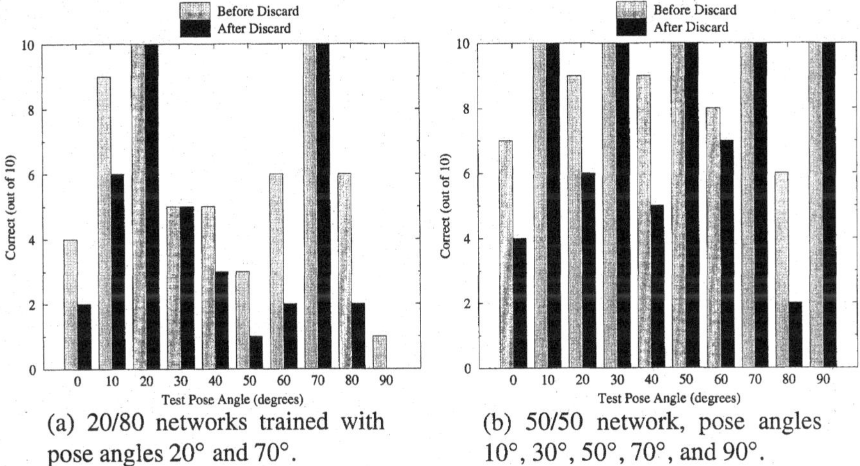

(a) 20/80 networks trained with pose angles 20° and 70°.

(b) 50/50 network, pose angles 10°, 30°, 50°, 70°, and 90°.

Figure 5. Learned Pose Invariance: number of correct classifications (out of 10) of test images at specific pose angles for interpolating RBF networks with DoG preprocessing.

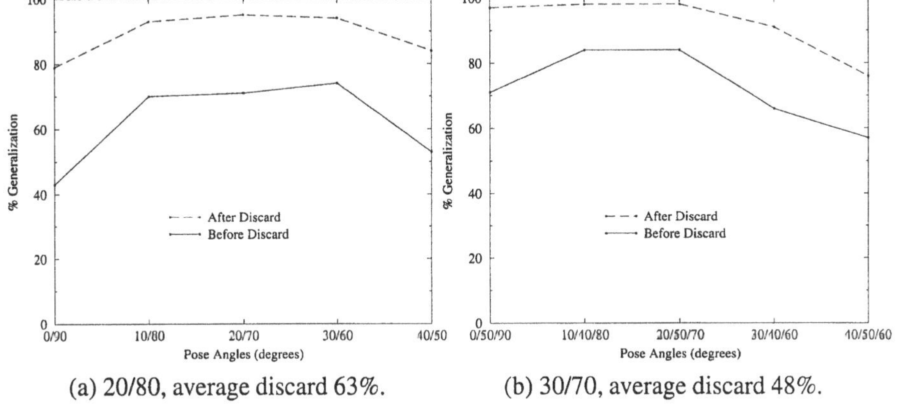

(a) 20/80, average discard 63%.

(b) 30/70, average discard 48%.

Figure 6. Learned Pose Invariance: test generalization with 20/80 (trained with two images per class) and 30/70 (three per class) interpolating RBF networks with Gabor preprocessing, varying over selections of pose angles: from left to right, widely to closely space intervals.

Summary

We have been able to show learned pose invariance in interpolating RBF networks, which have several training examples (each of different pose) for each class. These networks were able to generalize effectively when tested with images with head pose that lies between that of at least two of the training examples.

The increase in generalization performance from the two- (20/80) to three-example (30/70) networks indicates that a good level of pose invariance is provided by each RBF hidden unit over a pose range of $\pm 20°$, with $\pm 15°$ providing a high level of generalization.

4.3 Shift and Scale Invariance

This section tests the RBF network with some image variations that are likely to be encountered in real-life data, where automatic face localization will not always be exact. Two type of errors may occur in an automatic localization stage of the processing of face images:

1. The face may be incorrectly centered.
2. The face size may be incorrectly determined.

These errors correspond to the two specific modes of image variation under which we will be testing generalization:

1. A translational shift of the face, so that the face is no longer centered compared to the standard 'nose-centered' face position determined for the Sussex database (we assume this original position was correctly registered, see [14] for further details, and experiments with other centering algorithms).
2. A scale variation of a normally centered face, so that the face is no longer the same size compared to the standard face size determined for the Sussex database.

As mentioned earlier, it is important to know, in each case, how much invariance can be expected from the RBF network, so that trade-offs between explicit processing stages for specific types of invariance can be made, and the bounds on localization accuracy determined.

4.3.1 Shift- and Scale-Varying Data

In order that each specific mode of 2-D variation in the images could be studied separately, each were isolated by creating two new data sets of 500 images each from the original 100-image Sussex dataset:

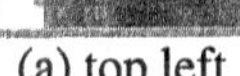

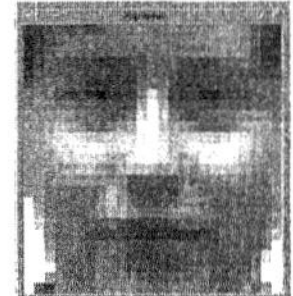
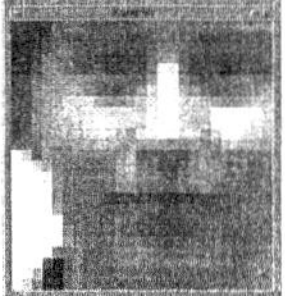

(a) top left (b) top right (c) normal view (d) bottom left (e) bottom right

Figure 7. Example shifted versions of the original front view of one individual from the Sussex database, used to test for shift invariance.

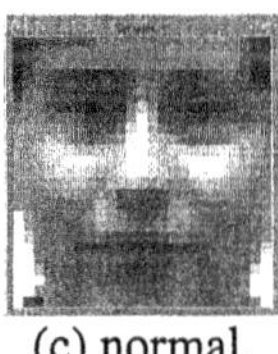
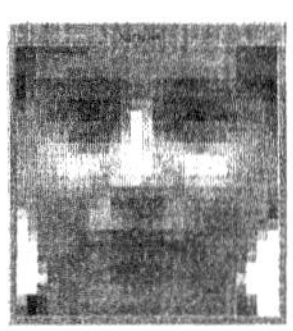

(a) +25%, 111×111 (b) +12.5%, 107×107 (c) normal, 100×100 (d) −12.5%, 94×94 (e) −25%, 87×87

Figure 8. Example scaled versions of the original front view of one individual from the Sussex database, used to test for scale invariance, with relative size to the normal sampling area, and size of window grabbed from (in pixels).

- A *shift-varying* data set with five copies of each image: one at the standard sampling 'window' position, and four others at the corners of a box where all x,y positions were ± 10 pixels from the center (see Figure 7).
- A *scale-varying* data set with five copies of each image: one at the standard sampling 'window' size of 100×100, and four re-scaled at $\pm 12.5\%$ and $\pm 25\%$ of its surface area, ranging from 87×87 to 111×111 (see Figure 8).

Similarly to the previous section, where we dealt with pose invariance, we experiment with the RBF network with two different types of data examples: the first searches for *inherent invariance* by training with original images only, the second is looking for *learned invariance* by training with shift and scale varying images.

4.3.2 Inherent Shift and Scale Invariance

The experiments in this section are testing for the inherent shift and scale invariance in the RBF network using the Sussex database. Inherent invariance is the generalization exhibited by the network to test images of a particular type of variation, in the absence of exposure to that variation through explicit training examples.

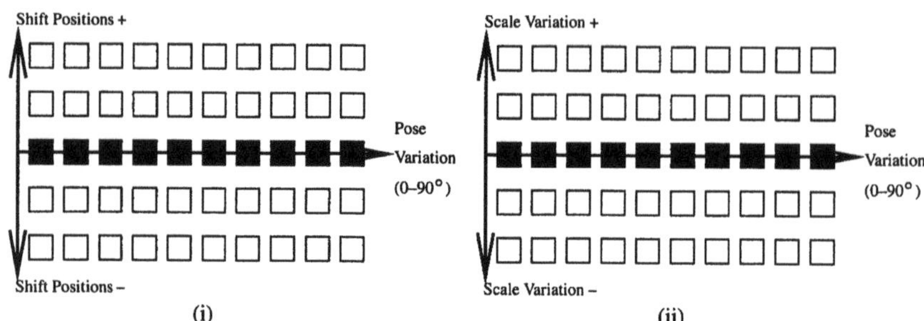

(a) *Inherent invariance* tests using original face images from all 10 pose angles: 10 training (black) and 40 test (white) images.

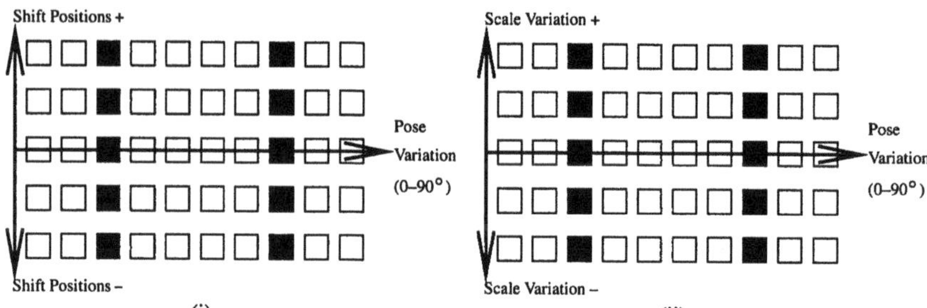

(b) *Learned invariance* tests with images from two pose angles: 10 training and 40 test images.

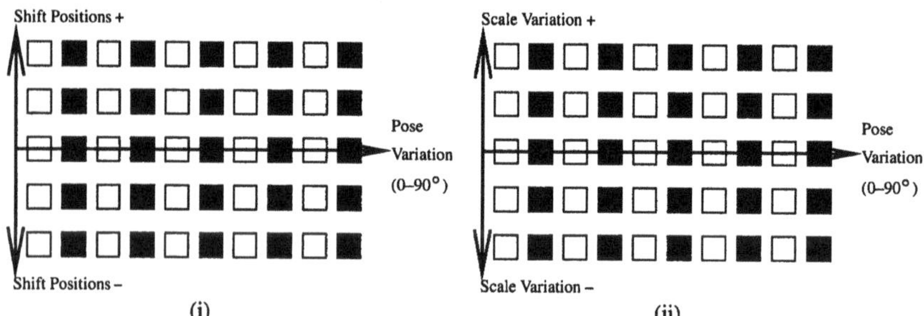

(c) *Learned invariance* tests with images from five pose angles: 25 training and 25 test images.

Figure 9. Selection of training and test data from the 50 images available for each person with the (i) shift and (ii) scale varying data.

To test for this intrinsic shift or scale invariance, only the original image from each group of five (see Figures 7 and 8) is used for training, the four varied ones being reserved for testing; see Figures 9(a)(i) and (ii) for a diagram of how this is done. This means that for all experiments in this section, there are 100 training and 400 test images.

Table 3. Inherent Shift and Scale Invariance: Effect on test generalization for the RBF network of different variations in the dataset with Gabor preprocessing, both before and after discarding of low-confidence classifications: networks trained with all ten non-varied versions of poses for each person and testing with varied versions (100 training and 400 test images).

Variation	Network	Initial %	% Discarded	% After Discard
Shift	100/400	35	82	47
Scale	100/400	83	36	88

Results

From the results in Table 3, it is immediately obvious that the RBF networks trained with no shift or scale variations performed very differently when tested with the shift rather than with the scale varying data.

In the absence of explicit training examples, the network using the shift-varying test data with Gabor preprocessing was only able to give a low level of useful generalization. In contrast, the scale-varying test data appears to be much easier for the network to generalize to, even without explicit training examples, and RBF network was able to give a high level of generalization performance, even without discard.

Summary

This section has shown that the RBF network has a significant inherent invariance to scale differences with the Gabor preprocessed face data from the Sussex database. In marked contrast, the shifted images were very much harder for the network to generalize to.

Figures 10(a) and (b) show the kind of differences that arise out of the choice of preprocessing, and that the scale transformation seems to alter the image vector less than the shift transformation. This is shown by the 'other class' line for the Gabor scaled images in Figure 10(b)(ii) being noticeably further away from the 'same class' line than for the other combinations of transformation and preprocessing.

4.3.3 Learned Shift and Scale Invariance

The experiments in this section test for learned shift and scale invariance. As before, they use a fixed selection of pose positions for training

Table 4. Learned Shift and Scale Invariance: Effect on test generalization for the RBF network of different variations in the dataset with Gabor preprocessing, both before and after discarding of low-confidence classifications: networks trained with all five shift or scale-varied versions of two (100/400) or five (250/250) equally spaced poses for each person.

Variation	Network	Initial %	% Discarded	% After Discard
Shift	100/400	69	60	89
	250/250	85	35	98
Scale	100/400	64	55	88
	250/250	90	26	97

examples, but this time use all five versions (4 varied, 1 unvaried) of each original image. This helps the network to learn about the shift and scale image variation during training and thus develop a learned invariance. The difference between the generalization performance found in the previous section (with inherent invariance) and in the tests in this section will be due to this learned invariance.

Two levels of training are used in this section, corresponding to the two- (Figures 9(b)(i) and (ii)) and five-example (Figures 9(c)(i) and (ii)) networks for pose invariance in Section 4.2.2. These use 10 and 25 training images for each class, creating 100/400 and 250/250 networks respectively.

The first level of training is used to allow a direct comparison with the results from the previous section, as it uses the same number of training examples. The second is used to establish whether the same level of performance improvement seen in Section 4.2.2 for five-example pose invariance networks over two-example networks (see Table 2) would be repeated for the shift and scale invariance networks.

Results

The results in Table 4 show that not only can the RBF network learn identity in spite of pose variations, but it can continue to be invariant to pose in the presence of other variations. In addition, it can learn an invariance to scale variation more easily than shift as shown by both the better classification performance and the lower discard rates.

Interestingly, the *inherent invariance* 100/400 network using Gabor preprocessed data, with a generalization rate of 83% before discard (Table 3), was able to perform better than the *learned invariance* 100/400 network, with only 69% before discard (Table 4).

Summary

These results suggest once more that the use of only two learned pose views for training the RBF network is not the most efficient arrangement for good pose generalization, especially when this is required in addition to scale invariance, and that three or more are required for robust performance. This is backed up by the superior performance exhibited by the 5-pose example 250/250 networks, which corresponds to the high performance obtained from the learned pose invariance 50/50 network (Table 2). This indicates that there are sufficient pose examples in the 250/250 networks to interpolate efficiently.

It should be noted that this discussion of an absolute number of examples required for good generalization is only relevant within the specific context of the 90° pose range encountered in the Sussex database, as other ranges in different data will obviously require differing amounts of training views.

4.3.4 The Contribution of Multi-Scale Preprocessing

The Euclidean distances graphs in Figures 10(a) and (b) indicate that the Gabor preprocessing does separate the within-class images from the other-class images more than the DoG preprocessing for the shift and scale varying data, although the effects appear quite small.

To investigate further why there is such a big difference between the two preprocessing techniques when using the shift and scale-varying data, further tests were made to determine if it was the multi-scale nature of the Gabor preprocessed representation that gave its advantage, rather than the design of the filters themselves. These used a variant on the DoG preprocessing schemes used previously:

Multi-scale DoG preprocessing This used 4 scale factors (0.15, 0.4, 0.8, and 1.3) to give 1556 samples per image (compared to 441 for the normal single scale representation).

Contrary to expectations, however, the results using the multi-scale DoG preprocessing for the shift and scale-varying data proved to be very similar to the original tests using the normal DoG and Gabor schemes, bearing in mind that more data samples were provided, which should have improved the learnability of the task. Of course, no amount of extra data will help if the representation is not appropriate to the task.

If it is not the different scales in the representation which are improving generalization, it must be the oriented nature of the Gabor preprocessed data which is significant. We have previously been able to show, however, that there is a finite limit to the usefulness of this, and that performance is not enhanced through the use of more than three orientations [14].

Summary

It was concluded that providing a range of scales in the DoG preprocessing stage will not, in itself, provide the representation with the same generalization power that the Gabor process did. This is backed up by the similarity of the Euclidean distance values between the single and multi-scale DoG preprocessed images in Figures 10(a) and (c).

4.4 Discussion

Section 4.2 showed that the RBF network has a limited inherent pose invariance, due to its poor extrapolation ability, although this can be improved via preprocessing. The key to enhanced performance, both in higher generalization and lower discard rates, is in providing training examples within the anticipated test pose range, using a suitably close interval between training pose angles, so that the RBF network can interpolate effectively.

In Section 4.3, we have shown that RBF networks seem to have quite powerful inherent scale invariance, but no inherent shift invariance. Both image variations could be learned to give a high level of generalization if given suitable training examples.

Gabor preprocessing allows greater invariance to these transformations than the DoG preprocessing. This effect is most pronounced with the scale variations, which is not surprising considering the multi-scale na-

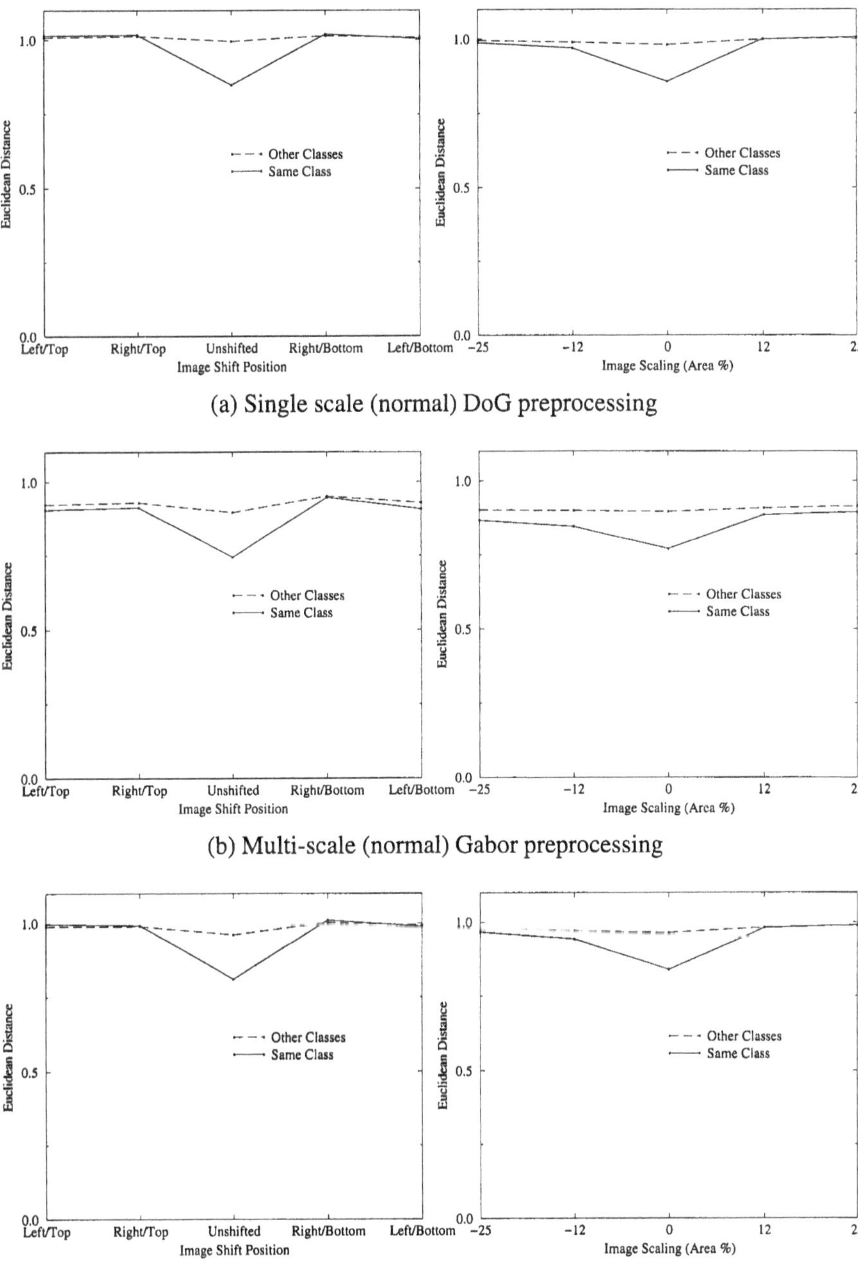

(a) Single scale (normal) DoG preprocessing

(b) Multi-scale (normal) Gabor preprocessing

(c) Multi-scale DoG preprocessing

Figure 10. Euclidean distances for images from the Sussex database to same- and other-class images, averaged over all classes, varying over specific shift and scale variations, (i) shift, (ii) scale, and different types of preprocessing.

ture of the data representation. However, we have discounted that it is this aspect alone of the Gabor preprocessing which gives it its power, as the tests using a multi-scale DoG representation showed that the explicit extra information at different scales gave no improvement in network performance over that obtained with training without these data values. Indeed, the RBF networks using the multi-scale DoG preprocessing were unable to improve on those using single scale DoG preprocessed data.

It might be expected that it was the oriented nature of the Gabor preprocessed data which gave it an advantage in learnability over the DoG preprocessed data. However, such an advantage can not be controlled through varying the number of orientations, as we have found that performance remains fairly constant in such circumstances. This does not mean it cannot be the oriented nature of the data that gives the advantage, but that there is a limit to how much useful information can be extracted with a single technique.

The next section will be concerned with how variations in the structure of the RBF network itself can enhance its performance and allow greater control over the discarding procedure.

5 Face Unit RBF Networks

This section describes a different approach to learning the face recognition task through the reorganization of the standard RBF networks into a group of smaller 'face recognition units', each trained to recognize a single person. This type of system organization allows flexible scaling up which can be used either by itself or in conjunction with a standard RBF network trained on all classes where the combined decisions might give greater reliability.

The concept of *face recognition units* was suggested in the perceptual frameworks for human face processing proposed by [13] and [6]. We are adopting this face unit concept as a useful way of developing a modular, scalable architecture, creating fast small RBF networks trained with examples of views of the person to be recognized. The face unit network uses these views of the person to be recognized as positive evidence together with selected confusable views of other people as the negative evidence, which are linked to just 2 outputs corresponding to 'yes' or 'no' decisions for the individual. This training using explicit negative examples is in contrast to the HyperBF network scheme used by [10], who preferred to use implicit negative evidence in their study.

For each individual, an RBF network is trained to discriminate between that person and others selected from the data set. Rather than using all the data available from the other classes to train the network against an individual, the strategy adopted was to use only negative data that was most similar (using an Euclidean distance metric) to the positive data.

The reduction in the size of the network using the face unit organization plus the use of negative knowledge should allow a more efficient coding of the information. Furthermore, people can be added to the data set of a trained set of networks by the creation of a new 'face unit' network for each new individual to be added without retraining the entire database, as the reorganized scheme is completely modular. In the standard RBF network, a new individual means a complete retraining with the expanded dataset.

5.1 The Face Unit Network Model

The face unit network is essentially a normal RBF network with two output units which produces a positive signal only for the particular person it is trained to recognize. It differs from the RBF networks used in previous sections only in the selection of training data, the data for the face unit network being manipulated to present a many-class problem as a two-class problem: (1) a particular class and (2) all others.

The fundamental process in training the face unit network is the splitting of the training data into two halves: class and non-class. The small size of the network is due to the limited amount of non-class data used for training, only those that are seen as hardest to distinguish with the class are included. This selection of negative evidence was based on Euclidean vector distance comparisons of the class face image with images of the same pose angle of non-class faces. In order to make the most efficient arrangement of training examples, the 'anti' evidence was taken from the class that was the closest (in Euclidean distance terms) to the 'pro' class,

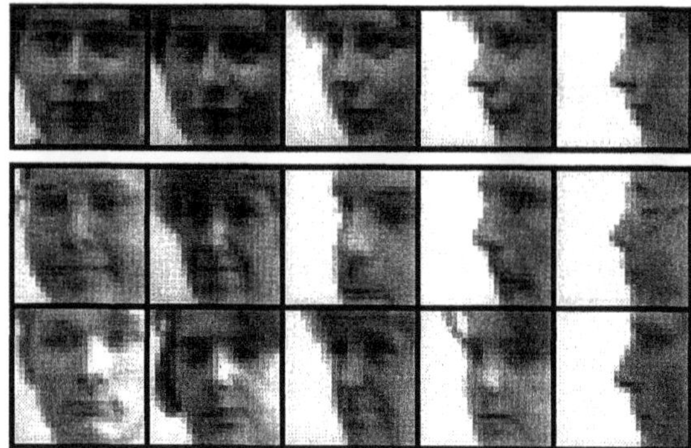

Figure 11. Example of the range of negative classes that can be selected during the training of a face unit RBF network. The top line shows the supporting, 'pro' evidence, the middle and bottom lines the differentiating, 'anti' evidence (middle line is the closest to the pro class, bottom line the second closest).

see Figure 11. As the RBF network's hidden units response is based on the same Euclidean distance comparison, it is important to distinguish the closest non-class examples, as these will be the most 'confusable' for the network, and any other non-class images further away will then be automatically excluded.

5.2 Face Unit Networks as Adjudicators

One potential drawback of using face unit networks is that the processing required to input the test image to every network may become excessive for large number of classes. It would be possible to take advantage of the specialized training characterized by each individual face unit network by using them in cooperation with other networks.

For instance, a single face unit network can be used to confirm or dispute a classification from a standard RBF network trained on all individuals. To do this, the initial output from the multi-class network is used to index into the group of face unit networks to identify which one was needed, and the outputs from the two networks used in conjunction. We have been able to show that such an approach can be used to give better, or at least as good, generalization performance, after discard, as that provided by the original confidence measure used with the standard RBF network alone, but that this superior performance is sometimes at the cost of higher proportion of discarded classifications [15].

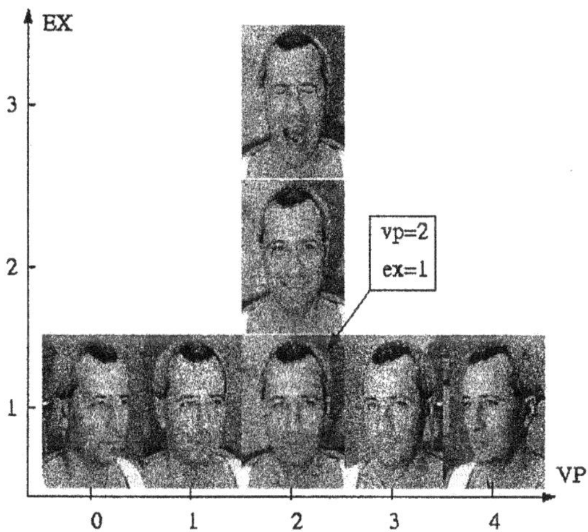

Figure 12. The expression (*EX*)/head pose (*VP*) dimensions of variation for one person in the Weizmann FaceBase (from [9]).

6 Learning Expression/Pose Classes

This section describes how to train generic expression and head pose models using RBF networks. The data used here is from the standard Weizmann FaceBase [23], which allows us to test identity generalization for RBF networks in the presence of expression as well as pose variation. Although the illumination conditions can be varied, we kept it constant for these tests. For the 28 people in the database, we used 15 images for each (420 total): 5 head pose positions, *VP*, (-34°, -17°, 0°, 17°, 34°) for each of 3 expressions, *EX*, (neutral, smile, yawn), as shown in Figure 12.

In each table in the results, the 'Initial %' column shows the initial generalization rate for the RBF network. This value can be modified with the 'low-confidence' measure, the '% Discarded' column indicating how many classifications were discarded in this way, and '% after Discard' shows the final generalization rate using only the resulting high-confidence output.

6.1 Expression Invariance

Our first experiment looks at identity recognition using pose- and expression-varying images. This establishes the ability of the RBF to

Table 5. Test generalization for RBF networks trained to classify by identity, using pose- and expression-varying images from the Weizmann FaceBase.

Train/Test (per Class)	Initial %	% Discarded	% After Discard
1/14	60	63	94
3/12	90	28	98
9/6	93	28	100

distinguish the data in terms of identity classes before we move onto 'generic' training of the network with non-identity classes.

The 'Train/Test (per Class)' in the tables shows how many training and test images were used for each class. Following our earlier tests on pose invariance in face recognition [17], we select training data by 'paving' the pose variation found in the data for each person with equally-spaced examples (-34°, 0°, 34°), using the others for testing (-17°, 17°). This approach has been shown to provide good levels of pose invariance for trained RBF networks, and will allow us to focus on the expression variation in the data. Within this framework, then, we can then check for 'inherent' expression invariance (see Section 4.2.1) by using training examples with neutral expression only (*3 train/12 test*), and 'learned' expression invariance by using training examples with all expressions (*9 train/6 test*).

Table 5 shows that the RBF network can provide good identity generalization over expression variation even without explicit examples of that variation.

In addition, we did a '1/14' test, where only one training example was used for each class. This is a harder task, as the network has to be invariant to both pose and expression, and can be compared with results in [9], where an error rate of 31% (69% correct) was reported. The major difference here is that we have not collected class-based knowledge about viewpoint and expression transformations, and therefore have only the individual training example. Such extrapolation is not a strength of RBF networks, as can been seen by the large improvement in performance when only two extra training examples per class are provided (the 3/12 test). In all cases, however, the discard measure allowed ambiguous re-

Table 6. Test generalization performance for generic RBF networks trained to classify (a) expression (EX) classes, using pose- and identity-varying images, or (b) head pose (VP) classes, using expression- and identity-varying images.

Type of Classes	Train/Test (Individuals)	Initial %	% Discarded	% After Discard
(a) Expression	21/7	67	41	79
(EX)	14/14	67	46	81
(3 classes)	7/21	52	53	61
(b) Head Pose	21/7	99	8	99
(VP)	14/14	95	19	98
(5 classes)	7/21	89	20	93

sults to be efficiently identified, as shown by high classification rates in the '% After Discard' column.

6.2 Classifying Expression and Pose

In addition to identifying individuals, we also wish to develop networks for other specific tasks. With the Weizmann data, we can train RBF networks to classify images in terms of expression and pose classes, without regard for identity.

For these tests, we took all 15 images for a number of individuals to use as training examples for either the 3 expression (EX) classes or the 5 head pose (VP) classes. The 'Train/Test (Individuals)' column shows how many of these were used for training and testing. Thus, the '7/21' test used 7×15 training examples in total (split into 35 for each expression class or 21 for each pose class).

Table 6 shows that very different results were obtained for the two types of network. The head pose (VP) classes (b) appear to be very much easier to generalize to than the expression (EX) classes (a), which failed to give good results even with large numbers of training examples. This may be due to expressions requiring higher resolution data for discrimination than head pose, which can easily be identified from low resolution images.

6.3 Discussion

Our tests with the Weizmann FaceBase demonstrate how computationally cheap RBF classifiers can be developed for particular static recognition tasks. These could be used in parallel to give a range of information about the current frame from live video input. A way to improve on the high level of error in the undiscarded generalization rates is to use class-based knowledge, e.g., [9].

7 Conclusion

This chapter has described practical work using radial basis function (RBF) networks on a pose-varying face recognition task, and shown how the control of training data can provide invariance to specific aspects in image data, such as lighting and inaccurate segmentation. This control can also be used to isolate and learn non-identity information, such as expression and head pose.

Section 2.1 presented an analysis of the Sussex face database in terms of Euclidean distance comparisons, showing how head pose affected intra- and inter-class distances for identity. Figure 2 illustrates how these distances are much less distinct for extreme pose angles (0° and 90°) than for the mid-range images (around 45°).

In addition, Figure 3 shows the differences for Euclidean distances for images compared with other within its class and with those from other classes. The distances to all the other classes are averaged and also when distances from five different images (rather than just one) are averaged together. This latter graph shows that extra examples of the class will widen the Euclidean distance distinction (on average, at least) between intra- and inter-class images, and implies that learning the identity classes with an RBF network will be much easier if several examples of each class are available for training.

Section 3 described our specific RBF network model and the confidence discard measure we use to improve generalization in noisy data.

Having shown in Section 2.1 how the representation used for input data can have a profound effect on the ability of the RBF network to generalize from a learned task, Section 4 went on to develop these ideas to analyze how specific variations in the image will affect such generalization.

The experiments in Section 4.2 looked at invariance to head pose, a complex 3-D image transformation. The results show that this is not inherent to the RBF network over any wide pose angle range, but that it can be effectively learned if appropriate training examples are available to give high levels of test generalization. What this implies is that even if we cannot create an image representation that is (inherently) pose-invariant over large angles, we can produce an RBF hidden layer representation with useful (learned) pose invariance.

Section 4.3 dealt with shift and scale transformations, both simple, 2-D image-plane variations. The experiments show that both can be learned and give high levels of generalization performance when using Gabor preprocessing. In marked contrast to its invariance to pose and shift variation, the RBF network has been shown to have a useful inherent scale invariance for this kind of data, as the Euclidean distances between intra-class and inter-class images are more distinct (Figures 3 and 10). This is clearly indicated by the good generalization (only slightly lower than the 5-example (250/250) learned rates) in conditions where the network completely failed with the shift-varying data. This means that fewer training examples need to be explicitly used to teach the network about image scale variation. In addition, although a rough approximation may be sufficient when localizing the face during preprocessing, it is important to correctly register it so that the face region is accurately centralized within the image.

Section 5 described how a face unit RBF network can learn to distinguish a single class from a range of other classes. This can be used either in groups, one for each class, or singly in conjunction with a multi-class network to give greater reliability to classification. Although the standard RBF network will give similar positive and negative information about classes, because of the fully interconnected hidden to output unit layer, the face unit network, by concentrating only on distinguishing one class at a time, allows the negative influences of such non-class connections to be more specialized, indeed optimized, to give the most effective 'one class against all others' partitioning in image space.

The modular approach using face unit RBF networks to learn identity is especially attractive for an unconstrained recognition task, as it allows the modification of the learned element of the system during use, and can give a secondary classification decision which can either confirm or dispute the primary RBF network output.

Finally, in Section 6, we showed how computationally cheap RBF classifiers can be developed for three particular static recognition tasks, identity, expression and pose, with the same training data. The flexibility of example-based learning with the RBF network means that, provided an appropriate representation is chosen for the data, re-learning for new tasks is both practical and computationally efficient.

References

[1] Ahmad, S. and Tresp, V. (1993), "Some solutions to the missing feature problem in vision," in Hanson, S.J., Cowan, J.D., and Giles, C.L. (Eds.), *Advances in Neural Information Processing Systems*, vol. 5, Morgan Kaufmann, San Mateo, CA, pp. 393-400.

[2] Beymer, D.J. and Poggio, T. (1996), "Image representations for visual learning," *Science*, vol. 272, pp. 1905-1909.

[3] Bishop, C.M. (1995), *Neural Networks for Pattern Recognition*, Oxford University Press, Oxford, U.K.

[4] Broomhead D.S. and Lowe, D. (1988), "Multivariable functional interpolation and adaptive networks," *Complex Systems*, vol. 2, pp. 321-355.

[5] Bruce, V., Valentine, T., and Baddeley, A.D. (1987), "The basis of the 3/4 view advantage in face recognition," *Applied Cognitive Psychology*, vol. 1, pp. 109-120.

[6] Bruce, V. and Young, A. (1986), "Understanding face recognition," *British Journal of Psychology*, vol. 77, pp. 305-327.

[7] Brunelli, R. and Poggio, T. (1991), "HyperBF networks for real object recognition," in Myopoulos, J. and Reiter, R. (Eds.), *Proceedings of International Joint Conference on Artificial Intelligence*, Morgan Kaufmann, Sydney, Australia, pp. 1278-1284.

[8] Chen, S., Cowan, C.F.N., and Grant P.M. (1991), "Orthogonal least squares learning algorithm for radial basis function networks," *IEEE Transactions on Neural Networks*, vol. 2, pp. 302-309.

[9] Duvdevani-Bar, S., Edelman, S., Howell, A.J., and Buxton, H. (1998), "A similarity-based method for the generalization of face recognition over pose and expression," in *Proceedings of IEEE International Conference on Automatic Face & Gesture Recognition*, IEEE Computer Society Press, Nara, Japan, pp. 118-123.

[10] Edelman, S., Reisfeld, D., and Yeshurun, Y. (1992), "Learning to recognize faces from examples," in Sandini, G. (Ed.), *Proceedings of European Conference on Computer Vision, Lecture Notes in Computer Science*, vol. 588, Springer-Verlag, Santa Margherita Ligure, Italy, pp. 787-791.

[11] Girosi, F. (1992), "Some extensions of radial basis functions and their applications in artificial intelligence," *Computers & Mathematics with Applications*, vol. 24, pp.61-80.

[12] Gong, S., McKenna, S.J., and Collins, J.J. (1996), "An investigation into face pose distributions," in *Proceedings of International Conference on Automatic Face & Gesture Recognition*, IEEE Computer Society Press, Killington, VT, pp. 265-270.

[13] Hay, D.C. and Young, A. (1982), "The human face," in Ellis, H.D. (Ed.), *Normality and Pathology in Cognitive Functions*, Academic Press, San Diego, CA.

[14] Howell, A.J. (1997), *Automatic face recognition using radial basis function networks*, Ph.D. thesis, University of Sussex.

[15] Howell, A.J. (1999), "Face unit radial basis function networks," in Jain, L.C., Halici, U., Hayashi, I., Lee, S.B., and Tsutsui, S. (Eds.), *Intelligent Biometric Techniques in Fingerprint and Face Recognition*, CRC Press, pp. 315-334.

[16] Howell, A.J. (1999), "Introduction to face recognition," in Jain, L.C., Halici, U., Hayashi, I., Lee, S.B., and Tsutsui, S. (Eds.), *Intelligent Biometric Techniques in Fingerprint and Face Recognition*, CRC Press, pp. 217-284.

[17] Howell, A.J. and Buxton, H. (1996), "Face recognition using radial basis function neural networks," in Fisher, R.B. and Trucco, E. (Eds.), *Proceedings of British Machine Vision Conference*, BMVA Press, Edinburgh, pp. 455-464.

[18] Howell, A.J. and Buxton, H. (1998), "Recognising people and behaviours," in Wechsler, H., Philips, P.J., Bruce, V., Fogelman-Soulié, F., and Huang, T. (Eds.), *Face Recognition: from Theory to Applications, NATO ASI Series F*, Springer-Verlag.

[19] McKenna, S.J. and Gong, S. (1996), "Tracking faces," *Proceedings of International Conference on Automatic Face & Gesture Recognition*, IEEE Computer Society Press, Killington, VT, pp. 271-276.

[20] McKenna, S.J., Gong, S., and Collins, J.J. (1996), "Face tracking and pose representation," in Fisher, R.B. and Trucco, E. (Eds.), *Proceedings of British Machine Vision Conference*, BMVA Press, Edinburgh, pp. 755-764.

[21] Moody, J. and Darken, C. (1988), "Learning with localized receptive fields," in Touretzky, D., Hinton, G., and Sejnowski, T. (Eds.), *Proceedings of 1988 Connectionist Models Summer School*, Morgan Kaufmann, Pittsburgh, PA, pp. 133-143.

[22] Moody, J. and Darken, C. (1989), "Fast learning in networks of locally-tuned processing units," *Neural Computation*, vol. 1, pp. 281-294.

[23] Moses, Y., Adini, Y., and Ullman, S. (1994), "Face recognition: the problem of compensating for illumination changes," in Eklundh, J.O. (Ed.), *Proceedings of European Conference on Computer Vision, Lecture Notes in Computer Science*, vol. 800, Springer-Verlag, Stockholm, Sweden, pp. 286-296.

[24] Musavi, M.T., Ahmad, W., Chan, K.H., Faris, K.B., and Hummels, D.M. (1992), "On the training of radial basis function classifiers," *Neural Networks*, vol. 5, pp. 595-603.

[25] Poggio, T. and Edelman, S. (1990), "A network that learns to recognize three-dimensional objects," *Nature*, vol. 343, pp. 263-266.

[26] Poggio, T. and Girosi, F. (1990), "Networks for approximation and learning," *Proceedings of IEEE*, vol. 78, pp. 1481-1497.

[27] Poggio, T. and Girosi, F. (1990), "Regularization algorithms for learning that are equivalent to multilayer networks," *Science*, vol. 247, pp. 978-982.

[28] Pomerleau, D.A. (1989), "ALVINN: an autonomous land vehicle in a neural network," in Touretzky, D.S. (Ed.), *Advances in Neural Information Processing Systems*, Morgan Kaufmann, San Mateo, CA, vol. 1, pp. 305-313.

[29] Press, W.H., Flannery, B.P., Teukolsky, S.A., and Vetterling, W.T. (1986), *Numerical Recipes in C*, Cambridge University Press, Cambridge.

[30] Rosenblum, M. and Davis, L.S. (1996), "An improved radial basis function network for autonomous road-following," *IEEE Transactions on Neural Networks*, vol. 7, pp. 1111-1120.

[31] Saha, A. and Keeler, J.D. (1990), "Algorithms for better representation and faster learning in radial basis function networks," in Touretzky, D.S. (Ed.), *Advances in Neural Information Processing Systems*, Morgan Kaufmann, San Mateo, CA, vol. 2.

[32] Stokbro, K., Umberger, D.K., and Hertz, J.A. (1990), "Exploiting neurons with localized receptive fields to learn chaos," *Complex Systems*, vol. 4, pp. 603-622.

[33] Ullman, S. and Basri, R. (1991), "Recognition by linear combinations of models," *IEEE Transactions on Pattern Analysis & Machine Intelligence*, vol. 13, pp. 992-1006.

Chapter 5

Classification of Facial Expressions with Domain Gaussian RBF Networks

J.M. Hogan, M. Norris, and J. Diederich

This chapter examines the problem of categorization of facial expressions through the use of a receptive field neural network model, based upon novel *domain Gaussian* network units trained through error back-propagation. Such networks are trained upon images derived from the Ekman and Friesen "Pictures of Facial Affect" database, and they are subsequently able to successfully generalize to images of unseen subjects, and provide qualitative replication of the perceptual confusions common to previous studies. By using digital morphing techniques to produce intermediate frames between the existing stills, we are able to study the space of transitions between endpoint expressions. Our results suggest that expressions unrelated to the endpoint images may be perceived during certain transitions, a path far more complex than direct translation through a neutral expression.

1 Introduction

This work is concerned with the application of novel neural network models to the problem of categorizing human facial expressions, and the extent to which such models may successfully replicate human performance and provide falsifiable predictions for novel images. The human category judgments are here obtained from the now classical Ekman and Friesen "Pictures of Facial Affect" study [3], the still images of their set of photographs partitioned by Ekman's subjects into one of the six classes of "Happiness", "Sadness", "Anger", "Fear", "Surprise", and "Disgust". The task of each of our networks is to recognize one of these categories from training upon positive and negative examples of that category, these consisting of preprocessed bitmaps derived from scanned versions of the Ekman stills.

As well as using Ekman images unseen by the network for generalization testing, we also examine network performance on novel images extracted as still pictures from a number of (linear) digital morphs between images derived from the Ekman slides. In this way we are able to identify both the crossover point in the transition 'movie' – the frame at which the final category activation exceeds that for the initial category – and to offer psychologically interesting predictions of perceptual confusion, with some sequences appearing to verge during the transition toward an unrelated category before returning to the appropriate endpoint.

The network is based upon novel receptive field units which map facial regions implicated in the encoding of expressions, allowing generalization to unseen subjects and some confidence measure of the degree of category membership for each image. These *domain Gaussian* units provide a strong weighting of the intensity of two-dimensional features within the image according to their distance from the nominal centre of the field, giving a sensitive but compact representation of local changes within the domain.

From the cognitive perspective, our model is closely allied with the *Lzero* project of Feldman *et al.* [4] in addressing the integration of linguistic and visual information. In the original Lzero task, a computational system is required to learn a small portion of a natural language – as defined by a set of associations between spatial relations terms such as *above* and cartoon pictures exemplifying each term – sufficiently well that it is able to judge whether an unfamiliar picture is an exemplar of a particular term. In the present work, we are able to establish an association between the semantics of terms such as "happy", and their denotation through the relevant facial expression, which we argue is identifiable through a specific spatial configuration within the image.

This chapter is organized as follows. Section 2 provides a brief summary of the problem of facial expression perception, with particular reference to the the relevant developmental literature. Section 3 discusses the network model and the receptive field units employed for each network, together with an account of the adaptive learning approach of Geva [5], which forms the basis of the training methods employed in this study. Details of the image preparation and the precise learning task are given in Section 4, and are followed by presentation of the learning and generalization results for unseen static images in Section 5. Section 6 examines the creation of transition movies between well-classified Ekman stills, and provides an initial characterization of the (potentially) complex space of transitions between categories. After discussion of these results in Section 7, we summarize our conclusions in Section 8.

2 Development of Facial Expression Perception

Perception of the human face has been of great scientific interest since the time of Galton, and categorization remains a central question in this research – notably in regard to the recognition of a familiar subject among distractors. In the present context, it is useful to consider both the development of sophisticated facial processing and the parallel development of language processing.

Young infants are known to scan faces on the basis of individual salient features [9], [6], [16], showing a marked preference for tracking facial stimuli as early as the first hour of life, suggesting some innate preference for conspecifics, which is refined to the infant's caregiver once visual acuity has developed sufficiently. This preference continues throughout the first month of life, subsequently declining significantly, only to re-emerge around a month later as a result of the maturation of primary visual cortex [9]. Corresponding development of the fovea and the resulting acuity allow greater resolution of facial components during this period, and by five months, a preference for facial stimuli is shown only if movement of constituent features is integrated into the pattern display [9]. One example of this is a minor adjustment to a line-drawn mouth. Hainline [6], reports further development of scanning from 7 weeks through to the establishment of an integrated facial percept by the end of the first year of life.

Studies of changes in performance on facial expression tasks with increasing age are limited, and variations in experimental approach make it difficult to trace development of this capability right through to adulthood. Some indication may be gleaned from the related case of face recognition, in which there is evidence of a near-monotonic improvement in performance from around five years to maturity [1]. What is clear, however, is that that by age 4-6, children may be trained to associate verbal descriptions (such as "happy") with line drawings of appropriate facial expressions [12], and that this capacity develops over time, being fully established well before adolescence (Dimitrovsky et al. [2]). However, this latter study also reports significant variations in the confusion rate across the categories, and in performance with respect to age among the more difficult judgments. Chung and Thomson [1] postulate that improved recognition performance may be the result of memorization of a greater number of facial features and feature relations, rather than involving a fundamental change in mechanism.

3 Radial Basis Functions

Networks of radial basis function units [13] have been applied to a wide variety of classification and function approximation tasks. While in theory the approach provides no representational advantage over sigmoid networks,[1] their strongly localized response offers some simplification of network construction and training, as learning need not depend upon a fine balance between units strongly active across much of the domain [5].

The RBF unit response to a particular input varies according to the (Euclidean) separation between the input vector and the unit centre, both being regarded as elements of the vector space of patterns. Such responses are usually weighted according to the spatial Gaussian of Equation 1, with influence decaying as the separation increases, but remaining strong within some local radius of the centre. Formally, given an input vector $x \in R^n$, and a centre $c \in R^n$, a Gaussian RBF unit in the general form given by Geva [5] has activation

$$G(x; T, c) = \exp(-||T(x-c)||_2^2), \qquad (1)$$

where $T \in R^{n \times n}$ is the *transformation matrix*, which determines the

[1] Hornik *et al.* [8] established that a two layer feedforward network of sigmoid neurons may approximate any continuous function $f : R^n \to R^m$, and a similar result for RBF units was established more recently by Hartmann *et al.* [7].

shape of the unit's footprint. Usually T is chosen to be diagonal

$$T = diag(1/r_1, \ldots, 1/r_n), \tag{2}$$

r_i being the local radius in direction e_i, the i-th component of the standard Euclidean basis. In the simplest case, $r_i = r, \forall i$, producing a radially symmetric receptive field.

3.1 Domain Response Units

The use of RBF units such as those described above for problems involving 2D images leads to a training problem of enormous dimension. For this reason, some mechanism for incorporating the influence of an entire region – without *a priori* geometric specification – must be found if bitmap representations are to be employed. Gaussian *Domain Response* units, introduced below, are one such approach.

Formally, we consider an image over a bounded domain $D \subset R^2$ with normalized intensity level:[2]

$$I(x) : D \rightarrow [0, 1], \tag{3}$$

at each point $x \in D$ within the region. Then the activation of the Domain Response Unit centered at c, with transformation matrix T, is defined by:

$$v(I; T, c) = \frac{1}{< G >} \int_D I(x) G(x; T, c) dx, \tag{4}$$

where

$$< G >= \int_D G(x; T, c) dx, \tag{5}$$

is the maximum unit response.

In this work we are concerned only with a 2D image map of dimension N^2, each location having identical nominal area, with constant intensity $I_{ij} = I(x_i, y_j)$ across this logical pixel. Equation 4 for the domain response is then re-cast to give

$$v(I; T, c) = \frac{1}{< G >} \sum_{i=1}^{N} \sum_{j=1}^{N} I_{ij} G(x_i, y_j; T, c), \tag{6}$$

[2]This need not be restricted to intensity and may include any suitably normalized scalar combination of image components.

with the corresponding modification to $< G >$. Here (x_i, y_j) is understood to be the centre of the logical pixel (i, j).

The network is trained according to the parameter-specific dynamic learning rate approach described in the next section, unit centers and radii being adjusted through backpropagation of error to provide receptive fields appropriate to the problem. While calculation of the activation for each unit is time-consuming, network training is less troublesome because of the dramatic reduction in the dimension of the search space.

3.2 Network Training Methods

Geva [5] investigated the use of fully connected RBF networks for function approximation, a layer of RBF units receiving activation from the inputs, and feeding a weighted response to a linear output unit to produce the function estimate. In contrast to the more usual clustering techniques,[3] Geva's approach provides receptive fields appropriate to the problem through error backpropagation adjustment of the unit centers and radii, sharing with the traditional methods gradient descent adjustment of the output weights.

Geva's work significantly extended the existing approaches in two key areas: through the generalization of the response function described above, and through the development of a training technique based upon the adaptive gradient descent method of Silva and Almeida [15]. Traditional neural network function approximation techniques – based upon backpropagation-trained multi-layer perceptrons – have long suffered from convergence problems in larger domains. One contributing factor to this problem is the use of a single global learning rate in spite of large variations in the magnitude of partial derivatives with respect to particular weights. The method of Silva and Almeida addresses this issue by providing for the adjustment of each weight through a learning rate set with reference to the relevant partial derivative.

While Geva remarks that Silva and Almeida's technique is unable to overcome the difficulties posed by a number of large MLP problems, he nevertheless establishes that the technique is well-suited to the train-

[3] See for example [11].

ing of an exponential response network, perhaps because of the purely local effect of parameter adjustment [5].

As is commonly the case in backpropagation approaches, the estimation error is given by the squared error cost function of Equation 8, with contributions summed over the entire set of P patterns. For each pattern, the true activation value on pattern p, y_p, is approximated by the network estimate

$$\hat{y_p} = \sum_{\mu=1}^{m} w_\mu v_\mu, \tag{7}$$

where v_μ is the output of domain response unit μ on pattern p, and w_μ the corresponding output layer weight.

Reliance on individual learning rates requires that we provide expressions for the partial derivates of the cost function with respect to each of the trainable parameters. The necessary expressions for a two dimensional map are developed as follows. As discussed above, the squared error cost function for the problem is defined by the equation

$$E = \frac{1}{4}\sum_{p=1}^{P}(\hat{y_p} - y_p)^2, \tag{8}$$

where the constant is chosen to provide cleaner derivative expressions. The derivatives with respect to output weights are then

$$\frac{\partial E}{\partial w_\mu} = \frac{1}{2}\sum_{p=1}^{P}(\hat{y_p} - y_p)^2 v_\mu(I_p; c^\mu, T^\mu), \tag{9}$$

where as before v_μ is the activation of the μth domain response unit. Use of the chain rule and some manipulation yields the remaining expressions for the partials with respect to the transformation matrix elements

$$\frac{\partial E}{\partial T_1^\mu} = \frac{-T_1^\mu}{< G >}\sum_{p=1}^{P}(\hat{y_p} - y_p) w_\mu \left(\sum_{i=1}^{N}\sum_{j=1}^{N} I_{ij}^p G(x_i, y_j; T^\mu, c^\mu)(x_i - c_1^\mu)^2\right), \tag{10}$$

and

$$\frac{\partial E}{\partial T_2^\mu} = \frac{-T_2^\mu}{< G >}\sum_{p=1}^{P}(\hat{y_p} - y_p) w_\mu \left(\sum_{i=1}^{N}\sum_{j=1}^{N} I_{ij}^p G(x_i, y_j; T^\mu, c^\mu)(y_j - c_2^\mu)^2\right); \tag{11}$$

together with those with respect to the field centers

$$\frac{\partial E}{\partial c_1^\mu} = \frac{(T_1^\mu)^2}{< G >}\sum_{p=1}^{P}(\hat{y}_p - y_p)w_\mu\left(\sum_{i=1}^{N}\sum_{j=1}^{N} I_{ij}^p G(x_i, y_j; T^\mu, c^\mu)(x_i - c_1^\mu)\right), \tag{12}$$

and

$$\frac{\partial E}{\partial c_2^\mu} = \frac{(T_2^\mu)^2}{< G >}\sum_{p=1}^{P}(\hat{y}_p - y_p)w_\mu\left(\sum_{i=1}^{N}\sum_{j=1}^{N} I_{ij}^p G(x_i, y_j; T^\mu, c^\mu)(y_j - c_2^\mu)\right). \tag{13}$$

As one would expect, these expressions are substantially more complex than those for Geva's units of Equation 1, the difference arising as a result of the summation over the pixels required to calculate the unit activation. However, domain response units share with more conventional RBF units the problem of large variations in gradient magnitudes – both through local variations in the pattern space and through substantial differences in functional form between the field centre and radius partials. Fortunately, the individual learning rates η may be successfully tuned for each of the adjustable weights, with modifications to the strategy described by Geva being limited to the initial unit array (see Section 4).

3.3 A Biological Interpretation

While the properties of the domain Gaussian representation are of themselves desirable, we may also view the units as a computationally convenient form of a biologically plausible receptive field, arising as a result of variations in the density of synaptic contacts. It has long been known [14], that the probability of synaptic connection is high in the immediate vicinity of each neuron, but is observed to decrease markedly with increasing spatial separation between the 'source' and 'target' cells. Let us now consider a target neuron, existing at the centre, c, of a logical 'canopy' over a large but finite group of randomly positioned source nodes as shown in Figure 1, such as might be the case if the target node resided in a different layer from the source nodes. Suppose that each of the source nodes projects a connection of fixed (and perhaps unit) weight to the target with probability $\alpha(r)$, where r is the radial separation between the source node at x and the target at c as normalized with respect

RF centered at c

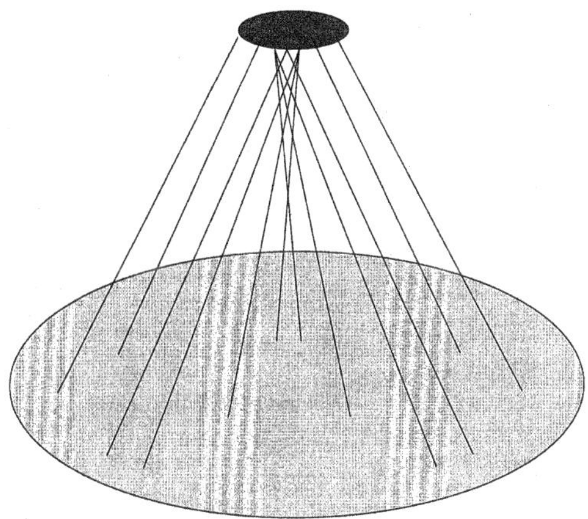

Figure 1. The "canopy" receptive field.

to some local radius R, and α is a non-increasing function of r.[4]

If we define a connectivity function $C(r)$ to be the cumulative fraction of connections to the target within radius r of the centre, the fraction contained within the area element of Figure 2 may be expressed through the equation

$$\{C(r+dr) - C(r)\}d\theta = r\alpha(r)drd\theta. \tag{14}$$

The corresponding connection density $c(r)$ is then

$$c(r) = \frac{dC}{dr} = r\alpha(r), \tag{15}$$

where α must be chosen so that

$$\int_0^\infty c(r)dr = 1. \tag{16}$$

If we make the mathematically convenient selection of

$$\alpha(r) = e^{-\frac{r^2}{2}}, \tag{17}$$

[4]There may of course be substantial angular variation in connection probability – corresponding in some respects to the elliptical footprint of the weighting function of Equation 1. For the sake of simplicity, we shall restrict our discussion to radially symmetric connection probability $\alpha(r)$ and intensity $I(r)$.

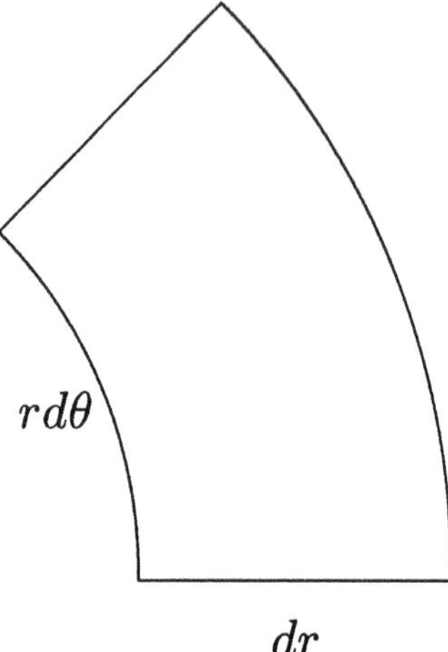

Figure 2. The element of area considered in Equation 14.

then the connection density is seen to be a weighting function for the map, with the effective influence of each feature upon the receptive field critically dependent upon its separation from the unit centre. The field response is then formally the expected value of the intensity, weighted with respect to the connection density across the domain

$$v(c) = \int_0^\infty I(r)c(r)dr, \tag{18}$$

with properties qualitatively similar to the more general response of Equation 4.

4 The Learning Task

In the present study, the 110 images of the "Pictures of Facial Affect" database were scanned from photographic slides to gray-scale pixel images and preprocessed to provide some alignment of facial features between frames, and to eliminate confounding detail. In all cases, the preprocessing operations have an identifiable counterpart within the visual system, and our aim was limited to that of reducing the scope of the facial expression task to that of comparison of images with facial features in gross-level correspondence. Each pixel map was manually scaled (preserving proportions) and cropped so that the face from chin to hairline and ear to ear fit as closely as possible within a 3 by 4 rectangle. The resulting images were bandpass filtered (using Photoshop 4.0) under a Gaussian blur with radius 3 pixels, followed by a high pass filter with radius 10 pixels. This filtering serves to remove fine textural detail and normalize across complexion, lighting, and hair colour. Images were then reduced using Gaussian compression to 30 by 30 pixels, a scale at which the facial expressions remain distinguishable by eye.

The resulting images were presented as input to the neural network models. Targets corresponding to each non-neutral expression were used for training, with target values of 1.0 indicating category membership (as judged by Ekman's human subjects), and 0.0 indicating non-membership. Each model network was initialized with 64 equally-spaced receptive fields which under training formed a small set of highly localized and redundant receptive regions.

For each of the six target expressions – "Happiness", "Sadness", "Fear", "Anger", "Surprise", and "Disgust" – eight separate networks were trained, with the best performed network in each category preserved as the 'judge' network. Such networks are subsequently referred to by their category name, respectively the "Happy" network, the "Sad" network and so on. An overall category judgment may be made through a winner-take-all across the networks.

Due to the paucity of data, the nets are trained on a leave-one-subject out approach, in which *all* of the six images of a single Ekman subject are reserved for testing, each net being trained on the remaining 104 frames.

5 Results for Static Images

Examples of raw generalization results are shown for unseen subjects NR,JJ,EM and GS, MF and MO, and JM in Tables 1 through 5. Each of the judge networks was trained on all the images remaining in the database, for 500 epochs in the case of NR and JJ, and 300 epochs for the remainder. As may be seen from the activations, the present task provides substantial variation in prototypicality across subjects, with some individual faces being naturally biased – or perhaps biased as a result of the limited technical proficiency of the actor – towards some categories and away from others. For example, the Happy pose (#14) for subject

Table 1. Network responses for the unseen subject NR, using judge networks trained for 500 epochs. Network categories run horizontally (Happiness, Sadness, Fear, Anger, Surprise, Disgust) and images vertically, the numbers being those from the Ekman photographs. Each numeric column refers to a category network trained on all other images. Note the correct detection of each category and the strong responses for Disgust (as 'perceived' by the Anger network), and Fear (Surprise).

NR	hp	sd	fr	ag	sr	ds
66: hp	0.60	−0.09	0.26	0.26	0.56	0.16
67: sd	0.30	0.72	0.36	0.54	0.14	0.34
68: fr	0.32	0.17	0.67	0.25	0.50	0.15
69: ag	0.50	0.57	0.13	0.83	−0.15	0.55
70: sr	0.27	0.05	0.46	0.38	0.62	0.45
71: ds	0.49	0.44	0.14	0.77	−0.30	0.86

Table 2. Network responses for the unseen subject JJ, after training for 500 epochs. As before, each numeric column refers to a category network trained on all other images. Note the strong generalization (see the elements of the main diagonal) and the WTA judgment that the 'angry' image should be perceived as 'disgusted'.

JJ	hp	sd	fr	hp	sd	sr
34: hp	0.62	0.16	0.50	0.38	0.29	0.42
36: sd	0.25	0.47	0.53	0.39	0.28	0.50
37: fr	0.25	0.35	0.73	0.30	0.37	0.39
38: ag	0.13	0.40	0.31	0.50	0.39	0.59
39: sr	0.18	0.31	0.57	0.24	0.73	0.39
40: ds	0.52	0.33	0.32	0.44	0.17	0.69

EM produces an activation of 0.96 in the relevant Happy network, while the corresponding task for GS (#22), yields only 0.55. Thus, absolute thresholds of classification performance are an unreasonably demanding measure in the present context, and we consider that the judge networks have generalized successfully to the unseen *subject* if the highest activation for a particular category network (for example the Anger network for unseen JJ) occurs on the unseen image of *that category* (here the Angry JJ or image 38). Note that while the example may show correct generalization, this does not of itself imply that the response of the appropriate category network (for #38: Anger: 0.50) must be the highest for that image (for #38: Disgust: 0.59). Indeed such confusions are part

Table 3. Network responses for the unseen subjects EM and GS, after network training for 300 epochs. While strong generalization performance is indicated for most categories, these judge networks also show the common difficulty in 'perceiving' anger, disgust and sadness, with comparable activations being observed across the three categories for appropriate stimuli. The confusion between anger and disgust is especially pronounced, and is consistent with the human subject literature. Unusually, these examples also exhibit an high degree of similarity between the three stated categories and fear, although this may disappear with further training. The activation of the Happy network for image 14 provides further evidence that this category is more cleanly defined than some of the others.

EM	**Hp**	**Sd**	**Fr**	**Ag**	**Sr**	**Ds**
14 : Hp	0.96	0.44	0.37	0.49	0.38	0.50
15 : Sd	0.33	0.54	0.58	0.40	0.25	0.40
16 : Fr	0.35	0.35	0.42	0.33	0.40	0.30
18 : Ag	0.54	0.49	0.47	0.64	0.48	0.55
19 : Sr	−0.08	0.26	0.13	0.00	0.65	0.11
20 : Ds	0.48	0.49	0.42	0.49	0.25	0.72

GS	**Hp**	**Sd**	**Fr**	**Ag**	**Sr**	**Ds**
22 : Hp	0.55	0.24	0.37	0.26	0.44	0.39
23 : Sd	0.40	0.64	0.34	0.42	0.14	0.47
24 : Fr	0.43	0.51	0.51	0.49	0.54	0.50
25 : Ag	0.32	0.40	0.18	0.55	0.05	0.43
26 : Sr	0.03	0.24	0.36	0.24	0.61	0.07
27 : Ds	0.42	0.42	0.44	0.45	0.44	0.46

and parcel of the problem, with the Ekman and Friesen study reporting confusion of a significant extent for a number of examples of Fear and Surprise, of Anger and Disgust, and to a lesser degree between Anger and Sadness.

While the networks of the present study do not thoroughly replicate the performance of Ekman's judges, they nevertheless display similar behaviour, with a more pronounced confusion in the 'perception' of Sadness. More detailed discussion of the performance on example networks is provided in the captions of Tables 1 to 5.

Table 4. Network responses for the unseen subjects MF and MO after training for 300 epochs. These results provide very strong indications of the classical confusions between fear and surprise (note in particular the Fear response to image 54, and the Anger response to image 64). The results are also noteworthy for the extraordinary prototypicality of the MO Happy and Fear images (respectively image number 57 with activation 0.91, and image number 60 with activation 0.96).

MF	**Hp**	**Sd**	**Fr**	**Ag**	**Sr**	**Ds**
48 : Hp	0.75	0.15	0.13	−0.03	0.20	0.23
49 : Sd	0.43	0.64	0.43	0.63	0.55	0.59
50 : Fr	0.33	0.32	0.67	0.38	0.37	−0.17
53 : Ag	0.42	0.40	0.31	0.47	0.43	0.55
54 : Sr	0.26	0.50	0.84	0.51	0.64	0.15
55 : Ds	0.10	0.09	0.01	0.28	0.03	0.64
MO	**Hp**	**Sd**	**Fr**	**Ag**	**Sr**	**Ds**
57 : Hp	0.91	0.23	0.19	0.18	−0.02	0.39
58 : Sd	0.28	0.56	0.30	0.40	0.45	0.35
60 : Fr	0.29	0.14	0.96	0.22	0.44	0.13
61 : Ag	0.25	0.70	0.04	0.67	0.30	0.31
63 : Sr	0.06	0.20	0.46	0.11	0.63	0.22
64 : Ds	0.39	0.48	0.29	0.60	0.28	0.57

Table 5. Network responses for the unseen subject JM, after training for 300 epochs. Results for subject JM provide strong generalization performance along with the usual similarity between Anger, Disgust and Sadness.

JM	**Hp**	**Sd**	**Ag**	**Sr**	**Ds**
42 : Hp	1.14	0.14	0.13	0.05	0.27
43 : Sd	0.53	0.72	0.62	0.27	0.68
44 : Ag	0.29	0.57	0.76	0.28	0.70
45 : Sr	−0.11	0.10	0.06	0.84	−0.05
46 : Ds	0.24	0.42	0.45	0.03	0.62

6 Digital Morphing and Dynamic Images

The Ekman and Friesen study is concerned solely with the classification of single still frames. While these images may exhibit substantial variation within classes, as we have discussed in the previous section, they do not support direct investigation of the category boundaries, the point at which a perturbation of an image of one category is sufficient for that judgment to be revised to another. One way of examining this problem is to create a movie of each possible category transition for a number of subjects, and thence present the individual frames to the category networks for judgment.

For each of the example subjects discussed above, digital morphing software was used to produce a series of 16 intermediate frames between the well-classified Ekman stills. Key frames were high resolution scaled, cropped and filtered as described above, with the 34 morphing control points chosen manually. Linear interpolation of distorting control points and linear pixel value crossfade results in a natural and gradual transition between expressions. Due to the small number of control points used, some details – notably teeth and lips – were seen to merge unnaturally, although the integrity of the image as a face with a recognizable expression was not impaired.

Each of the resulting 15 animated sequences (a linear morph between each possible category pairing for a given Ekman subject) is then presented in parallel to all of the model networks. As one might expect, the networks representing the initial and final categories of the morph showed respectively decreasing and increasing activation levels. However, for some of the subjects, the responses of the remaining categories suggest a perceptually confusing trajectory may be followed as the transition takes place, with significant activation of a number of the judgment networks. This is in contrast to our intuitive expectation of a cartesian category space, with transitions constrained to pass linearly through a conceptual origin – although there is more than a hint of this phenomenon in the strong intermediate response of the Sadness network for subjects MF, JM and EM, with Sadness known to be confused with Neutral in some of the Ekman and Friesen experiments.

In the absence of an exhaustive study involving leave-one-subject-out networks and presentation of all possible sequences, we must thus be cautious in our remarks, noting only that our results suggest that:

- the existence of complex transitions in which one or more apparently unrelated categories may compete for apprehension during the intermediate phases;

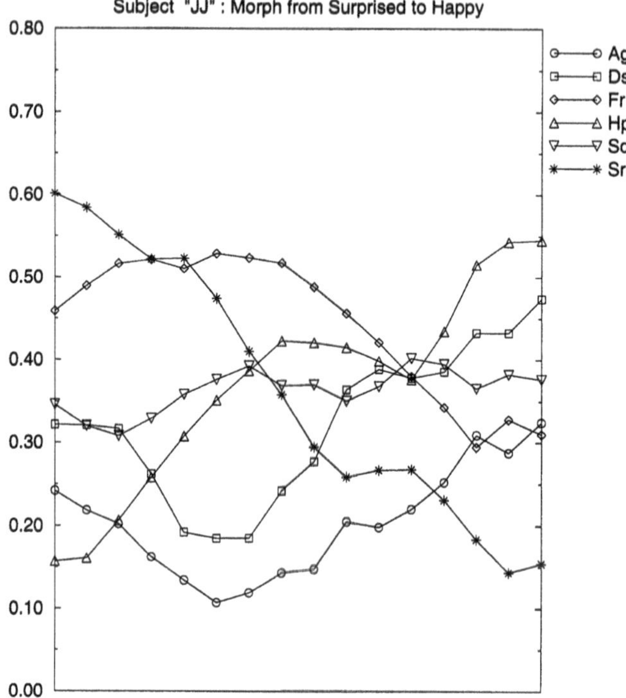

Figure 3. Network responses to the Surprise → Happy transition for subject *JJ*. This figure suggests the existence of a complex transition space between categories, with the prediction of an intermediate perception of *Fear* as the face changes expression between Surprise and Happiness. Moreover, the middle region suggests a substantial break between the often correlated responses of Anger, Disgust and Sadness.

- there is consistent qualitative – and to some degree quantitative – grouping of the responses for Fear with those for Surprise, as well as those for Anger, Disgust and Sadness, although these may be disrupted for particularly strong exemplars of a particular category.

Figures 3 through 8 show the response of each of the relevant category networks to the image transition indicated, with a more detailed discussion of the particular results being given in the associated caption. The implications of these results, and those for the static case are considered in the following section.

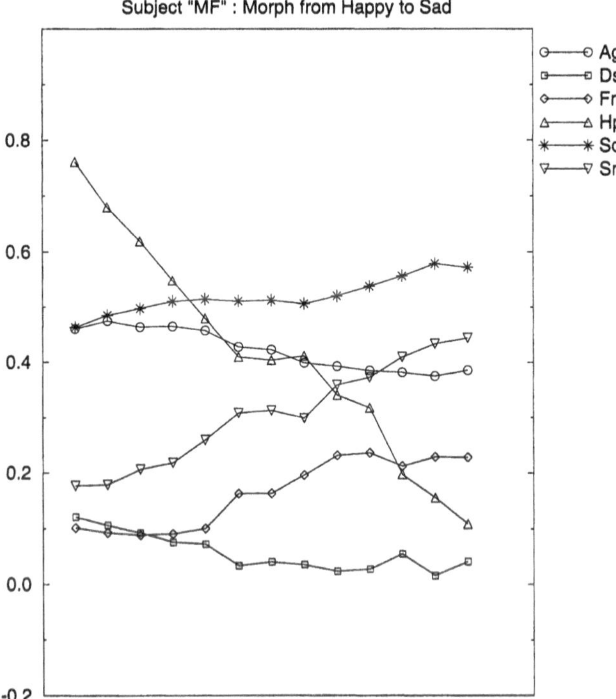

Figure 4. Network responses to the Happiness → Sadness transition for subject MF. This figure shows significant correlation between the Surprise and Fear networks, along with some lesser correlation between Disgust, Anger and Sadness. Indeed, Anger should here be taken as almost constant. Note the early onset of high activation for Sadness, due possibly to the similarity between Sadness and what Ekman and Friesen regarded as a Neutral category.

7 Discussion

In this work we have considered the problem of classification of facial expressions for an unseen subject within the categories employed by Ekman and Friesen [3]. Both the generalization results of Section 5 and the morphing studies of Section 6 provide some evidence that these categories may be broadly distinguished through a decomposition of the form

$$H_p \vee \{F_r, S_r\} \vee \{A_g, D_g, S_d\}.$$

This assertion is further supported by principal component analysis of the hidden unit activations, which suggests that as few as four dimensions may suffice to distinguish the categories. At the highest level, a decompo-

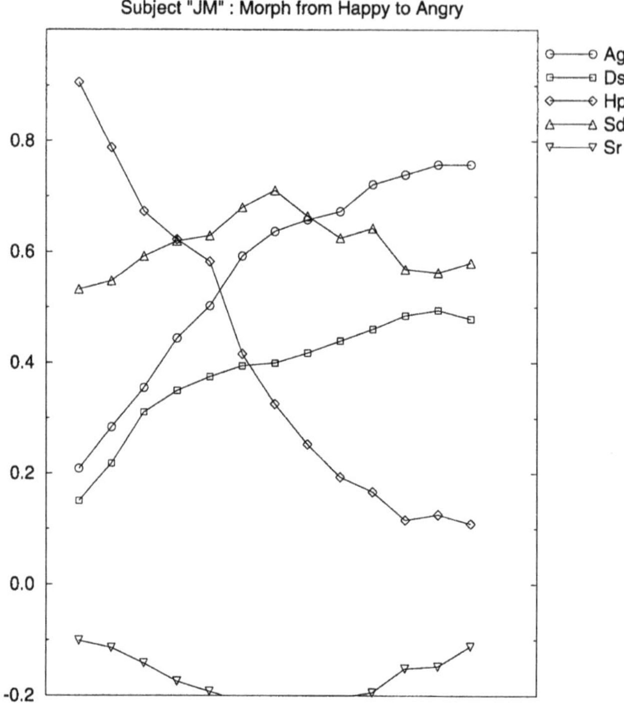

Figure 5. Network responses to the Happiness → Anger transition for subject JM. Here we observe behaviour qualitatively similar to the previous figure, with an intermediate Sadness peak and moderate correlation between Anger and Disgust. Note the negligible response of the Surprise network.

sition into $H_p \wedge \neg H_p$ is straightforward, with difficulty increasing as one attempts to distinguish between the Fear-Surprise and Anger-Disgust-Sadness sets, and finally between the elements themselves. In this latter case at least the targets are necessarily probabilistic, and while Ekman's human judges report lower confusion rates than the domain Gaussian nets of this study, they are nevertheless significant within these distinctions.

Such indeterminacy is a fundamental aspect of human categorization and the results of the present study are in some respects reminiscent of the confusion reported in Labov's seminal 'CUP' study [10], in which subjects were required to attach linguistic labels to non-deterministically combined features of cups, mugs and bowls. More technically, Labov's work was concerned with the fuzzy boundaries of *denotational* cate-

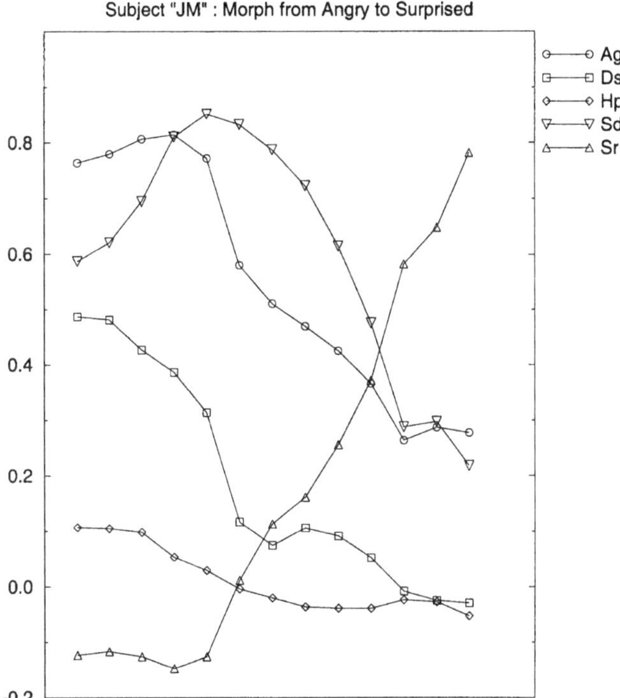

Figure 6. Network responses to the Anger → Surprise transition for subject JM. This set of plots shows again an intermediate peak for Sadness, but differs from the previous figure in preserving qualitative similarity between Sadness, Anger and Disgust.

gories,[5] and the 'CUP' study demonstrated that small variations in the features underlying such denotata will contribute to a gestalt judgment of greater or lesser – or equivalently, more or less prototypical – membership of the category. At some point, such gradual variations give way to hard categorical distinctions, and even the use of controlled linear frame interpolation provides no guarantee that the resulting category judgments will be any more predictable.

[5]Denotation is defined as the association of a linguistic label with a set of possible referents, in the present work the association between an expression label such as Happy and an acceptable range of facial feature configurations.

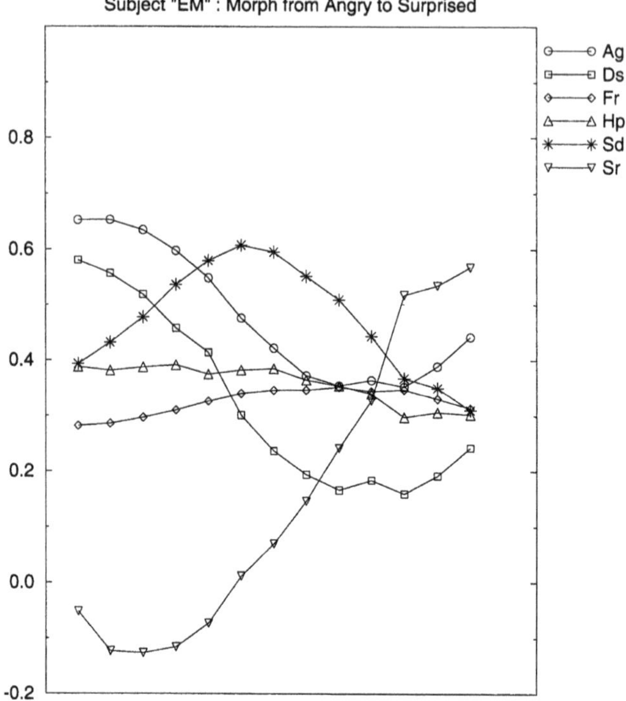

Figure 7. Network responses to the Anger → Surprise transition for subject EM. This transition is significant in showing a breaking of the nexus between Fear and Surprise, with Fear almost constant and, for this subject at least, correlated closely with Happy. Note the presence of the usual correlation between Anger and Disgust, and the curious phenomenon that the Anger network shows some increasing response as the transition is completed into Surprise.

8 Conclusions

In this chapter, we have introduced a new class of radial basis function unit and, through the exploitation of existing variable learning rate techniques, applied networks of such units to the problem of classification of facial expressions, as represented by the categories and images of the famous "Pictures of Facial Affect" study of Ekman and Friesen. Our models have successfully generalized to unseen subjects, providing clear classification within each subject while replicating the confusions of the earlier work. The novel use of morphing techniques to study the transitions between images suggests the existence of a complex perceptual transition space rather than a straightforward path through a conceptual origin.

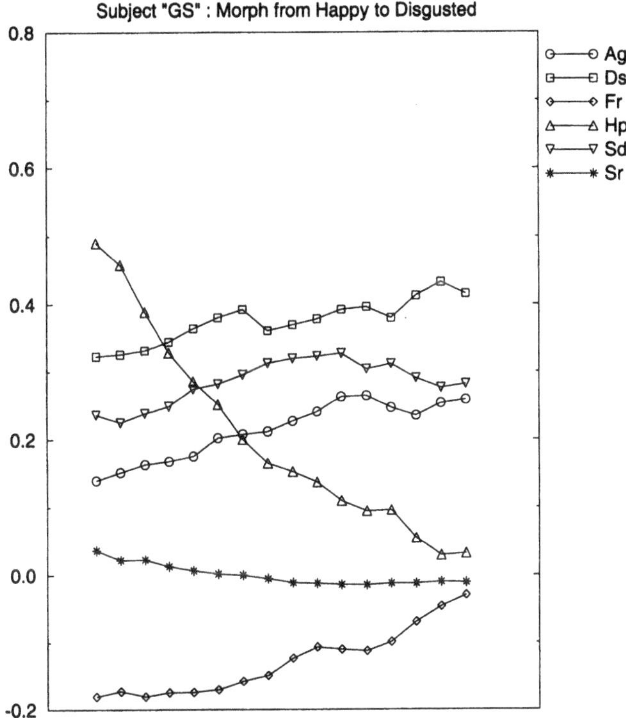

Figure 8. Network responses to the Happy → Disgust transition for subject GS. Note the bunching of responses for the Anger, Disgust and Sadness networks.

This space is the subject of ongoing computational and psychophysical investigation.

Acknowledgments

The authors would like to acknowledge helpful discussions with Claudia Brugman, and assistance with image processing from Sylvia Wyllie. This work was funded by a grant from the Australian Research Council.

References

[1] Chung, M.S and Thomson, D.M. (1995), "Development of face recognition," *Br-J-Psychol.*, vol. 86, no. 1, pp. 55-87.

[2] Dimitrovsky, L., Spector, H., Levy-Shiff, R., and Vakil, E. (1998), "Interpretation of facial expressions of affect in children with learning disabilities with verbal or nonverbal deficits," *Journal of Learning Disabilities*, vol. 31, no. 3, pp. 286-292.

[3] Ekman, P. and Friesen, W. (1975), *Unmasking the Face*, New York, Prentice Hall.

[4] Feldman, J.A., Lakoff, G., Stolcke, A., and Hollbach Weber, S. (1990), "Miniature language acquisition: a touchstone for cognitive science," Technical Report TR-90-009, International Computer Science Institute, Berkeley CA, U.S.A.

[5] Geva, S. (1992), *Exponential Response Artificial Neurons for Pattern Classification and Function Approximation*, Ph.D. Dissertation, Queensland University of Technology, Australia.

[6] Hainline, L. (1978), "Developmental changes in visual scanning of face and nonface patterns by infants," *Journal-of-Experimental-Child-Psychology*, vol 25, no. 1, pp. 90-115.

[7] Hartman, E.J., Keeler, J.D., and Kowalski, J.M. (1990), "Layered neural networks with Gaussian hidden units as universal approximations," *Neural Computation*, vol. 2, pp. 210-215.

[8] Hornik, K., Stinchcombe, M., and White, H. (1989), "Multi-layer feedforward networks are universal approximators," *Neural Networks*, vol. 2, pp. 359-366.

[9] Johnson, M.H. and Morton, J. (1991), *Biology and Cognitive Development: the Case of Face Recognition*, Oxford. Basil Blackwell.

[10] Labov, W. (1973), "The boundaries of words and their meanings," in Bailey, C.N.J. and Shuy, R. (Eds.), *New Ways of Analysing Variation in English*, Georgetown, VA. Georgetown University Press.

[11] Moody, J. and Darken, C.J. (1989), "Fast learning in locally-tuned processing units," *Neural Computation*, vol. 1, pp. 281-294.

[12] Murray, F.S. and Stanley, R.L. (1980), "Perceptual learning of cartoon faces by young children," *Bulletin-of-the-Psychonomic-Society*, vol. 16, no. 5, pp. 367-370.

[13] Poggio, T. and Girosi, F. (1990), "Networks for approximation and learning," *Proceedings of the IEEE*, vol. 79, pp. 1481-1497.

[14] Sholl, D.A. (1956), *The organization of the cerebral cortex*, London, Methuen.

[15] Silva, F.M. and Almeida, L.B. (1990), "Speeding up backpropagation," in Eckmiller, R. (Ed.), *Advanced Neural Computers*, North Holland, pp. 151-158.

[16] Tanaka, J.W. and Farah, M.J. (1993), "Parts and wholes in face recognition," *Q-J-Exp-Psychol-A*, vol. 46, no. 2, pp. 225-245.

Chapter 6

RBF Network Classification of ECGs as a Potential Marker for Sudden Cardiac Death

H.A. Kestler and F. Schwenker

Non-invasive risk assessment after myocardial infarction is a major but still unresolved goal in clinical cardiology. Various parameters such as ventricular late potentials, T-wave alternans, and repetitive ventricular extrasystoles have been shown to indicate an increased risk of sudden cardiac death. However, the practical use of these arrhythmic markers into clinical decision making remains difficult. In this chapter we will describe two approaches of risk stratification with RBF networks using high-fidelity ECG recordings. Based on these high-fidelity recordings different aspects of conduction defects are exemplarily investigated. The first utilizes established features derived from signal averaged QRS complexes (heartbeats) and the second investigation centers on capturing morphology changes within the QRS complex.

1 Introduction

The non-invasive risk stratification of patients prone to sudden cardiac death is an important problem in modern cardiology. The incidence of sudden cardiac death (SCD) in the area of Germany is about 80,000 to 160,000 cases per year. Apart from cases of ventricular fibrillation (VF) related to myocardial ischaemia, the main reason for SCD is the occurrence of ventricular tachyarrhythmias as a cause of a chronic arrhythmogenic substrate. Sudden cardiac death most often occurs in the presence of coronary artery disease (CAD) (90% of SCD patients). In a significant number of patients (13% – 20%) it is the initial symptom of CAD. Ventricular fibrillation emerges in most cases (70%) secondarily from a ventricular tachycardia.

Various parameters such as ventricular late potentials, T-wave alternans, and repetitive ventricular extrasystoles have been shown to indicate an increased risk of sudden cardiac death. However, the practical use of these arrhythmic markers into clinical decision making remains difficult. The positive predictive value of all non-invasive parameters is limited especially when not combined with a reduced left ventricular function. On the other hand the available therapeutic options, the implantable cardioverter defibrillator or long term amiodarone drug therapy, have side effects, strain the patient and are cost intensive, thus requiring a highly selective usage. Recently the MUSTT [1] and the MADIT [2], [3] study proved the effect of defibrillator therapy in post infarction patients preselected by a reduced left ventricular function and spontaneous non-sustained ventricular tachycardia, with inducible sustained ventricular tachycardia during electrophysiologic study. In this chapter we summarize the clinical results of the currently available methods for non-invasive risk assessment and describe two approaches of risk stratification with RBF networks based on high-fidelity ECG recordings. In post-infarction studies with animals it has been shown that the substrate for singular or repeated ventricular arrhythmias is a localized damaged myocardium with abnormal conduction characteristics [4]-[6]. This causes slow or irregular propagation of activation. It is possible to detect these delayed signals with the high-resolution electrocardiogram. Based on these high-fidelity recordings different aspects of conduction defects are exemplarily investigated. The first is based on established features derived from signal averaged QRS complexes (heartbeats) and mainly describes a prolongation of cardiac exitation that extends beyond the normal heartbeat (**late potentials**). The second investigation centers on capturing morphology changes of the QRS complex (segment of the ECG signal associated with depolarization) in beat-to-beat recordings.

Within this problem context of non-invasive risk stratification the topics of data acquisition, group description and evaluation are treated together with the initialization and training algorithms of the used RBF networks.

Table 1. Mortality rates after myocardial infarction (total deaths and sudden cardiac deaths) in the era of thrombolysis, as taken from the placebo arms of recent large randomized trials. Abbreviations: SCD: sudden cardiac death, FU: follow-up, yrs: years, AMI: acute myocardial infarction, LVEF: left ventricular ejection fraction, f/r VPBs: frequent (>10/h) or repetitive (≥3 beats) ventricular premature beats, HF: heart failure, CHF: congestive heart failure, AIRE: Acute Infarction Ramipril Efficacy study, SAVE: Survival And Ventricular Enlargement study, EMIAT: European Myocardial Infarct Amiodarone Trial, CAMIAT: Canadian Amiodarone Myocardial Infarction Arrhythmia Trial, AMIO: Amiodarone.

Author	Year	Study	Target	Number	Total	SCD	FU (yrs)
AIRE Investigators [11]	1993	AIRE	AMI + HF	992	23.0%	-	1.25
Lamas *et al.* [8]	1995	SAVE	AMI	946	6.6%	–	1 (3.5)
Julian *et al.* [9]	1997	EMIAT	AMI, LVEF ≤ 40%	743	12.0%	8.2%	1.75
Cairns *et al.* [10]	1997	CAMIAT	AMI, f/r VPBs	596	8.3%	5.2%	1.79
Amiodarone Trials Meta-Analysis Investigators [12]	1997	AMIO Meta Analysis (13 trials)	AMI + CHF	6553 (5101 + 1452)	12.3%	5.7%	1.4

2 Medical Background: Review of Non-Invasive Risk Stratification in Patients after Myocardial Infarction

Even in the thrombolytic era with its generally accepted reduction of hospital mortality, patients with acute myocardial infarction remain at an increased risk of sudden death at least in the first year after the acute event [7]. Based on large multi center studies post myocardial infarction there is still a remarkable rate of total death (7% to 23%) and sudden cardiac death (4% to 8%) within the first one or two years after infarction, particularly in patients with reduced left ventricular function, as seen from the placebo arms of several studies [8]-[12] (Table 1).

Various non-invasive tests have been developed and clinically evaluated for risk assessment after myocardial infarction to detect subgroups of high risk patients for preventive treatment. From the current concept ar-

Table 2. Association of certain electrocardiographic methods and parameters to cellular functions of the myocardium and to electrophysiological mechanisms of tachyarrhythmias. Abbreviations: ECG: electrocardiogram, SAECG: signal averaged surface ECG, VLP: ventricular late potentials, HR: heart rate, HRECG: high resolution ECG.

ECG - Parameter	Cellular Function	VT/VF – Mechanism
SAECG: VLP	Conduction delay (static)	Reentry Bystander area?
Holter-ECG: spontaneous arrhythmias	Trigger events	Abnormal automatism Reentry-induction
Real time-HRECG: QRS variability (QRV)	Dynamic conduction delay	Reentry
Real time-HRECG: variant VLP	Wenckebach conduction delay	Reentry Bystander area?
Surface ECG: QT-Dispersion	Dispersion of local repolarization	Reentry
Holter ECG: QT-Variability	Dynamic behaviour of action potential duration	Reentry Autonomic tone Triggered Activity
Surface ECG: T-wave alternans	Dynamic behaviour of repolarization	Reentry Autonomic tone
Holter ECG: HR-variability	Sympathetic-parasympathetic balance	Reentry? Autonomic tone

rhythmogenesis is an integrative process dependent on the existence of an arrhythmogenic substrate (the infarction zone with abnormal automatism and slowed conduction), the autonomic tone, spontaneous trigger events (ventricular extrasystoles) [13], and other modulating environmental factors (electrolytes, drugs). The available non-invasive tests cover different aspects of this scenario (Table 2). Late potential analysis concentrates on the detection of myocardium with slow conduction. Holter monitoring allows to measure the incidence and complexity of spontaneous trigger events. Baroreflex sensitivity and heart rate variability reflect the autonomic tone. Most recently T-wave alternans has been introduced into clinical application as a marker of repolarization abnormalities.

Ambulatory electrocardiography. With the ambulatory ECG the different types of ectopic beats can be documented that may trigger the initiation of ventricular tachycardias and/or fibrillation. Among those are frequent and repetitive ventricular premature beats (VPBs) up to non-sustained or sustained ventricular tachycardias. In addition to the quantification of spontaneous arrhythmias, modern Holter ECG equipment allows ST-segment analysis for ischaemia detection, heart rate variability analysis, the detection of ventricular late potentials by signal averaging, and QT variability analysis. Late potentials may be considered as a marker of delayed depolarization from areas of damaged ventricular myocardium, thus forming one prerequisite of a reentrant circuit. However, it has been claimed from both experimental and clinical studies that in a significant proportion late potentials may represent only bystander areas, which are not an essential anatomical part of the reentrant circuit. Because dynamic events of ventricular depolarization are lost by the averaging process, beat-to-beat real time high resolution ECG equipment have been developed and clinically tested [14], [15], and indeed increased beat-to-beat variations of the QRS-complex (QRV) and the T-wave have been demonstrated in patients at high risk for malignant arrhythmias [15]-[17].

Two new ECG methods have been extensively investigated in recent years, aimed at detecting repolarization inhomogeneities, namely QT-dispersion from the conventional 12-lead surface ECG [18] and QT-variability mainly from 24-hour ambulatory ECG recordings [19]. Most recently a special technique and algorithm has been described to detect beat by beat T-wave alternans at the microvolt level [20]. T-wave macro-alternans is a well known phenomenon in severe myocardial ischaemia, experimental myocardial infarction, vasospastic angina and other pathophysiological conditions (neuro-hormonal imbalance). Increased beat-by-beat micro-fluctuations of the amplitude and shape of the T-wave (repolarization process) are thought to reveal an increased local inhomogeneity of repolarization within the entire ventricular myocardium [21].

Assessment of imbalances of the autonomic nervous system. To detect influences of the autonomic nervous system, heart rate variability (HRV) has been tested in short term (5 minutes to hours) and long term (24 hours) approaches, using either surface ECG monitoring or 24 hour Holter recorders, both in the time and frequency domain [22]-[24]. A large number of time domain indices have been developed and clinically tested such as SDNN, SDANN, RMSSD, NN50 and pNN50 (all statistical methods), and HRV-triangular index, TINN, Differential index and Logarithmic index (all geometrical methods). According to the Task Force Committee on Heart Rate Variability both SDNN and HRV triangular index should be used for the assessment of overall HRV, whereas short term components of HRV may be estimated by SDANN and RMSSD [25]. Power spectral analysis using fast Fourier transform allows the separation of the total power spectrum into high frequency (HF), low frequency (LF), very low frequency (VLF) and the ultra-low frequency range (ULF). The physiological correlate to HF components is attributed to ventilation, of LF to baroreflexes, of VLF to sympathetic activity (?), and of ULF possibly to the activity of the Renin-Angiotensin system. The LF/HR ratio may reflect sympatho-vagal balance, sympathetic modulations or baroreflex activity [24]. It should be stressed that for physiological and mathematical reasons there are strong correlations between certain time and frequency parameters of heart rate variability: SDNN, HRV triangular index, and TINN correlate to the total frequency power spectrum; SDNN index correlates to mean 5-min total power; RMSSD, SDSD, NN50 count, pNN50, differential index and logarithmic index correlate to the HF spectrum [25]. Changes in HRV have been found in patients after myocardial infarction, in diabetic neuropathy, in transplanted hearts, in cardiac failure and in patients with tetraplegia [25]. A number of drugs like beta-adrenergic blockers, anti-arrhythmic drugs and muscarinic receptor blockers have been found to influence HRV. Beta blockers enhance HRV, antiarrhythmics like flecainide and propafenonene decrease HRV, and scopolamine paradoxically also decreases HRV. For risk stratification in post-MI patients both SDNN and HRV triangular index proved to be a powerful tool for predicting sudden cardiac death. In the study of Kleiger *et al.* [22] a SDNN cut-off value of 50-100 ms differentiated well between patients at low risk (50-100 ms) and those at high risk (<50 ms), as did a cut-off value of the HRV triangular index of 20 in the study of Malik *et al.* [23].

Electrophysiological testing (EPS). Between 1982 and 1992 a considerable number of studies have been published on the value of electrophysiological testing (EPS) for predicting the risk of sustained VT or SCD in post-MI patients [26]-[39]. The parameter used initially, repetitive ventricular response, namely (>3 VPBs following one or two ex-

Table 3. Prognostic significance of programmed ventricular stimulation (PVS) for the incidence of ventricular tachycardia (VT) or fibrillation (VF) and for sudden cardiac death (SCD) in the first to second year after acute myocardial infarction. Abbreviations: n: patient number studied, FU: follow-up, Ind +: inducible by PVS, Ind −: non-inducible by PVS, Rec: recurrences.

Author	Year	n	FU month	Ind+ (%)	Rec (%)	Ind− (%)	Rec (%)	Prognostic for SCD
Breithardt [26]	1982	132	15	46	16	54	4	+
Hamer [28]	1982	70	12	17	33	83	9	+
Richards [29]	1983	165	12	23	21	77	2	+
Marchlinski [30]	1983	46	18	22	6	78	14	−
Gonzalez [27]	1984	84	20	23	0	77	6	−
Waspe [31]	1985	50	23	34	41	61	0	+
Roy [32]	1985	150	10	23	6	72	2	−
Santarelli [33]	1985	50	11	46	0	54	0	−
Bhandari [34]	1985	45	12	44	10	56	3	−
Kowey [35]	1990	187	18	64	21	36	29	−
Iesaka [36]	1990	133	21	19	47	81	3	+
Bourke [37]	1991	1209	12	6	19	94	3	+
Bhandari [41]	1992	86	18	22	32	78	7	+
Steinbeck [39]	1992	152	11	16	13	84	2	+

trastimuli) proved to be too unspecific and over sensitive as a marker of ventricular electrical instability, and today only the induction of sustained VT is considered a meaningful and more specific risk marker for ventricular vulnerability [40]. Among 14 selected prognostic studies of EPS following acute myocardial infarction only 8 proved to be prognostic for SCD (Table 3). The positive predictive value of EPS following MI, ranges between 13% to 42%, whereas the negative predictive value is as high as 95% to 100%.

In the clinical setting the value of all non-invasive methods and risk markers on its own, including of programmed ventricular stimulation, is limited since the positive predictive values of all of theses methods range from 4% to 42% (Table 4), i.e., there is a significant number of false positive candidates with a pathological finding in either of these tests, who never will experience a sudden cardiac death in the first one or two years after myocardial infarction. A combination of two or more non-invasive

Table 4. Predictive value of different non-invasive and invasive markers for sudden cardiac death given with their corresponding cut-off values. Abbreviations: VTA: ventricular tachyarrhythmias, SCD: sudden cardiac death, ECG: electrocardiogram, VT: ventricular tachycardia, VPB: ventricular premature beat, QTD: QT-dispersion, TD: time domain, AE: serious arrhythmic event.

Method	Marker	Positive Predictive Value (%)	Negative Predictive Value (%)
Holter ECG	non-sustained VT Pairs $\geq$ 10/24h Salvos $\geq$ 2/24h frequent VPBs >10/h	10 – 20	70 – 90
Signal Averaged ECG (at rest, Holter)	Ventricular late potentials (2/3 Simson criteria positive)	4 – 30	95 – 99
12 lead ECG	QTD $\geq$ 80ms	inconsistent, 0 – 100 (see [46])	inconsistent, 0 – 100 (see [46])
Surface ECG	T-wave alternans ratio $\geq$ 3.0	54 (AE)	90 (AE)
Holter ECG	Heart Rate Variability SDNN $\geq$ 50ms (TD)	17	77
Electrophysiological Study	Repetitive ventricular response, sustained ventricular tachycardia	13 – 42	96 - 100

risk markers, e.g. left ventricular ejection fraction below 40%, ventricular late potentials, frequent and/or repetitive extrasystoles, may enhance the positive predictive value to 50% or more, but at the expense of sensitivity, which may drop below 50% [42]-[45].

Risk stratification in patients with cardiomyopathies and chronic congestive heart failure. Risk stratification in patients with hypertrophic obstructive cardiomyopathy (HOCM) or dilative cardiomyopathy (DCM) seems to be less substantiated, since at least PVS proved to be too insensitive and unspecific for differentiating patients at high risk of SCD. Therefore other risk markers for HOCM such as sudden unexpected death in family relatives, sudden unexplained syncope in the individual patient or syncope on exertion, the presence of sustained VT and a high pressure gradient with exaggerated septal hypertrophy seem to be more predictive [47]. For DCM the degree of left ventricular dysfunction, the clinical status of cardiac failure, and the presence of non-sustained

VT may be predictive of increased mortality. The degree of left ventricular dysfunction may also be useful for predicting reduced survival rates in patients with other types of chronic severe heart failure (CHF), which may be tested by the degree of exercise tolerance. This has been shown by Mancini *et al.* [48], who demonstrated that CHF patients on a waiting list for heart transplantation being able to perform an exercise work load with a peak oxygen uptake of >14 ml/kg/min had an equal survival rate compared to those who already had a heart transplant. In contrast, those patients with a peak exercise capacity of < 14 ml/kg/min had a one year survival rate of only 47%, and a two year survival rate of 32%. The role of left ventricular dysfunction and particularly of repetitive ventricular arrhythmias including non-sustained VT in predicting the risk of sudden arrhythmic death remains unclear in patients with severe CHF. At least in those with sustained VT or arrhythmic syncope an implantable cardioverter defibrillator (ICD) should be implanted prophylactically in order to bridge the patient alive to the time of heart transplantation.

Sequential non-invasive and invasive risk stratification protocols. Instead of an alternative application of non-invasive or invasive strategies, a two-step risk stratification procedure using non-invasive screening followed by an invasive electrophysiological study seems to be more appropriate, as has been proposed and investigated by Pedretti *et al.* [49]. In a total of 303 post-myocardial infarction patients a number of clinical risk markers such as age, previous myocardial infarction, non-Q-wave infarction, left ventricular dyskinesia, ejection fraction < 40%, filtered QRS duration of $\geq$ 115 ms (VLP), VPBs > 6/hour, presence of non-sustained VT, HRV index of < 29 and mean RR interval < 750 ms were tested by stepwise logistic regression analysis. The following markers proved to be most significant: EF < 40%, VLP present, and detection of repetitive VPBs. Patients with none or one non-invasive risk marker were classified as low risk patients and followed for a mean of 15 months post infarction. Those with two or three non-invasive risk markers were classified as intermediate to high risk and subjected to invasive electrophysiologic testing. Patients with inducible sustained VT were classified as high risk patients, and those without inducibility of sustained VT to the low risk group. The mortality rate for SCD was 13/20 (65%) in the group with inducible sustained VT, whereas mortality in the low risk group was 3/263 patients (1.1%). The sensitivity for predicting SCD by the two-step program was 81%, the specificity 89%, the positive predictive value was 65% and the negative predictive value was 99%, i.e., 65% of patients were correctly classified as SCD candidates. The study of Pedretti *et al.* [49] has been confirmed in essence by the publication of Zoni-Berisso *et al.* [50].

Current status. In daily practice the diagnosis of an increased arrhythmic risk has to be followed by the clinical decision whether the risk of the individual patient is high enough to require aggressive and cost intensive treatment strategies such as long term amiodarone or cardioverter defibrillator implantation. Despite the large number of studies dealing with risk assessment from different parameters, data concerning proven therapeutic consequences of risk assessment are still limited to very high risk patient groups. The MUSTT [1] and MADIT [2], [3] trials ascertain the use of a stepwise approach based on non-sustained ventricular tachycardia (nsVT) and a reduced left ventricular ejection fraction (EF) for the selection of patients for electrophysiologic testing (EPS). In patients with inducible sustained VT implantation of an cardioverter defibrillator was proven to be an effective therapy. Despite the fact that these studies could demonstrate the successful transposition of risk assessment into therapy, there are still many open questions. The level of risk as well as the optimum of equivalent combinations of risk factors have to be defined. Currently all risk assessment strategies are based on a significantly depressed left ventricular function. However it remains to be defined whether LV dysfunction needs to be always heavily reduced or whether certain combinations of risk parameters require treatment even with moderate or low LV-impairment. Only recently Ikeda *et al.* [51] showed that the combined assessment of T-wave alternans and late potentials is associated with a high positive predictive value for an arrhythmic event after acute MI. Furthermore current risk assessment strategies mostly serve as pre-screening of patients for subsequent programmed ventricular stimulation still regarded as the gold standard of risk evaluation. Although this might be acceptable in post MI patients, EPS does not capture all relevant mechanisms of malignant ventricular tachyarrhythmias [52]. Especially in patients with cardiomyopathy the inducibility of sustained VT during electrophysiological stimulation is less specific. In clinical practice a two step stratification program in post infarction patients seems to be an adequate and cost effective approach. The positive predictive value of all individual non-invasive parameters is limited. However the negative predictive value is relatively high (> 90%) and can be further increased by combining them using the OR relation. Thus pre-selection of high risk patients with a set of non-invasive markers will markedly enhance the specificity and predictive accuracy of the subsequent invasive electrophysiological test. A different test characteristic can be reached by combining several screening parameters in an AND relation resulting in an improved positive predictive value of the subsequent EPS. Furthermore the use of multiple pre-screening non-invasive tests allows to cover different pathophysiological aspects of arrhythmogenesis (see Table 2). A potential risk stratification strategy including both established parameters (EF $\leq$ 40%, non-sustained VT, see MUSTT, MADIT) and new non-invasive tests is shown in Figure 1. After myocardial infarction patients will first be studied for post-MI ischaemia (angina, ST-segment depression) and will be revascularized if needed (PTCA or bypass grafting). Two to three weeks post MI, left ventricular function will be measured (echo, angiogram, scintigraphy), and a Holter ECG will be recorded. In addition a set of new risk markers including ventricular late potentials, heart rate variability, T-wave alternans, and the recently described heart rate turbulence [53] can be recorded. In patients with EF $\leq$ 40% and non-sustained VT (which corresponds to MUSTT and MADIT) or a reduced LV function in combination with at least three other risk markers an electrophysiologic study will be performed. Patients not undergoing EP study as well as patients with a negative EP test result will receive beta blocker therapy. Patients with inducible VT (due to the protocol always on top of the above mentioned pre-screening risk factors) represent a true high risk population requiring ICD therapy. Further studies are necessary to clarify the role of long term amiodarone drug therapy plus beta blocker as an alternative to the ICD strategy in certain patient subgroups. New technologies of signal analysis have broadened our apparatus for risk assessment allowing to measure very diverse aspects of arrhythmogenesis. The above proposed strategy is a careful approach to include these new technologies into clinical practice although other combinations of risk markers might replace the reduced left ventricular ejection fraction [51]. Several studies with long term follow-up are necessary to clarify their final role in different patient subgroups and pathophysiological entities.

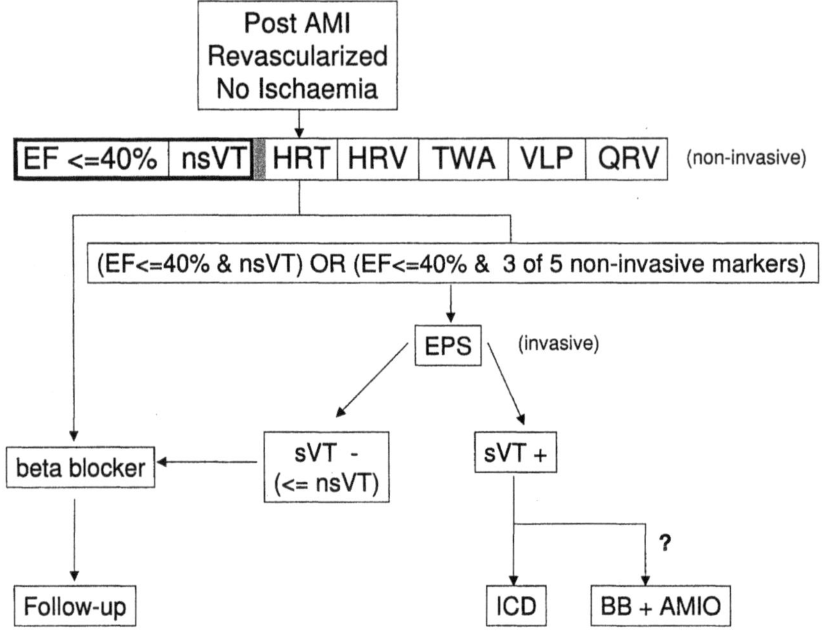

Figure 1. Flow chart showing the proposed two-step risk stratification procedure in patients after acute myocardial infarction (see text). Abbreviations: EF: ejection fraction, VEA: ventricular ectopic activity, HRT: heart rate turbulence, HRV: heart rate variability, TWA: T-wave alternans, VLP: ventricular late potentials, QRV: QRS microvariability, nsVT: non-sustained ventricular tachycardia, EPS: electrophysiological testing (by programmed ventricular stimulation), sVT: sustained VT, ICD: implantable cardioverter defibrillator, BB: beta blocking drug, AMIO: amiodarone.

3 Selected Methods for Training RBF Classifiers

In this section we present the different RBF initialization and training strategies used in this investigation.

In the classification scenario a neural network performs a mapping from a continuous input space X $(= \mathbb{R}^d)$ into a finite set of classes $Y = \{\omega_1, \ldots, \omega_l\}$. In the training phase the parameters of the network are determined from a finite training set: $S = \{(\mathbf{x}^\mu, \omega^\mu) | \mu = 1, \ldots N\}$, each feature vector $\mathbf{x}^\mu \in \mathbb{R}^d$ is labeled with its class membership $\omega^\mu \in Y$. In the recall phase further unlabeled observations $\mathbf{x} \in \mathbb{R}^d$ are presented to the network which estimates their class membership ω.

Here, we restrict ourselves to Gaussian basis functions [54] of the type

$$\phi_j(\mathbf{x}) = \exp\left(-\frac{||\mathbf{x} - \mathbf{c}_j||^2}{2\sigma_j^2}\right)$$

where $\mathbf{x}$ is the d-dimensional input vector with elements $x_i \in \mathbb{R}$, and $\mathbf{c}_j \in \mathbb{R}^d$ is the vector determining the center of the basis function ϕ_j and has elements $c_{ji} \in \mathbb{R}$, $||\,.\,||$ denotes the Euclidean norm. The radial basis function neural network mapping with M basis functions is then

$$y_k(\mathbf{x}) = \sum_{j=1}^{M} w_{kj}\phi_j(\mathbf{x}) + w_{k0}$$

where the w_{k0} denote the biases, which may be absorbed into the summation by including an extra basis function ϕ_0 whose activation is set equal to 1. This mapping can be represented as the network diagram of Figure 2 with the radial basis functions in the hidden layer and linear summation on the output layer. In our classification scenario the number of output units corresponds to the number of classes (1 of l coding). Categorization is performed by assigning the input vector $\mathbf{x}$ the class of the output unit with maximum activation:

$$\text{class}(\mathbf{x}) = \omega_{k^*} \quad \text{where} \quad k^* = \underset{k=1,\ldots,l}{\text{argmax}}\, y_k(\mathbf{x}).$$

To simplify notation and without any loss of generality we identify

$$\omega_k = k \quad \text{and thus} \quad Y = \{1, \ldots, l\}.$$

Typically, training an RBF network is separated into two phases:

1. Adaptation of the centers of the prototype with a supervised or unsupervised training procedure and

2. adaptation of the output layer together with the setting of the width of the RBF functions.

In the following methods for these two phases, which were applied in this investigation are described together with a procedure for the selection of initial prototypes.

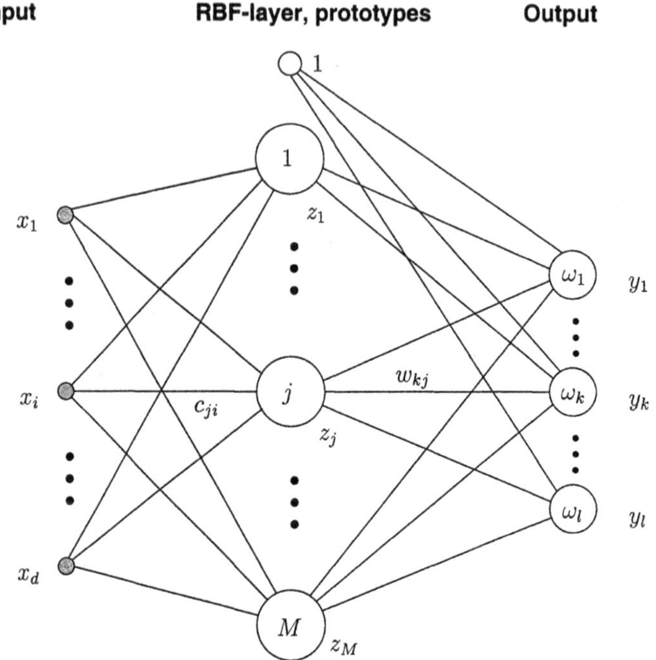

Figure 2. Architecture of the radial basis function neural network with Gaussian basis functions $z_j = \phi_j(\mathbf{x}) = \exp\left(-\frac{||\mathbf{x}-\mathbf{c}_j||^2}{2\sigma_j^2}\right)$ and linear output units $y_k(\mathbf{x}) = \sum_{j=1}^{M} w_{kj}\phi_j(\mathbf{x}) + w_{k0}$.

3.1 Selection of Seed Prototypes

Different methods for the selection or generation of seed prototypes are possible. One of them, a random selection of prototypes from the available training data does not fulfill the requirements of good seed prototypes in terms of their equal distribution among the classes and good classification properties within a reasonable neighborhood of their location. We therefore used an algorithm for finding seed prototypes from the training data which selects if possible an equal number of prototypes from each class with the additional requirement of having within the K nearest neighbors a majority of the same class. If that is not possible the neighborhood requirement is dropped. If that is still not possible a data point of any class is used as a seed prototype.

More formally we define:

$$d_j^\mu = ||\mathbf{x}^\mu - \mathbf{c}_j||$$

for $j \in \{1, \ldots, M\}$ and $\mu \in \{1, \ldots, N\}$.

With the sequence $\mu_1, \ldots, \mu_M$ and

$$d_j^{\mu_1} \leq d_j^{\mu_2} \leq \ldots \leq d_j^{\mu_M},$$

$$\mathcal{N}^K(\mathbf{c}_j) = \{\mathbf{x}^{\mu_1}, \ldots, \mathbf{x}^{\mu_K}\}$$

is the set of K nearest neighbors (data points) of prototype $\mathbf{c}_j$ and

$$\mathcal{N}_k^K(\mathbf{c}_j) = \left\{\mathbf{x}^\mu \in \mathcal{N}^K(\mathbf{c}_j) \mid \quad \text{class}(\mathbf{x}^\mu) = k\right\}$$

is the set of nearest neighbors (data points) of class k among the K nearest neighbors (data points) of prototype $\mathbf{c}_j$.

The procedure for the selection of seed prototypes is described in Algorithm 1.

Algorithm 1 Selection of seed prototypes

Require: K, M
  $C = \emptyset$
  for $m = 1$ to M **do**
    for $k = 1$ to l **do**
      for $\mu \in \{1, \ldots, N\} \backslash C$ **do**
        $\Delta_\mu = |\mathcal{N}_k^K(\mathbf{x}^\mu)| - \max\limits_{i \neq k} |\mathcal{N}_i^K(\mathbf{x}^\mu)|$
      end for
      $\mu^* = \underset{\mu}{\text{argmax}}\, \Delta_\mu$
      $C = C \cup \{\mu^*\}$
      $\mathbf{c}_m = \mathbf{x}^{\mu^*}$, class$(\mathbf{c}_m) = k$
    end for
  end for

3.2 Adapting the Prototype Location

Supervised: OLVQ1. Kohonen [55] proposed a supervised version of a vector quantization algorithm called Learning Vector Quantization

(LVQ). From the basic LVQ1 version, the OLVQ1, LVQ2, and LVQ3 competitive training procedures have been derived. In the following the OLVQ1 algorithm, which is used in the experiments, will be briefly illustrated. After the initialization of the prototypes $\mathbf{c}_j$ and upon the presentation of a feature vector from the training set $\mathbf{x}^\mu$, the location of the winning prototype $\mathbf{c}_{j^*}$ with

$$j^* = \underset{j}{\operatorname{argmin}} \, ||\mathbf{x}^\mu - \mathbf{c}_j||$$

is adapted according to the learning rule:

$$\Delta \mathbf{c}_{j^*} = \begin{cases} +\eta_{j^*}(t)(\mathbf{x}^\mu - \mathbf{c}_{j^*}), \text{ if class}(\mathbf{c}_{j^*}) = \text{class}(\mathbf{x}^\mu) \\ -\eta_{j^*}(t)(\mathbf{x}^\mu - \mathbf{c}_{j^*}), \text{ if class}(\mathbf{c}_{j^*}) \neq \text{class}(\mathbf{x}^\mu) \end{cases} .$$

In contrast to the LVQ1 algorithm, OLVQ1 exhibits an individual learning rate $\eta_j(t)$ for each prototype $\mathbf{c}_j$. Usually $\eta_j(t)$ is positively decreasing. The class labels of the prototypes are not changed during adaptation, they remain constant after initialization.

Unsupervised: Batch k-means. It is possible to adapt the prototype location in a non-trivial way without using any class information of the training patterns. This is done by utilizing the neighborhood relationships within the data points imposed by a distance measure. The k-means clustering procedure [56]-[58] is among the most popular methods in cluster analysis [59]. After initialization of the prototypes $\mathbf{c}_j$ their location is adapted after every epoch according to (batch k-means algorithm):

$$\mathbf{c}_j = \frac{1}{|C_j|} \sum_{\mathbf{x}^\mu \in C_j} \mathbf{x}^\mu$$

with

$$C_j = \left\{ \mathbf{x}^\mu \in X \mid j = \underset{i}{\operatorname{argmin}} \, ||\mathbf{x}^\mu - \mathbf{c}_i|| \right\}$$

being the set of hits at prototype $\mathbf{c}_j$ and $X = \{\mathbf{x}^1, \ldots, \mathbf{x}^N\}$ being the set of feature vectors of the training set S. It is easily shown that this update rule minimizes the error function:

$$E(\mathbf{c}_1, \ldots, \mathbf{c}_M) = \sum_{j=1}^{M} \sum_{\mathbf{x}^\mu \in C_j} ||\mathbf{x}^\mu - \mathbf{c}_j||^2 .$$

Dynamic LVQ. The previous two approaches for adapting the hidden layer require the a priori setting of the number of prototypes. Here, we present a simple data driven codebook generation scheme, which is similar to [60], [61]. Adaptation of the prototype location is done by OLVQ1 (although k-means could be used as well). During training a statistic for each prototype $\mathbf{c}_j$ is maintained, which contains the number of class specific hits h_{jk} with $k \neq \text{class}(\mathbf{c}_j)$. Based upon this statistic new prototypes are inserted, and if after the temporarily insertion of the new prototype the classification error does not decrease, the prototype inserted last is pruned from the network, see Algorithm 2 and Figure 3.

Algorithm 2 Dynamic LVQ

Require: R, ϵ, MAX
  OLVQ1 training: $\mathbf{c}_1, \ldots, \mathbf{c}_M$
  $E = \text{error}(\mathbf{c}_1, \ldots, \mathbf{c}_M)$
  while $(E \leq \epsilon)$ or $(M \geq MAX - 1)$ **do**
    Calculate all h_{jk} for $j \in \{1, \ldots, M\}$ and $k \in \{1, \ldots, l\} \setminus \text{class}(\mathbf{c}_j)$
    Sort h_{jk} such that $h_{j_1 k_1} \geq h_{j_2 k_2} \geq \ldots \geq h_{j_p k_p}$
    $\nu = 1$
    while $\nu \leq p$ **do**
      $\mathbf{c}^{\nu}_{j_\nu} = \frac{1}{h_{j_\nu k_\nu}} \sum_{\mathbf{x} \in C_{j_\nu k_\nu}} \mathbf{x}$
      $\text{class}(\mathbf{c}^{\nu}_{j_\nu}) = k_\nu$
      OLVQ1 $(\mathbf{c}_1, \ldots, \mathbf{c}_M, \mathbf{c}^{\nu}_{j_\nu})$
      if $E > (e = \text{error}(\mathbf{c}_1, \ldots, \mathbf{c}_M, \mathbf{c}^{\nu}_{j_\nu}))$ **then**
        $M = M + 1$, $E = e$
        $\mathbf{c}_M = \mathbf{c}^{\nu}_{j_\nu}$, $\text{class}(\mathbf{c}_M) = k_\nu$
      end if
      $\nu = \nu + 1$
    end while
    OLVQ1 training: $\mathbf{c}_1, \ldots, \mathbf{c}_M$
    $E = \text{error}(\mathbf{c}_1, \ldots, \mathbf{c}_M)$
  end while

For $j \in \{1, \ldots, M\}$ and $k \in \{1, \ldots, l\}$ we define

$$C_{jk} = \left\{ \mathbf{x}^\mu \in C_j \;\middle|\; \text{class}(\mathbf{x}^\mu) = k \right\}$$

and for $k \in \{1, \ldots, l\} \setminus \text{class}(\mathbf{c}_j)$ we set

$$h_{jk} = |C_{jk}|.$$

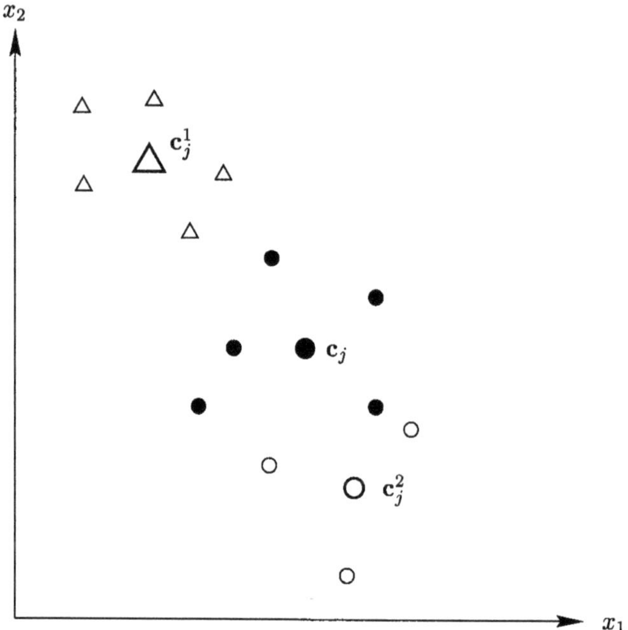

Figure 3. Illustration of prototype insertion with dynamic LVQ in a three class scenario ($\triangle$, $\circ$, $\bullet$). The prototype $\mathbf{c}_j$ makes five misclassifications with class $\triangle$ and three with class $\circ$. At first a new prototype is added at the center of gravity $\mathbf{c}_j^1$. If the overall classification rate does not rise, location $\mathbf{c}_j^2$ is tried.

Then, there exists a sequence $(j_1, k_1), \ldots, (j_p, k_p)$ with $p = M(l-1)$ such that

$$h_{j_1 k_1} \geq h_{j_2 k_2} \geq \ldots \geq h_{j_p k_p}.$$

Candidate prototypes for the temporary insertion into the codebook are defined as follows:

$$\mathbf{c}_{j_\nu}^{\nu} = \frac{1}{h_{j_\nu k_\nu}} \sum_{\mathbf{x} \in C_{j_\nu k_\nu}} \mathbf{x} \quad \text{and} \quad \text{class}(\mathbf{c}_{j_\nu}^{\nu}) = k_\nu.$$

3.3 Construction of the RBF Network

So far we have only dealt with different vector quantization schemes for the adaptation of prototype locations. For the transition to a RBF network these prototype locations are used as centers of the radial basis functions. Additionally the initial setting and possible adaptation of the kernel widths σ_j of the radial basis functions and of the hidden to output layer connections w_{kj} is required. Here, we restrict ourselves to initializing the output weights to 1 for 'prototype-of-that-class' to 'output-of-that-class' connections and the others to small values (see Section 5).

3.3.1 Setting of the Kernel Widths

The setting of the kernel widths is a critical issue in the transition to the RBF network. When the kernel width σ is too large the estimated probability density is over-smoothed and the nature of the underlying true density may be lost. Conversely, when σ is too small there may be an over-adaptation to the particular data set. In addition very small σ tend to cause numerical problems with gradient descent methods as their gradients vanish. We investigated three different schemes for the initial setting of the kernel widths in transition to the RBF network (γ is set heuristically):

1. The kernel width σ_j is set to the mean of the distance to the L nearest prototypes $\mathcal{P}_j(L)$ of prototype $\mathbf{c}_j$:

$$\sigma_j = \gamma \frac{1}{L} \sum_{\mathbf{c} \in \mathcal{P}_j(L)} ||\mathbf{c} - \mathbf{c}_j||$$

2. Use the distance to the nearest prototype with a different class label for initialization:

$$\sigma_j - \gamma \min_{\substack{i \neq j \\ class(\mathbf{c}_i) \neq class(\mathbf{c}_j)}} ||\mathbf{c}_i - \mathbf{c}_j||$$

3. All σ_j are set to the same value, which is proportional to the average minimal distance between all prototypes:

$$\sigma_j = \sigma = \gamma \frac{1}{M} \sum_{n=1}^{M} \min_{i \neq n} ||\mathbf{c}_i - \mathbf{c}_n||$$

3.3.2 Gradient Descent

The adaptation of the output weights and of the kernel widths was done with two gradient descent methods, i.e., plain back-propagation and back-propagation enhanced by Armijo line search.

Back-propagation. We give a brief summary of the use of error-back-propagation in the context of radial basis function network training, for a more detailed treatment see [54], [62], [63].

If we define as the error function of the network a differentiable function like the sum-of-squares error E,

$$E = \frac{1}{2} \sum_{\mu=1}^{N} \sum_{k=1}^{l} (y_k^\mu - t_k^\mu)^2$$

with y_k^μ and t_k^μ as the actual and target output values respectively, and we consider a network with differentiable activation functions – which we have see Figure 2 – then a necessary condition for a minimal error is that its derivatives with respect to the parameters center location $\mathbf{c}$, kernel width σ and output weights $\mathbf{w}$ vanish. The resulting equations are only solvable explicitly if the activation functions are linear and with a sum-of-squares error function. An iterative procedure for finding a solution to this problem is gradient descent. Here, the full parameter set $\mathbf{W} = (\mathbf{c}_j, \sigma_j, \mathbf{w}_j)$ is moved by a small distance η (the learning rate) – in their respective spaces – in the direction in which E decreases most rapidly, i.e., in the direction of the negative gradient $-\nabla E$:

$$\mathbf{W}^{(\tau+1)} = \mathbf{W}^{(\tau)} - \eta \nabla E(\mathbf{W}^{(\tau)}).$$

The update of the other parameters ($\mathbf{c}$, σ) is performed in a similar fashion. For the network of Figure 2 we obtain the following expressions for the derivatives of the error function with respect to the network parameters:

$$\frac{\partial E}{\partial \sigma_j} = \sum_\mu \sum_k (y_k^\mu - t_k^\mu) w_{kj} \exp\left(-\frac{||\mathbf{x}^\mu - \mathbf{c}_j||^2}{2\sigma_j^2}\right) \frac{||\mathbf{x}^\mu - \mathbf{c}_j||^2}{\sigma_j^3}$$

$$\frac{\partial E}{\partial c_{ji}} = \sum_\mu \sum_k (y_k^\mu - t_k^\mu) w_{kj} \exp\left(-\frac{||\mathbf{x}^\mu - \mathbf{c}_j||^2}{2\sigma_j^2}\right) \frac{x_i^\mu - c_{ji}}{\sigma_j^2}$$

$$\frac{\partial E}{\partial w_{kj}} = \sum_\mu (y_k^\mu - t_k^\mu) z_j^\mu.$$

Back-propagation with variable stepsize. Choosing the right learning rate or stepsize η is sometimes a critical issue in neural network training. If its value is too low convergence to a minimum is slow, conversely if it is chosen too high successive steps in parameter space overshot the minimum of the error surface. This problem can be avoided by a proper stepsize tuning. A procedure for obtaining such a stepsize was proposed by Armijo [64] in 1966. In the following very brief description of the method we draw heavily from the papers of Armijo [64] and Magoulas *et al.* [65], for details see the respective articles. Under mild conditions on the error function E, which are satisfied in our setting the following theorem holds:

Theorem (Armijo, 1966) If η_0 is an arbitrarily assigned positive number, $\eta_m = \frac{\eta_0}{2^{m-1}}, m = 0, 1, \ldots$. Then the sequence of weight vectors $\{\mathbf{W}^{(\tau)}\}_0^\infty$ with

$$\mathbf{W}^{(\tau+1)} = \mathbf{W}^{(\tau)} - \eta_{m_\tau} \nabla E(\mathbf{W}^{(\tau)}), \qquad \tau = 0, 1, 2, \ldots$$

where m_τ is the smallest positive integer for which

$$E(\mathbf{W}^{(\tau)} - \eta_{m_\tau} \nabla E(\mathbf{W}^{(\tau)})) - E(\mathbf{W}^{(\tau)}) \leq -\frac{1}{2}\eta_{m_\tau} ||\nabla E(\mathbf{W}^{(\tau)})||^2,$$

converges to the point $\mathbf{W}^*$ which minimizes (locally) E.

Using Armijo's theorem, Magoulas *et al.* [65] proposed a back-propagation algorithm with variable stepsize, see Algorithm 3.

4 Data

Subject groups. We compared a group of 51 healthy subjects (group A) with 44 cardiac patients at a high risk for malignant ventricular arrhythmias (group B, VT patients). All healthy volunteers (mean age 24.0±4.1 years) had a normal resting ECG and a normal echocardiogram, and no cardiac symptoms or coronary risk factors. The patients with a high-risk for malignant ventricular arrhythmias (mean age 61.2±8.9 years) were selected from our electrophysiologic database. Inclusion criteria were the presence of coronary artery disease, a previous myocardial infarction, a history of at least one symptomatic arrhythmia,

Algorithm 3 Back-propagation with variable stepsize

Require: E_{min}, η_{min}, τ_{max}
  Epochs: $\tau = 0$
  while $E(\mathbf{W}^{(\tau)}) > E_{min}$ & $\tau \leq \tau_{max}$ **do**
    if $\tau = 0$ **then**
      $\eta = 0.5$
    else
      $\eta = 0.5/(\|\nabla E(\mathbf{W}^{(\tau)}) - \nabla E(\mathbf{W}^{(\tau-1)})\|/\|\mathbf{W}^{(\tau)} - \mathbf{W}^{(\tau-1)}\|)$
    end if
    while $\eta < \eta_{min}$ **do**
      $\eta = 2\eta$
    end while
    while $E(\mathbf{W}^{(\tau)} - \eta\nabla E(\mathbf{W}^{(\tau)})) - E(\mathbf{W}^{(\tau)}) > -\frac{1}{2}\eta\|\nabla E(\mathbf{W}^{(\tau)}\|^2$ **do**
      $\eta = \eta/2$
    end while
    $\mathbf{W}^{(\tau+1)} = \mathbf{W}^{(\tau)} - \eta\nabla E(\mathbf{W}^{(\tau)})$
    $\tau = \tau + 1$
  end while

and inducible sustained ventricular tachycardia (> 30 seconds) at electrophysiologic testing. Patients with bundle branch block or atrial fibrillation were excluded. All patients of group B underwent coronary angiography and programmed right ventricular stimulation due to clinical indications. Stimulation was done from the right apex and the right outflow tract. The stimulation protocol included up to 3 extrastimuli during sinus rhythm and at baseline pacing with a cycle length of 500 ms, and a maximum of 2 extrastimuli at baseline pacing with cycle lengths of 430 ms, 370 ms, and 330 ms. Group B consisted of 10 patients with single vessel disease, 17 patients with double vessel disease, and 17 patients with triple vessel coronary artery disease. Nineteen patients had a previous posterior infarction, 14 patients had a previous anterior infarction, and 11 patients had both a previous anterior and a previous posterior infarction. Mean left ventricular ejection fraction was 44.0%±14.9%. Forty-one patients had a documented episode of spontaneous, sustained ventricular tachycardia or ventricular fibrillation. Out of the remaining three patients, 1 patient had syncopes and non-sustained ventricular tachycardias on Holter monitoring, and 2 patients had syncopes of presumed cardiac origin.

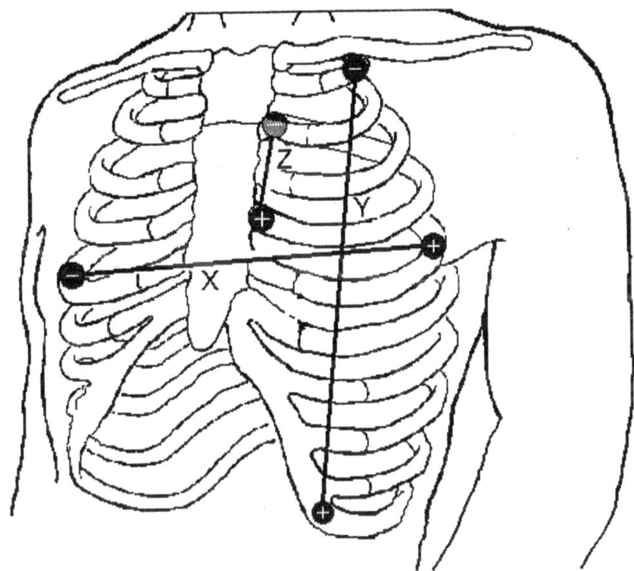

Figure 4. Placement of the three bipolar leads for the recording of high-resolution ECG's

Signal-Averaged ECG recordings. Ventricular late potential analysis (VLP) is a non-invasive method to identify patients with an increased risk for reentrant ventricular tachycardias and for risk stratification after myocardial infarction [66]-[68]. Techniques commonly applied in this purely time-domain based analysis are signal-averaging, high-pass filtering and late potential analysis of the terminal part of the QRS complex. The assessment of VLP's depends on three empirically defined limits of the total duration of the QRS and the duration and amplitude of the terminal low-amplitude portion of the QRS complex [69], [70].

High-resolution signal averaged electrocardiograms are recorded during sinus rhythm from three bipolar orthogonal X, Y, Z leads, see Figure 4. Before ECG recording antiarrhythmic drugs were stopped for at least four half-lives. The skin was carefully prepared and recordings were done with the subjects in reclining position in a Faraday cage, see Figure 5.

Sampling rate was 2000 Hz, A/D resolution was 16 bit, and an analog bandpass filter of 0.05-300 Hz was used (anti-aliasing). The ECG's were recorded with the Predictor system (Corasonix Inc., Oklahoma, USA). The three leads were averaged and combined into a vector magnitude

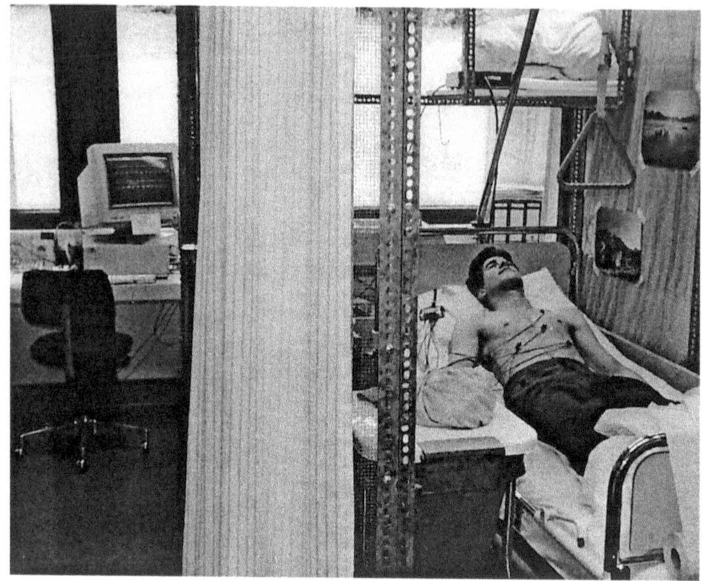

Figure 5. Picture of the high resolution ECG recording facilities. The subject is lying inside the Faraday cage.

signal $V = \sqrt{X^2 + Y^2 + Z^2}$ and bidirectionally filtered with a 4-pole Butterworth filter (40–250 Hz), see Figure 6.

From this vector magnitude signal V three features are extracted:

- QRSd (QRS duration):

$$QRSD := QRS_{offset} - QRS_{onset}$$

- RMS (Time A: $A := QRS_{offset} - 40ms$):

$$RMS := \sqrt{\frac{1}{QRS_{offset} - A} \sum_{i=A}^{QRS_{offset}} V_i^2}$$

- LAS (Duration of the low amplitude signal below 40μV):

$$LAS := QRS_{offset} - \text{argmax}\{i \mid V_i \geq 40\mu V\}$$

In standard late potential analysis a subject is termed "VLP positive" if 2 of the 3 following criteria are met: $QRSD > 115ms$, $RMS < 20\mu V$,

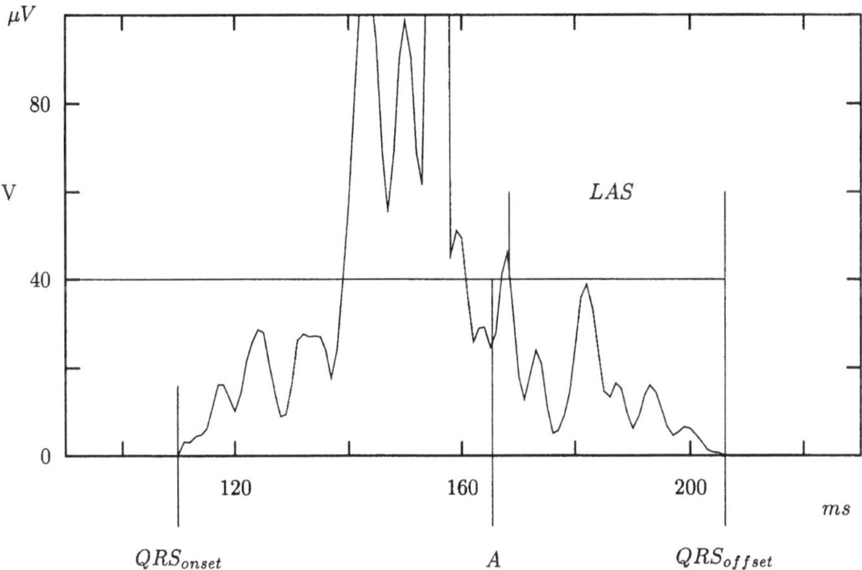

Figure 6. Signal averaged ECG: example of the vector magnitude signal V of a patient with late potentials.

$LAS > 38ms$, see Table 4. In this investigation these three features are used as inputs to a classifying RBF network, which is trained to predict the group status, see subject groups. Figure 7 (left) shows a 2-dimensional visualization of the complete dataset.

Beat-to-beat ECG recordings. High-resolution beat-to-beat electrocardiograms of 30 min duration were recorded during sinus rhythm from bipolar orthogonal X, Y, Z leads using the same equipment as with the signal-averaged recordings. Sampling rate was reduced to 1000 Hz. QRS triggering, reviewing of the ECG, and arrhythmia detection was done on a high-resolution ECG analysis platform developed by our group [72]. The three leads were summed into a signal $V = X + Y + Z$. From each recording 250 consecutive sinus beats preceded by another sinus beat were selected for subsequent beat-to-beat variability analysis.

In a first step the signals were aligned by maximizing the cross-correlation function [73] between the first and all following beats. Prior to the quantification of signal variability the beats were preprocessed to suppress the main ECG waveform, bringing the beat-to-beat micro-

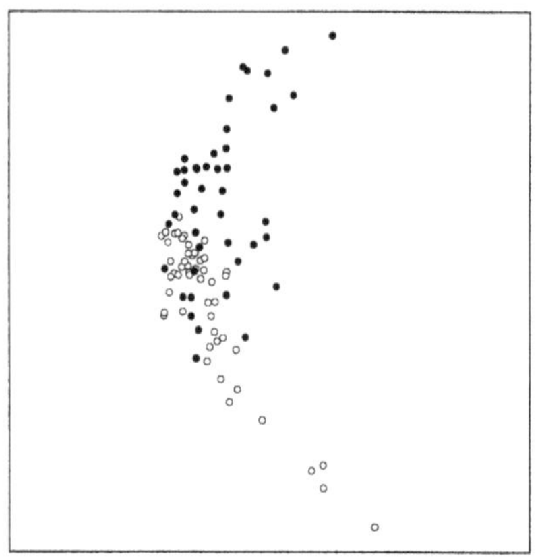
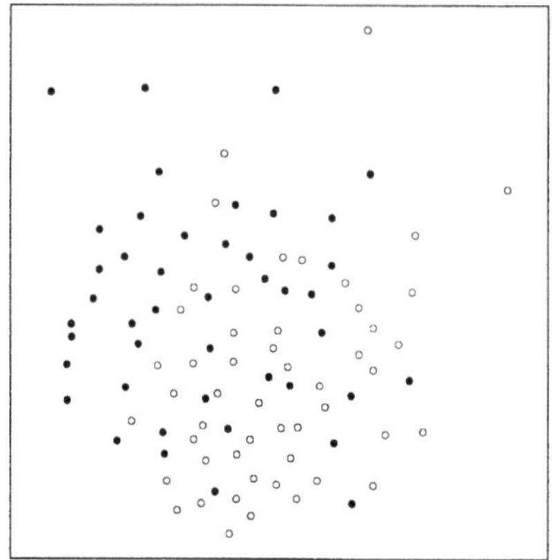

Figure 7. Mapping (Sammon mapping [71]) of the signal averaged ECG features (3-D, left) and the beat-to-beat QRS variability features (141-D, right) onto the 2-dimensional plane visualizing distance relations (using LVQ-Pak 3.1 Helsinki University of Technology). Samples from the healthy subject group are marked with • those from the VT patient group with ∘.

variations into clearer focus. To achieve this, the individual signal was subtracted from its cubic spline smoothed version (spline filtering, spline interpolation through every seventh sample using the not-a-knot end condition) [74], [75], compare Figure 8. This method resembles a waveform adaptive, high-pass filtering without inducing phase-shift related artefacts. Next, for each individual beat the amplitude of the difference signal was normalized to zero mean and a standard deviation of 1 μV. Beat-to-beat variation of each point was measured as the standard deviation of the amplitude of corresponding points across all 250 beats. For the QRS we used a constant analysis window of 141 ms which covered all QRS complexes of this series [17].

The resulting 141-dimensional variability vector was used as input for classification into subject group A or B. Figure 7 (right) shows a 2-dimensional visualization of the complete dataset.

5 Results

Different types of classification experiments with the Gaussian basis function networks of Section 3 were performed. The selection of seed

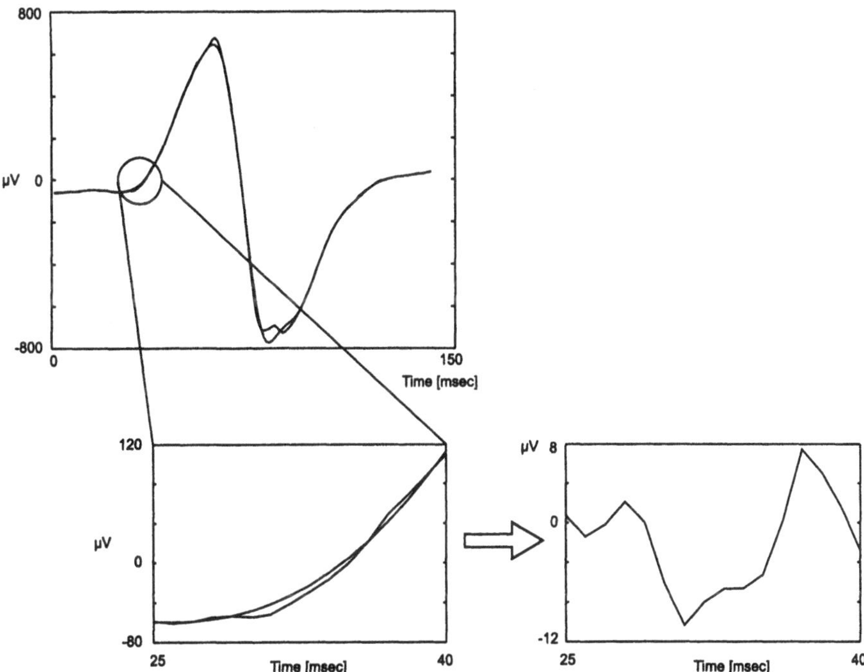

Figure 8. Diagram of the spline-filtering procedure. The upper panel shows both signals, the QRS-complex (sum of the three leads) and the cubic spline. A zoom-in makes the differences more apparent (lower left panel). The resulting signal difference is shown on the lower right panel (note the different scaling of the Y-axis).

prototypes was done with Algorithm 1 ($K = 5$).

The following taxonomy gives an overview of the experiments and the notation:

1. Adaptation of the prototype layer (see Section 3.2). Figures 9 and 10, and Tables 5 and 6 give the nearest neighbor classification results on the prototype layer.

   OLVQ1 : Initial and maximal learning rate was set to 0.3.
   Number of adaptation steps: $120M$.

   Batch k-means : Training until the assignment of data points to prototypes does not change with each epoch. Class labels are not used in this adaptation step. After training class labels are assigned to

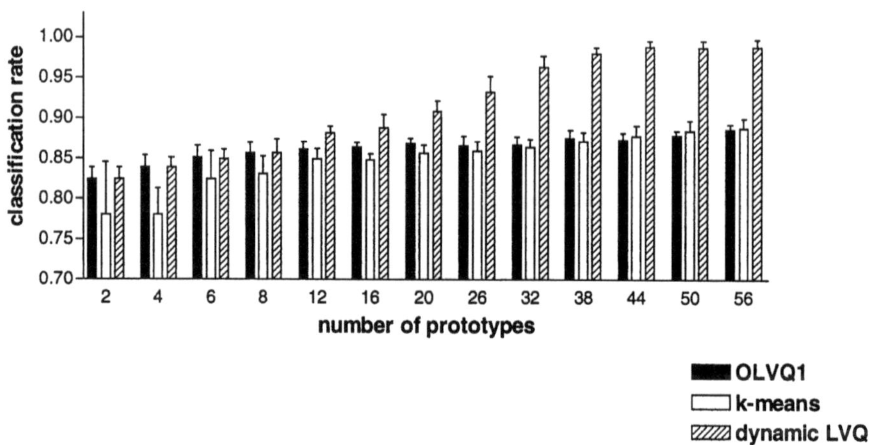

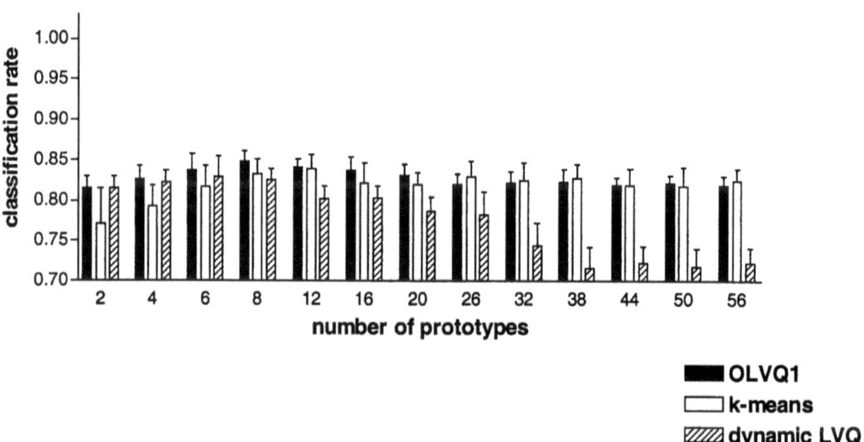

Figure 9. Signal-averaged 3D data: Re-classification (training and test set are the same) and 10-fold cross-validation results (accuracy) for the three prototype adaptation schemes (OLVQ1, k-means, dynamic LVQ) using the nearest neighbor rule on the hidden layer. Results are averages over 10 training and test runs for re-classification and over ten 10-fold cross-validation runs with their standard deviations.

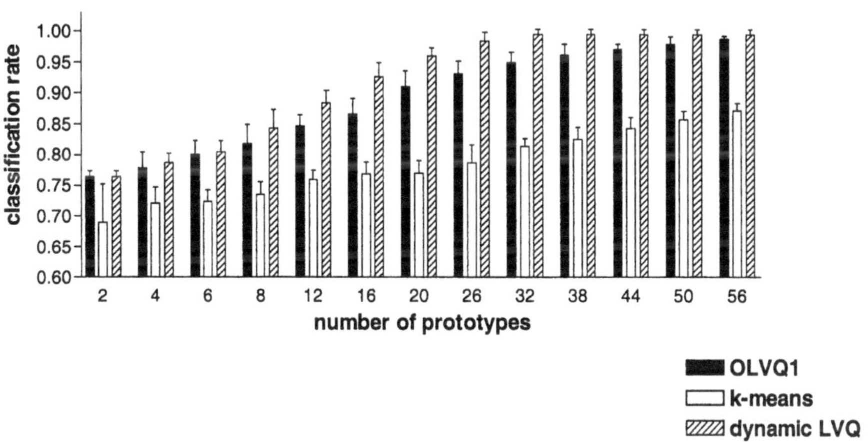

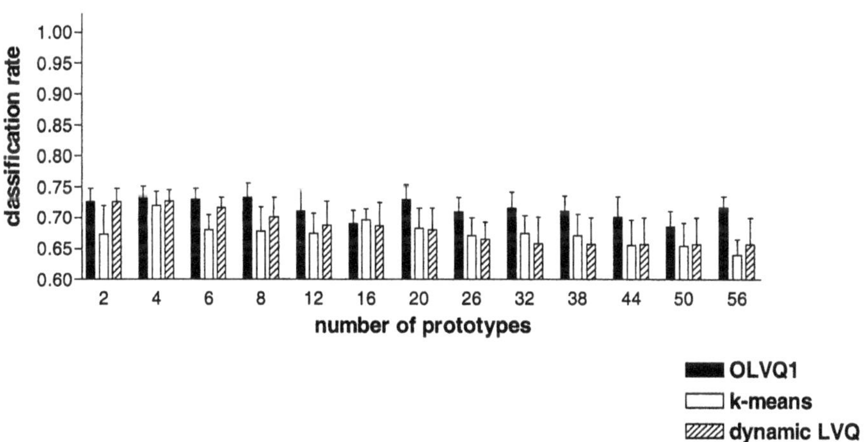

Figure 10. Beat-to-beat variability data: re-classification (training and test set are the same) and 10-fold cross-validation results (accuracy) for the three prototype adaptation schemes (OLVQ1, k-means, dynamic LVQ) using the nearest neighbor rule on the hidden layer. Results are averages over 10 training and test runs for re-classification and over ten 10-fold cross-validation runs with their standard deviations.

Table 5. Detailed classification results of the three prototype adaptation schemes for the signal averaged data (3-dimensional, 8 prototypes): re-classification and 10-fold cross-validation results are given (ten runs, mean ± standard deviation). Classification was performed on the prototype layer with the nearest neighbor rule.

Classification results on the prototype layer of the signal-averaged data (8 prototypes)

OLVQ1

	Acc	Sensi	Speci	PPV	NPV
Re-val	85.7% ± 1.3%	70% ± 3.2%	99.2% ± 1%	98.8% ± 1.6%	79.3% ± 1.6%
Cross-val	84.8% ± 1.3%	69.3% ± 2.9%	98.2% ± 1.4%	97.2% ± 2.3%	78.8% ± 1.5%

k-means

	Acc	Sensi	Speci	PPV	NPV
Re-val	83.1% ± 2.3%	67.7% ± 6.8%	96.3% ± 2.2%	94.3% ± 3.2%	77.7% ± 3.2%
Cross-val	83.3% ± 1.9%	67.7% ± 3.2%	96.7% ± 1.6%	94.6% ± 2.6%	77.7% ± 1.8%

dynamic LVQ

	Acc	Sensi	Speci	PPV	NPV
Re-val	85.7% ± 1.7%	71.4% ± 3.9%	98% ± 1.6%	97% ± 2.5%	79.9% ± 2.1%
Cross-val	82.5% ± 1.4%	69.8% ± 2.2%	93.5% ± 1.9%	90.4% ± 2.6%	78.2% ± 1.3%

prototypes by majority vote of those class labels of data points having minimal distance to the prototype.

Dynamic LVQ : List size p (see Algorithm 2) was set to 12. After every inserted prototype $20M$ OLVQ1 iterations were performed. Learning rate was set to 0.3. Following the growth process the prototypes were finally adapted with $120M$ OLVQ1 iterations. The initial number of prototypes was 2 in all cases and was bounded by the preset value. In some cases the preset number of prototypes was not attained. This occurred for $M \geq 44$ on the 3D data set and $M \geq 26$ on the 141D data set.

2. Training of the RBF network (see Section 3.3). Figures 11 and 12 give the classification results for the RBF networks with a re-training of the output layer only (online back-propagation). Kernel widths were set with the three methods given below. Figures 13 and 14, and Tables 7 and 8 show the classification results on the completely re-trained RBF network (σ initialization was done with method s_a) with Algorithm 3.

   (a) Initialization of RBF widths (see Section 3.3.1)
   γ was heuristically set to 2 in all cases.

Table 6. Detailed classification results of the three prototype adaptation schemes for the beat-to-beat data (141-dimensional, 8 prototypes): re-classification and 10-fold cross-validation results are given (ten runs, mean ± standard deviation). Classification was performed on the prototype layer with the nearest neighbor rule.

Classification results on the prototype layer of the beat-to-beat variability data (8 prototypes)

OLVQ1

	Acc	Sensi	Speci	PPV	NPV
Re-val	81.8% ± 3.1%	71.8% ± 6.7%	90.4% ± 3.3%	86.7% ± 3.6%	79% ± 3.7%
Cross-val	73.3% ± 2.4%	62.7% ± 4.9%	82.4% ± 2.6%	75.4% ± 2.7%	72% ± 2.6%

k-means

	Acc	Sensi	Speci	PPV	NPV
Re-val	73.5% ± 2%	60.7% ± 8.9%	84.5% ± 6.8%	78.7% ± 8.6%	71.6% ± 3%
Cross-val	67.8% ± 4%	52% ± 4.5%	81.4% ± 5.6%	71% ± 6.8%	66.3% ± 2.8%

dynamic LVQ

	Acc	Sensi	Speci	PPV	NPV
Re-val	84.3% ± 3%	76.1% ± 5.2%	91.4% ± 3.5%	88.5% ± 4.2%	81.7% ± 3.4%
Cross-val	70.1% ± 3.3%	61.4% ± 2.6%	77.6% ± 5.8%	70.7% ± 6.3%	69.9% ± 1.9%

s_a: σ_j were set to the average distance to the nearest three prototypes.

s_b: σ_j were set with the distance to the nearest prototype of a different class.

s_c: All σ_j were set to the same value, proportional to the average minimal distance between all prototypes.

(b) Initialization of the output weights w_{kj}: Output weights were always initialized to 1 for connections between prototypes of a class and their corresponding output unit, otherwise they were set to small random values (uniform distribution) in the range of [-1E-6, +1E-6].

(c) Gradient descent (see Section 3.3.2)

Back-propagation on the output layer: Online back-propagation training, i.e., weight update after every presentation of a training pattern (learning rate $\eta = 0.04/\mu$ for every epoch μ). Every epoch consisted of $N = 95$ random presentations of a training pattern. A total of 100 training epochs was performed.

Re-training of the complete network: Complete re-training of the network with back-propagation with variable stepsize (Algorithm 3) for 80 epochs. Every epoch consists of a complete presentation of the training data.

The classification performance is given in terms of **re-validation** and **10-fold cross-validation** results. Re-validation means training and test on the whole data set. 10-fold cross-validation means partitioning the whole data set into 10 disjoint subsets and carrying out 10 training and test runs always using 9 subsets as the training set and testing on the remaining one. The results are those on the test sets. Each of these re-validation or 10-fold cross-validation simulations was performed 10 times. The difference between subsequent simulations was the initialization of the random number generator and the random permutation of the data set.

The classification results of the different networks are summarized into five measures of performance:

Actual Condition of Population

Classification Result		Patients with Disease	Patients without Disease
	Positive	a (true-positives)	b (false-positives)
	Negative	c (false-negatives)	d (true-negatives)

Accuracy (Acc) = $(a + d) / (a + b + c + d)$
Sensitivity (Sensi) = $a / (a + c)$
Specificity (Speci) = $d / (b + d)$
Positive predictive value (PPV) = $a / (a + b)$
Negative predictive value (NPV) = $d / (c + d)$

6 Concluding Remarks

Several topics were touched in this investigation: the role of non-invasive risk assessment in cardiology, new signal processing techniques utilizing

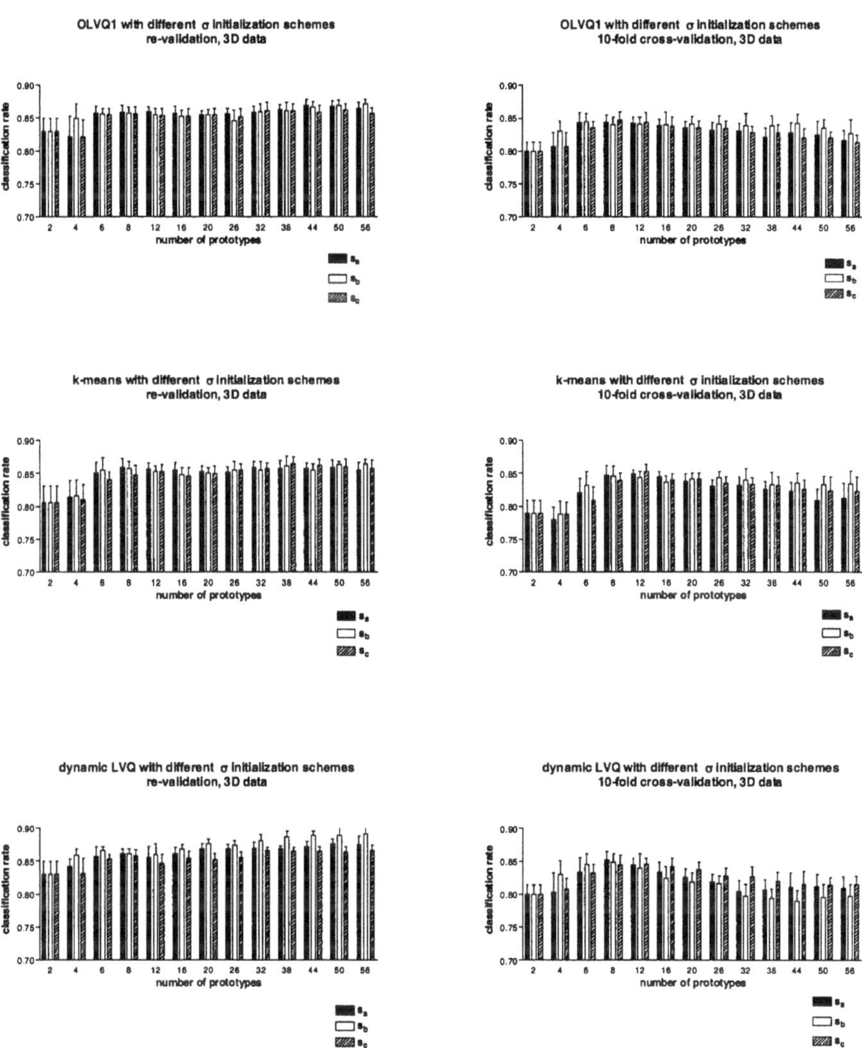

Figure 11. RBF results for the signal-averaged data. The figures show the results for the OLVQ1 (top row) prototype adaptation scheme, k-means (middle) and dynamic LVQ (bottom). Each figure gives the results for the three different σ initialization schemes (see text). Training of the output weights is done with back-propagation. Re-classification results are shown in the graphs on the left and cross-validation results in those on the right (accuracy, averages over ten runs and standard deviations are given).

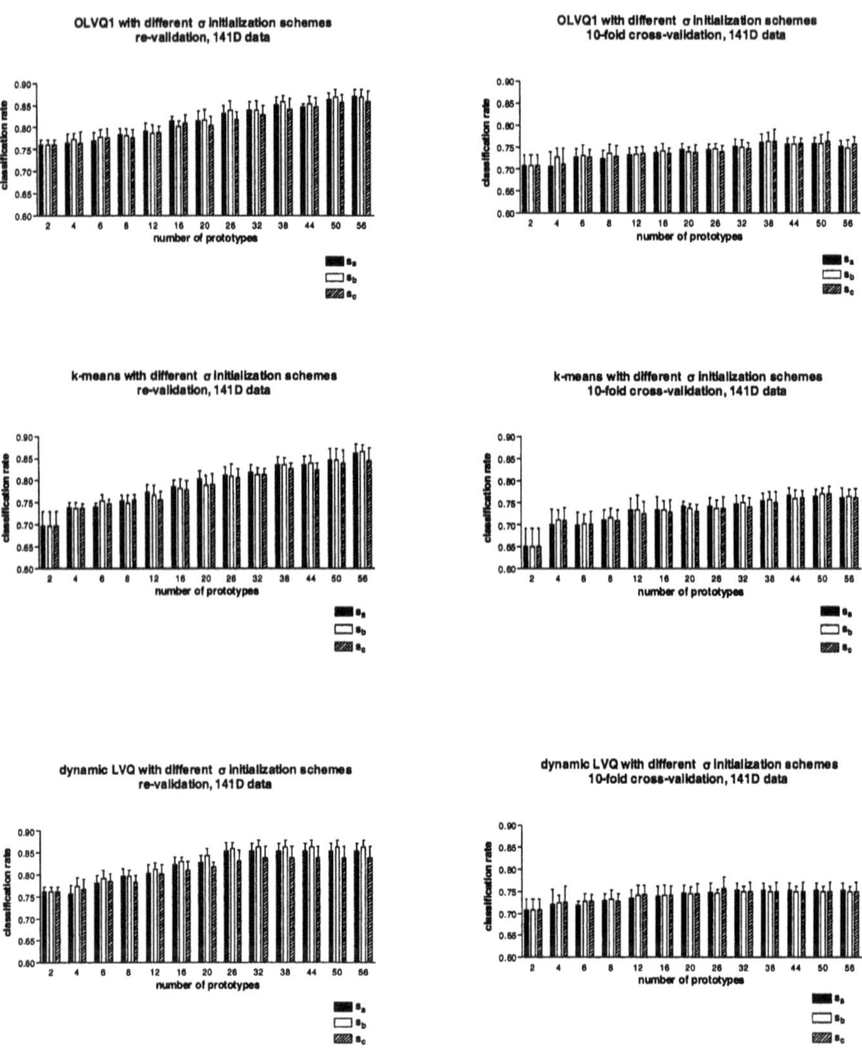

Figure 12. RBF results for the beat-to-beat variability data. The figures show the results for the OLVQ1 (top row) prototype adaptation scheme, k-means (middle) and dynamic LVQ (bottom). Each figure gives the results for the three different σ initialization schemes (see text). Training of the output weights is done with back-propagation. Re-classification results are shown in the graphs on the left and cross-validation results in those on the right (accuracy, averages over ten runs and standard deviations are given).

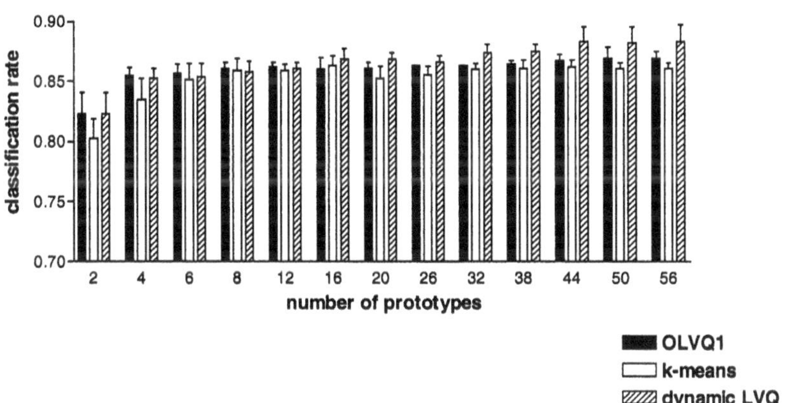

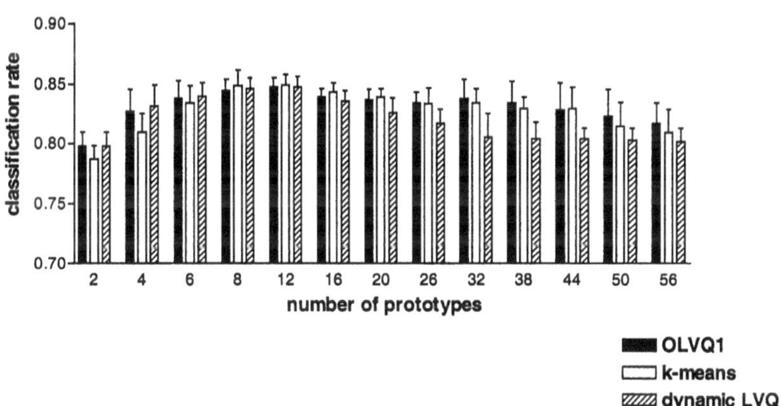

Figure 13. RBF results for the signal-averaged data. The graphs show the results for the OLVQ1 prototype adaptation scheme, k-means and dynamic LVQ for different numbers of hidden neurons. The widths of the RBF functions are initialized via their distance to the next three prototypes (see text). Output weights are initialized to 1 for connections between prototypes of one class and their corresponding output unit, otherwise small values. The complete network (σ_j, $\mathbf{c}_j$, $\mathbf{w}_k$) is re-trained with back-propagation with variable stepsize. Re-classification results are shown in the figure on the left and cross-validation results on the right (accuracy, averages over ten runs and standard deviations are given).

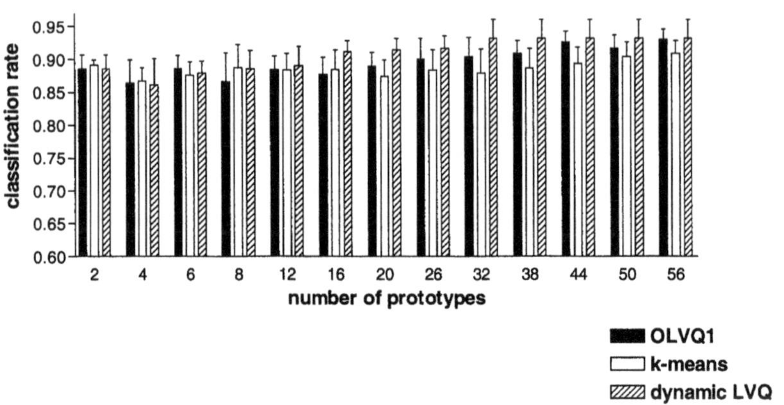

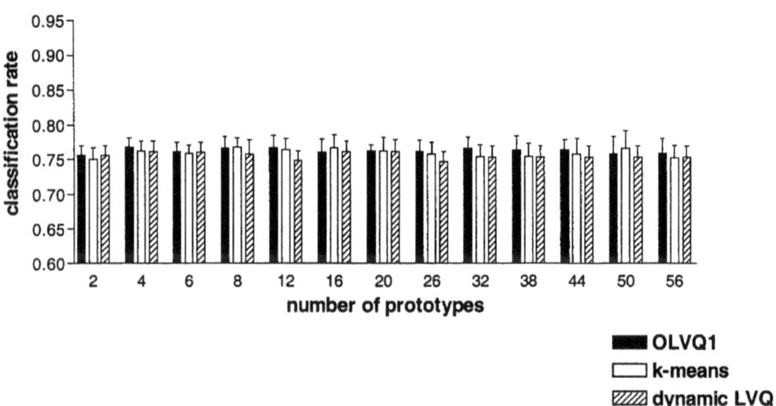

Figure 14. RBF results for the beat-to-beat variability data. The graphs show the results for the OLVQ1 prototype adaptation scheme, k-means and dynamic LVQ for different numbers of hidden neurons. The widths of the RBF functions are initialized via their distance to the next three prototypes (see text). Output weights are initialized to 1 for connections between prototypes of one class and their corresponding output unit, otherwise small values. The complete network $(\sigma_j, \mathbf{c}_j, \mathbf{w}_k)$ is re-trained with back-propagation with variable stepsize. Re-classification results are shown in the figure on the left and cross-validation results on the right (accuracy, averages over ten runs and standard deviations are given).

Table 7. Detailed RBF classification results of the three prototype adaptation schemes for the signal averaged data (3-dimensional, 8 hidden neurons): Re-classification and 10-fold cross-validation results are given (ten runs, mean ± standard deviation). The widths of the RBF functions are initialized via their distance to the next three prototypes (see text). The complete network (σ_j, $\mathbf{c}_j$, $\mathbf{w}_k$) is re-trained with back-propagation with variable stepsize.

RBF results for the signal-averaged data (8 hidden neurons)

OLVQ1

	Acc	Sensi	Speci	PPV	NPV
Re-val	86.1% ± 0.4%	70.9% ± 1.8%	99.2% ± 1.4%	98.8% ± 2%	79.8% ± 0.8%
Cross-val	84.4% ± 1%	69.8% ± 1.1%	97.1% ± 1.9%	95.4% ± 2.9%	78.8% ± 0.6%

k-means

	Acc	Sensi	Speci	PPV	NPV
Re-val	85.9% ± 1%	70% ± 1.4%	99.6% ± 0.8%	99.4% ± 1.4%	79.4% ± 0.9%
Cross-val	84.8% ± 1.3%	70.5% ± 1.1%	97.3% ± 2.1%	95.8% ± 3.2%	79.2% ± 0.8%

dynamic LVQ

	Acc	Sensi	Speci	PPV	NPV
Re-val	85.8% ± 0.9%	71.4% ± 1.2%	98.2% ± 1.4%	97.3% ± 2.2%	79.9% ± 0.7%
Cross-val	84.6% ± 0.9%	70.2% ± 0.7%	97.1% ± 1.7%	95.4% ± 2.4%	79.1% ± 0.4%

not only the three standard VLP parameters but processing sequences of beats, and the possible application of RBF networks in this assessment.

By using the more elaborate categorization methods of RBF networks compared to VLP assessment (see Section 4) on the 3-dimensional signal-averaged data an increase in accuracy of about 10% could be gained (VLP results: Acc = 72.6%, Sensi = 63.6%, Speci = 80.4%) in all cases of prototype based or RBF classification (scc Tables 5 and 7 and Figures 9,11 and 13). The increase from prototype based to RBF network categorization was moderate but still visible and was accompanied by a reduction of variance. All network classification results show only a slight difference between re-validation and cross-validation for a small number of prototypes or radial basis functions. This substantiates the robustness of the methods on this data. Surprisingly does the accuracy stagnate at about 86% for the re-validation case on all simulations, only the dynamic LVQ makes an exception and shows an over-adaptation to the data set, which is reflected in its poor generalization ability at higher prototype numbers. Unfortunately the sensitivity of all methods on the 3D data is still too low to qualify as a single screening test (see Section 2, Current status). Another issue of using signal-averaged features

Table 8. Detailed RBF classification results of the three prototype adaptation schemes for the beat-to-beat data (141-dimensional, 8 hidden neurons): Re-classification and 10-fold cross-validation results are given (ten runs, mean ± standard deviation). The widths of the RBF functions are initialized via their distance to the next three prototypes (see text). The complete network (σ_j, $\mathbf{c}_j$, $\mathbf{w}_k$) is re-trained with back-propagation with variable stepsize.

RBF results for the beat-to-beat data (8 hidden neurons)

OLVQ1

	Acc	Sensi	Speci	PPV	NPV
Re-val	86.6% ± 4.3%	83.6% ± 5.7%	89.2% ± 3.7%	87% ± 4.5%	86.4% ± 4.5%
Cross-val	76.5% ± 1.8%	69.8% ± 3.2%	82.4% ± 1.3%	77.3% ± 1.7%	76% ± 2%

k-means

	Acc	Sensi	Speci	PPV	NPV
Re-val	88.7% ± 3.5%	86.1% ± 5.8%	91% ± 3%	89.2% ± 3.6%	88.5% ± 4.2%
Cross-val	76.7% ± 1.4%	70.7% ± 2.5%	82% ± 1.2%	77.2% ± 1.5%	76.4% ± 1.6%

dynamic LVQ

	Acc	Sensi	Speci	PPV	NPV
Re-val	88.5% ± 2.8%	85.9% ± 4%	90.8% ± 2.3%	88.9% ± 2.8%	88.2% ± 3.1%
Cross-val	75.8% ± 2.1%	69.1% ± 3.7%	81.6% ± 1.4%	76.4% ± 1.9%	75.4% ± 2.4%

solely as predictors of SCD are their moderate positive predictive value (see Table 4) and, as far as the simulations of this paper are concerned, a problematic prognostic significance of the PVS result for SCD (see Table 3). The positive and negative predictive values presented here should be treated with care as the study population does not represent the true prevalence of SCD.

In the case of the 141-dimensional best-to-beat variability data there is also a substantial (7% - 15%) increase in classification accuracy (see Tables 6 and 8 and Figures 10, 12 and 14) compared to categorization via a single cut-off value on the sum of the variability features (re-val: Acc = 73.7%, Sensi = 68.2%, Speci = 78.4% [17]; 10-fold cross-val (mean ± stdev): Acc = 68.9% ± 5%, Sensi = 66.1% ± 8.7%, Speci = 71.4% ± 16.8%). Compared to the 3D data classification results drop when switching to the RBF network and training the output layer only. Interestingly, is the performance not influenced by the type of initialization of the kernel width in all cases on both data sets. Only on the high-dimensional data a re-tuning of the complete network seems to be mandatory to recover from and even increase, the performance compared to a purely prototype based classification.

All networks end, after being re-trained, in a comparable range of performance (within their prototype number), although this is not the case on the prototype layer. The difference between the supervised training methods of OLVQ1 and dynamic LVQ and the unsupervised k-means is most pronounced with the variability data (Figure 10). This is not too surprising as the 2-dimensional projection (Figure 7) also points in that direction.

The presented results indicate that both types of features are of a supplementary nature (results on sensitivity). This calls for studies in which both are combined. Further investigations into the uncertainty of the target classification (long term follow-up) are needed to assess the diagnostic and prognostic value of the presented methods, their combination and their applicability to different patient groups.

Acknowledgment

An investigation like the above would not be possible without the support of many people, in particular we would like to thank André Müller, and especially Dr. Martin Höher, Professor Vinzenz Hombach and Professor Günther Palm for providing an inspiring research environment.

References

[1] Buxton, A., Lee, K., Fisher, J., Josephson, M., Prystowsky, E., and Hafley, G. (1999), "A randomized study of the prevention of sudden death in patients with coronary artery disease. Multicenter Unsustained Tachycardia Trial Investigators," *N.Engl.J Med*, vol. 341, no. 25, pp. 1882-1890.

[2] Moss, A., Hall, W., Cannom, D., Daubert, J., Higgins, S., Klein, H., Levine, J., Saksena, S., Waldo, A., Wilber, D., Brown, M., and Heo, M. (1996), "Improved survival with an implanted defibrillator in patients with coronary disease at high risk for ventricular arrhythmia," *New Engl J Med*, vol. 335, pp. 1933-1940.

[3] Moss, A. (1997), "Update on MADIT: the Multicenter Autonomic Defibrillator Implantation Trial," *Am J Cardiol*, vol. 79, no. 6A, pp. 16-17.

[4] Sherif, N.E., Scherlag, B., Lazzara, R., and Hope, R. (1977), "Re-entrant ventricular arrhythmias in the late myocardial infarction period. 1. Conduction characteristics in the zone," *Circulation*, vol. 55, pp. 686-702.

[5] Sherif, N.E., Hope, R., Scherlag, B., and Lazzara, R. (1977), "Re-entrant ventricular arrhythmias in the late myocardial infarction period. 2. Patterns of initiation and termination of re-entry," *Circulation*, vol. 55, pp. 702-719.

[6] Ciaccio, E. (2000), "Localization of the slow conduction zone during reentrant ventricular tachycardia," *Circulation*, vol. 102, pp. 464-469.

[7] Antman, E. and Braunwald, E. (1997), "Acute myocardial infarction," in Braunwald, E. (Ed.), *Heart Disease - a Textbook of Cardiovascular Medicine*, W.B. Saunders Company, Philadelphia-London-Toronto-Montreal-Sydney-Tokyo, pp. 1184-1288.

[8] Lamas, G., Flaker, G., Mitchell, G., Smith, J., S.C., Gersh, B., Wun, C., Moye, L., Rouleau, J., Rutherford, J., and Pfeffer, M. (1995), "Effect of infarct artery patency on prognosis after acute myocardial infarction. The Survival and Ventricular Enlargement Investigators," *Circulation*, vol. 92, no. 5, pp. 1101-1109.

[9] Julian, D., Camm, A., Frangin, G., Janse, M., Munoz, A., Schwartz, P., and Simon, P. (1997), "Randomised trial of effect of amiodarone on mortality in patients with left-ventricular dysfunction after recent myocardial infarction: EMIAT. European Myocardial Infarct Amiodarone Trial Investigators" [published errata appeared in *Lancet*, 1997 Apr 19, vol. 349, no. 9059, p. 1180, and 1997 Jun 14, vol. 349, no. 9067, p. 1776]," *Lancet*, vol. 349, no. 9053, pp. 667-674.

[10] Cairns, J., Connolly, S., Roberts, R., and Gent, M. (1997), "Randomised trial of outcome after myocardial infarction in patients

with frequent or repetitive ventricular premature depolarisations: CAMIAT. Canadian Amiodarone Myocardial Infarction Arrhythmia Trial Investigators [published erratum appeared in *Lancet*," 1997 Jun 14, vol. 349, no. 9067, p. 1776] [see comments], *Lancet*, vol. 349, no. 9053, pp. 675-682.

[11] The Acute Infarction Ramipril Efficacy (AIRE) Study Investigators (1993), "Effect of ramipril on mortality and morbidity of survivors of acute myocardial infarction with clinical evidence of heart failure," *Lancet*, vol. 342, no. 8875, pp. 821-828.

[12] Amiodarone Trials Meta-Analysis Investigators (1997), "Effect of prophylactic amiodarone on mortality after acute myocardial infarction and in congestive heart failure: meta-analysis of individual data from 6500 patients in randomized trials," *Lancet*, vol. 350, no. 9089, pp. 1417-1424.

[13] Breithardt, G., Borggrefe, M., Martinez Rubio, A., and Budde, T. (1989), "Pathophysiological mechanisms of ventricular tachyarrhythmias," *Eur Heart J*, vol. Suppl.E, pp. 9-18.

[14] Hombach, V., Braun, V., Hopp, H., Gil-Sanchez, D., Scholl, H., Behrenbeck, D., Tauchert, M., and H., Hilger (1982), "The applicability of the signal averaging technique in clinical cardiology," *Clin. Cardiol.*, vol. 5, pp. 107-124.

[15] Hombach, V., Hocher, M., and Kochs, M. (1993), "Clinical significance of high resolution electrocardiography – sinus node, His bundle and ventricular late potentials," in Gomes, J. (Ed.), *Signal Averaged Electrocardiography, Concepts, Methods and Applications*, Kluwer Academic Publishers, Dordrecht-Boston-London, pp. 267-295.

[16] Hoeher, M., Axmann, J., Eggeling, T., Kochs, M., Weismuller, P., and Hombach, V. (1993), "Beat-to-beat variability of ventricular late potentials in the unaveraged high resolution electrocardiogram – effects of antiarrhythmic drugs," *Eur. Heart J*, vol. 14 (Suppl. E), pp. 33-39.

[17] Kestler, H.A., Wöhrle, J., and Höher, M. (2000), "Cardiac vulnerability assessment from electrical microvariability of the high-resolution electrocardiogram," *Medical & Biological Engineering & Computing*, vol. 38, pp. 88-92.

[18] Higham, P. and Campbell, R. (1994), "QT dispersion," *Br. Heart J*, vol. 71, no. 6, pp. 508-510.

[19] Algra, A., Tijssen, J., Roelandt, J., Pool, J., and Lubsen, J. (1993), "QT interval variables from 24 hour electrocardiography and the two year risk of sudden death," *Br. Heart J*, vol. 70, no. 1, pp. 43-48.

[20] Rosenbaum, D., Jackson, L., Smith, J., Garan, H., Ruskin, J., and Cohen, R. (1994), "Electrical alternans and vulnerability to ventricular arrhythmias," *New Engl J Med*, vol. 330, pp. 235-241.

[21] Smith, J., Clancy, E., Valeri, C., Ruskin, J., and Cohen, R. (1988), "Electrical alternans and cardiac electrical instability," *Circulation*, vol. 77, no. 1, pp. 110-121.

[22] Kleiger, R., Miller, J., Bigger-JT, J., and Moss, A. (1987), "Decreased heart rate variability and its association with increased mortality after acute myocardial infarction," *Am J Cardiol*, vol. 59, no. 4, pp. 256-262.

[23] Malik, M., Farrell, T., Cripps, T., and Camm, A. (1989), "Heart rate variability in relation to prognosis after myocardial infarction: selection of optimal processing techniques," *Eur. Heart J*, vol. 10, pp. 1060-1074.

[24] Bigger Jr, J., Fleiss, J., Steinman, R., Rolnitzky, L., Kleiger, R., and Rottman, J. (1992), "Frequency domain measures of heart period variability and mortality after myocardial infarction," *Circulation*, vol. 85, no. 1, pp. 164-171.

[25] Task Force of the European Society of Cardiology and the North American Society of Pacing and Electrophysiology (1996), "Heart rate variability: standards of measurement, physiological interpretation and clinical use," [see comments], *Circulation*, vol. 93, no. 5, pp. 1043-1065.

[26] Breithardt, G., Seipel, L., Meyer, T., and Abendroth, R. (1982), "Prognostic significance of repetitive ventricular response during programmed ventricular stimulation," *Am J Cardiol.*, vol. 49, pp. 693-698.

[27] Gonzalez, R., Arriagada, D., Corbalan, R., Chamorro, G., Fajuri, A., and Rodriguez, J. (1988), "Role of programmed electrical stimulation of the heart in risk stratification post-myocardial infarction," *Pacing Clin. Electrophysiol.*, vol. 11, pp. 283-288.

[28] Hamer, A., Vohra, J., Hunt, D., and Sloman, G. (1982), "Prediction of sudden death by electrophysiologic studies in high risk patients surviving acute myocardial infarction," *Am J Cardiol*, vol. 50, no. 2, pp. 223-229.

[29] Richards, D., Cody, D., Denniss, A., Russell, P., Young, A., and Uther, J. (1983), "Ventricular electrical instability: a predictor of death after myocardial infarction," *Am J Cardiol*, vol. 51, no. 1, pp. 75-80.

[30] Marchlinski, F., Buxton, A., Waxman, H., and Josephson, M. (1983), "Identifying patients at risk of sudden death after myocardial infarction: value of the response to programmed stimulation, degree of ventricular ectopic activity and severity of left ventricular dysfunction," *Am J Cardiol*, vol. 52, no. 10, pp. 1190-1196.

[31] Waspe, L., Seinfeld, D., Ferrick, A., Kim, S., Matos, J., and Fisher, J. (1985), "Prediction of sudden death and spontaneous ventricular tachycardia in survivors of complicated myocardial infarction: value of the response to programmed stimulation using a maximum of three ventricular extrastimuli," *J Am Coll Cardiol*, vol. 5, no. 6, pp. 1292-1301.

[32] Roy, D., Marchand, E., Theroux, P., Waters, D., Pelletier, G., and Bourassa, M. (1985), "Programmed ventricular stimulation in survivors of an acute myocardial infarction," *Circulation*, vol. 72, no. 3, pp. 487-494.

[33] Santarelli, P., Bellocci, F., Loperfido, F., Mazzari, M., Mongiardo, R., Montenero, A., Manzoli, U., and Denes, P. (1985), "Ventricular arrhythmia induced by programmed ventricular stimulation after

acute myocardial infarction," *Am J Cardiol*, vol. 55, no. 4, pp. 391-394.

[34] Bhandari, A., Rose, J., Kotlewski, A., Rahimtoola, S., and Wu, D. (1985), "Frequency and significance of induced sustained ventricular tachycardia or fibrillation two weeks after acute myocardial infarction," *Am J Cardiol*, vol. 56, no. 12, pp. 737-742.

[35] Kowey, P., Waxman, H., Greenspon, A., Greenberg, R., Poll, D., Kutalek, S., Gessman, L., Muenz, L., Friehling, T., Marinchak, R., Volosin, K., Beauregard, L., Kidwell, G., Kempf, F., and White, M. (1990), "Value of electrophysiologic testing in patients with previous myocardial infarction and nonsustained ventricular tachycardia," *Am J Cardiol.*, vol. 65, pp. 594-598.

[36] Iesaka, Y., Nogami, A., Aonuma, K., Nitta, J., Chun, Y., Fujiwara, H., and Hiraoka, M. (1990), "Prognostic significance of sustained monomorphic ventricular tachycardia induced by programmed ventricular stimulation using up to triple extrastimuli in survivors of acute myocardial infarction," *Am J Cardiol.*, vol. 65, pp. 1057-1063.

[37] Bourke, J., Richards, D., Ross, D., Wallace, E., McGuire, M., and Uther, J. (1991), "Routine programmed electrical stimulation in survivors of acute myocardial infarction for prediction of spontaneous ventricular tachyarrhythmias during follow-up: results, optimal stimulation protocol and cost-effective screening," *J Am Coll. Cardiol.*, vol. 18, pp. 780-788.

[38] Bhandari, A., Hong, R., Kotlewski, A., McIntosh, N., Au, P., Sankooikal, A., and Rahimtoola, S. (1989), "Prognostic significance of programmed ventricular stimulation in survivors of acute myocardial infarction," *Br. Heart J*, vol. 61, pp. 410-416.

[39] Steinbeck, G., Andresen, D., Bach, P., Haberl, R., Oeff, M., Hoffmann, E., and Von Leitner, E. (1992), "A comparison of electrophysiologically guided antiarrhythmic drug therapy with beta-blocker therapy in patients with symptomatic, sustained ventricular tachyarrhythmias," *New Engl J Med*, vol. 327, pp. 987-992.

[40] Denniss, A., Richards, D., Cody, D., Russell, P., Young, A., Cooper, M., Ross, D., and Uther, J. (1986), "Prognostic significance of ventricular tachycardia and fibrillation induced at programmed stimulation and delayed potentials detected on the signal-averaged electrocardiograms of survivors of acute myocardial infarction," *Circulation*, vol. 74, pp. 731-745.

[41] Bhandari, A., Widerhorn, J., Sager, P., Leon, C., Hong, R., Kotlewski, A., Hackett, J., and Rahimtoola, S. (1992), "Prognostic significance of programmed ventricular stimulation in patients surviving complicated acute myocardial infarction: a prospective study," *Am Heart J*, vol. 124, no. 1, pp. 87-96.

[42] Gomes, J., Horowitz, S., Millner, M., Machac, J., Winters, S., and Barreca, P. (1987), "Relation of late potentials to ejection fraction and wall motion abnormalities in acute myocardial infarction," *Am J Cardiol*, vol. 59, no. 12, pp. 1071-1074.

[43] Denniss, A., Richards, D., Cody, D., *et al.* (1987), "Correlation between signal-averaged electrocardiogram and programmed stimulation in patients with and without spontaneous ventricular tachyarrhythmias," *Am J Cardiol.*, vol. 59, pp. 586-590.

[44] Kuchar, D., Thorburn, C., and Sammel, N. (1987), "Prediction of serious arrhythmic events after myocardial infarction: signal-averaged electrocardiogram, Holter monitoring and radionuclide ventriculography," *J Am Coll. Cardiol.*, vol. 9, pp. 531-538.

[45] Camm, A. and Fei, L. (1995), "Risk stratification following myocardial infarction: heart rate variability and other risk factors," in Malik, M. and Camm, A. (Eds.), *Heart rate variability*, Futura, Armonk, NY, pp. 369-392.

[46] Zabel, M., Klingenheben, T., Franz, M., and Hohnloser, S. (1998), "Assessment of QT dispersion for prediction of mortality or arrhythmic events after myocardial infarction. results of a prospective, long-term follow-up study," *Circulation*, vol. 97, pp. 2543-2550.

[47] Fananapazir, L., McAreavey, D., and Epstein, N. (1995), "Hypertrophic cardiomyopathy," in Zipes, D. and Jalife, J. (Eds.), *Cardiac*

electrophysiology – from cell to bedside, 2nd edition, W.B. Saunders Company, Philadelphia, pp. 769-779.

[48] Mancini, D., Eisen, H., Kussmaul, W., Mull, R., Edmunds-LH, J., and Wilson, J. (1991), "Value of peak exercise oxygen consumption for optimal timing of cardiac transplantation in ambulatory patients with heart failure," *Circulation*, vol. 83, no. 3, pp. 778-786.

[49] Pedretti, R., Etro, M., Laporta, A., Braga, S., and Caru, B. (1993), "Prediction of late arrhythmic events after acute myocardial infarction from combined use of noninvasive prognostic variables and inducibility of sustained monomorphic ventricular tachycardia," *Am J Cardiol.*, vol. 71, pp. 1131-1141.

[50] Zoni-Berisso, M., Molini, D., Mela, G., and Vecchio, C. (1996), "Value of programmed ventricular stimulation in predicting sudden death and sustained ventricular tachycardia in survivors of acute myocardial infarction," *Am J Cardiol*, vol. 77, no. 9, pp. 673-680.

[51] Ikeda, T., Sakata, T., Takami, M., Kondo, N., Tezuka, N., Nakae, T., Noro, M., Enjoji, Y., Abe, R., Sugi, K., and Yamaguchi, T. (2000), "Combined assessment of T-wave alternans and late potentials used to predict arrhythmic events after myocardial infarction," *J Am Coll Cardiol*, vol. 35, pp. 722-730.

[52] Anderson, K., Shusterman, V., Brode, S., Gottipaty, V., Schwartzman, D., and Weiss, R. (1999), "Noninvasive testing for selection of patients for electrophysiological study," *Annals of Noninvasive Electrophysiology*, vol. 4, no. 4, pp. 434-442.

[53] Schmidt, G., Malik, M., Barthel, P., Schneider, R., Ulm, K., Rolnitzky, L., Camm, J., Bigger, J., and Schmig, A. (1999), "Heart rate turbulance after ventricular premature beats as a predictor of mortality after acute myocardial infarction," *Lancet*, vol. 353, pp. 1390-96.

[54] Bishop, C. (1995), *Neural Networks for Pattern Recognition*, Oxford University Press, Oxford, U.K.

[55] Kohonen, T. (1989), *Self-Organization and Associative Memory*, Springer-Verlag, Berlin.

[56] Lloyd, S.P. (1957), "Least squares quantization in PCMs," Tech. rep., Bell Telephone Laboratories Paper, Murray Hill, NJ.

[57] Linde, Y., Buzo, A., and Gray, R.M. (1980), "An algorithm for vector quantizer design," *IEEE Transactions on Communication*, vol. 28, pp. 84-95.

[58] MacQueen, J. (1967), "Some methods for classification and analysis of multivariate observations," *Proceedings of the Fifth Berkeley Symposium on Mathematical Statistics and Probability*, vol. 1, pp. 281-297.

[59] Backer, E. (1995), *Computer-Assisted Reasoning in Cluster Analysis*, Prentice Hall, New York.

[60] Odorico, R. (1997), "Learning vector quantization with training count (LVQTC)," *Neural Networks*, vol. 10, no. 6, pp. 1083-1088.

[61] Kestler, H.A., Farschtschi, A.A., and Wein, P.H. (1994), "Untersuchung und Simulation neuronaler Netze mit dynamischer Strukturänderung," *Automatisierungstechnische Praxis*, vol. 36, no. 2, pp. 47-51.

[62] Hertz, J., Krogh, A., and Palmer, R.G. (1991), *Introduction to the Theory of Neural Computation*, Addison Wesley, New York.

[63] Wasserman, P. (1993), *Advanced Methods in Neural Computing*, Van Nostrand Reinhold, New York.

[64] Armijo, L. (1966), "Minimization of functions having Lipschitz continuous first partial derivatives," *Pacific Journal of Mathematics*, vol. 16, no. 1, pp. 1-3.

[65] Magoulas, G., Vrahatis, M., and Androulakis, G. (1997), "Effective backpropagation training with variable stepsize," *Neural Networks*, vol. 10, no. 1, pp. 69-82.

[66] Gomes, J., Winters, S., Martinson, M., Machac, J., Stewart, D., and Targonski, A. (1989), "The prognostic significance of quantitative signal-averaged variables relative to clinical variables, site of myocardial infarction, ejection fraction and ventricular premature beats," *JACC*, vol. 13, pp. 377-384.

[67] Höher, M. and Hombach, V. (1991), "Ventrikuläre Spätpotentiale – Teil I Grundlagen," *Herz & Rhythmus*, vol. 3, no. 3, pp. 1-7.

[68] Simson, M. (1981), "Use of signals in the terminal QRS complex to identify patients with ventricular tachycardia after myocardial infarction," *Circulation*, vol. 64, no. 2, pp. 235-242.

[69] Breithardt, G. and Borggrefe, M. (1986), "Pathophysiological mechanisms and clinical significance of ventricular late potentials," *Eur Heart J*, vol. 7, pp. 364-385.

[70] Breithardt, G., Cain, M., El-Sherif, N., Flowers, N., Hombach, V., Janse, M., Simson, M., and Steinbeck, G. (1991), "Standards for analysis of ventricular late potentials using high resolution or signal-averaged electrocardiography," *Eur Heart J*, vol. 12, pp. 473-80.

[71] Sammon, J. (1969), "A nonlinear mapping for data structure analysis," *IEEE Transactions on Computers*, vol. C-18, pp. 401-409.

[72] Ritscher, D.E., Ernst, E., Kammrath, H.G., Hombach, V., and Höher, M. (1997), "High-resolution ECG analysis platform with enhanced resolution," *IEEE Computers in Cardiology*, vol. 24, pp. 291-294.

[73] Van Bemmel, J. and Musen, M. (Eds.) (1997), *Handbook of Medical Informatics*, Springer Verlag, Heidelberg / New York.

[74] De Boor, C. (1978), *A Practical Guide to Splines*, Springer Verlag.

[75] Kestler, H.A., Höher, M., Palm, G., Kochs, M., and Hombach, V. (1996), "Time domain variability of high resolution beat-to-beat recordings classified by neural networks," in Murray, A. and Arzbaecher, R. (Eds.), *Computers in Cardiology*, IEEE Computer Society, pp. 317-320.

Chapter 7

Biomedical Applications of Radial Basis Function Networks

A. Saastamoinen, M. Lehtokangas, A. Värri, and J. Saarinen

An important and interesting group of applications of Radial Basis Function (RBF) networks lies on the field of biomedical engineering. These applications include intelligent signal and image analysis techniques ranging from classification and waveform detection methods to decision making and decision support systems. This chapter begins with a review on the biomedical applications of radial basis function networks. After that, we discuss some general design considerations based on our experiences on the field. Finally, as an example on the design process in general, we present our recent contribution on biomedical waveform detection.

1 RBF Networks in Medicine

During recent years, the number of biomedical applications using radial basis function (RBF) networks has been steadily growing. To give an impression on the wide applicability of RBF networks in various biomedical applications, this chapter will start with a literature review, followed by a discussion on the design process of biomedical pattern recognition systems.

1.1 ECG Signal Processing

The electrocardiogram (ECG) is one of the most important tools both in the intensive and long time care of cardiac patients. This is due to the fact that ECG can clearly point out different changes in cardiac pathology. In various ECG signal processing applications reliable detection of QRS complexes is of vital importance. Therefore, many methods for QRS detection have been presented in recent years. The following is a brief review of a method presented by Downes [8] where RBF networks and ART II-masking fields approaches are used to detect and classify QRS complexes.

According to Downes, previous experience has shown that the use of time delay vectors as inputs produces faster training and prediction of RBF networks. According to Taken's theorem, attractors were reconstructed from the time series by plotting time delay vectors in phase space by picking samples between a time delay τ into the attractor vector. This time delay was determined by using Fraser's mutual information method to ensure that the points of the attractor are maximally independent. The appropriate dimension for attractor reconstruction was determined by inspecting the singular spectrum of the system.

Two types of RBF networks were used in these experiments. In addition to the standard RBF network, the adaptive RBF network architecture by Mel and Omohundro was tested. Both networks were trained with a data set containing 100 QRS examples on each of the different pathological classes found in the data set. A separate network was trained for each output class. The mean predictive error for the both networks with 100 centers was found to be 0.005.

1.2 Ischemia Classification

In the intensive care of cardiac patients, one of the most important skills is the reliable detection of ischemia, i.e., the detection of decreased blood flow to the myocardium. This dangerous condition, that may be caused by vessel occlusion or muscle injury, can be detected on the ECG as ST-segment depressions or elevations. In the literature, a number of methods for the detection of this state have been presented. Traditionally, these methods have been based on digital filtering, syntactic methods and temporal properties of the first derivative of the recorded ECG.

Recently, Stamkopoulos *et al.* [32] have presented a new method based on the application of nonlinear principal component analysis and neural networks. Before feature extraction the recorded ECG was preprocessed by determining first the R-peaks of the ECG based on the algorithm presented by Pan and Tompkins. After that, for each heart cycle a sample vector containing the ST-segment was extracted. These input patterns were of predetermined length according to the recommendations of the European ST-T database. Feature extraction was then performed by determining the differences between the ischemic ST-segments and the normal ST-segment template, that was constructed for each recording as the average of the 10 first normal ST-segments in the recording. The averaging not only reduces the effect of noise but also makes the algorithm insensitive to the inter-patient differences and changes in the leads used during the recordings.

Before feeding the input patterns into the Radial Basis Function network classifier, nonlinear Principal Component Analysis (NLPCA) realized with an NLPCA neural model was performed to reduce the dimensionality of the input data. The resulting principal components were used as inputs for the RBF network. Network centers and widths of the Gaussian hidden neurons were selected by using a self-organizing algorithm and the delta rule was applied for the determination of the weights between the hidden layer and the output neuron. After the construction of the network, a threshold value for the output of the classifier was selected in such a way that 80% of the training patterns were correctly classified.

Several files of the European ST-T database were used as the basis for data used during the experiments. Each of these files contains more than 4000 heart cycles with normal, elevated and depressed ST-segments. For the training set, only the normal ST-segments were used. Thus, the problem could be considered a one-class problem where the ischemic ST-segments and artefacts formed the other output class. The training was performed separately for each patient. Depending on the file used, classification accuracy for abnormal beats was found to be between 60.6% and 99.6% with an average value of 81.9% when classification accuracy for the normal segments was approximately 80%.

1.3 Diagnostics of Hypertrophy and Myocardial Infarction

Fraser *et al.* [10] have presented an automated method for the diagnostics of myocardial infarction based on the application of electrocardiographic data and clinical history of the patient. Their data set contained the clinical details of 500 patients admitted to a coronary care unit. In addition to ECG parameters containing ST elevation, ST depression and T- and Q-wave properties, a set of clinical symptoms were used as input information. In total, feature vectors contained 27 elements. The correct diagnosis was determined by a consultant physician in the conventional manner. The training set consisted of 200 cases while the remaining 300 cases were used for validation.

For the classification, back-propagation (BP) and radial basis function networks were compared. For the BP network, optimum results were obtained with a network having 6 hidden neurons. For the RBF network, 40 gaussian hidden units were used. The results were slightly better for the RBF network with a sensitivity of 85.7% and a specificity of 86.1%. To examine the dependence between sensitivity and specificity of the classifier, Receiver Operating Characteristic (ROC) analysis was performed. Based on the ROC curve quite a successful performance was obtained.

Bortolan *et al.* [2] have described a hybrid architecture combining fuzzy preprocessing with traditional neural network approach for diagnostic ECG classification. Instead of traditional quantitative data description and feature extraction they describe the input feature space with Gaussian radial basis functions that can be considered as fuzzy member functions. Final diagnostic classification results are obtained by classifying the fuzzy input descriptions by means of a traditional Multi-Layer Perceptron (MLP) network.

In the presented experiments, a large database of rest ECG recordings was used. The data set contained in total 3266 12-lead rest ECG recordings each of them falling to one of seven classes: normal, left ventricular hypertrophy, right ventricular hypertrophy, biventricular hypertrophy, inferior myocardial infarction, anterior myocardial infarction, and mixed myocardial infarction. From this data set, 2446 recordings were randomly selected to form the training set whereas the other 820 recordings were reserved for testing. Input parameters for the system were selected through a two-phase feature reduction process. For each lead of a recording, 45 parameters derived mainly from the properties of QRS complexes, T waves, and ST segments were first computed. This original feature set containing 540 parameters was reduced on a clinical basis to a set of 166 parameters. Finally, 39 statistically most discriminating parameters were selected amongst the reduced data set to form the input feature set for fuzzy preprocessing.

For fuzzy data abstraction, Gaussian membership functions in two different configurations were applied. In Multi-RBF approach, all the input parameters were fed to Gaussian membership functions related to each seven diagnostic classes. Initial values for the RBF units related to jth input feature were determined by estimating sample means and standard deviations for the jth input parameter in each diagnostic class. Fine-tuning of initial RBF parameters was then performed by applying delta rule based training. In Single-RBF approach, only one RBF function for each input feature was utilized. In this case, statistical properties of normal class were used as initial values for the RBF units. Output values of these activation functions were then fed to the traditional Multilayer Perceptron Network (MLP) that was used to determine the final classification results. MLP network was trained by using a modified back-propagation algorithm. For comparison, corresponding experiments for traditional MLP network without fuzzy preprocessing were also performed. For Single-RBF and traditional MLP approaches, networks with 30 hidden neurons were applied. In Multi-RBF approach, MLP network with 50 hidden neurons was applied instead. Initially, all the MLP weights were set to be equal to 1.

In the experiments, four different classification strategies, denoted as strategies A, B, C, and D were compared. First, all the output classes for which the corresponding output was greater than 0 were considered as possible classes (A). This rule was then modified in such a way, that in those cases where all the calculated outputs were negative, the input pattern was assigned either as normal (B) or as a member of the class corresponding to the highest output (C). In addition to these three rules, maximum rule was also used (D). Classification strategies C and D were found to give the best performance. Effects of the training of RBF parameters and MLP weights on the final performance of the classifier were also investigated. This was done by going through all the different combinations on using initial and trained RBF units and MLP weights and comparing system performance between the cases. Additionally, effect of the widths of RBF units was investigated by comparing the results with initial standard deviations to those obtained with the first three integer multiples of the initial standard deviation. The results showed that the output error converges slower, when MLP weights are trained and when the widths of RBF units increase. Best results were obtained in those cases where only MLP weights or RBF parameters were trained or the initial values of these parameters were used. In addition to the comparison on the basis of output error values, ROC analysis was also applied. In general, specificity of over 90 % was reached whereas sensitivity varied between 45 % and 70 % depending on the selected classification strategy.

During the experiments, possibility for decreasing the complexity of the MLP part of neuro-fuzzy classifier was also investigated. Network pruning process was carried on by adding a punishment term in the back-propagation algorithm in order to generate a network with small connection weights. All the neurons with weights smaller than a predetermined threshold were then removed from the network. To investigate the effect of pruning on the performance of the system, performance of the pruned network on several pruning threshold levels was compared. It was found that heavy pruning especially deteriorates the sensitivity of the classifier, particularly in multi-RBF approach.

1.4 Image Matching

Image matching is a method where a correction is applied to one of a pair of images of the same or similar scene in such a way, that the two images become more alike. In the easiest sense, this means simple translation or rotation correction. However, in many cases a deformable mapping is needed leading to a complex transformation. This is the case for example when head MRI images are compared to a brain atlas image, when images acquired before and after administration of some contrast enhancing pharmaceutical are compared and when images acquired a considerable time apart or in different physiological conditions are compared [7].

One way to determine the transformation between two images is to apply the landmark based approach [7]. In this method, a set of corresponding pixels in different images are first selected as landmarks. After that, coordinate transformation between the image spaces is determined in such a way that the landmarks in the image to be matched are mapped to the landmarks in the reference image and other pixels are interpolated in an optimal way. However, manual selection of landmarks makes this method very time-consuming. Additionally, for example in biomedical applications, the anatomy of the imaged organs varies from patient to patient making the selection of landmarks extremely complicated or impossible.

Davis *et al.* [7] have proposed a method for matching 3D magnetic resonance images of the breast for use in the diagnosis of breast cancer. Instead of the typical landmark based approach, they applied the RBF network with thin-plate spline hidden neurons to determine the coordinate transformation. The desired coordinate transformation was determined by selecting the RBF network centers and weight factors in such a way that the normalized correlation between the two images was optimized by using the gradient descent method. In this way, the selection of landmarks could be avoided. At the beginning of the training, RBF center locations were selected in such a way that their distribution in the image was uniform and all the weight factors were set to zero. Thus, initially there was no deformation. The method was also tested with head MRIs with slightly different initialization.

Three-dimensional breast MRI images with dimensions of $256 \times 256 \times 128$ from four different subjects were used for evaluating the method. As similarity measures mean squared error, mean average error and correlation coefficient were used. These values were provided for uncorrected and corrected image pairs for the networks with 10, 20, 50, and 200 hidden units. Although the best results were obtained for the network with 20 hidden units, almost equal results were obtained for all of the network architecture. When MSE, MAE and the correlation coefficient for the uncorrected image pair were 360.6, 10.07, and 0.79, respectively, after correction these values were around 152.2, 6.96, and 0.91, respectively. Thus, this method can be considered successful.

1.5 Image Segmentation

The main objectives of biomedical imaging are to inspect and localize various regions and to measure different parameters. Before this is possible the image must be segmented into separate regions consisting of different tissue types. Image segmentation is also the first step in automated contextual analysis and image understanding. Kovacevic and Loncaric [21] have presented an automated segmentation method for computerized tomography (CT) head images. With their method the image is partitioned into background and four tissue classes that include skull, brain, calcifications, and intracerebral brain hemorrhage. After segmentation it is possible to determine various parameters, such as size and position, of the detected hemorrhagic regions.

The segmentation algorithm consists of three phases. The first phase consists of image brightness normalization and feature extraction using the receptive field approach. Elements of the feature vectors for the pixels are calculated from the brightness values of the current pixel and selected pixels in its neighborhood that belong to the receptive field. The receptive field consists of several receptive rings with a fixed number of pixels. For each receptive ring, mean and standard deviation of the brightness values are computed. Following this, pixels are classified into the different tissue classes with a radial basis function network. Final segmentation results are formed by merging the pixels belonging in the same tissue class into regions with an expert system based on assumptions related to minimal region sizes and on possible region neighborhood relations.

In the experiments done by Kovacevic and Loncaric real images with 512×512 pixels and 256 gray levels were used. Images were obtained by digitizing CT films with a camera. Several experiments were performed to find the optimal size of the receptive field and optimal number of hidden neurons in the RBF network. The best results were obtained with network topology 12-30-5. Depending on the type of hidden function used, the segmentation error varied between 1.5% (Gaussian) and 2.8% (multi-quadratic). The segmentation performance of the RBF network was also compared to the MLP network with comparable complexity. Although the segmentation error in the training set was significantly smaller for the MLP network, the results for the RBF network in the generalization test were remarkably better than those obtained for the MLP network.

1.6 Source Localization

Bioelectromagnetism is a discipline that is related to the measurement of electric and magnetic fields caused by the activity of neural and muscle cells of excitable tissues and the localization of these sources based on measured field distributions. For the forward problem, i.e., for field distribution in the body, an analytical solution for an appropriate head or torso model can be found when the parameters of the source causing the field distribution are known [24]. For the determination of electrical potentials, methods known as finite element method (FEM) or boundary element method (BEM) can be used. However, localization of the sources of bioelectrical and biomagnetic fields based on noninvasive measurements of electric potentials or magnetic field distributions outside the body is in general an extremely complicated problem. For this inverse problem there is no analytical solution. Therefore, problem of source localization can be solved only numerically and only under certain conditions [24]. In general, the iterative algorithms used for this purpose require an extremely large amount of computing power and processing time.

Schlang *et al.* [31] presented a method for speeding up the reconstruction of underlying dipole sources by applying neural networks. With this method a large amount of computing power is needed only during the training phase of the system, whereas the hardware requirements during practical application are remarkably lower. The main objective of this method is to reconstruct the parameters of the underlying sources based on the recorded magnetoencephalogram (MEG), i.e., the magnetic field generated by the active neurons in the brain [24]. The method is based on the assumption of a single electric current dipole situating focally somewhere inside the head. The field distributions that are not generated by a dipole-like source distribution are considered to be noisy inputs. Therefore, in addition to the exact localization of the sources of noise-free field distributions, the aim is to optimally extrapolate the noisy field distributions by relating them to the most similar noise-free distributions.

To generate the training data for the RBF network they performed a large set of forward calculations of the magnetic fields caused by single dipole sources that were uniformly distributed inside the head model. These simulated magnetic fields were sampled at 37 sensor locations in accordance with the montage definition used by Siemens KRENIKON recorder. Field intensities at these locations and the corresponding dipole parameters, i.e., location and magnitude of the dipole source, were used as the basis of the training data. In total, the training data set contained 10,000 patterns of noise-free dipole maps.

During the experiments, various network architectures were used. In addition to the standard RBF network, the RBF network with Partitioning to One (PTO) approach was applied. All of the networks were trained with a noise-free training set. For the conventional RBF networks of 50 and 200 hidden neurons and a RBF network with PTO of 500 hidden neurons and 15 inputs after PCA, localization accuracy without noise was 0.32 cm, 0.23 cm, and 0.27 cm, respectively. Localization accuracy was defined as the distance in centimeters within which half of the dipoles were correctly localized. When the noisy generalization set was used, localization accuracy was 1.7 cm, 1.3 cm, and 1.1 cm, respectively. These results were similar to those reported for the iterative Levenberg-Marquardt (LM) algorithm (less than 0.1 cm without noise and 1 cm for noisy data) and remarkably better than the results obtained for MLP networks of 50 and 200 hidden neurons. For noise-free generalization data the localization accuracy was 0.7 cm and 0.6 cm, whereas for noisy data the accuracy was 2.9 cm and 4.1 cm, respectively. The authors conclude that this method speeds up the source localization by one to three orders of magnitude compared to the conventional LM algorithm.

1.7 Performance Monitoring

Vigilance studies form an important branch of sleep medicine. The main purpose of these studies is to examine a subject's tendency to get tired or fall asleep during some monotonous task such as driving a vehicle at night or monitoring an industrial process. Changes in vigilance can be monitored by performing a monotonous reaction time test combined with a simultaneous recording of several electrophysiological variables such as electroencephalography (EEG), eye movement activity (EOG), and mental or submental muscle activity (EMG). Typically, the elecrophysiological recording is first scored by a neurophysiologist to find changes in the subject's vigilance. Following this, correlation between the state of vigilance and the performance of the subject in the reaction test can be estimated.

Kirk and LaCourse [18] have proposed a method for predicting subject's responses to given stimuli based on the power spectrum of the recorded EEG. Their reaction test is based on a set of eight colored matrices. Two of these randomized color matrices used as test stimuli contain an inlaid diamond. To be able to track relatively fast changes in vigilance the colored matrix on the screen is changed twice per second. The subject has 1800 milliseconds to respond. Otherwise the stimulus is considered to be missed. The subject is asked to press a button after recognizing a diamond on the screen. Each test contains three 30-minute sessions, during which the stimuli are presented in random order. The first half of the first test session is reserved for getting accustomed to the method and this part is discarded before the analysis.

During each test session, four channels of data sampled at 120 Hz are recorded. These include bipolar occipital lead O1-O2, electro-oculogram (EOG) for eye movement detection and correction, stimulus onsets and subject's responses. The channels containing stimulus markers and subjects responses are combined to form a single channel showing recognized and missed stimuli. The recorded data are processed in 15-second windows. The number of missed stimuli inside each window is divided by the total amount of stimuli inside the window. This error measure, referred to as the local error ratio, is used as the target output for the RBF classifier.

The inputs for the classifier are determined in the following way. First, FFTs of the EEG and EOG signals after windowing with Kaiser window are computed and the unaliased frequencies are packed into thirty 1-Hz bins. Following this, eye movement correction proportional to the correlation between the EEG and EOG is performed. Principal Component Analysis is then applied to the filtered EEG spectrum to find the frequencies that contain the largest amount of information. Final input frequencies used as the input features for the RBF network are determined based on the bispectrum analysis.

Two different training methods were applied. Initially, each input and target was given a neuron. Because this led to a very large network, orthogonal least squares training was used instead. Half of the data from the first two tests were used as training data whereas the remaining data were reserved for testing. The ability of the network to simulate the actual local error ratio was found to be dependent on the subject's ability to properly perform the tests.

1.8 Neural Control of Drug Delivery Systems

Recently, neural networks and fuzzy systems have been increasingly applied in various control engineering applications. In the care of several diseases, administration of certain drugs is used to control the key physiological variables. Hence, neural control methods have also gained applications in the control of various drug delivery systems. Due to the extreme complexity and inherent non-linearities of the physiological control system, traditional closed-loop control methods have given inaccurate results. Although the application of neural networks for determining these non-linearities has been found to be a successful method, determination of accurate mathematical models for physiological control systems is still an extremely complicated process.

Normally, the pancreas performs an important role in the control of the blood-glucose level by producing insulin. However, in patients with diabetes this process has been disordered, either totally or in part. Therefore, due to decreased or totally blocked production of insulin, the blood-glucose level must be maintained within the desired limits by frequent insulin injections. For at least ten years, research has been conducted on finding methods for controlling the blood-glucose level, e.g., with an intelligent insulin pump that continuously monitors changes in the blood-glucose level and injects a small amount of insulin when needed.

Trajanoski and Wach [34] proposed a method for neural control of the blood-glucose level based on an RBF network and nonlinear predictive controller. Due to recent advances in the development of monomeric insulin analogues, new methods for the measurement of subcutaneous blood-glucose, and efficient algorithms for the control of nonlinear systems, they have been able to develop an alternative for currently known approaches. In their method, subcutaneous tissue glucose monitoring is performed by inserting a double lumen cannula in the subcutaneous tissue and perfusing an isotonic ion-free solution at a rate of 2 μl/min through the inner lumen in the tissue. This perfusion fluid reacts chemically with subcutaneous fluid. Part of this fluid is then collected through the outer lumen and analyzed for glucose and conductivity. Subcutaneous glucose can then be calculated from the measured glucose, conductivity of the recovered perfusate and subcutaneous fluid conductivity.

Continuous infusion of monomeric insulin analogues in subcutaneous tissue was simulated with a pharmacokinetic model for different infusion profiles. For the control of subcutaneous glucose, a control strategy based on the combination of a neural network and a predictive neural controller was successfully applied. The purpose of the neural network was to perform an off-line identification of the glucoregulatory system. For system identification, a nonlinear autoregressive model with exogenous inputs (NARX) was selected. The unknown nonlinear function to determine the system output for a given set of inputs was approximated by using an RBF network. A nonlinear predictive controller was then applied to perform multiple step-ahead predictions of the previously identified system. Based on this model, control law for the predictive controller was derived by solving a nonlinear optimization problem. In their numerical studies with simulated data, subcutaneous glucose could be monitored for 24 hours with a single *in vitro* calibration and no *in vivo* calibrations.

Polycarpou and Conway [29] presented a method for modeling and control of mean arterial pressure through the intravenous infusion of sodium nitroprusside. To improve the performance of linear control law they applied an RBF network for modeling the non-linearities of the physiological control system in order to tune the controller to the response characteristics of a specific patient. In their control model, a change in the mean arterial pressure can be obtained as a linear combination of the change of mean arterial pressure at the previous time instant and the infusion rates at earlier time instants related to initial transportation delay and recirculation delay.

The weight parameters of the control model vary between patients and within the same patient with different conditions and were assumed to be functions of blood pressure. These weights were formulated as sums of a known constant and an unknown nonlinear function of the mean arterial pressure. To estimate these nonlinear parts at time instant k, separate RBF networks for each of the weight parameters were used. As the input parameter for these networks, the change in the mean arterial pressure at time instant k-1 was applied. The RBF networks were trained adaptively starting with zero weights between the hidden layer and output layer. Thus, a fully linear control system was initially applied. In the current model, transportation and recirculation delays were assumed to be constant and known, although in practice this is not necessarily the case. All three RBF networks contained 21 fixed Gaussian hidden neurons equally distributed to cover the range of blood pressure changes from -60 mmHg to 0 mmHg. The weights between the output connections were adaptively updated during training using a gradient approach.

In the first phase of these experiments, the capability of the neural networks to learn the nonlinearities of the system in an open loop approach was examined. In the second phase, these networks were used in a closed loop control system to examine their ability to improve the dynamic response of the controller. In both phases, the performance of the adaptive neural controller was found to be superior compared to the simple linear controller. Steady state errors and significant fluctuations in the regulated pressure that were reported in the case of the linear controller could not be found in the neural controller. Instead, the blood pressure was accurately controlled in reasonable time. In addition, the adaptive neural controller has an important advantage compared to the linear model as it is able to retain in its memory situations that have been encountered in the past.

1.9 Nonstationary Signal Estimation

Traditionally, estimation of evoked potential waveforms has been based on the ensemble averaging of a large amount of noisy evoked potentials. This approach is based on the assumption that the waveforms and latencies are identical and the on-going EEG activity can be considered zero-mean random noise. Because these assumptions do not generally hold perfectly, alternative methods for denoising have been investigated. Jemili and Westerkamp [17] have presented a method that is based on the classification of time-frequency representations of noisy evoked potentials by using radial basis function network. Time-frequency representations were obtained by applying discrete wavelet transform (DWT) to the contaminated EEG patterns. RBF network was then trained to recognize the time-frequency components of the corrupted evoked potentials and to suppress the components of the ongoing EEG. Finally, estimated evoked potentials were obtained by performing inverse DWT for the outputs of the RBF network. In case the input pattern did not contain an evoked potential, the network was trained to give zero output.

For the testing and validation of the proposed noise reduction system, 100 human EEG patterns and simulated evoked potentials were generated by using the raised cosine model. Each of the simulated evoked potentials contained four peaks at latencies of 73.31 ms, 113.79 ms, 166.40 ms, and 199.58 ms with standard deviations of 8.76 ms, 10.97 ms, 5.72 ms, and 11.72 ms and peak amplitudes of 5.17 μV, –12.42 μV, –3.19 μV, and 11.16 μV, respectively. To generate contaminated evoked potentials, human EEG noise was added to the simulated evoked potentials. During the experiments, 64-point data vectors, 4-tap Daubechies' wavelets, and RBF networks with 64 hidden neurons were used. As performance measures, normalized mean square error (NMSE), bias factor and noise reduction factor were used. Bias factor gives the normalized mean square error between the desired output and the calculated output in the case when desired output is used as system input. Noise reduction factor is the ratio between the input and output power in the case where system input contains only the noise. These performance measures were determined for an original SNR of –5.61 dB. The proposed system was reported to perform better than ensemble averaging and other referred methods with NMSE of 12.7% on average, noise reduction factor of –12dB on average and bias factor around 0.06 %.

1.10 Nonlinear Time Series Prediction

In neural network literature, time series prediction has traditionally been one of the most extensively used way of model benchmarking and performance estimation. Due to the highly nonlinear nature of many natural time series, linear prediction methods often turn out to be insufficient. Therefore, nonlinear methods for signal prediction are often needed. As an example of nonlinear prediction methods we review the work of Nisbet *et al.* [26] on RBF based nonlinear signal prediction. Their aim has been to simplify the method originally presented by Wiener. Based on a set of n samples, the task is to model the unknown system and to estimate the next sample in the sequence. In the original method, probability density function (pdf) of the predictor state vector is first estimated. After that, a set of orthogonal functions is constructed. Finally, the set of coefficients to form the weights of the series is determined. Due to the theoretical problems in the calculation of probability distribution functions, an alternative method has been presented in which the estimation of the pdf is not needed. This method is based on the determination of a set of orthogonal polynomials through eigenvalue analysis of the associated autocorrelation matrix. A finite series of infinite orthonormal functions can then be obtained. To obtain an estimate for the next sample in the sequence for a given sample vector, standard RBF network was applied to approximate the next sample as a sum of a bias term and a weighted sum of 83 thin plate spline functions. The centers of the RBF hidden neurons were randomly selected amongst the available data either by generating vectors from the available time series through time-delay mechanism or by picking them from the space containing the trajectory of the equation.

The presented algorithm was tested by trying to predict two time series generated by the Duffing's equation. Depending on the parameters of the equation, the resulting time series can be periodic or chaotic. System performance in both cases was investigated by solving the equation by a fourth order Runge-Kutta method with stepsize of 0.1 and comparing the results to those obtained through RBF based prediction system. In both cases, at least some amount of stationarity in the time series was reported. When the predictor performance was investigated based on the normalized mean square error, it was found, that remarkably better results (about –44 dB *vs.* –36 dB) were obtained in the case where the centers were randomly selected from the space containing the trajectory of the equation.

1.11 Diagnostics of Low Back Disorders

As in the case of all the fields of medical diagnostics, obtaining a specific and reliable diagnosis of low back pain and sciatica as early as possible is extremely important. This is because some back disorders may require immediate medical care. In general, diagnostics of low back disorders is a complicated task because the symptoms present with the patients suffering from serious spinal problems can also be present with patients with less serious problems. Non-organic symptoms, that may also be present, make the situation even more complicated.

Bounds *et al.* [3] have applied different pattern recognition methods to the automated diagnostics of low back disorders. In addition to MLP and RBF networks, K-nearest neighbor statistics (K-NN), Closest Class

Mean Classifier (CCM) and a fuzzy logic based classifier have been used. The results obtained with automated methods have also been compared to the opinions of three different groups of doctors. In the presented work, low back disorders are classified into four groups including simple backache, nerve root compression pain, spinal pathology due to tumor, inflammation, or infection, and back pain with significant psychological overlay. Patients can have either simple low back pain, root pain, or spinal pathology, either with or without any psychological overlay. All the 200 patients, who were selected to take part in the study, were asked to fill a tick sheet where all the relevant clinical features were listed. Each subject belonged to one of the four diagnostic groups each of which contained 50 subjects. These classifications were considered correct because all patients were followed up until the final clinical diagnosis was ready. Tick sheet entries combined with the clinical diagnosis formed the basis for the data used in the experiments. In addition to the full set of 145 tick sheet entries, a reduced set of 86 entries was also used. Input database was divided at random into training and validation sets of 100 patients in such a way, that both sets contained 25 examples on all the four diagnostic classes. All the answers of the tick sheet were numerically coded into an 85-element feature vector (50 elements in case of the reduced input set).

For comparison, two different architectures for MLP networks were applied. These included networks designed for the direct classification of all the four diagnostic classes and combinations of four subnetworks designed to recognize a single diagnostic class. In the latter case, both separate output units for all the classes and binary output coding were used. However, most of these experiments were performed by using binary output coding. Different network topologies having a different number of neurons in one or two hidden layers were also tested to find the architecture with optimal performance. All the MLP networks were fully connected without any connections within layers and trained with standard back-propagation algorithm. During the training phase, network weights were updated after presenting one example from all the four diagnostic classes to the network and the training was continued until the calculated outputs for all the training patterns differed less than 0.5 from the target value. All the RBF networks used were designed to directly classify the input patterns into the four diagnostic classes. Effects of the RBF neuron types, RBF parameters and network topologies on the performance of the system were investigated. A typical network was reported to have 50 centers chosen randomly amongst the input feature set. Several variations of Closest Class Mean and K-Nearest Neighbor classifiers were also tested. In adddition to the traditional Euclidian distance metric, the scalar product between training and test vectors was used. Finally, the results obtained for the different classifiers were compared to the results presented earlier for a fuzzy logic classifier.

When the effect of the number of hidden neurons on the performance of different classifiers was investigated, MLP and RBF performances were found to be quite stable over a wide range of network topologies. Also, in case of network-of-networks approaches, changes in the network topology were found to have just minor effect on the system performance. However, single networks capable of classifying the input features directly to four clinical classes were found to perform slightly better than the network-of-networks classifiers. Best single MLP and RBF networks were also found to perform better than all the three groups of clinicians. In case of spinal pathology, which is the most important class to get right, the networks were much better. Clinicians outperformed the networks only in the classification of simple low back pain. The results for CCM classifier, K-NN classifier and fuzzy classifier were almost identical than those for the best RBF and MLP networks. As regards to the dimension of input feature vector, application of the full data set had remarkable effect only on the classification accuracy of simple low back pain. In most cases, the amount of correct classifications was found to be over 80 % from all the classifications.

1.12 Digital Mammography

Breast cancer is the most common type of cancer amongst women in the world. One of the most important signs of breast cancer in its earliest stage with an efficient treatment is the formation of clusters of microcalcifications in the breast tissue. Therefore, in many countries, mammographic screenings are routinely performed for all women of certain age. Due to the vast amount of mammographic images that need to be analyzed, it is an important matter to investigate the possibilities to somehow automate the diagnostics. In the following discussion we review two scientific works from the same laboratory related to automated detection of microcalcifications in mammographic images.

Hojjatoleslami *et al.* [15] have presented a detection method that is based on the estimation of probability density functions for normal and abnormal classes with RBF network as a finite mixture of uncorrelated Gaussians. The estimated class densities could then be used for decision making and for determining whether the image data follows a certain distribution. Before classification, raw image data was first preprocessed to find the suspected image regions by using a three-step method based on the application of top-hat transform, local adaptive thresholding and region-growing algorithm. After that, 39 independent features were extracted from the gradient and contrast peak boundaries and associated regions of the suspected blobs in the images. When the two distributions had been estimated, detected regions were classified as either normal or abnormal through the Bayes rule. Those points, for which both of the probabilities were smaller than some predefined thresholds, were considered as outliers, i.e., as points that should be classified neither normal nor abnormal due to insufficient amount of information.

In the presented work, database of 227 digital mammograms has been used. From these images, 205 were normal mammograms whereas the rest 22 images were diagnosed abnormal. Training set was generated by picking 320 microcalcifications from three abnormal images and 960 detected regions from five normal images. The performance of the classifier was extensively evaluated with a database of two gigabytes of mammographic data. During the experiments, maximum penalized likelihood classifier was compared with K-nearest neighbor classifier, Gaussian classifier and standard MLP. To find a suitable combination of input features for the experiments, Sequential Forward and Backward Floating Algorithms were used to maximize the performance of K-NN and Gaussian classifiers. This way, four different feature sets were determined. These same sets were used to build RBF and MLP networks and the networks with best performance within the training set were used to test the performance for the independent test set. MLP network had 13 inputs, a single hidden layer with 9 hidden units and two output units. RBF networks for estimating the normal and abnormal distributions had 13 and 7 hidden neurons, respectively. To estimate the accuracy of each classifier, ROC analysis for cluster detection and image identification was performed. As regards to the detection of clusters of microcalcifications, MLP network was found to have the best performance. However, when the performance of the image identification between the different classifiers were compared, RBF based approach was found to give the best results.

Kittler *et al.* [19] have also investigated the detection of microcalcifications in digital mammograms. Their aim has been to create a reliable method for labeling suspected image regions as either normal or abnormal. Instead of traditional neural network based approach, they have studied the possibility to combine several different classifiers with partly shared and partly distinct input feature sets. In addition to the custom decision rule based on the Bayesian estimation theory, radial basis function network, multi-layer perceptron network and K-nearest neighbor statistics were combined. Total number of input features for different classification strategies including the four shared features were 17, 7, 13, and 11, respectively.

In this work, training examples were generated in a similar way than in the work by Hojjatoleslami *et al.* [15]. These eight images were then removed from the image database and the remaining images were divided into two sets. One of these sets was first used to determine the prior probabilities for the Bayesian classifier that would guarantee the detection of all microcalcifications in the set. The final classification results were then determined with the other set and the role of the sets was interchanged. As performance measures, rate of clusters of at least three false positive microcalcifications inside a predefined radius and the percentage of normal images misclassified as abnormal were used. In general, it was found that the lowest detection rate of false positive microcalcifications was obtained for the combination of the four classifiers. However, in terms of specificity of the classifier, identical or even slightly better results were obtained with RBF classifier alone.

1.13 Glaucoma Diagnostics

As regards to the number of blindness cases, glaucoma is one of the most severe eye diseases in the western industrial countries. Therefore, early and reliable detection of glaucoma has been an important branch in ophthalmology. Zahlman *et al.* [40] have presented a neuro-fuzzy glaucoma monitor intended to detect the early glaucomatous changes in the patient's ophthalmologic data sets in primary care environment. Clinical decision of medical experts is based on parameter estimations, verbal descriptions and direct measurement of intraocular pressure and perimetry data. Perimetry is a method, where the status of the visual field of the patient is determined by special devices that detect the loss of light sensitivity at different stimulus points around the retina. The subject is asked to press a button after each detected stimulus. Although the method is somewhat subjective, it is considered as best available method today. Another problem is that there is no gold standard for perimetry. Therefore, because the data could not be verified by an objective reference method, four medical experts were asked to independently classify the same data set of 244 perimetry recordings. In the presented work, classification results of two medical experts were compared to illustrate the problems in perimetry classification.

Perimetry data consisted of 59-dimensional feature vectors. To investigate the distributions of feature vectors and classification agreements and disagreements of medical experts, Sammon mapping was used. This method can be applied for approximating local geometric relations of the features in a two-dimensional plot. Based on these results, reliable classification of perimetry data was found to be a complicated task. As additional inputs, papilla descriptions and subject's own verbal reports and descriptions about the changes in the clinical status were used. Based on these data the ophthalmologist has to make a decision whether these findings are glaucomatous and how the results should be reacted. In the presented work, the main goal has been to model this decision process and to give decision support for the ophthalmologist. The design of the neural classifier was based on the classification tree approach. All the networks were trained only with those input patterns for classification of which they were intended. For the input feature dimensionality reduction, special feature selection algorithm was developed. Outputs of the networks were used as inputs for the fuzzy post-processing part that was used for determining the final output of the system.

All the six neural networks belonging to the classification tree were trained by using about 67 % of the recordings. The rest of the recordings were reserved for validation. When the performances of the specialized neural networks were investigated, all the networks were found to give equal or better results when the custom feature selection algorithm was applied. The overall decision was obtained by using a two-stage fuzzy rule set. In the first rule level, intra-ocular pressure and the properties of papillas were used as inputs. Output values were obtained through the min-max decision rule and these outputs were used as inputs for the second stage. As additional inputs for the second stage, perimetry data classifications were used. This preclassification was performed through the application of neural network classifier tree but it could have also been performed by a medical expert. The final decision was performed in the second rule level. These outputs were directly used without defuzzification to produce messages that are aimed to give a description of the clinical state of the subject. The first results for the classifier were reported to be acceptable to the medical user. However, separation between pathological but not glaucomatous and early glaucomatous changes based on perimetry data alone was found to be extremely difficult, when papilla descriptions and intra-ocular pressure did not give additional information. A more thorough validation of the system and the development of the messaging system were reported to be in progress.

1.14 Cancer Diagnostics

According to the American Cancer Society, cervical carcinoma is the most common type of cancer in women after breast cancer. It is very important to improve the methods used for diagnostics, because early detection remarkably lowers the risk of mortality. Currently, Pap smear test, which is based on the cytologic examination of cell samples of cervical epithelium, does not concurrently achieve both high sensitivity and specificity. Therefore, a patient with a Pap smear test interpreted as possibly abnormal, will be conducted for further examination with colposcopy. It includes microscopic examination of cervix, biopsing of the suspicious tissue sites and histological examination of these samples. This method is known to have high sensitivity. However, because of the lower specificity the amount of tissue samples needed may be unnecessarily high. Also, due to the histological nature of the test, diagnosis is not immediate. For this reason, Tumer *et al.* [35] have presented a detection technique that is based on laser induced fluorescence spectroscopy and an ensemble of radial basis function networks. For comparison, multivariate statistical algorithm (MSA) and multi-layer perceptron networks were also tested for classification.

Laser induced fluorescence spectroscopy is quick non-invasive way to probe the biochemical and morphological changes in tissue based on the spectral characteristics of the measured fluorescence. During the measurements, a portable fluorimeter system was used to measure fluorescence spectra from cervix at three excitation wavelengths. A randomly selected group of non-pregnant patients referred to colposcopy study was asked to participate in the fluorescence spectroscopy study. Fluorescence spectra were acquired from each patient on several normal and abnormal sites totalling in 361 recordings from 95 patients. Consisting of three spectra at 337 nm, 380 nm, and 460 nm excitation wavelengths with 59, 56, and 45 emission wavelength-intensity pairs, respectively, all the recordings contained a total of 160 initial measurements.

For statistical classification, full-parameter and reduced-parameter multivariate statistical algorithms were tested. Both of them were based on the two-stage approach in which the input patterns were first classified as clearly normal or possibly pre-cancerous. Pre-cancerous patterns were then further classified as normal or abnormal. Full-parameter MSA was started by normalizing the fluorescence spectra in the first stage or normalizing and mean-scaling the spectra in the second stage. After that, dimensionality reduction through Principal Component Analysis and selection of diagnostically relevant principal components through the unpaired, one-sided student's t-test was performed. Finally, logistic discrimination of these diagnostically relevant input features was carried out and performance of the classifier was evaluated. However, due to the large amount of input parameters, a reduced-parameter approach was desired. This was also motivated by the possibility to use simpler and more cost-effective imaging system for the final classifier. By determining correlations between the clinically relevant principal components and the preprocessed fluorescence spectra at each excitation-emission wavelength pair it was possible to reduce the number of input parameters to 13 with a minimal decrease in classification accuracy.

In the presented study, performance of the statistical algorithms has been compared to the performance of ensembles of Multi-Layer Perceptron Networks and Radial Basis Function Networks. The outputs of separate classifiers were combined with mean and median combiner before making the final decision. Comparison of different classification strategies was performed in three phases. First, suitability of neural network based methods for the classification task was investigated by developing two-stage classifiers comparable to MSA approach using full-parameter data sets, diagnostically relevant principal components and reduced-parameter data sets. After that, possibility to reduce the two-step algorithm into a single-step neural network classifier was examined. Finally, classification accuracy and reliability of neural network methods were compared with the results obtained for MSA, Pap smear and colposcopy. As in the case of MSA, the task was reported to be impossible using the full-parameter approach mainly due to the small amount of training patterns. Therefore, three diagnostically relevant principal components were used as inputs for the two-stage neural classifier. Both MLP and RBF networks had one hidden layer with three hidden units.

When the ensemble results of 20 different neural classifiers initialized with random parameters and using mean and median combiners were combined with MSA results, it was found, that RBF based combiners provided higher specificity for a similar sensitivity. For the two-stage classification with reduced parameter set, neural networks with a single hidden layer having 10 hidden neurons were utilized. RBF kernels were initialized by selectively picking them from the data set and adjusting only part of the kernel parameters during the training. This was done to ensure, that the distribution of the kernels in input space follows the distribution of the data. Again, ensemble results of 20 networks showed that RBF based combiners provided higher specificity than MSA whereas MLP outperformed MSA only in the first stage of the classifier. In the second stage, remarkably lower sensitivity was obtained. Therefore, the authors concluded that RBF networks fit better for the presented classification task and performed the further comparisons only between MSA and RBF ensemble approaches.

Next, the possibility of performing RBF based single-step classification with reduced parameter set was examined. For MSA and MLP networks, this was found to be unsatisfactory. Due to the differences in the preprocessing between the stages in two-stage approach, the two reduced feature sets were concatenated to form a single set of feature vectors with 26 elements. By using k-means algorithm again, ten kernels were initialized by using a trimmed set of input feature vectors containing equal amount of examples from all the diagnostic classes. During the training, RBF centers and widths were not adjusted any more to preserve the initial distribution of hidden neurons. To estimate the variability between the ensembles, average and median combiner results for the ensembles of 20 RBF networks were determined ten times. When compared to two-step MSA, remarkable increase in the sensitivity was obtained with similar or even slightly higher specificity. One-step RBF method led to a dramatical improvement of almost 30 % in sensitivity with minimal effects on the specificity. As regards to colposcopy, an improvement of almost 20 % in specificity was obtained with almost identical sensitivity. Therefore, the method has potential to significantly reduce the number of pre-cancerous cases missed by Pap smear and the number of normal tissue samples misdiagnosed with colposcopy.

2 Design of Biomedical Pattern Recognition Systems

During recent decades, research has been conducted in the field of medical diagnosis automation. Many suitable methods for biomedical pattern classifiers have been proposed. Conventionally, pattern classifiers have been based on different linear approaches such as linear discriminant analysis and simple perceptrons, statistical methods, for example Bayesian methods, and syntactic and rule-based classifiers. Recently, there has been greater use of different classification schemes like neural networks, fuzzy systems and their combinations. The main goals of these classification methods have been to equip the classifiers with the ability to learn complex input-output relationships from limited amount of examples, to perform associative operations, and to add memory to the conventional classifiers.

In general, training of neural classifiers can be performed either using supervised or unsupervised training algorithms. Supervised training algorithms have often been preferred in biomedical classification tasks as the purpose is to train the network to observe clinically relevant input-output relations in the training data set. However, unsupervised training methods may offer noteworthy alternatives for conventional cluster analysis algorithms. Due to the large number of competitive classification schemes the selection of the most suitable method for a certain application may not be straightforward. Practical comparison of different approaches for the same problem is a safe approach. This allows the best method to be selected after comparing the actual performance of different alternatives.

Although different neural network based methods may seem to have very attractive properties at first glance, it must be mentioned that they cannot be regarded as panacea for all pattern recognition problems. Neural networks do not automatically solve any design problems and they also contain aspects that must be taken into account during the design process. However, when these pitfalls are carefully considered, neural systems may reach superior performance compared with traditional methods. Perhaps the most important advantage of neural network based methods is the fact that the threshold values inherent, e.g., in fuzzy systems or rule-based systems need not be set by the designer. This is an especially useful property in biomedical applications where even the normal values of various tests and measures often have considerable variation. In the following section we discuss some important design considerations based on our experiences in the field. Although we concentrate on the design of RBF based biomedical pattern recognition systems, most of the ideas presented below fit equally well into the general pattern classifier design.

The design process of neural network based pattern recognition systems can be roughly divided into the following stages:

1. Detailed specification of the problem
2. Data acquisition and morphological analysis
3. Preprocessing and feature extraction
4. Selection of the neural network paradigm
5. Training and validation

In the following section we have attempted to point out the most important design considerations in each phase.

2.1 Detailed Specification of the Problem

Detailed specification of the problem at hand is the first prerequisite for the successful design of all systems. In biomedical problems this should contain, at least, clinical, architectural and data set definitions. Typically, the first to be considered is the clinical problem itself. This is an extremely important phase as the formulation of the clinical problem greatly affects the whole design process. Architectural specification is related to the selection of classification principles and types of classifiers to be used. Data set specification includes the gold standard definition and the definitions of the rules according to which the training and validation data will be generated.

From the clinical point of view, biomedical pattern recognition problems can be regarded either as one-class or multi-class problems depending on whether the positive and negative patterns can be divided into several separate subclasses. Therefore, it is very important to find the most efficient way to define the classes to be separated. In some cases defining the positive and negative output classes and formulating the problem as a one-class problem is straightforward. This is the case, for example, when the main objective of the classifier is to work as a preprocessor or as a part of a larger classification system. The one-class approach is also well suited to applications where the output classes consist of several clinically different subclasses but their separation is not needed in the application. However, there are many applications where the output classes cannot be combined. This is especially true with classifiers targeted for differential diagnosis of different diseases where the multi-class approach must be applied. In some cases it is reasonable to keep part of the subclasses separate and to combine the others. This approach may ease the design and speed up training although a multi-class classifier is still needed.

After clinical formulation of the problem the architecture of the classification system can be sketched. In the case of one-class problems this is quite an easy process. Generally, some kind of problem-dependent feature extraction block precedes the neural network classifier. However, when the multi-class approach is needed, the architecture of the classifier has to be considered more carefully. Generally there are three possibilities for the basic architecture of the classifier. These include single networks with multiple outputs, parallel classifiers and classifier trees. Examples of these network architectures are depicted in Figure 1.

A single network with multiple outputs may be the simplest possibility, as only one training run for the whole classifier is needed. However, the dimensionality of the network and computational complexity in the training phase may become too high to manage. Tree classifiers and parallel classifiers tend to reduce the computational load by partitioning the classifier into several smaller sub-classifiers. In tree classifiers the final classification results are formed through a series of one-class sub-classifications. This resembles the diagnostic reasoning of a physician. In parallel classifiers the separate sub-networks perform independent classifications whether the input pattern belongs to a certain output class or not. Thus the multi-class problem can be reduced to a set of parallel one-class problems. The output values can be considered as probabilities of certain physiological states. Typically the output neuron having the maximum output value determines the clinical state of the input pattern.

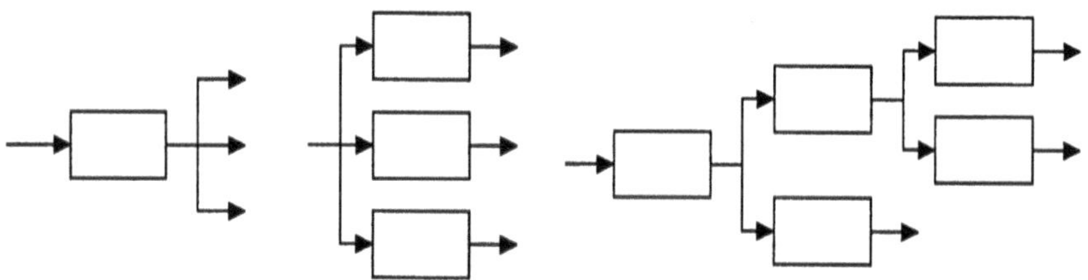

Figure 1. Examples of the most typical classifier architectures for multi-class pattern recognition tasks. From left to right: Single classifier with multiple outputs, parallel classifier, and classifier tree.

The architectural specification of the neural classifier must also contain definitions for the types of hidden neurons and the output units. Although there are several possibilities for the radial basis function, at least in biomedical applications the Gaussian function is almost always used. In some cases the thin-plate spline functions have been applied. With regard to the output units of the network, these can be selected to be either Boolean or real-valued. In the typical classification tasks real-valued outputs between 0 and 1 sound reasonable.

When the basic architecture of the network has been fixed, rules that control the generation of the training and validation data must be specified. An important consideration is the selection of the gold standard for the network output values. One of the characteristic problems for clinical classifiers is the fact that even normal values of different tests and diagnostic measures contain a remarkable variation. On the other hand, in various waveform detection problems for example, the determination of the exact duration of an event is often impossible. For this reason the target output values for training are often chosen based on visually scored recording data. To reduce the subjectivity of the markings the consensus scoring approach is often applied. The recordings that will be used for the formation of data sets are first analyzed independently by a group of physicians. These independent scorings are then compared by an experienced physician responsible for the final assignment of the target output values.

Another important factor to remember is the problem caused by different interferences, often referred to as artefacts, that are present in the recordings. In the data set definition the way in which these patterns will be handled should also be defined. In general, it would be easier to exclude these patterns from the training and validation data sets because they obviously complicate the design of the classifier. However, as these artefacts are unavoidable in many cases, classifiers that do not have any capability for handling artefacts can be regarded useless in practice.

2.2 Data Acquisition and Morphological Analysis

After specification of the rules governing the formation of the input data set, the acquisition and processing of the data for training and validation of the classifier can be started. Generation of labeled input-output pairs is one of the most time-consuming steps during the design process of the neural network classifier. Typical problems in this phase include the rare and often unpredictable occurrence of the events that need to be recorded, the excessive amount of work that is needed for the visual scoring of sufficient amount of data and problems in the exact definition of the onset and termination of the events to be scored. Practical recordings often also include some border-line cases that cannot be easily assigned to only one certain output class. Therefore the participation of at least one medical expert is an essential prerequisite for a successful project.

The main objective in the design of biomedical pattern classifiers is to assist physicians in medical decision making or even automate some phases in the diagnostic process. For this reason medical classification systems should be designed in such a way that they mimic the diagnostic reasoning of physicians. This also reduces suspicion of medical experts towards automated methods. In the case of neural network based classifiers, this aim can be achieved by importing diagnostic reasoning to the feature extraction stage of the classifier. This can be done by finding the properties on which the medical diagnosis is based through discussions with medical experts and through careful visual and morphological analysis of input patterns. The feature set used as the input for the classifier should be selected in such a way that the features effectively reflect the clinical differences between input patterns and form clearly separable clusters in the feature space.

2.3 Preprocessing and Feature Extraction

As previously mentioned, the main purpose of the preprocessing and feature extraction block design is to equip the classifier with clinical reasoning. Another extremely important requirement for the features is their robustness in view of the large number of possible signal morphologies related to a certain clinical state, inter-patient variations, and device parameters like montages and amplifier and filter settings. Careful consideration of all these aspects makes preprocessing and feature extraction challenging task. As the preprocessing and feature extraction stages in biomedical neural classifiers are strictly problem-dependent, it is impossible to list any generally working feature set. However, some guidelines for finding the appropriate set of features can be obtained through careful visual analysis of the data. In the following we present some feature groups that may be useful in biomedical applications.

In connection with automated signal and image analysis problems, features based on the temporal properties of 2-D signals or on the spatial properties of images form an important and widely used class of network input parameters. Temporal features may include, for example, latencies and amplitudes of different peaks and waves as well as estimates of amplitude range, rise time, fall time, slope, area, duration and symmetricity of the waves. These parameters can be used for classifying bioelectric and biomagnetic recordings, such as the activity of the heart and the brain and event related potentials such as evoked potentials and motor unit action potentials. In image processing applications features reflecting various changes in a local neighborhood of a pixel can be used, for example, for image segmentation, image analysis and image understanding. Temporal features may also include parameters based on the estimation of correlation. Correlation can be computed either as auto-correlation to find some hidden periodicities in the input signal, as cross-correlation between the signal segments in different channels or as cross-correlation between an input pattern and a template of a signal pattern.

Another important feature class is based on the estimation of spectral properties of the input signal patterns. Although short-term Fourier transform based parameters are generally the most widely used, autoregressive models and wavelet transform based methods have also been applied. If real power values are not needed, there are also several simpler methods for obtaining a rough but often sufficient estimate, for example, through the application of simple high-pass filters. Spectral methods are typically used for estimating signal power, either in total or on some selected frequency band. Often, monitoring of changes in power ratios between the selected frequency bands is an efficient method. For the estimation of spectral correlation between separate input signal patterns or between channels coherence may also be applied. Spectral methods also include the processing of the input signal patterns by utilizing various application-dependent linear and nonlinear filters.

Often it is also helpful to investigate various statistical properties of input patterns. The most well-known statistical parameters include mean, median, standard deviation, variance and higher order moments. Additionally, in the literature, a number of advanced linear and nonlinear estimators have been presented. In some applications, efficient estimators can be obtained by introducing some measures based on the distribution of input signal patterns. Later in this chapter, an example on this type of estimator is presented.

2.4 Selection of the Neural Network Paradigm

When considering neural network based classifiers, multilayer perceptron networks and radial basis function networks are the two most commonly used feedforward network paradigms [14]. Both MLP and RBF structures have been shown to be capable of universal approximation [16], [27]. However, considering the characteristic features of biomedical applications, radial basis function network can be considered a more viable choice. This is because the observed phenomena in biomedical applications usually form a large number of clusters of various shapes in the pattern space. As it can be seen from these clusters, the decision boundaries can become very complex. It is widely known that MLP networks are not very good at learning complex decision boundaries. On the other hand, RBF networks are based on the use of local radially symmetric kernel functions which make them well suited to these types of problems [14].

Secondly, recent studies have shown that it is hard to train an MLP to draw closed separation surfaces in the pattern space [11]. Hence, in many cases MLPs are unable to model patterns distributed in typical clusters. This problem is especially critical in biomedical applications as new recordings may contain unforeseen artefacts or other phenomena. In these cases an MLP with open separation surfaces would yield unpredictable behavior or operation. However, due to the local nature of RBF neurons, it is easy to show that RBF networks inherently draw closed separation surfaces. Therefore, the choice of using RBF networks instead of MLP networks in biomedical applications appears to be well justified.

Like other feedforward networks, radial basis function networks can also be trained using supervised training algorithms. However, it has been reported that with a pure gradient descent based training approach, certain locality problems may occur due to the local nature of RBF neurons [25]. This has led to the development of hybrid approaches where both supervised and unsupervised training are used. Usually unsupervised learning methods are used in the context of training RBF neurons while supervised learning methods are used in the context of training the weights feeding the output units.

One of the most effective and widely known hybrid method is the Orthogonal Least Squares algorithm [5], [6]. In this training procedure a large set of candidates for the hidden neurons are generated from the input data set. In simplest form these candidates can be randomly picked from the input features. Alternatively, a set of candidates can be generated by applying a clustering algorithm like the well-known k-means clustering [33] and using the resulting cluster centers as the centers for candidate neurons. The width parameters for the candidates can be determined, for example, by using the k-nearest neighbor statistics [25]. Following this, a desired number of candidate neurons are selected to be installed into the network based on certain performance measures. In addition, the weight factors feeding the output units are optimized simultaneously in the least mean square sense.

Some similar but computationally more simple hybrid approaches have also been recently investigated [23]. Such methods can be very useful in biomedical applications where the amount of data can be extremely large. The amount of data and the available computational resources can play a critical role when specific network structures and training algorithms are considered. It should also be noted that the performance of the final classifier may depend on the training algorithm used. Therefore, if possible, it would be a good idea to experiment with several training methods.

2.5 Training and Validation

Depending on the architecture of the neural system, training of the system can be performed in various ways. Training can be conducted either by using both positive and negative groups or by applying only one of them. In any case, the number of training examples must be much higher than the number of weight factors in the network to minimize the risk of overfitting. In principle, it is impossible to give any exact recommendations for the ratio between the number of network weights and the number of input patterns. However, many authors consider the amount of not more than one tenth of the total amount of training examples to be a safe choice. On the other hand, too small a number of processing neurons in the hidden layer may lead to severe underfitting of the data. Therefore, careful validation of the classifier after training with a comprehensive validation data set is a vitally important task. In general, performance of different automated pattern recognition systems can be validated in many different ways. In the following discussion, several widely used methods will be discussed.

The easiest way to estimate performance may be to utilize various error measures between real and desired outputs of the system. If d is the desired output and y is the actual output of the classifier, then the most typical error measure, the standard error (SE), is:

$$SE = d - y.$$

Error measure quite similar to SE is the absolute error (AE):

$$AE = |d - y|.$$

Based on these basic definitions, sum squared error (SSE), mean square error (MSE), mean absolute error (MAE) and normalized mean square error (NMSE) can be defined with the following equations:

$$SSE = \sum_{i=1}^{N} \left(d_i - y_i\right)^2 \qquad MSE = \frac{1}{N}\sum_{i=1}^{N} \left(d_i - y_i\right)^2$$

$$MAE = \frac{1}{N}\sum_{i=1}^{N} \left|d_i - y_i\right| \qquad NMSE = \frac{1}{N\sigma}\sum_{i=1}^{N} \left(d_i - y_i\right)^2$$

These measures are often used as performance indices during the training of neural networks. However, these measures do not fit well with the estimation of classification performance of automated classifiers. This is due to the fact that excluding standard and absolute error, these error measures reflect more the global deviation of the calculated output values from the desired output values than the correctness of separate classifications. For this reason, a better method for model validation is to use the measures based on the Receiver Operating Characteristics (ROC) analysis. This approach is explained below.

As previously mentioned, the design of different biomedical data classifiers is typically based on the utilization of visually scored physiological data. Based on the scorings made by a specialized physician, a set of desired output values for the corresponding set of input feature vectors is calculated. These desired output values are then compared with the actual output values of the classifier. These actual classifications are then divided into four separate classes that are true positive (TP), true negative (TN), false positive (FP) and false negative (FN) classifications. True positive and true negative classes contain correctly classified patterns. The class of false positives contains those classifications in which negative patterns are misclassified as positive patterns. In a similar way, false negative classifications include those classifications where positive patterns are misclassified as negative patterns.

Based on the above, several measures reflecting the performance and accuracy of automated pattern recognition systems can be defined. The most typical measures are sensitivity (true positive rate, TPR) and specificity (true negative rate, TNR). These values can be obtained by applying the following equations:

$$TPR = \frac{TP}{TP + FN} \qquad TNR = \frac{TN}{TN + FP}$$

Thus, sensitivity and specificity of the classifier determine the percentages of correct classifications for those patterns that were scored to be positive and negative, respectively, by the human scorer. Other useful measures for the estimation of performance include positive and negative predictive values (PV_{pos}, PV_{neg}) and the diagnostic accuracy and diagnostic ability of the classifier. Predictive values can be determined using the following equations:

$$PV_{pos} = \frac{TP}{TP + FP} \qquad PV_{neg} = \frac{TN}{TN + FN}$$

These parameters clearly determine estimates of the probabilities for cases where an input pattern classified either as positive or negative really is a positive or negative pattern, respectively. Diagnostic accuracy is defined as the total probability of correct classification as follows:

$$D_{acc} = \frac{TP + TN}{N}$$

where N is the number of input vectors fed to the network. Diagnostic ability that gives an estimate for the average probability of the correct classification can be obtained using the following equation:

$$D_{abl} = \frac{TPR + TNR}{2}$$

When considering the comparison between desired and actual output values based on these measures, it is important to note that the direct comparison between desired and actual outputs is not always possible. For example, actual output may be a real value between zero and one while the desired value is a Boolean variable and the network was trained to give Boolean output. For this reason, the calculated outputs must often be thresholded before the determination of these measures.

Of course, the selection of threshold level critically affects the results obtained for the performance measures defined above. For this reason, it is reasonable to determine sensitivities and specificities of the classifier for a set of different threshold levels. The comparison of performance at different threshold levels may be simplified by plotting these results in a graphical form. By plotting specificities of the system as a function of sensitivities, we get the well-known ROC curve. On the other hand, by plotting both sensitivities and specificities as a function of the threshold level in the same figure we get the performance curve, which effectively reflects the dependence of performance on the output threshold level. Based on these two curves it is easy to select an appropriate threshold value to use for thresholding the real-valued output of the neural network to a Boolean decision.

An important extension for ROC analysis is n-fold cross-validation. This is based on a large set of input feature vectors and corresponding output values that are divided into n smaller sets. From these n data sets, one set is selected at the time. The other n-1 sets are used to train the network and the small data set selected is used for validation. In this way, it is possible to perform n different validation runs for the classifier. After training and validation of the network with these n data sets, ROC curves and performance curves for each of the data sets can be plotted. Based on these figures it is possible to make conclusions on the generalization properties of the classifier.

In the above discussion, several different methods for validation of automated pattern classifiers were presented. However, none of them describe the type of patterns that were incorrectly classified. For this purpose, visual comparison of the original scorings and the calculated outputs is needed. Although visual analysis as such is not sufficient for model validation, it is the only way to gain valuable information on the morphological properties of the incorrectly classified patterns and on the severity of the misclassifications.

3 Case Study: Automated Detection of Interference Waveforms in EEG Recordings

As an example on the design process of a biomedical pattern classifier we describe our recent contribution on the automated detection of interference waveforms, i.e., artefacts in EEG recordings related to the diagnosis of epilepsy [30]. We start our discussion with an introductory section concentrating briefly on the clinical background of the problem. After that, we proceed according to the design guidelines presented in the previous section.

3.1 Clinical Background

For a long time, automated detection and classification of different waveforms in physiological recordings has been one the most intensively studied applications of signal processing in clinical medicine. In neurology and clinical neurophysiology, one of the most important tools for the examination of the electric activity of the brain is electroencephalography (EEG). Although EEG has been in use for many decades, EEG analysis and interpretation is still one of the least automated fields in clinical medicine.

The first experiments and scientific contributions on the recording of the electrical activity of the brain date back to 1875 when Richard Caton reported his experiments on recording the electrical activity of the brain in animals [20]. Due to the low technical level of measurement instrumentation at that time these findings can be considered extremely noteworthy. The first experiments on the recording of human EEGs were published by Hans Berger in 1929. During his research from 1924 to 1938 he laid the foundation for the use of EEG recording in clinical practice. He was the first to observe that the recorded brain waves contain some regularities and periodicities and these waves change in a recognizable way as a result of changes from a relaxed to an alert state. He also noticed the connection between slower waves during drowsiness and sleep and faster waves during active, waking states. He even found that the recorded EEG waveforms change remarkably during convulsive seizures [20]. However, in spite of these remarkable results, Berger's findings did not arouse very much attention until Adrian and Mathews published their paper verifying Berger's results in 1934. After this, the results were generally accepted.

During recent decades, the EEG has been found to be a powerful tool in neurology and clinical neurophysiology as the EEG effectively reflects different neurological states of the brain. For this reason, multi-channel long-term EEG recordings that are carefully inspected by a specialized physician have been widely applied in diagnosis and treatment planning for different neurological disorders. When combined with other clinical tests, the EEG can also be used for differentiating between disorders of neurological and non-neurological origin. As the visual inspection of long-term EEG recordings is generally a very time-consuming process, many methods have been proposed to facilitate the diagnosis and reduce the time needed for analysis [12], [13]. These methods have mainly been intended for the automated detection of epileptic activity in long-term EEG recordings, automated sleep stage scoring and sleep analysis, classification of event-related potentials and diagnosis of different sleep disorders.

In the most common setting, the EEG is recorded by attaching Ag-AgCl electrodes onto the scalp. To keep the electrode impedance sufficiently low, conductive paste is used as an electrolyte at the electrode-scalp interface. In routine EEG recordings of about half an hour duration, the electrode montage generally referred as 10-20 electrode system is the most commonly used [4]. During long-term recordings, extended electrode montages and sphenoidal electrodes are sometimes used. In the diagnosis of epilepsy, the main objective is to record EEG during suspected epileptic attacks. As these attacks may not happen very often, various activating procedures, including photic stimulation with a flash light, hyperventilation or sleep deprivation, are often used in an attempt to provoke the onset of an attack. Two main areas in sleep research are the diagnosis of nocturnal apnea episodes and the examination of vigilance and daytime sleepiness. Evoked potentials can be used, for example, for the examination of the visual, auditory and sensory systems. Due to the wide applicability of the EEG in clinical work there are also many potential applications of RBF networks in the automation of EEG analysis.

3.2 Detailed Specification of the Problem

Perhaps the most important reason for the low amount of automation in EEG analysis is the extreme complexity of the field. In addition to the wide variability of the recorded EEG signal morphologies, one of the most critical problems in automated EEG analysis is the summation of different interference waveforms, i.e., artefacts within the original EEG activity. The most common reasons for these artefacts include movement of the subject during the recording session and the normal electrical activity of the heart, muscles and eyes. Typically these waveforms radically complicate the design of various automated classifiers as they often resemble clinically relevant signal patterns. Thus, artefacts result in a risk of serious misclassification. This reduces the clinical applicability of automated EEG classifiers. In this study the main objective has been to introduce a simple and reliable method for the detection of the most common artefact types in long-term EEG recordings to improve the diagnostic applicability of the systems proposed earlier [9], [22], [28], [36].

Traditionally, different artefact processing methods have been based on the application of various conventional signal processing techniques including the application of high-pass filters for the reduction of high-frequency contaminations, various correlation based subtraction methods for eye movement artefact minimization and different statistical, syntactical and rule-based classifiers [1]. In this study we have selected a radial basis function network based classifier as the basis for the neural classification system. In general, neural network based detection of artefacts is a new approach. The only comparative study we know is the method presented by Wu *et al.* [39]. In this study, autoregressive spectrum estimates and cross-correlation methods are utilized for feature extraction and several Multilayer Perceptron (MLP) Networks are utilized for different artefact types for data classification. In our method, only one RBF network following the feature extraction block is used as a classifier. Thus, our approach is somewhat simpler.

With regard to the accuracy requirements for an artefact detector, the most important requirement is robust operation for negative patterns. This means that automated artefact detectors must be designed in such a way that the clinically relevant patterns, such as patterns with epileptic activity, are not incorrectly classified as artefacts. Although the artefact detection rate should be as high as possible, correct classification of negative patterns is a more important requirement for a clinically useful artefact detector. As the classifier was intended to be used as an artefact preprocessor for various clinical waveform detectors, the class of negative patterns contained both normal and epileptic signal patterns. This is possible and reasonable due to the fact that during preprocessing the separation of normal and epileptic patterns is not needed. This is the task for the classifier following the artefact detector.

To define the basis of the gold standard for the determination of target values, the artefactual patterns found in the recordings were visually scored by a medical expert before application. Based on these scorings, the desired output values for the input patterns were determined. For the totally artefactual and cerebral EEG activity, desired output values of 0 and 1 were used, respectively. In the cases where the segments were marked to be only partly artefactual, a real value between 0 and 1 giving the percentage of the genuine cerebral activity inside the whole segment was used as the desired output.

3.3 Data Acquisition and Morphological Analysis

The EEG recordings used in our experiments were recorded at the Intensive Monitoring Laboratory at Tampere University Hospital, Tampere, Finland and at Vaajasalo Epilepsy Unit at Kuopio, Finland. During visual analysis of signal morphologies several characteristic features for different artefactual pattern classes were found. In the following section we discuss and exemplify these properties for currently investigated classes including electromyography (EMG), movement and saturation artefacts. Although electrical activity of the eyes also produces interferences in the recorded EEG, we have not taken these into account as these artefacts can be found only on a few frontal channels. Moreover, we already have a reliable method for eye movement detection [37], [38].

3.3.1 Movement Artefacts

Skeletal movements of the subject during the recording session result in movements of the measurement cables and electrodes. Based on the nature of these movements the resulting interference waveforms can be easily recognizable or more subdued. General characteristics of these waveforms include very sharp transients with remarkably high amplitude levels compared to the spontaneous background activity. Due to the extremely low amplitude values of the background EEG the amplifier gains are sometimes set in such a way that the amplifiers saturate during these events. Another possible reason for signal saturation is insufficient dynamic range of the amplifiers or A/D converters. As a consequence of the inherent increase in muscle activity during skeletal movements EMG activity can also be observed. An example of interference waveforms observed during movements is shown in Figure 2.

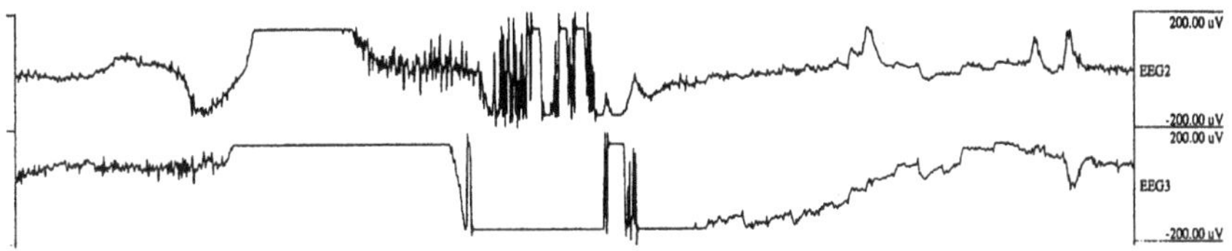

Figure 2. Movements of the subject typically consist of sharp transients with very high amplitude values compared to the background EEG. Often, EMG contamination can also be detected.

3.3.2 Saturation Artefacts

Saturation artefacts (Figure 3) form a class of signal patterns in which the signal amplitude levels are stuck at a certain amplitude level for a considerable length of time. Based on the amplitude level of the saturated signal these patterns can be divided into several subgroups, such as zero-level saturation, DC offset saturation, and amplifier saturation. Typical reasons for saturation artefacts include incorrect amplifier settings such as too high or too low gain, and problems caused by loose electrode connections or broken measurement cables. In case of electrode and cable problems various burst-like interference patterns can also be detected. A characteristic property of this pattern class is the flatness and minimal or zero variance of the data. However, the DC power of these patterns may still be remarkable, e.g., due to offset voltage problems or in the case of amplifier saturation.

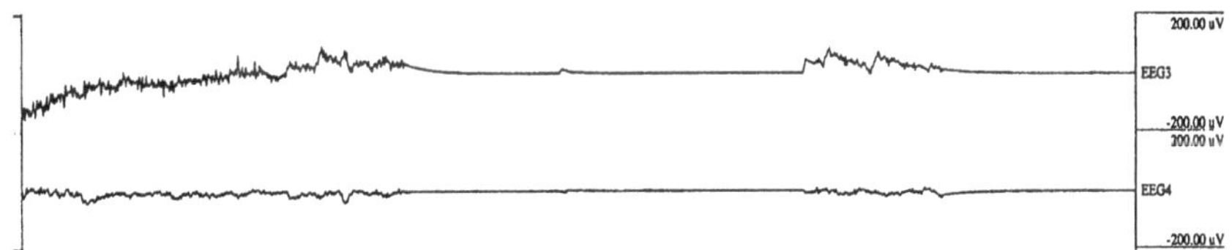

Figure 3. Saturation artefacts related to electrode problems.

3.3.3 EMG Artefacts

Electromyography (EMG) artefacts originate in EEG recordings as a consequence of increased muscle activity in the head area. Typical reasons include chewing, frowning and eating. The most characteristic property of this pattern class is the superposition of high frequency contamination with higher amplitudes than those of background activity (Figure 4). Thus, EEG with EMG artefacts contains more power on higher frequencies and the variance of the corrupted signal is higher than that of the spontaneous EEG activity. This is also true for the other types of high frequency contaminations.

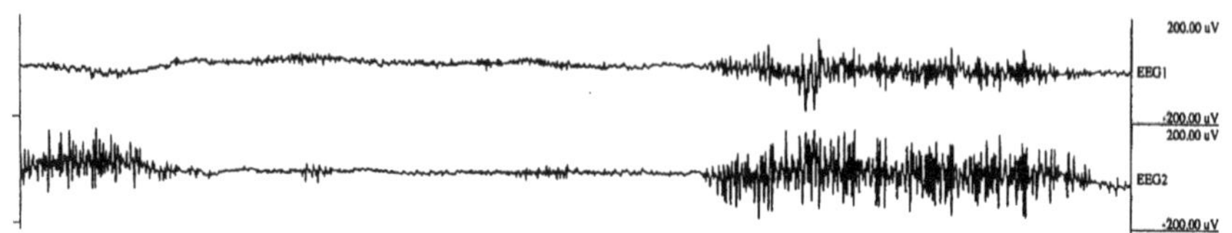

Figure 4. Example of two EEG channels containing EMG activity.

3.3.4 Epileptic Signal Patterns

Epileptic patterns typically contain sharp spikes and slower waves either as combined spike-and-wave complexes as shown in Figure 5 or as separate spikes and waves. During generalized grand mal epileptic attacks the recordings consist of high-amplitude, irregularly shaped high-frequency activity. As the main aim of this study has been to introduce a reliable artefact preprocessor to be used in connection with automated detectors of epileptic activity, it is crucial that epileptic patterns are not classified as artefacts. Therefore, the significance of preprocessing and feature extraction cannot be exaggerated.

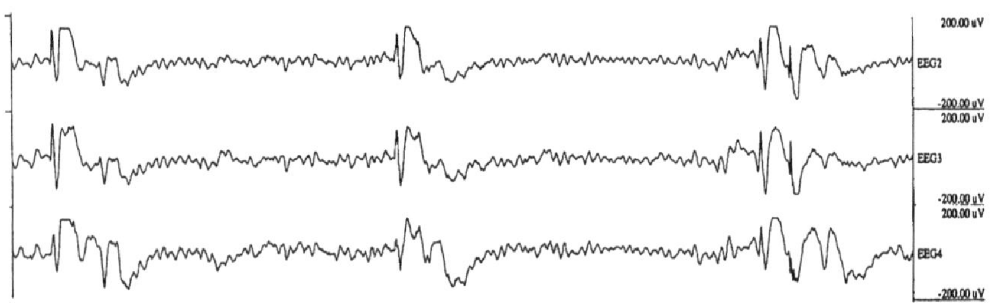

Figure 5. An example of epileptic waveforms. In this figure, a series of recurring spike-and-wave complexes can be observed. To be clinically applicable, the classifier must not classify these patterns as artefacts.

3.4 Preprocessing and Feature Extraction

As previously mentioned, the main goal of the preprocessing and feature extraction stage of a classifier is to calculate some measures that effectively reflect the characteristic properties of different pattern classes. In the following discussion we describe the implementation of preprocessing and feature extraction stages of our neural classifier.

In the current version of our classifier we first divided the recorded EEG into segments of 100 samples. As the sampling frequency of the data used in the experiments was 200 Hz, the duration was 0.5 seconds. To ensure reasonable time resolution for artefact onset detection, the segmentation window was moved in steps of 25 samples. For each segment, various measures intended to describe the morphology of the patterns were then computed. In the following discussion we concentrate on the definition of these measures.

3.4.1 Movement Artefacts

During morphological analysis the most characteristic features of movement artefacts were found to be sharp step-like transients related to severe amplifier saturation. This means that amplitude distribution of the patterns strongly concentrates in the vicinity of some high positive or negative amplitude value. Therefore, we can obtain a simple measure for estimating the concentration of the amplitude distribution of input patterns starting from the definition of histogram.

Let $\boldsymbol{x}$ denote an EEG segment with m samples for which the standard n-bar histogram can be obtained by sorting the sample values in increasing order and forming n bars of m/n samples. If the histogram is now scaled in such a way that the total area is equal to 1, we obtain a rough estimate for the probability distribution function. If s_i is the spread of the ith bar of the histogram, the height h_i for this bar is simply:

$$h_i = \frac{1}{ns_i}.$$

Although the heights provide a reliable measure for amplitude concentration by giving the highest values for those bars with smallest spread, this direct approach is problematic in case of zero spreads. This can be avoided by adding a nonzero bias to the spreads s_i and calculating the heights according to the following equation:

$$h_i = \frac{1}{n(s_i + bias)}.$$

If we now set $bias = 1/n$ we limit the maximum height of a bar in the case of zero spread to $h_{max} = 1$. Now let w_i be the mean value of the amplitudes inside the ith bar of the histogram. By using these mean amplitudes as weight factors in the weighted sum of the heights h_i we can define a nonlinear filter with output:

$$y = \sum_{i=1}^{n} w_i h_i = \sum_{i=1}^{n} \frac{w_i}{ns_i + 1}.$$

We call this filter a Weighted Histogram Filter (WHF) due to the connection to the histograms of the input patterns. Note that in the case of widely spread bars, the output of the filter will be quite close to zero. In the case of movement artefacts where the amplitude values tend to concentrate strongly in the vicinity of a high positive or negative value, the spreads are close to or equal to zero and the output of the filter is close to the sum of the mean amplitudes w_i. On the other hand, although the spreads for the spontaneous background activity may be close to zero, the output of the filter is still close to zero due to the low mean amplitudes related to the background EEG. In rare cases of two-sided steps with positive and negative mean amplitudes close to each other the filter output may become close to zero. When needed, this condition can be easily avoided by replacing the mean amplitudes with absolute mean amplitudes.

3.4.2 Saturation Artefacts

Saturation artefacts are typically related to electrode, measurement cable and offset voltage problems. Although these artefacts generally do not cause any misclassifications, it is important to develop a method for their detection as it may be used for the control of technical quality of the recordings, for example.

For this project we have divided saturation artefacts into two separate classes, namely zero-level saturation and low-amplitude saturation. A simple estimate of zero-level saturation can be easily defined based on the signal energy. Let L denote the length of the segment and let x_i denote the ith value inside the segment. By using the following equation a simple measure for the zero-level saturation or dead-electrode condition can be obtained.

$$D = \frac{1}{\left(1 + \sum_{i=1}^{L} |x_i|\right)^2}$$

In much the same way we can define an estimator for low-amplitude saturation based on the sorted pattern vector generated during the calculation of WHF output. By using the difference of the minimum and maximum amplitudes inside a segment as a simple range estimate we can define a saturation estimator S as:

$$S = \frac{1}{[1 + (x_{\max} - x_{\min})]^2}.$$

However, this estimator is sensitive to even single outliers inside the segment. A more robust estimator can be defined by subtracting first the mean from the segment and applying the equation used for dead electrode detection. Thus, we can rewrite the low-amplitude saturation estimator as:

$$S_R = \frac{1}{\left[1 + \sum_{i=1}^{L} |x_i - \mu_x|\right]^2}.$$

Although these estimators respond well to saturation at all amplitude levels, we call them low-amplitude saturation estimators as this type of saturation cannot be detected by the WHF filter or zero-level saturation estimator due to the low mean amplitudes or remarkable DC power in the case of offset voltage problems. In the experiments described here the equation based on simple range estimation was used for detection of low-amplitude saturation.

3.4.3 Muscle Artefacts and Other HF Contaminations

Electromyography (EMG) artefacts that are related to increased muscle activity are perhaps the most important example of different high-frequency noise components. Other examples of this class include 50 Hz/60 Hz mains noise, various irregular waveforms related to electrode and measurement cable problems and different capacitively or inductively connected noise components, such as HF noise components from adjacent poorly shielded monitors. As the corrupted EEG contains more power at higher frequencies during these periods, the simplest way to determine the amount of HF contamination is to filter the segment with a high pass filter and compute then the energy of the filtered signal. One computationally effective estimate can be obtained by simply computing the energy of the absolute differences between the consecutive samples of the segments using the following equation:

$$H = \frac{1}{2}\sum_{i=2}^{L}\left|x_i - x_{i-1}\right|.$$

This equation was used for feature extraction in the experiments described here. When desired, this estimate can also be easily rewritten in a normalized form as:

$$H_{norm} = \frac{H}{H+1}.$$

3.5 Selection of the Neural Network Paradigm

After definition of the preprocessing and feature extraction stages, training and validation of the neural classifier was performed. The RBF network was used instead of the MLP network for the reasons explained in the previous section. The training of the RBF network was performed by the use of the Orthogonal Least Squares (OLS) algorithm [5]. In this case study the amount of data used was low enough and computational resources were large enough to enable this choice to be made.

3.6 Training and Validation

During OLS training, we first used K-means clustering and 2-nearest neighbor statistics to generate the centers and widths for 300 candidate neurons [25]. The initial cluster centers for the K-means algorithm were randomly selected in such a way that their distribution in the four-dimensional input space would be uniform. When the centers and widths had been selected, their parameters were frozen and the 25 most efficient candidate neurons were selected amongst the candidate set by applying the OLS algorithm. In OLS training, neuron selection is based on the ability of the candidate neurons to reduce the variance between the desired and calculated output values. In addition to neuron selection, the connection weights between the hidden and output layers are also determined during training.

Final classification results for the input patterns were formed by hard-limiting the network output around a predetermined threshold value. The patterns for which the output of the network was smaller than the threshold were classified as artefacts while the remainder were classified as negative patterns, i.e., either normal or epileptic patterns. The selection of this threshold value was optimized through the application of ROC analysis in such a way that the detection rate for normal patterns was kept as high as possible while also ensuring a sufficiently high artefact detection rate in order for the classifier to be clinically applicable.

For validation of the classifier, four-fold cross-validation was used. The cross-validation data set contained in total slightly greater than 47,000 signal patterns of which about half contained artefacts. Thus, each training and validation set contained about 35,250 and 11,750 training and validation patterns, respectively. According to the discussion above, sensitivity and specificity were used as performance indices. During the experiments, RBF networks with different numbers of hidden neurons were tested. In Table 1, results of different cross-validation runs for the network with 25 hidden neurons are shown. These results show that for the selected threshold level of 0.5 negative patterns are correctly classified at the rate of approximately 95% while the rate of correct classification for the artefacts is over 75%.

Table 1. Sensitivity and specificity of the radial basis function classifier.

Performance	**Sensitivity (TPR)**	**Specificity (TNR)**
Validation set 1	77.38%	94.79%
Validation set 2	75.51%	94.84%
Validation set 3	76.42%	94.45%
Validation set 4	76.39%	94.55%
Average	**76.42%**	**94.65%**

The results of four-fold cross-validation for the classifier with 25 hidden neurons are shown in terms of average ROC curve and average performance curves in Figures 6 and 7, respectively. The ROC curve depicts the correct classification rate of negative (either normal or epileptic) patterns as a function of the correct artefact detection rate. Performance curves show the dependence of classification rates on the threshold value used in the output neuron. Thus, performance curves can be effectively used for the optimization of threshold value selection.

3.7 Discussion

It can be seen from the performance curves for the neural classifier that setting the threshold higher results in an increased number of artefacts being detected correctly. However, as this would happen at the cost of lower classification accuracy for true EEG, a lower threshold was selected to ensure a sufficient specificity for our classifier. To test real performance of the classifier in the presence of epileptic activity, the training and validation data sets contained a number of epileptic signal patterns. As almost all of the normal segments were correctly classified with the detection rate of over 75% for the artefacts, the results seem to be promising. However, more thorough validation, possibly with data recorded with other systems, would be needed. On the other hand, visual analysis of incorrectly classified patterns would also be needed to determine whether there is a possibility of increasing the detection rate by changing the threshold value used at the network output.

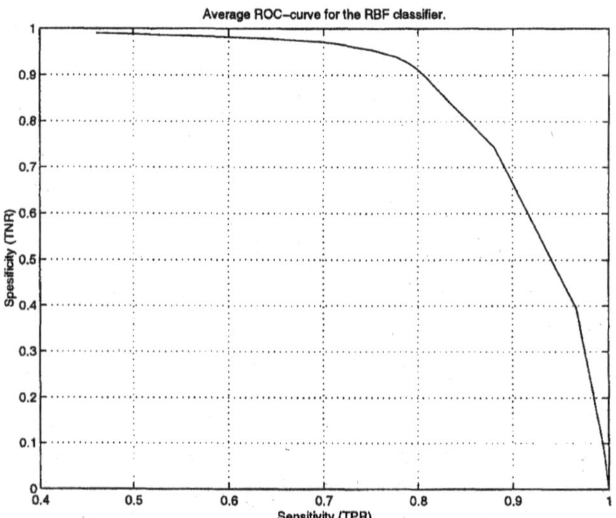

Figure 6. Average ROC curve for the RBF classifier with 25 hidden neurons. The ROC curve shows the dependency between the sensitivity and specificity of the classifier.

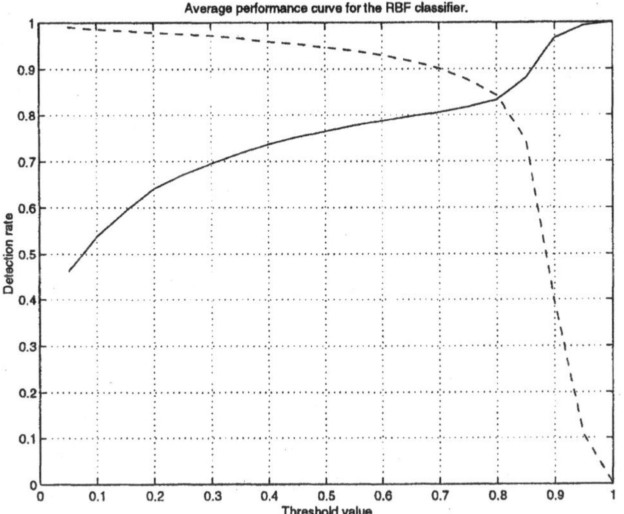

Figure 7. Average performance curves for the RBF classifier. These reflect the performance of the classifier as a function of the threshold level. The solid and dashed lines show the dependence of the correct classification rate for the artefacts and negative patterns, respectively.

Acknowledgements

This study has been financially supported by the Academy of Finland, Technology Development Centre of Finland and the European Union Healthcare Telematics Project European Neurological Network (ENN). This support is gratefully acknowledged. The authors also wish to thank the reviewers for their valuable comments on the manuscript.

References

[1] Barlow, J.S. (1986), "Artefact processing (rejection and minimization) in EEG data processing," in Lopes da Silva, F.H., Storm van Leeuven, W., and Rémond, A. (Eds.), *Handbook of Electroencephalography and Clinical Neurophysiology, Volume 2, Clinical Applications of Computer Analysis of EEG and other Neurophysiological Signals*, Elsevier Science Publishers, pp. 15-62.

[2] Bortolan, G., Silipo, R., and Marchesi, C. (1997), "Fuzzy pattern classification and the connectionist approach," *Pattern Recognition Letters*, vol. 17, pp. 661-670.

[3] Bounds, D.G., Lloyd, P.J., and Mathew, B.G. (1990), "A comparison of neural network and other pattern recognition approaches to the diagnosis of low back disorders," *Neural Networks*, vol. 3, pp. 583-591.

[4] Bronzino, J.D. (1986), *Biomedical Engineering and Instrumentation: Basic Concepts and Applications*, PWS Engineering, Boston.

[5] Chen, S., Cowan, C.F., and Grant, P.M. (1991), "Orthogonal least squares learning algorithm for radial basis function networks," *IEEE Trans. Neural Networks*, vol. 2, pp. 302-309.

[6] Chen, S., Grant, P., and Cowan, C. (1992), "Orthogonal least squares algorithm for training multioutput radial basis function networks," *IEE Proceedings-F*, vol. 139, no. 6, pp. 378-384.

[7] Davis, M.H., Khotanzad, A., and Flamig, D.P. (1996), "3D image matching using a radial basis function neural network," *WCNN'96, World Congress on Neural Networks, International Neural Network 1996 Annual Meeting*, San Diego, CA, USA, pp. 1174-1179.

[8] Downes, P. (1994) "QRS complex recognition using nld and neural networks," *World Congress on Neural Networks, International Neural Network Society Annual Meeting*, San Diego, CA, USA, vol. 1, pp. I-138-142.

[9] Elo, P., Saarinen, J., Värri, A., Nieminen, H., and Kaski, K. (1992), "Classification of epileptic EEG by using self-organized maps," in Aleksander, I. and Taylor, J. (Eds.), *Artificial Neural Networks*, 2nd ed, *Proceedings of International Conference on Artificial Neural Networks (ICANN 92)*, Brighton, United Kingdom, Elsevier Science Publishers, pp. 1147-1150.

[10] Fraser, H.S., Pugh, R., Kennedy, R.L., Ross, P., and Harrison, R.F. (1994) "A comparison of back propagation and radial basis functions, in the diagnosis of myocardial infarction," *Proceedings of the International Conference on Neural Networks and Expert Systems in Medicine and Healthcare*, Plymouth, UK, pp. 76-84.

[11] Gori, M. and Scarselli, F. (1998), "Are multilayer perceptrons adequate for pattern recognition and verification?" *IEEE Trans. on Pattern Analysis and Machine Intelligence*, vol. 20, no. 11, pp. 1121-1132.

[12] Gotman, J. (1986), "Computer analysis of the EEG in epilepsy," in Lopes da Silva, F.H., Storm van Leeuven, W. and Rémond, A. (Eds.), *Handbook of Electroencephalography and Clinical Neurophysiology, Volume 2, Clinical Applications of Computer Analysis of EEG and other Neurophysiological Signals*, Elsevier Science Publishers, Amsterdam, pp. 171-204.

[13] Gotman, J. (1986), "Computer analysis during intensive monitoring of epileptic patients," in Gumnit, R.J. (Ed.), *Advances in Neurology, Vol. 46, Intensive Neurodiagnostic Monitoring*, Raven Press, New York, pp. 249-269.

[14] Haykin, S. (1999), *Neural Networks: A Comprehensive Foundation*, 2nd ed., Prentice Hall, New Jersey.

[15] Hojjatoleslami, A, Sardo, L., and Kittler, J. (1997) "An RBF based classifier for the detection of microcalcifications in mammograms with outlier rejection capability," *1997 International Conference on Neural Networks, Proceedings*, Houston, TX, USA, vol. 3, pp. 1379-1384.

[16] Hornik, K. (1991), "Approximation capabilities of multilayer feedforward networks," *Neural Networks*, vol. 4, no. 2, pp. 251-257.

[17] Jemili, K., and Westerkamp, J.J. (1995) "A kernel based system for the estimation of nonstationary signals," *1995 International Conference on Acoustics, Speech, and Signal Processing, Conference Proceedings*, Detroit, MI, USA, Vol. 5, pp. 3423-3426.

[18] Kirk, B.P., and LaCourse J.R. (1997) "Performance monitoring from the EEG power spectrum with a radial basis function network," *Proceedings of the IEEE 23rd Northeast Bioengineering Conference*, Durham, NH, USA, pp. 19-20.

[19] Kittler, J., Hojjatoleslami, A., and Windeatt, T. (1997) "Strategies for combining classifiers employing shared and distinct pattern representations," *Pattern Recognition Letters*, Vol. 18, pp. 1373-1377.

[20] Kondraske, G.V. (1986), "Neurophysiological measurements," in Bronzino, J.D. (Ed.) *Biomedical Engineering and Instrumentation: Basic Concepts and Applications*, PWS Engineering, Boston, pp. 138-179.

[21] Kovacevic, D. and Loncaric, S. (1997) "Radial basis function-based image segmentation using a receptive field," *Proceedings, Tenth IEEE Symposium on Computer-Based Medical Systems*, Maribor, Slovenia, pp. 126-130.

[22] Krajca, V., Petranek, S., Patakova, I., and Värri, A. (1991), "Automatic identification of significant graphoelements in multichannel EEG recordings by adaptive segmentation and fuzzy clustering," *Int. J. Biomedical Computing*, vol. 28, pp. 71-89.

[23] Lehtokangas, M., Saarinen, J., and Kaski, K. (1995), "Accelerating training of radial basis function networks with cascade-correlation algorithm," *Neurocomputing*,vol. 9, pp. 207-213.

[24] Malmivuo, J. and Plonsey, R. (1995), *Bioelectromagnetism: Principles and Applictions of Bioelectric and Biomagnetic Fields*, Oxford University Press, New York.

[25] Moody, J. and Darken, C. (1989), "Fast learning in networks of locally-tuned processing units," *Neural Computation*, vol. 1, pp. 281-294.

[26] Nisbet, K.C., McLaughlin, S., and Mulgrew, B. (1991), "Nonlinear time-series prediction," *Second International Conference on Artificial Neural Networks*, Bournemouth, UK, pp. 354-358.

[27] Park, J. and Sandberg, I. (1991), "Universal approximation using radial basis function networks," *Neural Computation*, vol. 3, pp. 246-257.

[28] Pietilä, T., Vapaakoski, S., Nousiainen, U., Värri, A., Frey, H., Häkkinen, V., and Neuvo, Y. (1994), "Evaluation of a computerized system for recognition of epileptic activity during longterm EEG monitoring," *Electroencephalography and Clinical Neurophysiology*, vol. 90, pp. 438-443.

[29] Polycarpou, M.M. and Conway, J.Y. (1995) "Modeling and control of drug delivery systems using adaptive neural control methods," *Proceedings of the American Control Conference*, Seattle, Washington, pp. 781-785.

[30] Saastamoinen, A., Pietilä, T., Värri, A., Lehtokangas, M., and Saarinen J. (1998), "Waveform detection with RBF network – application to automated EEG analysis," *Neurocomputing*, vol. 20, pp. 1-13.

[31] Schlang, M., Haft, M., and Abraham-Fuchs, K. (1994) "Neural networks for reconstruction of focal events from bioelectric/biomagnetic potentials," *1994 IEEE International Conference on Neural Networks, IEEE World Congress on Computational Intelligence*, Orlando, FL, U.S.A., vol. 6, pp. 3467-3471.

[32] Stamkopoulos, T., Maglaveras, N., Diamantaras, K., and Strintzis, M. (1997) "Ischemia classification techniques using an advanced neural network algorithm," *Computers in Cardiology 1997*, Lund, Sweden, pp. 351-354.

[33] Tou, J.T. and Gonzales, R.C., (1981), *Pattern Recognition Principles*, Addison-Wesley, London.

[34] Trajanoski, Z. and Wach, P. (1997) "Evaluation of subcutaneous route for closed-loop control of insulin delivery: numerical and

experimental studies," *1995 IEEE Engineering in Medicine and Biology 17th Annual Conference and 21st Canadian Medical and Biological Engineering Conference*, New York, NY, U.S.A., vol. 2, pp. 1357-1358.

[35] Tumer, K., Ramanujam, N., Ghosh, J., and Richards-Kortum, R. (1998) "Ensembles of radial basis function networks for spectroscopic detection of cervical pre-cancer," *IEEE Trans. Biomedical Engineering.*

[36] Värri, A., Hirvonen, K., Hasan, J., Loula, P., and Häkkinen, V., (1992), "A computerized analysis system for vigilance studies," *Computer Methods and Programs in Biomedicine*, vol. 39, pp. 113-124.

[37] Värri, A., Kemp, B, Rosa, A.C., Nielsen, K.D., Gade, J., Penzel, T., Hasan, J., Hirvonen, K., Häkkinen, V., Kamphuizen, A.C., and Mourtazev, M.S. (1995), "Multi-centre comparison of five eye movement detection algorithms," *Journal of Sleep Research*, vol. 4, pp. 119-130.

[38] Värri, A., Hirvonen, K., Häkkinen, V., Hasan, J., and Loula, P., (1996), "Nonlinear eye movement detection method for drowsiness studies, *Int. J. Biomedical Computing*, vol. 43, pp. 227-242.

[39] Wu, J., Ifeachor, E.C., Allen, E.M., and Hudson, N.R. (1994), "A neural network based artefact detection system for EEG signal processing," *Proceedings of the International Conference on Neural Networks and Expert Systems in Medicine and Healthcare*, Plymouth, UK, pp. 257-266.

[40] Zahlmann, G., Scherf, M., and Wegner, A. (1997) "A neuro-fuzzy-classifier for a knowledge-based glaucoma monitor," *Artificial Intelligence in Medicine, 6th Conference on Artificial Intelligence in Medicine Europe, AIME '97, Proceedings*, Grenoble, France, pp. 273-284.

Chapter 8

3-D Visual Object Classification with Hierarchical Radial Basis Function Networks

F. Schwenker and H.A. Kestler

In this chapter we present a 3-D visual object recognition system for an autonomous mobile robot. This object recognition system performs the following three tasks: Object localization in the camera images, feature extraction, and classification of the extracted feature vectors with hierarchical radial basis function (RBF) networks.

1 Introduction

The recognition of 3-D objects from 2-D camera images is one of the most important goals in computer vision. There is a large number of contributions to this field of research from various disciplines, e.g. artificial intelligence and autonomous mobile robots [1], [2], artificial neural networks [3]-[5], computer vision and pattern recognition [6]-[10], psychophysics and brain theory [11]-[13]. Due to the increasing performance of current computer systems and the increasing development of computer vision and pattern recognition techniques several 3-D object recognition systems have been developed [14]-[17]. Among these many different approaches to 3-D object recognition two main streams can be detected: structural-based or primitives-based approaches and view-based methods.

In primitives-based approaches the 3-D objects are modeled using a small set of 3-D volumetric primitives (cubes, cylinders, cones, etc.) in a CAD-like model. In the recognition phase the most important step is to identify the primitives that are visible in the camera image. This approach is derived from the *recognition-by-components* theory developed by Biederman in [18], [19]. It seems that this approach is reasonable for CAD applications, but has its limitations for the recognition of free-form objects, for example in face recognition.

Psychophysical results achieved during the last years have shown that humans are able to learn to recognize 3-D objects from different characteristic 2-D views. In these view-based approaches a set of 2-D views of each object is stored or learned in order to build an internal object representation of the 3-D object. In the recognition phase of such a view-based system a single 2-D view of an object is compared to the learnt 2-D views. This processing step is related to methods like template matching and nearest neighbor classification. One of the main tasks in these view-based approaches is the selection of characteristic object views. The objects have to be recorded from various viewpoints, in different poses and with different illumination in order to build a recognition system which is robust under all such transformations.

Artificial neural network models can be used to learn to recognize 3-D objects on the basis of a small set of 2-D camera images which are recorded from distinct view points [4]. Based on a training set of feature vectors, the network learns a discrimination function in the high-dimensional feature space. For this kind of classification task supervised network training procedures must be utilized.

Often synthetic images or well prepared data sets ignoring problems which are present at lower processing levels have been used in order to simplify the recognition problem, e.g., the 3-D objects are always in the center of the camera images. We attempt to solve a more realistic problem and use camera images recorded from real 3-D objects for training and testing the recognition system. In the recognition phase scenes with multiple 3-D objects may be presented to the recognition system.

The recognition of a 3-D object consisted of the following three subtasks which will be discussed throughout this chapter:

1. **Localization of objects in the camera image.**

   In this processing step the entire camera image is segmented into regions. Each region should contain exactly one single 3-D object. Only these marked regions, which we call the regions of interest (ROI), are used for further image processing. Color-based approaches for the ROI-detection are used.

2. **Extraction of characteristic features.**

   From each ROI within the camera image a set of features is computed. For this, the ROIs are divided into subimages and for each subimage an orientation histogram with eight orientation bins is calculated from the gray valued image. The orientation histograms of all subimages are concatenated into the characterizing feature vector.

3. **Classification of the extracted feature vectors.**

   The extracted feature vectors together with the target classification are used in a supervised learning phase to build the neural network classifier. After network training novel feature vectors are presented to the classifier which outputs the estimated class labels.

We address all these three topics in this chapter, but we will focus on the classification task. The chapter is organized in the following way: in Section 2 the methods for 3-D object localization and feature extraction are described. RBF networks and support vector learning in RBF networks including multiclass SVM classifiers are discussed in Section 3. The construction of binary classifier trees is the topic of Section 4. In Section 5, we present some numerical classification results for the recognition system and finally a conclusion is given.

2 Object Localization and Feature Extraction

2.1 Visual Attention — Regions of Interest in the Camera Image

The classification of visual 3-D objects in camera images requires their reasonable delimitation from background. A possible way to achieve this is to locate regions of interest within the camera image. For this visual attention task biologically motivated models, like saliency-based methods have been intensively investigated during the last years [20]-[22]. In our case the regions of interest should contain areas of single objects. From the subimages enclosed by these regions, features are then extracted for the object classification. Because computational requirements are tight, we currently use a color-based approach for object detection, see [23] and

Figure 1. After downsampling the original camera image the resulting image is transformed from RGB (red, green, blue) to HSV-color space (hue, saturation, value) [24]. HSV color space is used, because this color model makes it very easy to describe color ranges independent of saturation and lightness. Downsampling has the effect of a low pass filtering and also reduces the computational complexity. After downsampling and color space transformation, each pixel inside a valid color range is labeled, and sets of connected labeled pixels (so-called color blobs) are calculated. For every found color-blob the color range and number of pixels is determined. If the number of pixels of a color-blob is larger then a predefined threshold value, a bounding box for this blob is calculated.

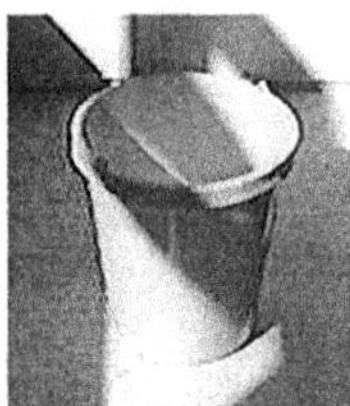

Figure 1. Examples of class `bucket` of the data set (left) and the calculated region of interest (right)

In addition to these processing steps, the following heuristics for merging regions are applied:

1. In the first step, bounding boxes which are contained in larger ones are merged. This is typically applied to objects, whose color range does not match a single valid range, but matches two or more valid color ranges.

2. After this preprocessing step, the distances between centers of regions within the same color range are calculated. If the distance between two regions is less than a predefined value, they will be merged. This is useful for merging small color blobs, for example bottles, whose color regions are usually separated by the label of the bottle.

3. In a last processing step, the bounding boxes determined on the downsampled image are rescaled to the original image size and are slightly enlarged.

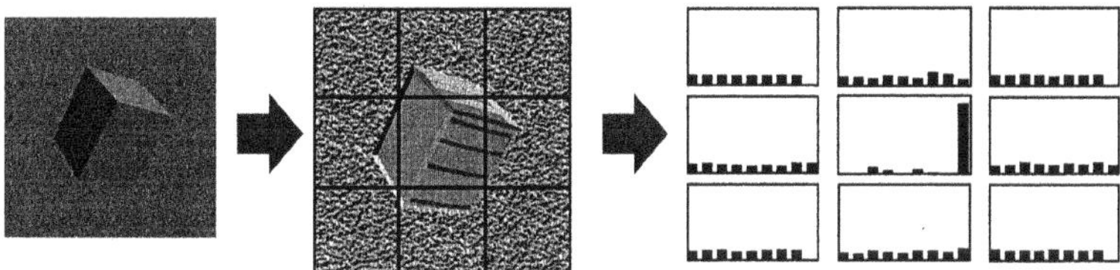

Figure 2. Elements of the feature extraction method. The grey valued image (left) is convolved with the masks S_x and S_y (see text) resulting in the gradient image (center; absolute value of the gradient). Orientation histograms (right) of non-overlapping subimages constitute the feature vector.

2.2 Feature Extraction

The image within the region of interest is divided into $n \times n$ non-overlapping subimages and for each subimage the orientation histogram of eight orientations (range: $0-2\pi$, dark/light edges) is calculated [25] from the gray valued image. The orientation histograms of all subimages are concatenated into the characterizing feature vector.

The gradient of an image $f(x, y)$ at location (x, y) is the two-dimensional vector

$$\begin{pmatrix} G_x \\ G_y \end{pmatrix} = \begin{pmatrix} \frac{\partial f}{\partial x} \\ \frac{\partial f}{\partial y} \end{pmatrix} \approx \begin{pmatrix} f * S_x \\ f * S_y \end{pmatrix}$$

where $*$ denotes the convolution operation. Gradient directions (S_x, S_y) were calculated with 3×3 Sobel operators. The gradient directions are calculated with respect to the x-axis:

$$\alpha(x, y) = \text{atan2}\,(f * S_y, f * S_x)$$

The *atan2* function corresponds to the *atan* but additionally uses the sign of the arguments to determine the quadrant of the result. The eight bins of the histogram all have equal size ($2\pi/8$). The histogram values are calculated by counting the number of angles falling into the respective bin. Histograms are normalized to the size of their subimages.

3 Learning in RBF Networks

RBF networks were introduced into the neural network literature by Broomhead and Lowe in 1988 [26]. The RBF network model is motivated by the locally tuned response observed in biological neurons. Neurons with a locally tuned response characteristic can be found in several parts of the nervous system, for example cells in the auditory system selective to small bands of frequencies or cells in the visual cortex sensitive to bars oriented in a certain direction. These locally tuned neurons show response characteristics bounded to a small range of the input space.

The theoretical basis of the RBF approach lies in the field of interpolation of multivariate functions. We consider multivariate functions $f : \mathbb{R}^d \to \mathbb{R}^m$. Without loss of generality we may assume that m is equal to 1. The goal of interpolating a set of tuples $(x^\mu, y^\mu)_{\mu=1}^M$ is to find a function $F : \mathbb{R}^d \to \mathbb{R}$ with $F(x^\mu) = y^\mu$ for all $\mu = 1, \ldots, M$, where F is an element of a predefined set (often a vector space) of functions. In the RBF approach the interpolating function F is a linear combination of basis functions:

$$F(x) = \sum_{\mu=1}^{M} b_\mu h(\|x - x^\mu\|) + p(x) \tag{1}$$

where $\| \cdot \|$ denotes the Euclidean norm, $b_1, \ldots, b_M$ are real numbers, h a real valued function, and p a polynomial $p \in \Pi_n^d$ (polynomials of degree at most n in d variables). The degree of the polynomial term has to be fixed in advance. The interpolation problem is to determine the real coefficients $b_1, \ldots, b_M$ and the polynomial term $p := \sum_{l=1}^{D} a_l p_j$ where $p_1, \ldots, p_D$ is a basis of Π_n^d and $a_1, \ldots, a_D$ are real numbers. The function F has to satisfy the conditions:

$$F(x^\mu) = y^\mu, \quad \mu = 1, \ldots, M$$

and

$$\sum_{\mu=1}^{M} b_\mu p_j(x^\mu) = 0, \quad j = 1, \ldots, D.$$

Sufficient conditions for the unique solvability of the interpolation problem were given by several authors e.g. see results due to Micchelli, Powell, or Light [27]-[29]. The function h is called a *radial basis function* if the interpolation problem has a unique solution. In some cases the polynomial term in equation (1) can be omitted, then the interpolation problem is equivalent to the matrix equation

$$Hb = y \tag{2}$$

where $b = (b_1, \ldots, b_M)$, $y = (y^1, \ldots, y^M)$, and $M \times M$ matrix H defined by

$$H = (h(\|x^\nu - x^\mu\|))_{\mu,\nu=1,\ldots,M}.$$

Provided the inverse of H exists, the solution of the interpolation problem has the form:

$$b = H^{-1}y. \tag{3}$$

Examples for radial basis functions h often used in applications are:

$$\begin{aligned} h(r) &= e^{-r^2/\sigma^2} \\ h(r) &= (r^2 + \sigma^2)^{1/2} \\ h(r) &= (r^2 + \sigma^2)^{-1/2} \end{aligned}$$

Here, σ is a positive real number which we call the scaling parameter or the width of the radial basis functions. The most popular and widely used radial basis function is the Gaussian function $h(\|x - c\|) = exp(-\|x - c\|^2/\sigma^2)$ with peak at center $c \in \mathbb{R}^d$ and decreasing as the distance from the center increases.

The solution of the exact interpolating RBF mapping passes through every data point (x^μ, y^μ). In the presence of noise in the data the exact solution of the interpolation problem is typically a function oscillating between the given data points. An additional problem with the exact interpolation procedure is that the number of basis functions is equal to the number of data points and so calculating the inverse of the $M \times M$ matrix H becomes intractable in practice. In applications, where we have to deal with many thousands of noisy data points an approximative solution to the data is more desirable than an interpolative one. Broomhead and Lowe [26] first proposed to reduce the number of basis functions in order to reduce the computational complexity. This technique produces a solution approximating instead of interpolating the data points. Furthermore, in [26] an interpretation of the RBF method as an artificial neural network model is given. It consists of three neural layers: a layer of input neurons feeding the feature vectors into the network, a hidden layer of RBF neurons, calculating the outcome of the basis functions, and a layer of output neurons, calculating a linear combination of the basis functions. Under some additional conditions to the basis function h the set of RBF networks with free adjustable prototype vectors are shown to be universal approximators, so that any continuous function can be approximated with arbitrary precision [30]. This implies that RBF-networks with adjustable prototypes can also be used for classification tasks [31].

3.1 Support Vector Learning

Three different training procedures to train an RBF network are known: Two-stage training, Backpropagation training, and Support vector training. We concentrate on support vector learning [32]-[34]. The support vector machine (SVM) was initially developed by Vapnik to classify data points of a linear separable data set. In this case a training set consisting of M examples (x^μ, y^μ), $x^\mu \in \mathbb{R}^d$, and $y^\mu \in \{-1, 1\}$ can be divided up into two sets by a separating hyperplane. Such a hyperplane is determined by a weight vector $b \in \mathbb{R}^d$ and a bias or threshold $\theta \in \mathbb{R}$ satisfying the separating constrains

$$y^\mu \ \left[\langle x^\mu, b\rangle + \theta\right] \geq 1 \quad \mu = 1, \ldots, M.$$

The distance between the separating hyperplane and the closest data points of the training set is called the margin. Intuitively, the larger the margin, the higher the generalization ability of the separating hyperplane. The optimal separating hyperplane with maximal margin is unique and can be expressed by a linear combination of those training examples lying exactly at the margin. These data points are called the support vectors. The separating hyperplane has the form

$$H(x) = \sum_{\mu=1}^{M} \alpha_\mu^* y^\mu \langle x, x^\mu\rangle + \alpha_0^*$$

where $\alpha_1^*, \ldots, \alpha_M^*$ is the solution optimizing the functional

$$Q(\alpha) = \sum_{\mu=1}^{M} \alpha_\mu - \frac{1}{2} \sum_{\mu,\nu=1}^{M} \alpha_\mu \alpha_\nu y^\mu y^\nu \langle x^\mu, x^\nu\rangle$$

subject to the constraints $\alpha_\mu \geq 0$ for all $\mu = 1, \ldots, M$ and $\sum_{\mu=1}^{M} \alpha_\mu y^\mu = 0$. Then a training vector x^μ is a support vector if the corresponding coefficient $\alpha_\mu^* > 0$. Then $b = \sum_{\mu=1}^{M} \alpha_\mu y^\mu x^\mu$ and the bias α_0^* is determined by a single support vector (x^s, y^s):

$$\alpha_0^* = y^s - \langle x^s, b \rangle.$$

The SVM approach has been extended to the nonseparable situation and to the regression problem. In most applications (regression or pattern recognition problems) linear solutions are insufficient. For example, in real world pattern recognition problems it is common to define an appropriate set of nonlinear mappings $g := (g_1, g_2, \ldots)$, each g_j defined as a real valued function, transforming the input vectors x^μ to a vector $g(x^\mu)$ which is element of a new feature space $\mathcal{H}$. Then the separating hyperplane can be constructed in the feature space $\mathcal{H}$ and can be expressed by

$$H(x) = \sum_{\mu=1}^{M} \alpha_\mu y^\mu \langle g(x), g(x^\mu) \rangle + \alpha_0.$$

Provided $\mathcal{H}$ is a Hilbert space, the explicit mapping $g(x)$ does not need to be known since it can implicitly be defined by a kernel function

$$K(x, x^\mu) = \langle g(x), g(x^\mu) \rangle$$

representing the inner product of the feature space. With a suitable choice of a kernel function the data can become separable in feature space despite being not separable in the input space. Using a kernel function K satisfying the condition of Mercer's theorem (see [34] for details), the separating hyperplane is given by

$$H(x) = \sum_{\mu=1}^{M} \alpha_\mu y^\mu K(x, x^\mu) + \alpha_0.$$

The coefficients α_μ can be found by solving the optimization problem

$$Q(\alpha) = \sum_{\mu=1}^{M} \alpha_\mu - \frac{1}{2} \sum_{\mu,\nu=1}^{M} \alpha_\mu \alpha_\nu y^\mu y^\nu K(x^\mu, x^\nu)$$

subject to the constrains $0 \leq \alpha_\mu \leq C$ for all $\mu = 1, \ldots, M$ and

$$\sum_{\mu=1}^{M} \alpha_\mu y^\mu = 0$$

where C is a predefined positive number. An important kernel function satisfying Mercers condition is the Gaussian kernel function

$$K(x,y) = e^{-\frac{\|x-y\|_2^2}{\sigma^2}}.$$

The separating surface obtained by the SVM approach is a linear combination of Gaussian functions located on the support vectors. The SVM reduces to an RBF network. In contrast to RBF networks trained by backpropagation learning the centers are located at the data points of the training set. Furthermore, the number of centers is automatically determined in the SVM approach.

3.2 Multiclass Classification

In many real world applications, e.g. speech recognition or optical character recognition, a multi-class pattern recognition problem has to be solved. The SVM classifiers as previously described are formulated as binary classifiers. Various approaches have been developed in order to deal with multi-class classification problems. The following strategies can be applied to build N-class classifiers utilizing binary SVM classifiers:

1. N ***one-against-rest*** **classifiers.**

   In this approach N different classifiers are constructed, one classifier for each class. Here the l-th classifier is trained on the whole training data set in order to classify the members of class l against the rest. For this, the training examples have to be re-labeled: Members of the l-th class are labeled to 1; members of the other classes to -1. In the classification phase the classifier with the maximal output defines the estimated class label of the current input vector.

2. $N(N-1)/2$ ***one-against-one*** **classifiers.**

   For each possible pair of classes a binary classifier is calculated. Each classifier is trained on a subset of the training set containing only training examples of the two involved classes. As for the *one-against-rest* strategy the training sets have to be re-labeled. All $N(N-1)/2$ classifiers are combined through a majority voting scheme to estimate the final classification [35], [36]. Here the class with the maximal number of votes among all $N(N-1)/2$ classifiers is the estimation.

3. **Extension of the original SVM formulation to the N-class classification problem.**

   Weston and Watkins proposed in [37] a natural extension to the binary SVM approach to solve the N-class classification problem directly. Here re-labeling of the training data is not necessary. All the N classes are considered at once, and the separating conditions are integrated into the same optimization problem. As for the *one-against-rest* classifiers, the result is a N-class classifier with N weight vectors and N threshold values. The recall phase is organized as for the *one-against-rest* classifier strategy.

4. **Hierarchies or trees of binary SVM classifiers.**

   Here the multi-class classification problem is decomposed into a series of binary classification sub-problems organized in a hierarchy, see Figure 3. We discuss this approach in the next section.

4 SVM Classifier Trees

One of the most important problems in multi-class pattern recognition problems is the existence of confusion classes. A confusion class is a subset of the set of the classes $\{1, \ldots, N\}$ in which very small differences in the feature vectors may lead to misclassifications. For example, in OCR the measured features for members of the classes `o`, `O`, `0` and `Q` are typically very similar, so $\{$`o, O, 0, Q`$\}$ defines a confusion class. The major idea of hierarchical classification is to make a coarse discrimination between confusion classes first and a finer discrimination within the confusion classes later [38].

In Figure 3, examples of hierarchical classifiers are depicted. Each node within the graph represents a SVM classifier discriminating feature vectors of a confusion class into one of two smaller confusion classes or possibly into individual classes. The terminal nodes of the graph (called leaves) represent these individual classes, and the other nodes are classifiers performing a binary decision task, thus these nodes have exactly two children. Nodes within the graph may have more than one incoming edge. Figure 3a shows a tree-structured classifier, where each node has exactly one incoming edge. In Figure 3b, a more general classifier struc-

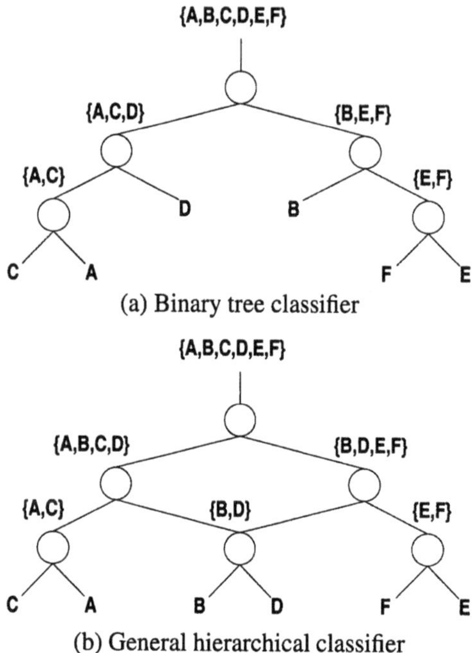

(a) Binary tree classifier

{A,B,C,D,E,F}

{A,B,C,D}

{B,D,E,F}

{A,C}

{B,D}

{E,F}

C A B D F E

(b) General hierarchical classifier

Figure 3. Two examples of hierarchical classifiers. The graphs are directed acyclic graphs with a single root node at the top of the graph and with terminal nodes (leaves) at the bottom. Individual classes are represented in the leaves, the other nodes within the graph are classifiers performing a binary decision task, which is defined through the annotations at the incoming and the outgoing edges.

ture defined through a special directed acyclic graph is depicted. In the following we restrict our considerations to SVM trees.

The classification subtask is defined through the annotations at the incoming and outgoing edges of the node. Let us consider for example the SVM classifier at the root of the tree in Figure 3a. The label of the incoming edge is $\{A, \ldots, F\}$, so for this (sub-)tree a 6-class classification task is given. The edges to the children are annotated with $\{A, C, D\}$ (left child) and $\{B, E, F\}$ (right child). This means that this SVM has to classify feature vectors into confusion class $\{A, C, D\}$ or $\{B, E, F\}$. To achieve this, all members of the six classes $\{A, \ldots, F\}$ have to be re-labeled: Feature vectors with class labels A, C, or D get the new label -1 and those with class label B, E, or F get the new label 1. After this re-labeling procedure the SVM is trained as described in the previous section. Note, that re-labeling has to be done for each classifier training.

So far we have not answered the question how to construct the hierarchy of subsets of classes. In some cases it may be a priori defined. For example in applications where the set of classes is hierarchically arranged based on some kinds of symbolic properties which are in general different from the measured features. In OCR for example, the set of characters can be divided into digits and letters, etc., and further the letters into upper and lower case letters.

An attempt to design a hierarchy of confusion classes is to consider the confusion matrices. Let K be a set of classes that should be divided into two disjoint subsets K_1 and K_2. A partition has to be evaluated by some kind of error function counting the number of errors made through the current class assignments of K_1 and K_2:

$$E(K_1, K_2) := \sum_{\substack{(i\in K_1 \wedge j\in K_2)\vee \\ (j\in K_1 \wedge i\in K_2)}} q_{ij}$$

here q_{ij} is the frequency of feature vectors from class i classified to class j. To design the whole hierarchy this procedure has to be applied until all confusion classes have exactly a single class.

This approach has two main disadvantages: a) The whole N-class classification problem has to be solved to determine the confusion matrix. To determine the confusion matrices, either classifiers have to be trained by supervision or the confusion matrices have to be calculated by k-nearest-nieghbor procedures. b) The exact evaluation of all possible partitions is computational expensive for large N, because the number of possible binary partitions is equal to $2^{N-1} - 1$. For large N an exact enumeration of all possible binary partitions is intractable, and so the confusion classes have to be calculated heuristically [23].

Another approach is the partition of classes K into subsets K_1 and K_2 by clustering or vector quantization methods. In clustering and vector quantization a set of representative prototypes $\{c_1, \ldots, c_k\} \subset \mathbb{R}^d$ is determined by unsupervised learning from the feature vectors $x^\mu, \mu = 1, \ldots, M$ of the training set. For each prototype c_j the Voronoi cells R_j

and clusters C_j are defined by

$$R_j = \{x \in \mathbb{R}^d \;:\; j = \text{argmin}_i \|c_i - x\|\}$$

and

$$C_j = R_j \cap \{x^\mu \;:\; \mu = 1, \ldots, M\}.$$

The relative frequency of members of class i in cluster j is

$$p_{ij} = \frac{|\Omega_i \cap C_j|}{|C_j|}.$$

For class i the set Ω_i is defined by

$$\Omega_i = \{x^\mu \;:\; \mu = 1, \ldots, M,\; y^\mu = i\}$$

where y^μ denotes the teacher signal of feature vector x^μ. The k-means clustering with $k = 2$ cluster centers c_1 and c_2 defines a hyperplane within the feature space $\mathbb{R}^d$ separating two sets of feature vectors. From the corresponding clusters C_1 and C_2 a partition of the set of classes K into two subsets K_1 and K_2 can be achieved through the following assignment:

$$K_j = \{i \in K \;:\; j = \text{argmax}\,\{p_{i1}, p_{i2}\}\}, \quad j = 1, 2.$$

Recursively applied, this procedure leads to a binary tree of confusion classes as depicted in Figure 3a, where each node within the tree is labeled with a confusion class and defines a partition into two sub-confusion classes. This assignment scheme can be extended in several directions, e.g. for schemes with $k > 2$ cluster centers or for non-binary trees.

5 Data and Classification Results

5.1 Data Sets

Two different data sets were used in performance evaluation of the classifier, artificially generated and a data set of real camera images.

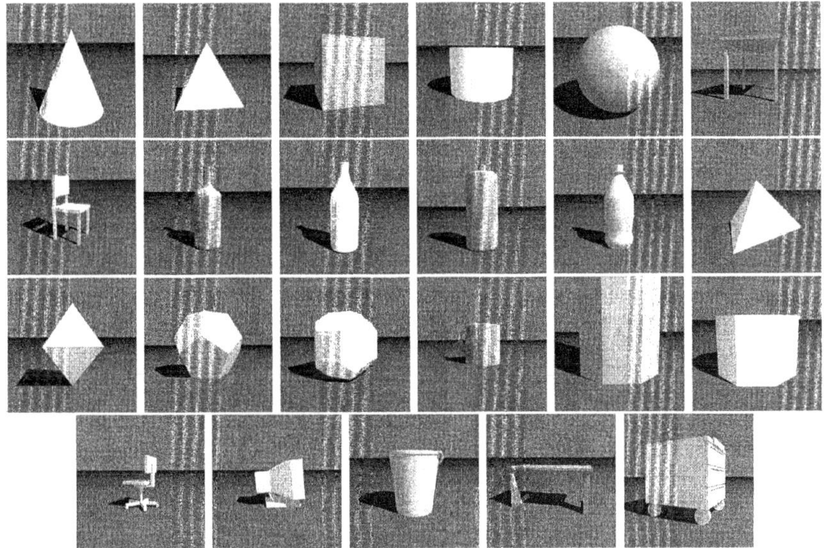

Figure 4. Examples of all 23 classes. Labels are from top left to right bottom: cone, pyramid, cube, cylinder, ball, table, chair, bottle 1 to 4, tetrahedron, octahedron, dodecahedron, gem, coffee mug, column, clipped column, office chair, monitor, bucket, office table and drawer.

5.1.1 Artificial Data

Images of 23 different objects were generated with the raytracing software PoV-Ray. Examples of the 5920 objects (class 0 to 5: 250 images; class 6 to 22: 260 images) are given in Figure 4. Images (256×256 pixel) were created through a virtual helical movement of the observer around the object (constant distance). The anzimut angle, was varied in steps of 36°(0°to 360°) with reference to the object. The declination angle was varied in steps of 1.5°(0°to 15°). A point light source made the same circular movement 45°ahead of the observer but at a constant declination angle of 45°. During this "movement" the objects were rotated at random (uniform distribution) around their vertical axis, the scaling of the objects (x,y,z -axis) was varied uniformly distributed in the range of 0.7 to 1.3 and the ambient light was varied at random (uniform) in the range of 0.2 to 0.6. An example of the variation within one class is given in Figure 5. From all images, 5×5 histograms (see Section 2 and Figure 2) were concatenated into a feature vector that serves as input to the classifier.

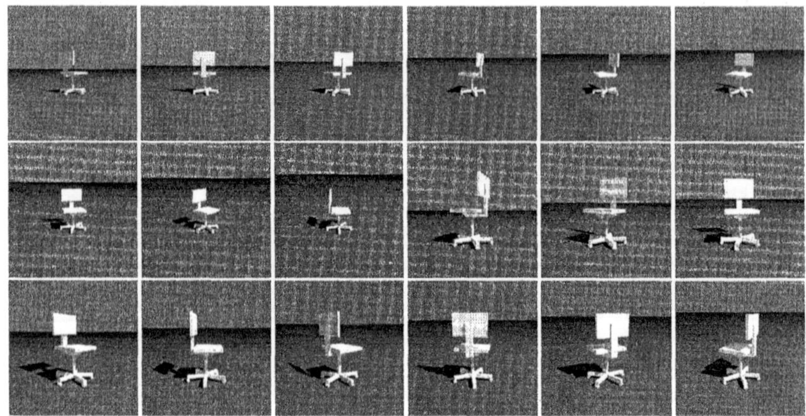

Figure 5. Examples illustrating the variation inside the class `office chair`.

5.1.2 Real-World Data Set of Camera Images

Camera images were recorded for six different 3-D objects (orange juice bottle, small cylinder, large cylinder, cube, ball and bucket) with an initial resolution of 768×576 pixels. To these five objects nine classes were assigned (bottle lying/upright, cylinders lying/upright). The test scenes were acquired under mixed natural and artificial lighting. Regions of interest where calculated from 1800 images using the color-blob detection method. These regions where checked and labeled by hand, 1786 images remained for evaluation. Regions of interest are detected using three color ranges, one for red (bucket, cylinder, ball), blue (cylinder) and yellow (cylinder, bucket, orange juice). The image in Figure 1 gives an example of the automatically extracted regions of interest. Feature vectors were calculated concatenating 5×5 orientation histograms calculated through 3×3 Sobel operator, see Section 2 and Figure 2.

5.2 Results

In order to get an overview over the underlying structure of the data, two data analysis tools are briefly mentioned. They are useful to explore large sets of high-dimensional feature vectors:

1. **Clustering** of the high dimensional feature vectors utilizing for example the k-means clustering algorithm in order to get a smaller set

Figure 6. Examples illustrating the real-world data set. Labels are from top left to right bottom: class 0/1: orange juice bottle upright/lying, class 2/3: large cylinder upright/lying, class 4/5: small cylinder upright/lying, class 6: cube, class 7: ball, class 8: bucket.

of representative prototypes. The feature vectors from each class are clustered separately leading to a set of prototypes, each representing a certain class. For the union of all prototypes a distance matrix is calculated. This distance matrix can be plotted as a matrix of gray values (see Figure 7) and used for further data analysis.

The distance matrix of $6 \times 9 = 54$ k-means prototypes of the recorded camera images is shown in Figure 7. Small distances can be observed between prototypes within the classes $\{2, 3, 4, 5, 6, 8\}$ and within $\{0, 1\}$. The prototypes of class 7 seem to be separated from the others, but some smaller distances to prototypes of classes $\{0, 1, 4, 5, 6\}$ can be detected. These smaller distances between prototypes of different classes typically lead to misclassifications.

2. **Nonlinear distance preserving projections** of the data points into a low-dimensional projection space (typically $\mathbb{R}^2$) may be used to explore the data set. The projection of large data sets is computational

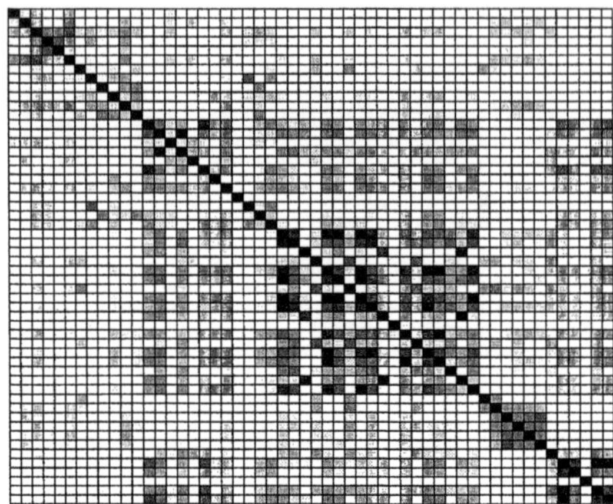

Figure 7. A 54 × 54 (Euclidean) distance matrix for 54 k-means prototypes (6 prototypes per class) of the recorded camera images. The 54 prototypes are sorted by its class memberships in such a way that the prototypes $c_1, \ldots, c_6$ are members of class 0, $c_7, \ldots, c_{12}$ have class label 1, etc. Distances between prototypes have been encoded into gray values (small distances black, large distance white).

expensive and intractable, therefore only the prototypes are projected which gives a rough overview over the data (see [39] for some more details on clustering and visualization of large and high-dimensional data sets). In Figure 8 the 54 prototypes of the k-means cluster procedure are shown as projections (with class labels) to $\mathbb{R}^2$. Here, in the lower left part of Figure 8 the projections of the prototypes of classes $0, 1$ and 7 are located, the prototypes of the other classes cover the rest of the projection area. This is a similar observation as already seen for distance matrix of the cluster centers. This result is not surprising because Spearman's rank order coefficient of the two sorted distance sequences (distances in feature space vs. distances in projection space) has been determined to $r_s = 0.98$. The value of Spearman's rank order coefficient r_s is within the interval $[-1, 1]$, where larger values close to 1 indicate similar rank orders of the sequences, so that the calculated value of $r_s = 0.98$ shows that the order of the distances between the cluster centers in the feature space are fairly well represented by the distances of the corresponding projections in $\mathbb{R}^2$. For a more detailed visualization of the data set clustering and projection algorithms have to be applied to the feature vectors of the confusion classes.

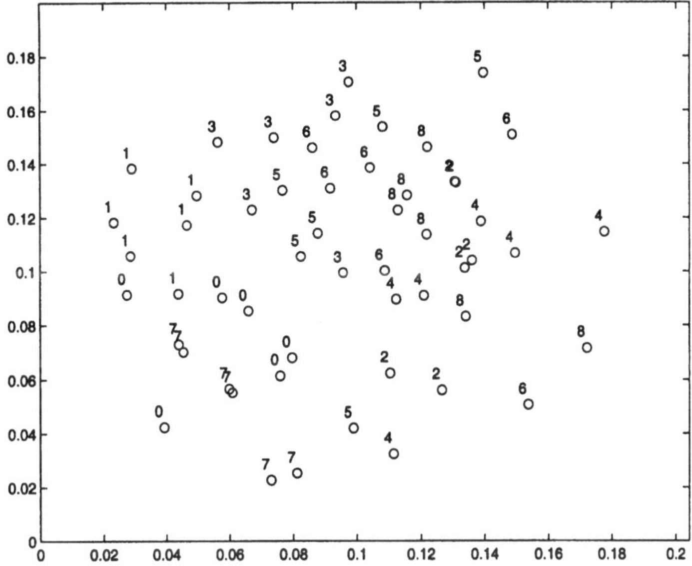

Figure 8. A distance preserving 2-D projection of the 54 prototypes (see text). The class membership of a prototype is used to annotate of its 2-D projection.

In Figure 9 the structure of the confusion classes for the real-world data set of recorded camera images is given. The binary tree of the confusion classes has been determined by 2-means clustering followed by the assignment scheme previously described. For a partition of a certain confusion class, 5 clustering runs have been applied to the feature vectors of this confusion class. Each clustering run has been initialized with a randomly selected subset of the data set serving as initial setting of the cluster centers. Except for the confusion class $\{4,5,6\}$, always the same split of the confusion classes has been found. For confusion class $\{4,5,6\}$ the partition $\{4,5\}$ and $\{6\}$ which is shown in Figure 9 has been found once, the trivial partition $\{4,5,6\}$ and $\emptyset$ has been found in the other four clustering runs. In the nodes the classification accuracies of the particular classification task are given. As already observed for the distance matrix of the class specific prototypes and in the 2-D projection of the prototypes the two confusion classes $\{0,1,7\}$ and $\{2,3,4,5,6,8\}$ may be defined and have been determined by the 2-means clustering procedure at the root level.

The classification results of four different classifiers are presented for both data sets:

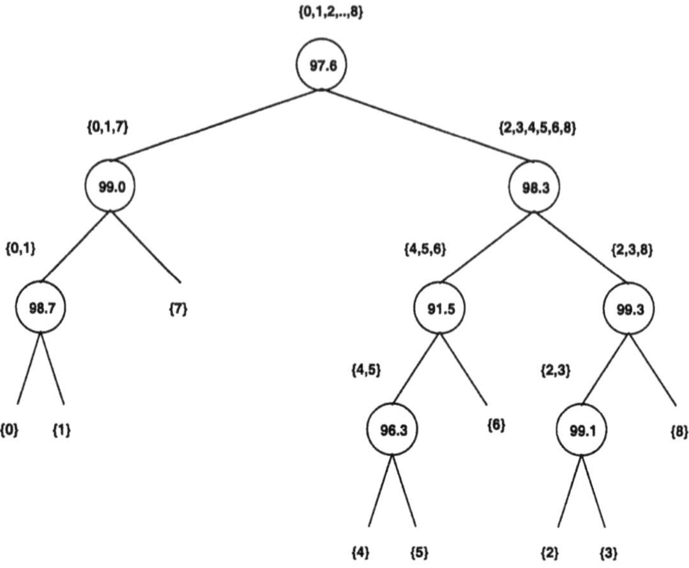

Figure 9. Binary tree classifier for the set of feature vectors derived from the ROIs of the camera images from the real-world data set. Each node within the tree is labeled with a confusion class and the classification rate of the defined sub-classification problem (mean of three 5-fold crossvalidation runs). In the leaves, the original individual classes are represented.

1NN: 1-nearest neighbor classifier with Euclidean distance.

LVQ: 1-nearest neighbor classifier trained by Kohonen's software package OLVQ1 and LVQ3 training each algorithm for 50 training epochs; 10 prototypes per class.

RBF-SVM: A set of support vector networks each with Gaussian kernel function; N-against-rest learning/voting strategy; NAG library for optimization.

RBF-SVM-HC: A binary tree of support vector networks each with Gaussian kernel function; a binary tree of confusion classes is determined with 2-means clustering; NAG library for optimization.

The classification results given in Table 1 are the means of three 5-fold crossvalidation runs. The classification rates of the SVM classifiers are significantly higher than the accuracies for the **1NN** and **LVQ** classifiers. For the real world data set the results of the SVM tree classifier are remarkably good, slightly better as for the flat SVM classifier with the N-

Table 1. Classification accuracies of the real-world camera images and the artificially generated PoV-RAY data set for the 1-nearest-neighbor classifier, an LVQ-classifier trained by OLVQ1 and LVQ3 with $k = 90$ prototypes (for the camera images) respectively $k = 230$ (for the POV-RAY data set) prototypes, an RBF network trained by support vector learning (N-against-rest strategy), and a binary tree of RBF classifiers each trained by support vector learning. The mean of three 5-fold crossvalidation runs is given.

Classifier	**Camera Images**	**PoV-RAY Data**
1NN	91.04	92.45
LVQ	92.44	92.80
RBF-SVM	93.89	93.32
RBF-SVM-HC	94.28	93.06

against-rest strategy. It can be observed in Figure 9 that many misclassifications appear by discriminating between the classes $\{4, 5, 6\}$, because the extracted feature vectors looked very similar. In such cases different features have to be extracted, e.g., edges, colors or texture.

6 Conclusion

In this chapter, we presented a 3-D visual object recognition system for a mobile robot. The components of this system perform the subtasks: (1) localization of the 3-D objects in the camera images based on color blob detection, the ROIs in the camera images, (2) extraction of low-level features within the determined ROIs — a set of orientation histograms calculated from the ROIs, and (3) classification of the extracted feature vectors utilizing a tree of RBF-classifiers, each classifier trained by support vector learning. Classification results based on crossvalidation have been presented for 1-NN, LVQ, SVM, and SVM-trees. We have assessed the potential of nonlinear SVMs and trees of nonlinear SVMs in the problem of recognizing 3-D objects from a single object view. In comparison to other algorithms, it appears that the classification results of SVM tree classifiers are remarkably good. The proposed SVM tree classifier is a flexible classifier architecture which is able to deal with different sets of features which may be useful in applications with many thousands of different objects to classify. Future work in this area includes the integration of additional features like edges, colors, and texture, where different features should be used in the visual attention module and in particular for the hierarchical classifier.

Acknowledgments

The research described here was part of the Collaborative Research Center (SFB 527) and is supported by the German Science Foundation (DFG). We thank Professor Günther Palm for many fruitful discussions and Axel Baune, Steffen Simon and Florian Vogt for help with data acquisition and labeling.

References

[1] Brooks, R. (1983), "Model-based three-dimensional interpreations of two-dimensional images," *IEEE Transactions on Pattern Analysis and Machine Intelligence*, vol. 5, pp. 140-149.

[2] Lowe, D. (1987), "Three-dimensional object recognition from single two-dimensional images," *Artificial Intelligence*, vol. 31, pp. 355-395.

[3] Little, J., Poggio, T., and Gamble, E. (1988), "Seeing in parallel: The vision machine," *International Journal of Supercomputing Applications*, vol. 2, pp. 13-28.

[4] Poggio, T. and Edelman, S. (1990), "A network that learns to recognize tree-dimensional objects," *Nature*, vol. 343, pp. 263-266.

[5] Schiele, B. and Crowley, J. (1996), "Probabilistic object recognition using multidimensional receptive field histograms," *Proc. of the 13th Int. Conf. on Pattern Recognition*, IEEE Computer Press, pp. 50-54.

[6] Marr, D. and Nishihara, H. (1978), "Representation and recognition of the spatial organization of three dimensional structure," *Proceedings of the Royal Society of London B*, vol. 200, pp. 269-294.

[7] Marr, D. (1982), *Vision*, Freeman, San Fransisco.

[8] Ullman, S. (1996), *High-level Vision. Object Recognition and Visual Cognition*, The MIT Press, Cambridge.

[9] Basri, R. (1996), "Recognition by prototypes," *International Journal of Computer Vision*, vol. 19, pp. 147-168.

[10] Edelman, S. and Duvdevani-Bar, S. (1997), "A model of visual recognition and categorization," *Phil. Trans. R. Soc. London B*, vol. 352, pp. 1191-1202.

[11] Edelman, S. and Bülthoff, H. (1992), "Orientation dependence in the recognition of familiar and novel views of three-dimensional objects," *Vision Research*, vol. 32, pp. 2385-2400.

[12] Bülthoff, H., Edelman, S., and Tarr, M. (1995), "How are three-dimensional objects represented in the brain?" *Cerebal Cortex*, vol. 5, pp. 247-260.

[13] Logothetis, N. and Scheinberg, D. (1996), "Visual object recognition," *Annual Review of Neuroscience*, vol. 19, pp. 577-621.

[14] Mel, B. (1997), "SEEMORE: combining colour, shape, and texture histogramming in a neurally-inspired approach to visual object recognition," *Neural Computation*, vol. 9, pp. 777-804.

[15] Zhu, S. and Yuille, A. (1996), "FORMS: aFlexible Object Recognition and Modeling System," *International Journal of Computer Vision*, vol. 20, pp. 1-39.

[16] Murase, H. and Nayar, S.(1995), "Visual learning and recognition of 3D objects from appearance," *International Journal of Computer Vision*, vol. 14, pp. 5-24.

[17] Lades, M., Vorbrüggen, J., Buhmann, J., Lange, J., von der Malsburg, C., Würtz, R., and Konen, W. (1993), "Distortion invariant object recognition in the dynamic link architecture," *IEEE Transactions on Computers*, vol. 42, pp. 300-311.

[18] Biederman, I. (1987), "Recognition by components: a theory of human image understanding," *Psychol. Review*, vol. 94, pp. 115-147.

[19] Biederman, I. (1985), "Human image understanding: recent research and a theory computer vision," *Graphics and Image Processing*, vol. 32, pp. 29-73.

[20] Itti, L., Koch, C., and Niebur, E. (1998), "A model of saliency-based visual attention for rapid scene analysis," *IEEE Transactions on Pattern Analysis*, vol. 20, no. 11, pp. 1254-1259.

[21] Koch, C. and Ullman, S. (1985), "Shifts in selective visual attention: towards the underlying neural circuitry," *Human Neurobiology*, vol. 4, pp. 219-227.

[22] Niebur, E. and Koch, C. (1994), "A model for the neuronal implementation of selective visual attention based on temporal correlation among neurons," *Journal of Computational Neuroscience*, vol. 1, pp. 141-158.

[23] Kestler, H., Simon, S., Baune, A., Schwenker, F., and Palm, G. (1999), "Object classification using simple, colour based visual attention and a hierarchical neural network for neuro-symbolic integration," in Burgard, W., Christaller, T., and Cremers, A. (Eds.), *KI-99: Advances in Artificial Intelligence*, Springer Verlag, pp. 267-279.

[24] Smith, A.R. (1978), "Color gamut transform pairs," in Phillips, R.L. (Ed.), *5th Annual Conf. on Computer Graphics and Interactive Techniques*, ACM, New York, pp. 12-19.

[25] Roth, M. and Freeman, W. (1995), "Orientation histograms for hand gesture recognition," Technical Report 94-03, Mitsubishi Electric Research Laboratorys, Cambridge Research Center.

[26] Broomhead, D. and Lowe, D. (1988), "Multivariable functional interpolation and adaptive networks," *Complex Systems*, vol. 2, pp. 321-355.

[27] Micchelli, C. (1986), "Interpolation of scattered data: distance matrices and conditionally positive definite functions," *Constructive Approximation*, vol. 2, pp. 11-22.

[28] Light, W. (1992), "Some aspects of radial basis function approximation," in Singh, S. (Ed.), *Approximation Theory, Spline Functions and Applications*, Kluwer, vol. 365 of *Kluwer Mathematical and Physical Sciences Series*, pp. 163-190.

[29] Powell, M.J.D. (1992), "The theory of radial basis function approximation in 1990," in Light, W. (Ed.), *Advances in Numerical Analysis*, Oxford Science Publications, vol. II. pp. 105-210.

[30] Park, J. and Sandberg, I.W. (1993), "Approximation and radial basis function networks," *Neural Computation*, vol. 5, pp. 305-316.

[31] Poggio, T. and Girosi, F. (1990), "Networks for approximation and learning," *Proceedings of the IEEE*, vol. 78, pp. 1481-1497.

[32] Cristianini, N. and Shawe-Taylor, J. (2000), *An introduction to support vector machines*, Cambridge University Press.

[33] Schölkopf, B., Burges, C., and Smola, A. (1998), *Advances in Kernel Methods — Support Vector Learning*, MIT Press.

[34] Vapnik, V. (1998), *Statistical Learning Theory*, John Wiley and Sons.

[35] Friedman, J. (1996), "Another approach to polychotomous classification," Tech. Rep., Stanford University, Department of Statistics.

[36] Kreßel, U. (1999), "Pairwise classification and support vector machines," in Schölkopf, B., Burges, C., and Smola, A. (Eds.), *Advances in Kernel Methods*, The MIT Press, chap. 15. pp. 255-268.

[37] Weston, J. and Watkins, C. (1998), "Multi-class support vector machines," Tech. Rep. CSD-TR-98-04, Royal Holloway, University of London, Department of Computer Science.

[38] Nadler, M. and Smith, E. (1992), *Pattern Recognition Engineering*, John Wiley and Sons.

[39] Schwenker, F., Kestler, H.A., and Palm, G. (2000), "An algorithm for adaptive clustering and visualisation of highdimensional data sets," in Riccia, G., Kruse, R., and Lenz, H.J. (Eds.), *Computational Intelligence in Data Mining*, Springer, pp. 127-140.

Chapter 9

Controller Applications Using Radial Basis Function Networks

K. Takahashi

Methods of designing a radial-basis-function-network-based (RBFN) controller and implementing it for servo controlling mechanical systems are presented. Focusing on the derivative of sigmoid function, we derive an RBFN controller by applying a differential operator to a neural servo controller. Applications for controlling a flexible micro-actuator and a 1-degree-of-freedom robot manipulator using RBFN controller are also described.

1 Introduction

Many studies of servo controllers using neural networks (NNs) have been undertaken to apply both the nonlinear mapping and learning abilities of NNs to control systems [1]-[5]. On the other hand, a network using a radial basis function (RBF) has been proposed [6] in order to achieve fast convergence of a network's learning of complex nonlinear functions/mappings. The RBF networks (RBFNs) are simple compared to NNs, and fast linear algorithms such as the least squares algorithm can be applied in the learning process of RBFNs; therefore, RBFNs are expected to be used in signal processing applications instead of NNs, and there has been interest in using RBFNs for control of nonlinear systems in the last few years [7]-[11].

This chapter presents servo controller applications of RBFN. First, a method of designing an RBFN controller based on a NN controller is described. In general, a sigmoid function is used as the neuron activation function of NNs. Study of the sigmoid function shows that the shape of the derivative of a sigmoid function is similar to that of a Gaussian function. Therefore, a network which uses the derivative of a sigmoid function as the activation function can be treated as a kind of RBFNs. Focusing on this characteristic of the sigmoid function, the RBFN controller is derived by applying a differential operator to the NN controller. Since the proposed RBFN controller relates to the NN controller by means of a differential operator, our design should make it possible to create an interface between an NN controller and an RBFN controller.

Next, application examples for controlling a flexible micro-actuator using the RBFN controller are presented. Micro-actuators which are capable of executing motions in the micron or submicron range play a key role in micro-robots and have applications in semiconductor and microchip manufacturing, biomedical research, biosubstance processing, micro-biological research, and micro-robotics. There is a need in the area of micro-robotics and micro-mechanism for light fast compact actuators. To develop such a micro-actuator, a flexible micro-actuator using the piezoelectric effect in PVdF(poly vinylidene fluoride) was proposed [12], [13] because the piezoelectric device is flexible, light, tough and can be easily fabricated into unusual designs. In order to achieve good control performance of the flexible micro-actuator with conventional controllers, the mathematical model of the objective system was necessary. However, it is difficult to obtain the mathematical model exactly because (1) a flexible micro-actuator is a distributed parameter system having a theoretically infinite number of vibration modes, (2) physical parameters of the actuator varies since piezoelectlic effect of PVdF is easily affected by the thermal condition of the environment, (3) input/output characteristics of the actuator is nonlinear with the piezoelectlic hysteresis of PVdF, and (4) the dynamics of the actuator is affected by nonlinear/uncertain disturbances in the environment. Therefore, using the fast learning ability and nonlinear mapping ability of RBFNs is an effective way to design a control system for a flexible micro-actuator which lacks a priori knowledge or a model of the system. In this study, simulations are performed to investigate both the feasibility and the characteristics of the RBFN controller for controlling the flexible micro-actuator.

Finally, experiments using 1-degree-of-freedom robots are presented to demonstrate the effectiveness of the RBFN controller for controlling actual systems. In our experiments, the force control of an axial robot and the angular position control of a robot arm are carried out. The robots have nonlinear input/output characteristics because the servo actuators of the robots are affected by nonlinear disturbances, such as solid friction, backlash and deadzone. Moreover, it is hard to obtain physical parameters of the robots exactly. By using the RBFNs, however, a servo control system of the robots can be designed without a priori knowledge of the system. Experimental results indicate both the usefulness and flexibility of the RBFN controller.

2 RBFN Controller Design

In this section, a method of designing an RBFN controller is described. First, we design a direct NN controller with the objective SISO system expressed by the following equation.

$$y(k+1) = G[\, y(k)\; y(k-1) \;\; \cdots \;\; y(k-n)\; u(k)\; u(k-1) \; \cdots \; u(k-m)\,] \tag{1}$$

Here $G(\cdot)$ is a function that expresses the system characteristics, $y(k)$ is the system output, $u(k)$ is the control input, k is the sampling number, and n and m are the system orders. Here, we assume that the orders n and m are known and that the inverse of the system $G^{-1}(\cdot)$ exists and is stable. The NN for the controller is three layers with no inner feedback loops and no direct connection from the input layer to the output layer. A sigmoid function $f(\cdot)$ defined by the following equation is used to activate the hidden layer neurons.

$$f(x) = \frac{1 - e^{-x/a}}{1 + e^{-x/a}} \tag{2}$$

Here a is the parameter that changes the shape of the sigmoid function. The NN input vector $\boldsymbol{I}_c(k)$ is defined by the following equation.

$$\boldsymbol{I}_c^T(k) = [\;\; y(k) \;\;\; y(k-1) \; \cdots \; y(k-n+1)\; u(k-1) \; u(k-2) \; \cdots \; u(k-m)\; y_d(k+1)\; 1\,] \tag{3}$$

where $y_d(k)$ is the desired system output. A constant value 1 is included in the element of the input vector $\boldsymbol{I}_c(k)$ as a threshold for the hidden layer neuron. The NN output which is the control input $u(k)$ to the objective system can be determined using the following equation.

$$u(k) = \boldsymbol{W}^{oh}(k)\boldsymbol{f}[\boldsymbol{W}^{hi}(k)\boldsymbol{I}_c(k)] \tag{4}$$

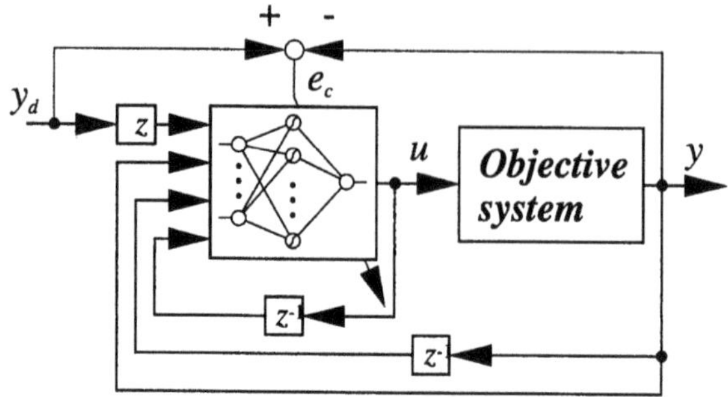

Figure 1. Block diagram of direct NN controller (n = 2, m = 1).

Here $\boldsymbol{W}^{hi}(k)$ is the weight matrix($q\times s$, $s = n + m + 2$) from the input layer to the hidden layer, $\boldsymbol{W}^{oh}(k)$ is the weight matrix($1\times q$) from the hidden layer to the output layer, and q is the number of neurons in the hidden layer. These weight matrices are updated during each sampling using the generalized δ-rule to minimize the square of the control error $e_c(k)$.

$$e_c(k) = y_d(k) - y(k) \tag{5}$$

Figure 1 shows a block diagram of the direct NN controller applied to a second-order system ($n = 2, m = 1$).

Next, we show how the RBFN controller can be derived from the NN controller. When the NN has a sufficiently high number of neuron units, we can assume the existence of weights $\boldsymbol{W}_0^{hi}(k)$ and $\boldsymbol{W}_0^{oh}(k)$ which satisfy $e_c(k)\approx 0$. The control error $e_c(k)$ can then be rewritten by using an arbitrary function $g(\cdot)$ which approximates the inverse of the system as the following form.

$$e_c(k+1) = g[\boldsymbol{I}_c(k)] - u(k) \tag{6}$$

If the function $g(\cdot)$ is differentiable by every component of the vector $\boldsymbol{I}_c(k)$, the following relation is derived by applying the differential operator $\partial/\partial\boldsymbol{I}_c(k)$ to Equation (6).

$$[\frac{\partial e_c(k+1)}{\partial \boldsymbol{I}_c(k)}]^T\boldsymbol{I}_c(k) = [\frac{\partial g[\boldsymbol{I}_c(k)]}{\partial \boldsymbol{I}_c(k)}]^T\boldsymbol{I}_c(k) - [\frac{\partial u(k)}{\partial \boldsymbol{I}_c(k)}]^T\boldsymbol{I}_c(k) \tag{7}$$

From Equation (4), the partial differentiation $[\partial u(k)/\partial\boldsymbol{I}_c(k)]^T\boldsymbol{I}_c(k)$ is calculated as follows.

$$[\frac{\partial u(k)}{\partial \boldsymbol{I}_c(k)}]^T \boldsymbol{I}_c(k) = \sum_{i=1}^{q} W_i^{oh}(k) T_i(k) f'[\sum_{j=1}^{s} W_{ij}^{hi}(k) I_{c_j}(k)] \tag{8}$$

$$T_i(k) = \sum_{j=1}^{s} W_{ij}^{hi}(k) I_{c_j}(k) \tag{9}$$

Here $W_{ij}^{hi}(k)$ is the component of the weight $\boldsymbol{W}^{hi}(k)$, $W_i^{oh}(k)$ is the component of the weight $\boldsymbol{W}^{oh}(k)$, and $I_{c_j}(k)$ is the component of the input vector $\boldsymbol{I}_c(k)$. Assuming the existence of weights $\boldsymbol{W}_0^{hi}(k)$ and $\boldsymbol{W}_0^{ho}(k)$ which satisfies

$$g[\boldsymbol{I}_c(k)] \approx \boldsymbol{W}_0^{oh}(k) \boldsymbol{f}[\boldsymbol{W}_0^{hi}(k) \boldsymbol{I}_c(k)], \tag{10}$$

we can obtain the following relation from Equation (7) if $\boldsymbol{W}^{hi}(k) \approx \boldsymbol{W}_0^{hi}(k)$ and $\boldsymbol{W}^{ho}(k) \approx \boldsymbol{W}_0^{oh}(k)$.

$$[\frac{\partial g[\boldsymbol{I}_c(k)]}{\partial \boldsymbol{I}_c(k)}]^T \boldsymbol{I}_c(k) \approx [\frac{\partial u(k)}{\partial \boldsymbol{I}_c(k)}]^T \boldsymbol{I}_c(k) \tag{11}$$

$$[\frac{\partial e_c(k+1)}{\partial \boldsymbol{I}_c(k)}]^T \boldsymbol{I}_c(k) \approx 0 \tag{12}$$

As a result, from Equations (8) and (11), the RBFN controller can be described in the following form.

$$u(k) - \boldsymbol{W}^{oh}(k) \boldsymbol{T}(k) \boldsymbol{\phi}[\boldsymbol{W}^{hi}(k) \boldsymbol{I}_c(k)] \tag{13}$$

$$\boldsymbol{T}(k) = \boldsymbol{diag}[T_i(k)], (i = 1, 2, ..., q) \tag{14}$$

Here $\phi(\cdot)(= f'(\cdot))$ is the derived RBF defined by the following equation (its shape is shown in Figure 2).

$$f(x) = \frac{2e^{-x/a}}{a(1 + e^{-x/a})^2} \tag{15}$$

Consequently, the RBFN controller approximates a derivative of function $g(\cdot)$ as described in Equation (11), and the system output can approach the desired output with a different integration constant. To approximate the function and compensate for the difference, the learning process of the RBFN controller was carried out according to the generalized δ-rule.

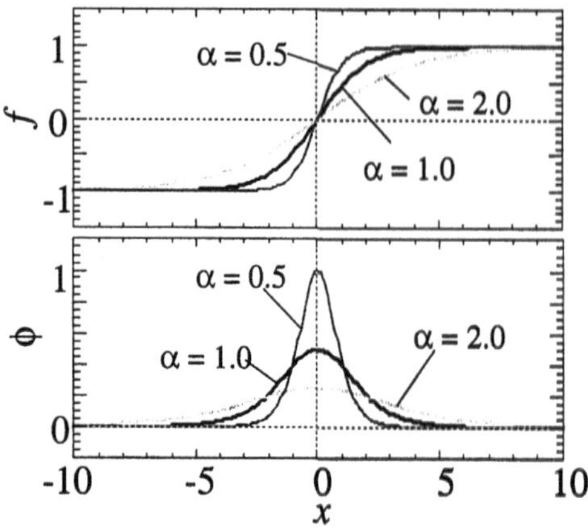

Figure 2. Function shapes.

To minimize the cost function $J_c(k)$ in Equation (16), the learning rule is defined in the following equations.

$$J_c(k) = \frac{1}{2}e_c^2(k) \tag{16}$$

$$\begin{aligned} \boldsymbol{W}^{hi}(k+1) &= \boldsymbol{W}^{hi}(k) - \eta\frac{\partial J_c(k)}{\partial \boldsymbol{W}^{hi}(k-1)} \\ &= \boldsymbol{W}^{hi}(k) + \eta e_c(k)\lambda(k) \\ &\quad \times[\boldsymbol{\Phi}(k-1) + \boldsymbol{T}(k-1)\boldsymbol{\Psi}(k-1)] \\ &\quad \times \boldsymbol{W}^{ho^T}(k-1)\boldsymbol{I}_c^T(k-1) \end{aligned} \tag{17}$$

$$\begin{aligned} \boldsymbol{W}^{oh}(k+1) &= \boldsymbol{W}^{oh}(k) - \eta\frac{\partial J_c(k)}{\partial \boldsymbol{W}^{oh}(k-1)} \\ &= \boldsymbol{W}^{oh}(k) + \eta e_c(k)\lambda(k)\boldsymbol{\phi}^T[\boldsymbol{W}^{hi}(k-1)\boldsymbol{I}_c(k-1)] \\ &\quad \times \boldsymbol{T}^T(k-1) \end{aligned} \tag{18}$$

Here η is the convergence factor, $\lambda(k)(= \partial y(k)/\partial u(k-1))$ is the system Jacobian, and the matrices $\boldsymbol{\Phi}(k)$, $\boldsymbol{\Psi}(k)$ are defined as follows.

$$\boldsymbol{\Phi}(k) = \boldsymbol{diag}[\phi[\sum_{j=1}^{s} W_{ij}^{hi}(k)I_{c_j}(k)]], (i = 1, 2, ..., q) \tag{19}$$

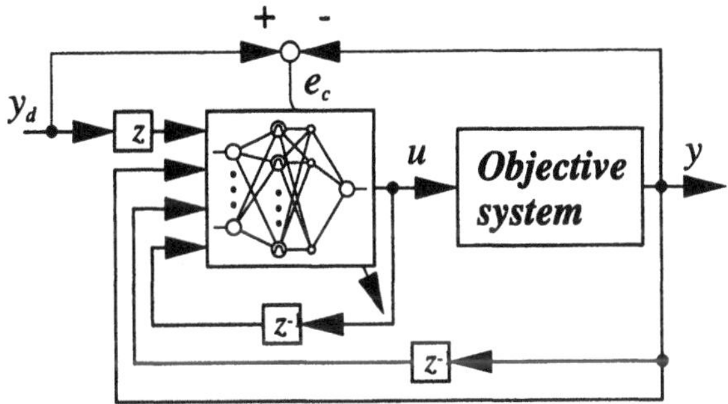

Figure 3. Block diagram of RBFN controller (n = 2, m = 1).

$$\Psi(k) = \boldsymbol{diag}[\phi'[\sum_{j=1}^{s} W_{ij}^{hi}(k) I_{c_j}(k)]], (i = 1, 2, ..., q) \tag{20}$$

Here $\phi'(\cdot)$ is the derivative of the derived RBF. As shown in Equations (17) and (18), the network weights and the RBF center parameters are updated simultaneously, since the RBF center parameters are expressed as network weights between an input layer and a hidden layer of the RBFN. To calculate Equations (17) and (18), the value of the Jacobian is required. In this study, we assume that the Jacobian equals 1 and that both the sign and magnitude of the Jacobian are compensated for by tuning the convergence factor to simplify the control system. Figure 3 shows a block diagram of the RBFN controller when it is applied to a second-order system ($n = 2, m = 1$).

3 Simulation Study

In this section, the RBFN controller was numerically investigated to determine its characteristics and feasibility for controlling a flexible micro-actuator [15].

3.1 Model of Flexible Micro-Actuator

Figure 4 shows a schematic of the flexible micro-actuator which consists of two layers of piezopolymer film cemented to an elastic metal shim in proper polarity. When an electric voltage is applied to the actuator terminals, one film expands and the other contracts, causing the actuator

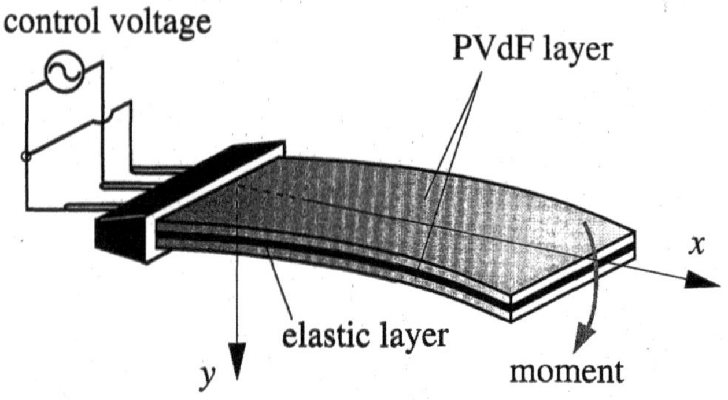

Figure 4. Schematic figure of flexible micro-actuator.

to bend. Assuming linear characteristics of PVdF, the equation of motion for the flexible micro-actuator is given by [14]

$$\begin{aligned} EI(1+\gamma\frac{\partial}{\partial t})\frac{\partial^4 w(x,t)}{\partial x^4} &+ m_a\frac{\partial^2 w(x,t)}{\partial t^2} \\ &= NV(t)[\delta'(x)-\delta'(x-L)] \end{aligned} \quad (21)$$

where E is Young's modulus, I is the moment of inertia of the actuator, γ is the structural damping coefficient, m_a is the mass per unit length of the actuator, L is the length of the actuator, x is the distance from the fix end, t is time, $w(x,t)$ is the bending displacement, N is the coefficient of the generated moment by the piezoelectric effect, $V(t)$ is the control input voltage and $\delta'(x)$ is the derivative of Dirac's delta function. Solving Equation (21), we finally obtain the following discrete-time transfer function of the flexible micro-actuator.

$$y(k) = \frac{z^{-d}[b_0 + \sum_{i=1}^{m} b_i z^{-i}]}{1+\sum_{i=1}^{n} a_i z^{-i}} u(k) \quad (22)$$

Here the output $y(k)$ is the tip displacement of the flexible micro-actuator, the input $u(k)$ is the control input voltage, z^{-1} is the time delay operator, d is dead-time, and a_i and b_i are order coefficients defined with the physical parameters of the flexible micro-actuator and the sampling rate.

In the actual flexible micro-actuator, two major nonlinearities are observed: (1) the coefficient N varies with respect to time because it is

Table 1. Physical properties of flexible micro-actuator.

Young's modulus E_{PVdF} (N/m^2)	2.0 10^9
E_{metal} (N/m^2)	6.56 10^{10}
Length L (m)	0.029
Width b (m)	0.0164
Thickness c_{PVdF} (m)	2.8 10^{-7}
c_{metal} (m)	1.4 10^{-7}
Piezoelectric constant d_{PVdF} (m/m)/(V/m)	23 10^{-12}
Total mass m_a (kg)	4.92 10^{-6}

easily affected by the nonlinear characteristics and uncertainties in the environment, and (2) the piezoelectric effect hysteresis exhibits. In the following study these nonlinearities are considered and simulated.

3.2 Simulation Results

In our simulation studies, the goal of the control was to make the system output $y(k)$ (i.e., tip displacement of the flexible micro-actuator) track the desired output $y_d(k)$. The physical parameters of the flexible micro-actuator are shown in Table 1. The damping coefficient of the model was determined by comparing the calculated result with the experimental one [14]. In the simulation, a model of the flexible micro-actuator with two elastic modes was used. Further, a sampling rate of 500 Hz was used with values for the coefficients in the discrete-time transfer function Equation (22) as listed in Table 2. The number of neurons in the input, hidden, and output layers was 9, 18, and 1, respectively. The initial weight matrices were randomly selected from the interval [-0.1, 0.1]. The RBF shape parameter a was 0.2 and the convergence factor η was 0.045. These parameters were chosen in order to keep both the control system and the RBFN learning stable and were found by trial and error. The desired output was a rectangular wave in order to take account of the frequency richness. The period of the rectangular wave was 1 sec. In the results that follow, the system output $y(k)$ was normalized by the desired output $y_d(k)$.

Initially, in order to establish the feasibility of the RBFN controller, it was used to control a linear model of the flexible micro-actuator. Figure 5 shows the learning process of the RBFN controller by plotting

Table 2. Coefficients for transfer function when two flexible mode is considered.

index i	a_i	b_i
0	*	4.513×10^{-7}
1	1.848	-2.144×10^{-7}
2	-1.212	-3.438×10^{-8}
3	0.5942	2.482×10^{-7}
4	-0.3306	*

the normalized cost function which is an average of the cost function $J_c(k)$ within one period of the desired output. As shown in Figure 5, the normalized cost function converged as learning progressed. Figure 6 shows the time response of the system at the 20th period. The RBFN controller was able to track the displacement quickly and precisely. This result shows the feasibility of the RBFN controller.

As a reference for comparing the results of the RBFN controller, both an NN controller [14] and an LQI controller [16] were simulated. Figure 7 shows the learning process of the NN controller and Figure 8 is the time response of the system at the 20th period. Here the NN controller's parameters are the same as those of the RBFN controller except for the convergence factor. The convergence factor of the NN controller was 0.02. As Figure 8 shows, residual vibration with the second elastic mode is observed in the displacement response, but the displacement tracks the desired output after convergence of the NN learning. Figure 9 shows the time response of the system controlled with the LQI controller.

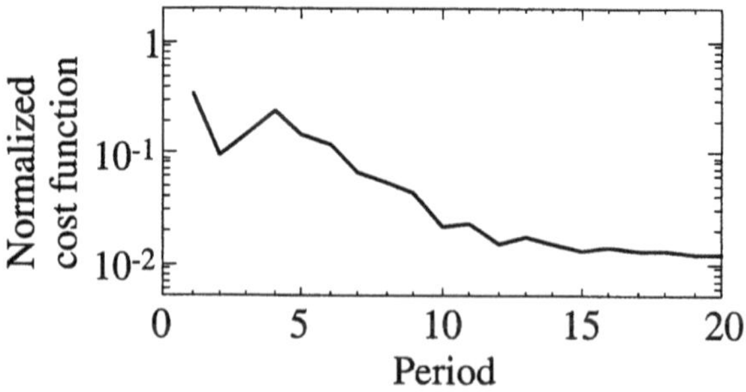

Figure 5. Learning process of RBFN controller.

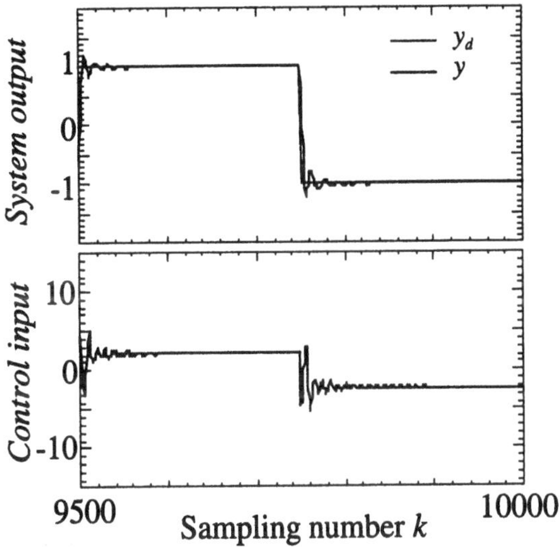

Figure 6. Response of system with RBFN controller.

The feedback gains of LQI controller were designed to minimize the cost function J_{lqi}.

$$J_{lqi} = \frac{1}{2}\sum_{k=0}^{\infty}[e_c^2(k+1) + r\Delta u^2(k)] \tag{23}$$

Here r is the weight of the control input and $\Delta u(k)(= u(k) - u(k-1))$ is the difference of the control input. As shown in Figure 9, the displacement tracks the desired output with relatively large overshooting and residual vibration with the first elastic mode. Table 3 compares the performance of these controllers. Here, CP is the average of the cost function within one period of the desired output, and AP is the average of the squared control input within one period of the desired output. The

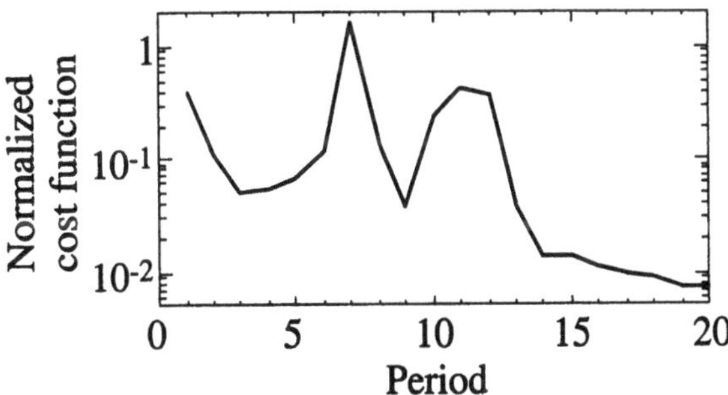

Figure 7. Learning process of NN controller.

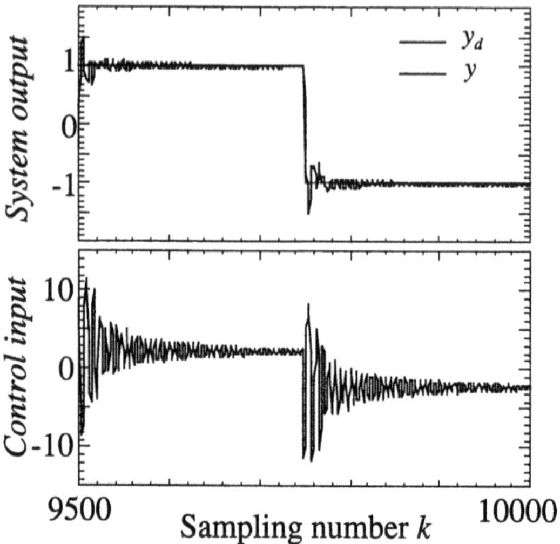

Figure 8. Response of system with NN controller.

CP and AP of the RBFN or NN controllers are the average values of those obtained with 10 different initial weight matrices, and those at the 20th period were evaluated. The optimal control parameters for converging the learning process of both the single-layer RBFN controller [19]

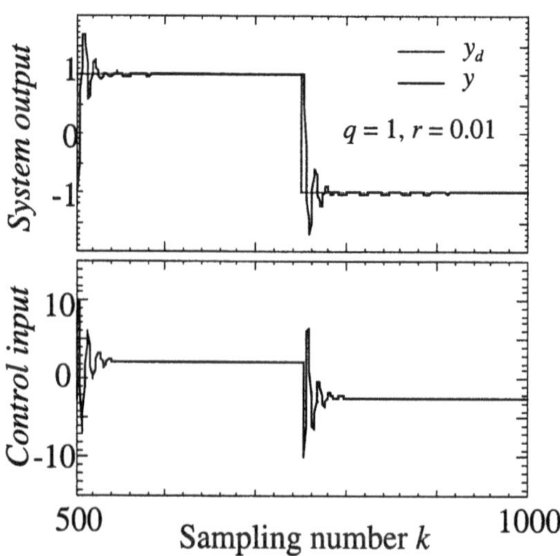

Figure 9. Response of system with LQI controller.

Table 3. Comparison of control performance.

controller	CP	AP
RBFNC	0.0134	2.8345
2-layer RBFCN	*	*
NNC	0.0074	4.7780
linear NNC	*	*
LQI	0.0263	3.2439

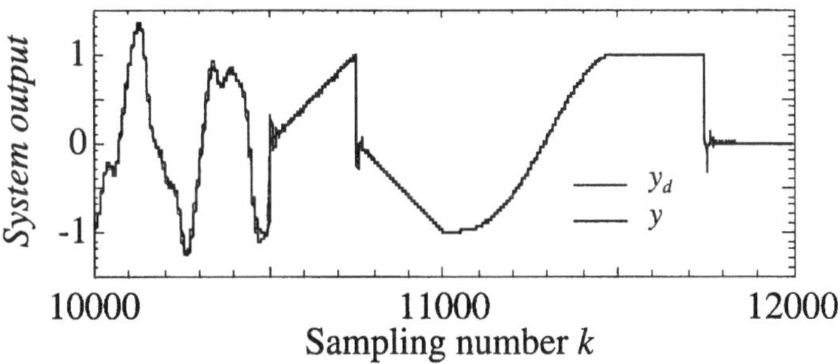

Figure 10. Tracking results for changing reference trajectory.

and the linear NN controller [17] could not be determined. The AP of the RBFN controller is minimal as can be seen in Table 3 and good tracking results were obtained as shown in Figure 6. Although the CP of the NN controller is minimal, residual vibration with the second elastic mode remains, as shown in Figure 8. These results indicate the effectiveness of using an RBFN controller.

Next, to investigate the robustness of the RBFN controller, we first tested how it handled changes in the desired output. After the RBFN controller's learning had been completed as shown in Figure 6, the desired output changed after every 500 samplings. The order of the desired output is the synthesized sine wave, the triangular wave, the 3rd power of sine wave, and the rectangular wave. As shown in Figure 10, the RBFN controller is robust to changes in the desired output. The performance of the RBFN controller in relation to the variation of the desired output frequency was then investigated. After the RBFN controller's learning converged for the

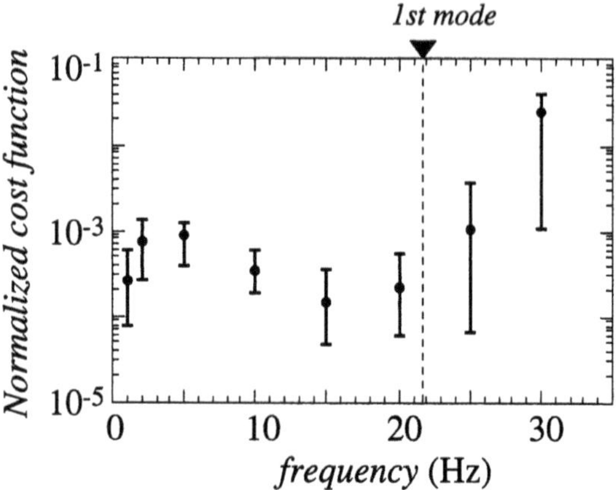

Figure 11. Relationship between control performance and desired output frequency.

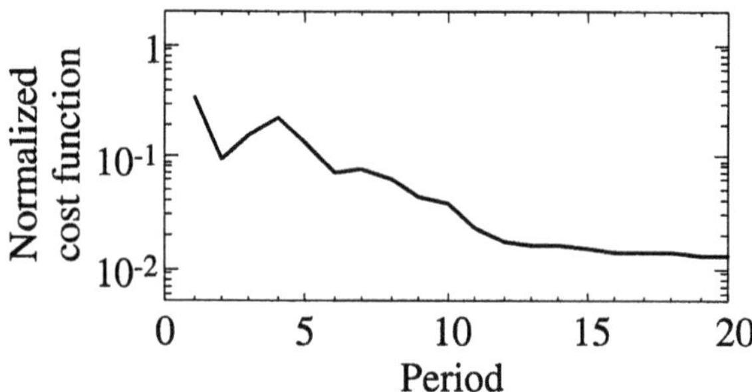

Figure 12. Learning process of RBFN controller under variation of moment coefficient.

rectangular wave, the desired output was changed to the sine wave and its frequency was varied after every 500 samplings. Figure 11 shows the relationship between the desired output frequency and the normalized cost function. Here the normalized cost function is the average of the values obtained with 10 different initial weight matrices. As is shown, the RBFN controller is robust at lower frequencies relative to the 1st elastic mode frequency, but it is not robust at higher frequencies. This shows that the RBFN controller can control a flexible micro-actuator under limited-bandwidth conditions.

Next, the ability of the RBFN controller to compensate for nonlinearities

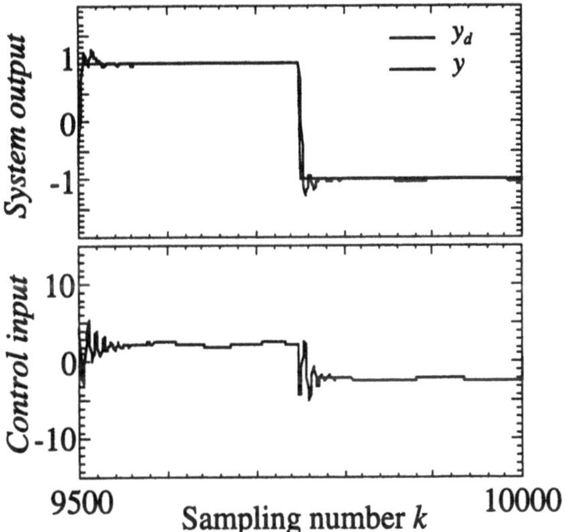

Figure 13. Response of system with RBFN controller under variation of moment coefficient.

of the objective system was tested. The time variation of the coefficient N was modeled with the additive perturbation form defined by sine function: $N = N_0 + N_v \sin 2\pi pt$, where N_0 is the nominal value, N_v is the amplitude of the additive perturbation and p is the frequency of the perturbation. Figure 12 shows the learning process and Figure 13 shows the time response of the system at the 20th period. In these figures, the parameters of the additive perturbation were $N_v = 0.1$ and $p = 4$. As shown in Figure 12, the normalized cost function converged as learning progressed. Comparing Figure 13 with Figure 6 reveals that the control input from the RBFN controller varies periodically to compensate for the additive perturbation and to maintain quick and precise tracking of the displacement.

Next, compensation for hysteresis of the actuator was tested. Assuming an ideal condition of hysteresis, the hysteresis was defined by using a backlash model [18]. Figure 14 shows the learning process and Figure 15 shows the time response of the system at the 20th period. In these figures, the bandwidth of the hysteresis was 0.4. The normalized cost function converged as learning progressed and the quick and precise tracking of the displacement was achieved. These results show that

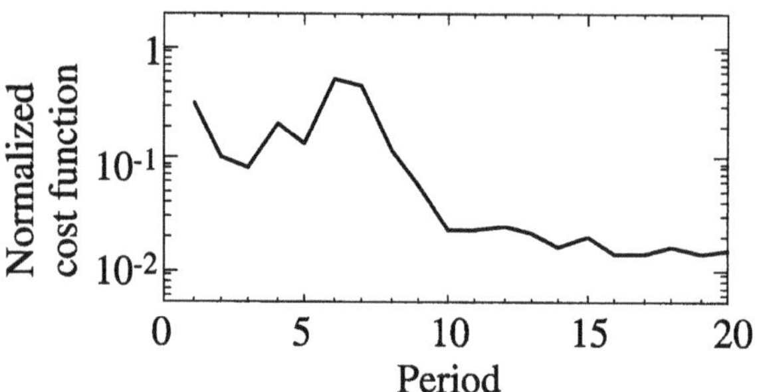

Figure 14. Learning process of RBFN controller under hysteresis of actuator.

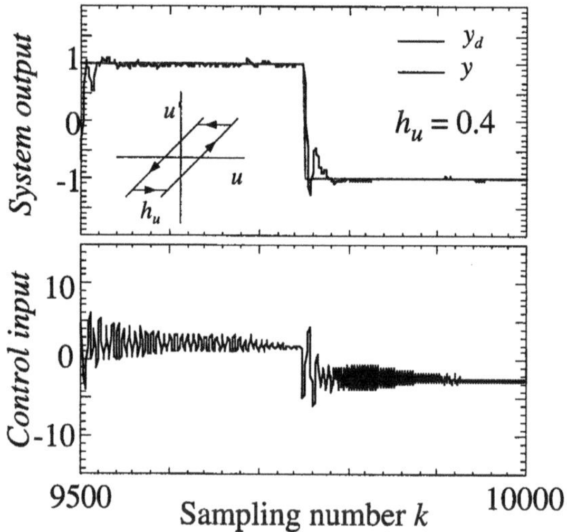

Figure 15. Response of system with RBFN controller under hysteresis of actuator.

the RBFN controller can control the flexible micro-actuator even under existing nonlinearities.

4 Experiment

In this section, experimental investigation of the RBFN controller was described to determine its feasibility for controlling actual systems [19].

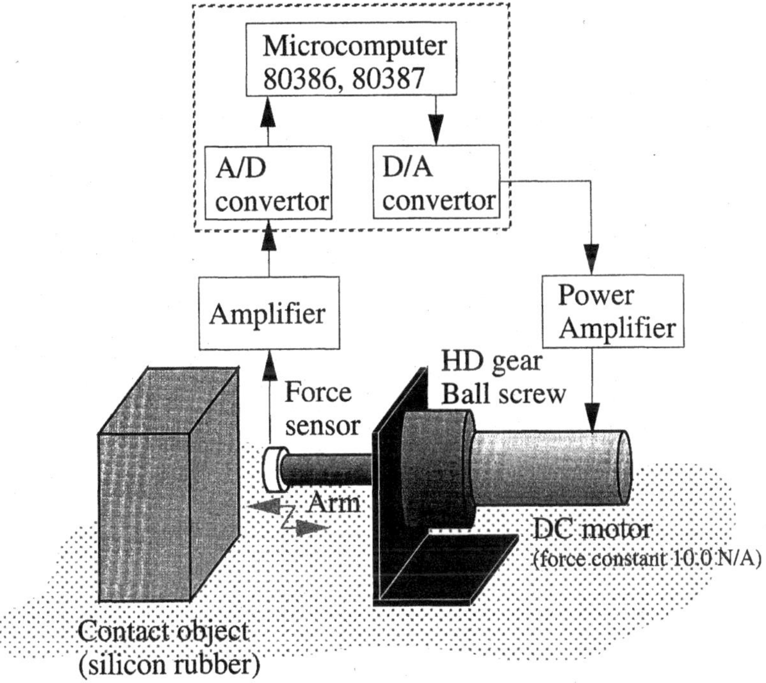

Figure 16. Experimental setup for force control of axial robot.

4.1 Force Control of a 1-Degree-of-Freedom Robot

Figure 16 shows the configuration of the experimental equipment. It consists of an axial robot, a force sensor, amplifiers, a microcomputer, and a contact object. The axial robot is a translational mechanism driven by a ball screw of which rotation is controlled using a DC motor. The contact force at the tip of the robot arm is measured using the force sensor. The signal from the force sensor is filtered using a low-pass filter with a 10 Hz cut-off frequency. The motor has a dead zone of approximately ± 0.12 A resulting from the harmonic-drive gear friction. The armature current of the motor is controlled directly by the microcomputer. Since this force control system can be approximated by a second-order system, the structure of the RBFN controller is the same as that shown in Figure 3. The RBFN controller was implemented by the microcomputer. The sampling time was 40 msec. The initial values of the weights were randomly selected in the interval [-1, 1], and the values of the controller parameters were set to $a = 1.0$ and $\eta = 0.04$. The contact object was made of sil-

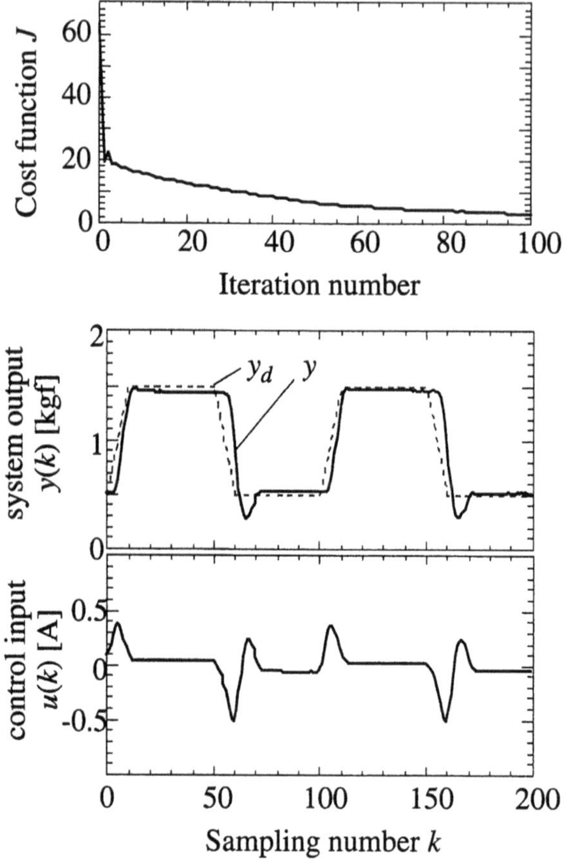

Figure 17. Experimental result for force control of axial robot(top: Learning process of RBFN controller. bottom:Response of system with RBFN controller).

icone rubber. In the experiment, the aim of the control is to make the force sensor output $y(k)$ track the desired contact force $y_d(k)$. The top of Figure 17 shows the learning process; the cost function decreases as learning progresses. The bottom of Figure 17 shows the system response at the 100th period; a small control error remains because of the dead zone in the motor current. However, the force sensor output $y(k)$ converges with the desired contact force $y_d(k)$.

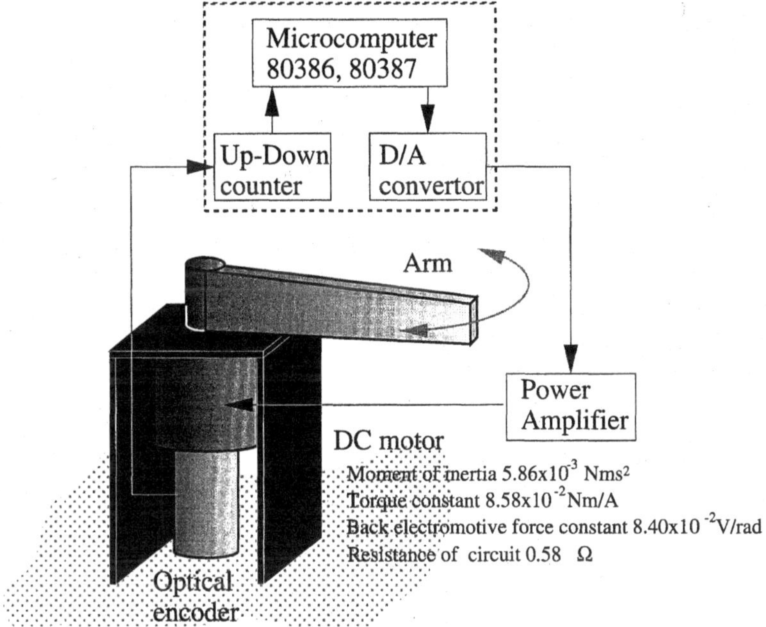

Figure 18. Experimental setup for joint angle tracking control of robot arm.

4.2 Angular Position Control of 1-Degree-of-Freedom Robot

Figure 18 shows the experimental setup. It consists of a DC motor, an optical encoder, an amplifier, a robot arm, and the microcomputer. One end of the arm is directly attached to the motor shaft, and the arm rotates in a horizontal plane. The rotation angle of the motor (joint angle) is measured using the optical encoder. The motor has a dead zone of approximately ± 0.36 A resulting from the solid friction at the joint. The armature current of the motor is controlled directly by the microcomputer with a sampling time of 40 msec. The aim of the control was to make the joint angle $y(k)$ track the desired output $y_d(k)$. Since this robot arm system is considered to be a second-order system, the structure of the RBFN controller and the controller parameters are the same as those in Section 4.1. The top of Figure 19 shows the learning process and the bottom of Figure 19 shows the system response at the 100th period. As shown in Figure 19, the cost function converges as learning progresses.

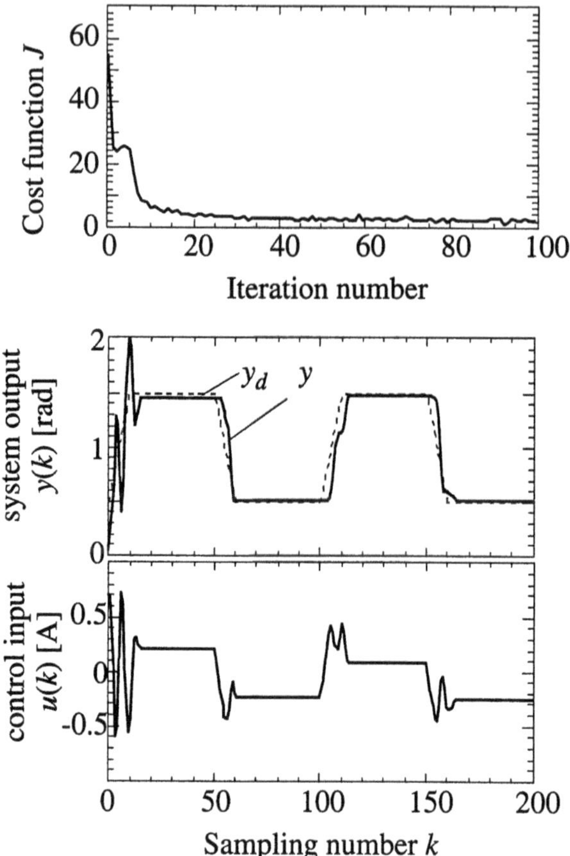

Figure 19. Experimental result for joint angle tracking control of robot arm(top: Learning process of RBFN controller. bottom: Response of system with RBFN controller).

A small control error remains because of the dead zone in the motor current. However, the joint angle $y(k)$ tracks the desired output $y_d(k)$ after convergence of the RBFN controller learning.

These experimental results indicate that the RBFN controller is effective in an actual system.

5 Conclusions

This chapter described a design method for an RBFN controller and presented a method for implementing it to control mechanical systems. By focusing on a sigmoid function derivative, we obtained the RBFN controller by applying a differential operator to a multi-layer NN controller. Simulation of tracking control for a flexible micro-actuator using the proposed controller demonstrated the feasibility and characteristics of the RBFN controller and the following results were obtained: (1) Using its learning ability, the RBFN controller can control the flexible micro-actuator without a priori knowledge. (2) The controller is robust to changes in the desired output, and the tracking of the tip position to the desired output is quick and precise until the frequency approaches the first elastic mode of the micro-actuator. (3) The controller can compensate for nonlinearities of the flexible micro-actuator, such as parameter variations and hysteresis. Experimental results for force control of an axial robot and angular position control of a robot arm demonstrated the effectiveness of the RBFN controller for controlling practical systems.

Acknowledgments

Thanks are due to Dr. Takayuki Yamada of NTT Access Network Systems Laboratories and Dr. Minoru Sasaki of Gifu University for their helpful comments.

References

[1] Kawato, M., Uno, Y., Isobe, M., and Suzuki, R. (1987), "A hierarchical model for voluntary movement and its application to robotics," *Proceedings of 1987 IEEE International Conference on Neural Networks*, vol. IV, pp. 573-582.

[2] Jordan, M.I. (1989), "Generic constraints on underspecified target trajectories," *Proceedings of IJCNN89*, pp. 217-225.

[3] Narendra, K.S. and Parthasarathy, K. (1990), "Identification and control of dynamic systems using neural networks," *IEEE Transactions on Neural Networks*, vol. 1, no. 1, pp. 4-27.

[4] Chen, F.C. and Khalil, H.K. (1992), "Adaptive control of nonlinear system using neural networks," *International Journal of Control*, vol. 55, no. 6, pp. 1299-1317.

[5] Takahashi, K. and Yamada, I. (1994), "Neural-network-based learning control of flexible mechanism with application to a single-link flexible arm," *ASME Journal of Dynamic Systems, Measurement, and Control*, vol. 116, no. 4, pp. 792-795.

[6] Poggio, T. and Edelman, S. (1990), "A network that learns to recognize three-dimensional objects," *Nature*, vol. 343, no. 18, pp. 263-266.

[7] Sanner, R.M. and Slotine, J.-J.E. (1992), "Gaussian networks for direct adaptive control," *IEEE Transactions on Neural Networks*, vol. 3, no. 6, pp. 837-864.

[8] Chen, S., Billings, S.A., and Grant, P.M. (1992), "Recursive hybrid algorithm for nonlinear system identification using radial basis function networks," *International Journal of Control*, vol. 55, no. 5, pp. 1051-1070.

[9] Mukhopadhyah, S. and Narendra, K.S. (1993), "Disturbance rejection in nonlinear systems using neural networks," *IEEE Transactions on Neural Networks*, vol. 1, no. 1, pp. 63-72.

[10] Gorinevsky, D.M. (1997), "Sampled-data indirect adaptive control of bioreactor using affine radial basis function network architecture," *ASME Journal of Dynamic Systems, Measurement, and Control*, vol. 119, no. 1, pp. 94-97.

[11] Yamada, T. (1997), "An application of radial basis function derived from neural network to servo control," *Proceedings of EUFIT '97*, pp. 2074-2078.

[12] Sasaki, M. and Okugawa, M. (1995), "Motion control of a piezopolymer bimorph flexible micro actuator," *Journal of Robotics and Mechatronics*, vol. 7, no. 6, pp. 467-473.

[13] Okugawa, M., Sasaki, M. and Fujisawa, F. (1996), "Robust motion control of a flexible micro-actuator using H control method," *Proceedings of the 11th KACC*, pp. 397-400.

[14] Takahashi, K. and Sasaki, M. (1997), "Neural-network-based controller with application to a flexible micro-actuator (direct neural controller and its extension to an open-loop neural controller)," *IEICE Transactions on Electronics*, vol. 80, no. 2E-C, pp. 246-254.

[15] Takahashi, K., Yamada, T., and Sasaki, M. (1998), "A radial-basis-function-network-based controller with application to controlling a flexible micro-actuator," *The Transaction of The IEE of Japan*, vol.118-E, no. 1, pp. 14-21.

[16] Takahashi, Y. (1978), *Systems and Control*, Iwanami Shyoten, (in Japanese).

[17] Yabuta, T. and Yamada, T. (1992), "Neural network controller characteristics with regard to adaptive control," *IEEE Transactions on Systems, Man, and Cybernetics*, vol. 22, no. 1, 1992, pp. 170-177.

[18] Takahashi, Y. (1992), *Adaptive Predictive Control of Nonlinear Time-Varying Systems using Neural Networks*, Kagaku Gijyutsu Co.

[19] Takahashi, K. and Yamada, T. (1997), "A radial-basis-function-network-based controller derived from a neural-network-based controller and its application to controlling mechanical systems," *JSME International Journal*, series C, vol. 40, no. 1, pp. 42-51.

Chapter 10

Model-Based Recurrent Neural Network for Fault Diagnosis of Nonlinear Dynamic Systems

C. Gan and K. Danai

A model-based recurrent neural network (MBRNN) is presented for modeling dynamic systems and their fault diagnosis. This network has a fixed structure that is defined according to the linearized state-space model of the plant. Therefore, the MBRNN has the ability to incorporate the analytical knowledge of the plant in its formulation. Leaving the original topology intact, the MBRNN can subsequently be trained to represent the plant nonlinearities through modifying its nodes' activation functions, which consist of contours of Gaussian radial basis functions (RBFs). Training in MBRNN involves adjusting the weights of the RBFs so as to modify the contours representing the activation functions. The performance of the MBRNN is demonstrated via several examples, and in application to the IFAC Benchmark Problem. The results indicate that MBRNN requires much shorter training than needed by ordinary recurrent networks. This efficiency in training is attributed to the MBRNN's fixed topology which is independent of training. In application to fault diagnosis, a salient feature of MBRNN is that it can be formulated according to the present model-based fault diagnostic solutions as its starting point, and subsequently improve these solutions via training by adapting them to plant nonlinearities. The diagnostic results indicate that the MBRNN performs better than 'black box' neural networks.

1 Introduction

The need for modeling complex industrial systems demands modeling methods that can cope with high dimensionality, nonlinearity, and uncertainty. As such, alternatives to traditional linear and nonlinear modeling methods are needed. One such alternative is neural network modeling. Artificial neural networks are powerful empirical modeling tools that can be trained to represent complex multi-input multi-output nonlinear systems. Neural networks are also pattern classifiers, so they provide robustness to parameter variations and noise.

Various types of neural networks have been used for modeling dynamic systems. Multi-layer perceptrons have been used to provide an input-output representation of the plant in auto-regressive moving average (ARMA) form for cases where the past values of the plant inputs and outputs are available as network inputs [1]. Another network used for modeling dynamic systems is the cerebellar model articulation controller (CMAC) [2], noted for its ability to represent the spacial aspects of the system and for its fast learning that is desired for on-line applications [3]. Multilayer perceptrons and CMAC networks, however, are feedforward networks that only provide static mapping between inputs and outputs. A more suitable network for representing dynamic systems is the recurrent network which has the inherent format to internally represent the autoregressive aspect of dynamic systems [4]-[7].

Regardless of their type, however, neural networks are generally disadvantaged by their 'black box' format. They need training for defining their structure (number of nodes) as well as their connection weights [7]. Therefore, these networks require prohibitively extensive training, and are hard to interpret once trained. One variant to these networks is the diagonal recurrent neural network proposed by Ku and Lee [8] that provides a simpler structure than the fully connected network, and therefore is an easier network to train. Another variant is a simplified network that is initiated based on representative patterns in the training data [9].

While the above solutions have led to reduced demand for training, they have not been significant, mostly due to their reliance on empiricism. Ideally, neural networks should be less empirical, to reduce the demand for training, and more transparent, to provide insight into their representation. A step toward such an ideal solution for modeling dynamic systems is using sub-networks to represent separately the autoregressive and moving average parts of the plant, and selecting the complexity of these networks according to linearity/nonlinearity of these parts [10]. Although this modular solution takes advantage of the existing knowledge of the plant to reduce the complexity of the overall network and, consequently, reduces the demand for training, it does not contribute to improving the transparency of the network, as it still uses a black box format for the individual sub-networks.

Perhaps a more fundamental step towards the ideal solution has been in the area of neuro-fuzzy inference systems [11], [12] and knowledge-based artificial neural networks (KBANN) [13], [14]. In the neuro-fuzzy approach, the heuristic knowledge of the process is expressed in the form of rules between inputs and outputs, and incorporated in a feedforward network with several layers, where each layer performs a step of inference. An important feature of neuro-fuzzy networks is their equivalence to Gaussian radial basis function (RBF) networks [11], which makes possible the use of learning algorithms associated with RBF networks to modify the rules. Knowledge-based artificial neural networks (KBANN) are formulated by symbolic rules in the form of propositional logic [13]. Both the neuro-fuzzy system and KBANN provide methods for incorporating the existing knowledge of the plant in a neural network. However, they require that this knowledge be formulated as heuristics or propositional logic. Given that most plant models are developed from first principles and are in analytical form, these methods would either ignore the existing analytical models or require the extra step of converting these models into heuristics or propositional logic.

The objective of this chapter is to introduce a method of incorporating the analytical knowledge of the plant in a recurrent neural network. This model-based recurrent neural network (MBRNN) will be formulated according to a linearized state-space model of the dynamic system. It will then be trained to adapt its activation functions to the nonlinearities of the plant as reflected in the training data. As such, the topology of the MBRNN will remain intact, and adaptation to nonlinearities will be confined to the activation functions of individual nodes. The activation functions in MBRNN are defined as contours of the RBFs that comprise the node, therefore, adaptation entails changing the weight of individual RBFs within each node.

2 Methodology

The model-based recurrent neural network (MBRNN) is structured according to a linearized state-space model of the plant. It, therefore, assumes that an analytical model of the plant is available which can be linearized about an operating point. If the discrete-time nonlinear state-space model of the plant is defined as:

$$\mathbf{x}(k+1) = \mathbf{\Phi}[\mathbf{x}(k), \mathbf{u}(k)] \tag{1}$$

$$\mathbf{y}(k) = \mathbf{\Psi}[\mathbf{x}(k), \mathbf{u}(k)] \tag{2}$$

where $\mathbf{u}(k)$, $\mathbf{x}(k)$, and $\mathbf{y}(k)$ represent the sampled values of the inputs, states, and outputs at time k, respectively, then the linearized state-space model has the form:

$$\mathbf{x}(k+1) = \mathbf{A}\mathbf{x}(k) + \mathbf{B}\mathbf{u}(k) \tag{3}$$

$$\mathbf{y}(k) = \mathbf{C}\mathbf{x}(k) + \mathbf{D}\mathbf{u}(k) \tag{4}$$

The above model can be formulated as a recurrent neural network, having the same number of inputs and outputs. An example of such a network is shown in Figure 1 for the second-order model:

$$\begin{bmatrix} x_1(k+1) \\ x_2(k+1) \end{bmatrix} = \begin{bmatrix} a_{11} & a_{12} \\ a_{21} & a_{22} \end{bmatrix} \begin{bmatrix} x_1(k) \\ x_2(k) \end{bmatrix} + \begin{bmatrix} b_1 \\ b_2 \end{bmatrix} u(k) \tag{5}$$

$$\begin{bmatrix} y_1(k) \\ y_2(k) \end{bmatrix} = \begin{bmatrix} c_{11} & c_{12} \\ c_{21} & c_{22} \end{bmatrix} \begin{bmatrix} x_1(k) \\ x_2(k) \end{bmatrix} + \begin{bmatrix} d_1 \\ d_2 \end{bmatrix} u(k) \tag{6}$$

Note that the nodes of this initial MBRNN have a gain of 1 (i.e., their output equals their input) to initially represent the linearized model (see Figure 1), but the activation functions of these nodes are subsequently adapted during training into nonlinear functions so as to represent the plant nonlinearity. As such, adaptation in MBRNN is performed by only changing the form of the activation functions, leaving the connection weights intact. In order to provide adaptability, the activation functions in MBRNN are defined as contours of radial basis functions that comprise the node. If the output of each RBF is defined as

$$o_i = \exp(-|x_j - c_i|^2/\sigma^2) \tag{7}$$

to represent a normal distribution with localized characteristics, then the activation function of the node will have the form,

$$O_j = \sum_{i=1}^{N} \theta_i o_i = \sum_{i=1}^{N} \theta_i \exp(-|x_j - c_i|^2/\sigma^2) \tag{8}$$

While the activation function O_j can be composed of an array of any basis function that can be adapted on-line, it is desirable that the basis function should have a localized characteristic so that the activation function can be modified locally without affecting the value of the function at neighboring points.

The above formulation represents a modular format for MBRNN where each module consists of an RBF network denoting a node. Training consists of adjusting the weights θ_i of individual RBFs to shape the node's activation function. The above second-order network with an adaptable set of activation functions has the form:

$$\begin{Bmatrix} x_1(k+1) \\ x_2(k+1) \end{Bmatrix} = \begin{bmatrix} a_{11} \sum_{i=1}^{N_{a_{11}}} \theta_i^{a_{11}} \exp(-|x_1(k) - c_i^{a_{11}}|^2/\sigma^2) \\ a_{21} \sum_{i=1}^{N_{a_{21}}} \theta_i^{a_{21}} \exp(-|x_1(k) - c_i^{a_{21}}|^2/\sigma^2) \end{bmatrix} + \begin{bmatrix} a_{12} \sum_{i=1}^{N_{a_{12}}} \theta_i^{a_{12}} \exp(-|x_2(k) - c_i^{a_{12}}|^2/\sigma^2) \\ a_{22} \sum_{i=1}^{N_{a_{22}}} \theta_i^{a_{22}} \exp(-|x_2(k) - c_i^{a_{22}}|^2/\sigma^2) \end{bmatrix} + \begin{bmatrix} b_1 \sum_{i=1}^{N_{b_1}} \theta_i^{b_1} \exp(-|u(k) - c_i^{b_1}|^2/\sigma^2) \\ b_2 \sum_{i=1}^{N_{b_2}} \theta_i^{b_2} \exp(-|u(k) - c_i^{b_2}|^2/\sigma^2) \end{bmatrix} \tag{9}$$

$$\begin{bmatrix} y_1(k) \\ y_2(k) \end{bmatrix} = \begin{bmatrix} c_{11} \sum_{i=1}^{N_{c_{11}}} \theta_i^{c_{11}} \exp(-|x_1(k) - c_i^{c_{11}}|^2/\sigma^2) \\ c_{21} \sum_{i=1}^{N_{c_{21}}} \theta_i^{c_{21}} \exp(-|x_1(k) - c_i^{c_{21}}|^2/\sigma^2) \end{bmatrix} + \begin{bmatrix} c_{12} \sum_{i=1}^{N_{c_{12}}} \theta_i^{c_{12}} \exp(-|x_2(k) - c_i^{c_{12}}|^2/\sigma^2) \\ c_{22} \sum_{i=1}^{N_{c_{22}}} \theta_i^{c_{22}} \exp(-|x_2(k) - c_i^{c_{22}}|^2/\sigma^2) \end{bmatrix} + \begin{bmatrix} d_1 \sum_{i=1}^{N_{d_1}} \theta_i^{d_1} \exp(-|u(k) - c_i^{d_1}|^2/\sigma^2) \\ d_2 \sum_{i=1}^{N_{d_2}} \theta_i^{d_2} \exp(-|u(k) - c_i^{d_2}|^2/\sigma^2) \end{bmatrix} \tag{10}$$

The RBFs in each node of MBRNN are evenly distributed across the expected range of state or input space. For the initial MBRNN, the values of parameters θ_i are selected to produce linear activation functions as

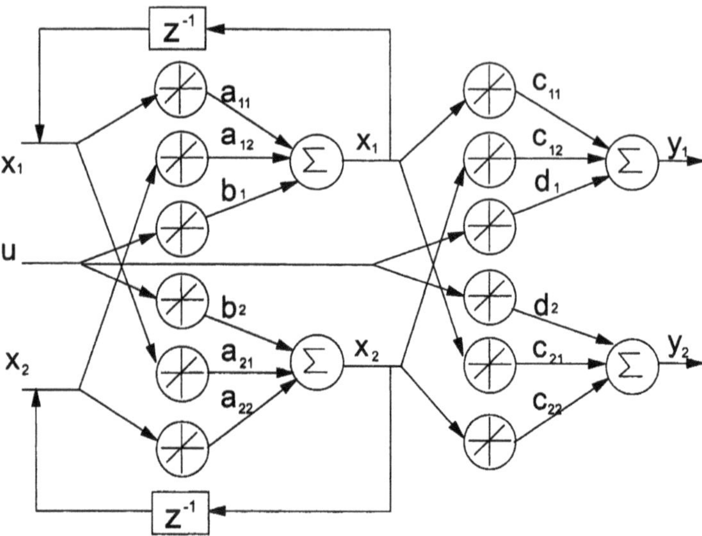

Figure 1. A model-based recurrent neural network (MBRNN) representing a second-order plant.

their contours, so as to depict the linearized model of the plant. Subsequently, these parameters are modified during a training phase to adapt the MBRNN to plant nonlinearities. Note that MBRNN is formulated such that the activation functions are linear in terms of parameters θ_i, so training is tractable. Based on Eqs. (9) and (10), if the states are measurable, then training of the parameters associated with each of the states and inputs can be carried out separately by the least-squares method. In cases where the states are not accessible, as is often the case, alternative forms of training such as dynamic backpropagation or extended Kalman filtering can be used. In either case, after training the activation functions may have forms very different from their initial linear form, as shown in Figure 2 for a hypothetical case. The construction of the MBRNN's nodes by normally distributed RBFs provides it with the distinct characteristic of "spacial localization" [15]. Because of one-to-one relationship between input-output pairs, each adaptation iteration in MBRNN is confined to a limited number of θ_i that are associated with the excitation input. This, in addition to providing efficient training, enables MBRNN to accommodate localized nonlinearities within limited ranges of the input space.

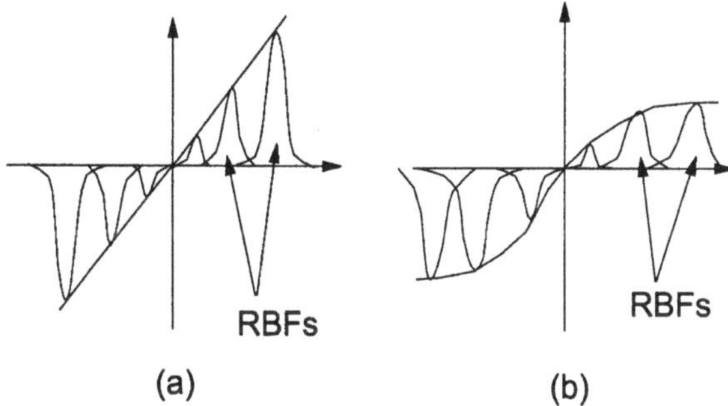

Figure 2. An initial linear activation function of MBRNN formed from the contour of RBFs in the node (a), and the trained activation function obtained by modifying the weights of various RBFs (b).

In its present form, the initial MBRNN represents the first-order approximation of the nonlinear plant, and it maintains this first-order representation while allowing the individual components of the linearized model to incorporate nonlinearity through training. As such, this format does not allow inclusion of bilinear terms. For example, if the actual x_1 in our example of Eqs. (5) and (6) had the form $x_1(k+1) = F(x_1(k), x_2(k))$, and was then approximated by a Taylor Series Expansion, as

$$F(x_1, x_2) = F(x_1, x_2)|_0 + \sum_{r=0}^{1} \binom{1}{r} \frac{\partial F}{\partial x_1^r \partial x_2^{1-r}}(x_1, x_2)(x_1 - x_1|_0)^r (x_2 - x_2|_0)^{1-r} + \ldots + \sum_{r=0}^{n} \binom{n}{r} \frac{\partial^n F}{\partial x_1^r \partial x_2^{n-r}}(x_1, x_2)(x_1 - x_1|_0)^r (x_2 - x_2|_0)^{n-r} + \ldots$$

where $\binom{n}{r} = \frac{n!}{r!(n-r)!}$ denote the binomial coefficients and all the derivatives are evaluated at $(x_1, x_2)|_0$, then the MBRNN constructed according to the first-order approximation of function F, would exclude the coupling between x_1 and x_2, represented by $\sum_{r=1}^{n} \binom{n}{r} \frac{\partial^n F}{\partial x_1^r \partial x_2^{n-r}}(x_1, x_2)$. Therefore, when this coupling is not negligible, MBRNN, in its present form, will not be able to approximate the nonlinear plant satisfactorily. In order to include such significant coupling terms, additional nodes may be added into the feedforward path of MBRNN to represent specific couplings. One stand-alone node that can represent a coupling term is shown in Figure 3, where the nodes with circular arrows pointing to themselves

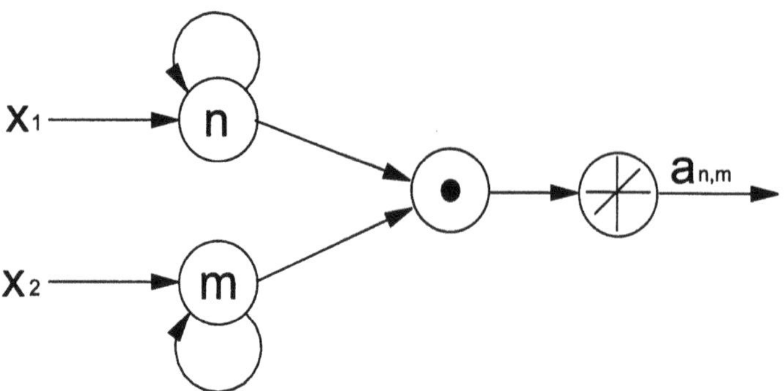

Figure 3. A possible modification to MBRNN to accommodate coupling between x_1 and x_2. The nodes with circular arrows pointing to themselves represent the repetitive multiplication of the input variable, i.e., the node with x_1 as input to the node enclosing n would output x_1^n, and the node with a dot inside signifies the product of the input variables.

represent the repetitive multiplication of the input variable (e.g., the node with x_1 as input to the node enclosing n would output x_1^n), and the node with a dot inside signifies the product of the input variables. Although the inclusion of such coupling terms in MBRNN is straightforward, it poses two constraints: (1) it requires a knowledge of the dominant coupling between the plant variables, and (2) it adds to the complexity of MBRNN and its demand for learning.

A central issue in MBRNN is the number of RBFs needed within each node. Initially, the activation functions should be linear with slopes of 1 so as to provide a uniform gain of unity at all inputs for an accurate representation of $x = y$. A perfect linear activation function, however, would require a large number of RBFs. Therefore, a method needs to be devised to limit the number of RBFs within the expected ranges of inputs and states. One method for selecting the number of RBFs is cross validation, where the available input-output data is divided into two parts, one part used for training and the other for testing. The selection criterion in this case is the generalization ability of the network based on the test set [16], [17]. For each modular RBF network representing a node, the average of mean-square-error over the training set can be defined as [18]:

$$\hat{\sigma}^2_{GCV_j} = \frac{p\hat{\mathbf{y}}_j^T \mathbf{P}_j^2 \hat{\mathbf{y}}_j}{trace(\mathbf{P}_j)^2} \tag{11}$$

where $\hat{\sigma}^2_{GCV_j}$ represents the generalized cross-validation (GCV), p denotes the number of patterns used in training, $\mathbf{P}_j$ represents the square matrix which projects p-dimensional vectors onto the m_j-basis subspace spanned by the RBFs within the node, and $\hat{\mathbf{y}}_j$ denotes the output of the node. Since each node in MBRNN can be perceived as a separate RBF network, GCV can be used to determine the number of RBFs within each MBRNN node. For this, each set of outputs from the p patterns corresponding to each node is projected to the m_j-dimension spanned by the RBFs within that node, so as to represent its optimal representation in least-squares sense. The projection matrix $\mathbf{P}_j$ for MBRNN is defined as:

$$\mathbf{P}_j = \mathbf{I}_p - \mathbf{O}_j \mathbf{A}_j^{-1} \mathbf{O}_j^T \tag{12}$$

where $\mathbf{O}_j$ represents the matrix of RBFs o_i for each node (see Eq. (7))

$$\mathbf{O}_j = \begin{bmatrix} o_1(s_1) & o_2(s_1) & \cdots & o_{m_j}(s_1) \\ o_1(s_2) & o_2(s_2) & \cdots & o_{m_j}(s_2) \\ \vdots & \vdots & \ddots & \vdots \\ o_1(s_p) & o_2(s_p) & \cdots & o_{m_j}(s_p) \end{bmatrix} \tag{13}$$

where s_i represents the input value associated with pattern i, and $\mathbf{A}_j^{-1}$ denotes the variance matrix of $\mathbf{O}_j$ obtained as

$$\mathbf{A}_j^{-1} = (\mathbf{O}_j^T \mathbf{O}_j + \lambda_j \mathbf{I}_\mathbf{p})^{-1} \tag{14}$$

In the above equation, λ_j denotes the regularization parameter associated with each node. Regularization parameters are integral parts of training the activation functions by dynamic backpropagation, so they are included in the formulation of GCV to define the rationale for their selection.

Generalized cross-validation is a measure of the network's ability in mapping a set of inputs to a desired set of outputs. As such, GCV can be used to determine the value of the regularization parameter and the number of RBFs for each node to provide an accurate representation of $y = x$ initially. The typical values of GCV obtained for different numbers of RBFs, with a constant regularization parameter, are shown in Figure 4(a). The results indicate that the increasing number of RBFs has a diminishing effect on the GCV value, so the GCV value can be used as the basis

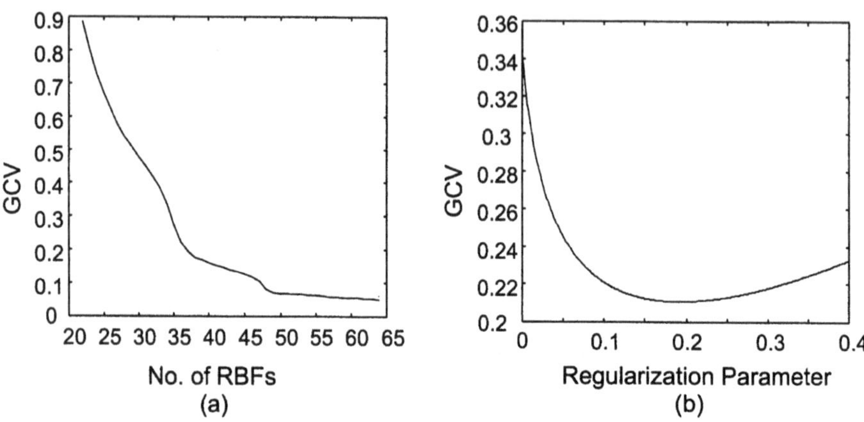

Figure 4. Effect of the number of RBFs (a) and the regularization parameter (b) on the generalized cross-validation (GCV) value.

of selecting the RBF numbers. Similarly, the effect of the regularization parameter on the GCV value of the node, with a fixed number of RBFs, is shown in Figure 4(b). The results indicate that the accuracy of each node's output (as represented by the GCV value) is directly affected by the regularization parameter, and that an 'optimal' value for it can be selected based on the GCV value. Of course, one should note that there is a correlation between the number of RBFs and the value of regularization parameter, and that by determining each independent of the other there is no assurance that their optimal values have been selected. Experience, however, indicates that selecting the number of RBFs and the regularization parameter separately leads to satisfactory results.

3 Training

An important feature of MBRNN is the linearity of its activation functions in terms of the RBF weights, which makes possible adapting the RBF weights by various linear regression methods. An important objective of MBRNN design is to adhere to its initial format which is structured according to the state-space model of the plant. In order to satisfy this objective, limited changes should be made to the shape of the activation functions during training, so as to (1) avoid drastic deviations from the initial structure of MBRNN, and (2) avoid creation of limit cycles. Two adaptation methods that can implement such a restriction, based on dynamic backpropagation [19], [20] and extended Kalman filter (EKF) [21], [15], [7] are described here, to estimate the network parameters θ_Φ and θ_Ψ in the MBRNN representation of the nonlinear plant, as

$$\hat{\mathbf{x}}(k+1) = \mathbf{\Phi}_{net}[\hat{\mathbf{x}}(k), \mathbf{u}(k), \theta_\Phi] \tag{15}$$

$$\hat{\mathbf{y}}(k) = \mathbf{\Psi}_{net}[\hat{\mathbf{x}}(k), \mathbf{u}(k), \theta_\Psi] \tag{16}$$

where $\mathbf{x} \in \mathcal{R}^n$, $\mathbf{u} \in \mathcal{R}^m$, and $\mathbf{y} \in \mathcal{R}^q$.

3.1 Training by Dynamic Backpropagation

For the p input-output training pairs, the objective function can be defined as:

$$J = \sum_{i=1}^{p} (\hat{\mathbf{y}}_i - \mathbf{y}_i)^2 \tag{17}$$

where $\hat{\mathbf{y}}$ denotes the vector of network outputs and $\mathbf{y}$ the corresponding plant outputs. Although this objective function is suitable for adaptation of the network parameters, it does not satisfy the goal of preserving its structure. This restriction on the extent of parameter changes can be imposed by including a regularization term in the objective function, as

$$J = \sum_{j=1}^{p} (\hat{\mathbf{y}}_j - \mathbf{y}_j)^2 + \sum_{j=1}^{N} \lambda_j \sum_{i=1}^{m_j} (\theta_i - \theta_{i0})^2 \tag{18}$$

where N denotes the number of nodes in MBRNN, m_j represents the number of RBFs in individual nodes, θ_i denotes the weight of each RBF during training, θ_{i0} represents the initial weight of each RBF, and λ_j denotes the regularization parameter of each node (see Eq. (14)).

MBRNN consists of two parts (see Figure 1): a recurrent part, which emulates the state equations (Eq. (1)), and a feedforward part, that represents the output equations (Eq. (2)). Training of the recurrent part can be performed by backpropagation (BP) over time (dynamic BP), to estimate θ_Φ, whereas the the static part can be trained by regular BP, to estimate θ_Ψ. The objective of training is to determine the vector θ^* which minimizes the objective function J in Eq. (18) by moving the parameter vector along the negative gradient of the objective function with respect to θ, as [22]

$$\theta(k+1) = \theta(k) - \eta \nabla_\theta J(k) \tag{19}$$

where η denotes the learning rate, $\nabla_\theta J$ represents the gradient of the objective function, and $\theta(k)$ represents the current value of the RBFs weight vector.

For the dynamic part of MBRNN, the change in a weight at time k will result in a change in the output $\hat{\mathbf{y}}(t)$ for all $t \geq k$. This means that the present value of the output $\hat{\mathbf{y}}(t)$ is not only affected by the current value of the weight vector $\theta_\Phi(k)$, for $k = t$, but by all the past values of $\theta_\Phi(k)$, for $0 \leq k \leq t$, as well. This implies that weight adaptation should be performed with regard to past adaptations, as reflected in the estimate of the gradient of the objective function, computed from Eqs. (15) and (16):

$$\frac{\partial \hat{\mathbf{x}}(k+1)}{\partial \theta_\Phi(k)} = \frac{\partial \mathbf{\Phi}_{net}(\hat{\mathbf{x}}(k), \mathbf{u}(k), \theta_\Phi(k))}{\partial \hat{\mathbf{x}}(k)} \frac{\partial \hat{\mathbf{x}}(k)}{\partial \theta_\Phi(k)} + \frac{\partial \mathbf{\Phi}_{net}(\hat{\mathbf{x}}(k), \mathbf{u}(k), \theta_\Phi(k))}{\partial \theta_\Phi(k)} \tag{20}$$

$$\frac{\partial \hat{\mathbf{y}}(k)}{\partial \theta_\Phi(k)} = \frac{\partial \mathbf{\Psi}_{net}(\hat{\mathbf{x}}(k), \mathbf{u}(k), \theta_\Phi(k))}{\partial \hat{\mathbf{x}}(k)} \frac{\partial \hat{\mathbf{x}}(k)}{\partial \theta_\Phi(k)} + \frac{\partial \mathbf{\Psi}_{net}(\hat{\mathbf{x}}(k), \mathbf{u}(k), \theta_\Phi(k))}{\partial \theta_\Phi(k)} \tag{21}$$

The components of the above equations can be computed at each instant k to yield $\partial \hat{\mathbf{y}} / \partial \theta_\Phi$ as the gradient of the objective function with respect to the RBF weights. Dynamic BP can then be used to adapt the parameter vector θ_Φ according to the learning rule in Eq. (19). Note that Eqs. (20) and (21) define a state-space representation of the gradient of the objective function $\nabla_{\theta_\Phi} J$ used in Eq. (19). The drawback of backpropogation is that it is often too slow for practical application. There are many variations on backpropogation that speed up the training, such as the Levenberg-Marquardt algorithm, BP with Momentum, etc. [23]. Also, in order to eliminate the spikes during training, a low-pass filter can be incorporated in training.

Another issue in training by backpropagation is the proper choice of the learning rate η (see Eq. (19)). Usually small values of η guarantee convergence, but at a very low speed. Larger values of η, on the other hand, may lead to instability. It is possible to determine analytically the range of η to guarantee stability.

3.2 Training by the Extended Kalman Filter

The MBRNN can also be trained by the Extended Kalman Filter (EKF) [7], [15], which has the added appeal of being applicable to both the recurrent and feedforward parts of the network. EKF-based training is also faster than dynamic BP, and is less prone to noise.

In application to MBRNN, the network states are augmented with auxiliary states that correspond to the RBF weights. As such, EKF-based training of MBRNN consists of simultaneous parameter and state estimation. Since the network inputs lie in $\Re^{m+n}$ (see Eqs. (15) and (16)), the augmented input space of the network $\mathbf{w}^T = [\mathbf{x}\ \mathbf{u}]$ belongs to $\mathcal{R}^{m+n}$. In this case, part of the augmented space $\mathbf{u}$ will be extraneous, and $\mathbf{x}$ will be constrained by the network dynamics. In the EKF algorithm, the system dynamics are first linearized about the current state and parameter estimates. The traditional Kalman filter is then used to update the state and parameter estimates of this linearized system.

The formulation of the EKF algorithm as applied to the MBRNN is as follows:

$$\hat{\mathbf{x}}(k+1) = \mathbf{\Phi}_{net}[\hat{\mathbf{x}}(k), \mathbf{u}(k), \theta_\Phi] + \zeta(k) \tag{22}$$

$$\hat{\mathbf{y}}(k) = \mathbf{\Psi}_{net}[\hat{\mathbf{x}}(k), \mathbf{u}(k), \theta_\Psi] + \nu(k) \tag{23}$$

where $\zeta(k)$ and $\nu(k)$ are zero-mean, independent Gaussian random variables representing the process and measurement noise, respectively. If the augmented parameter vector θ is defined as $\theta^T = [\theta_\Phi\ \theta_\Psi]$, and the augmented state vector $\mathbf{z}$ representing the unknown parameters of the network as $\mathbf{z}^T = [\hat{\mathbf{x}}\ \theta]$, then the network model can be defined as:

$$\begin{aligned} \mathbf{z}(k+1) &= \begin{bmatrix} \mathbf{\Phi}_{net}[\hat{\mathbf{x}}(k), \mathbf{u}(k), \theta_\Phi(k)] \\ \theta(k) \end{bmatrix} + \begin{bmatrix} \zeta(k) \\ \beta(k) \end{bmatrix} \\ &\equiv \mathbf{F}(\mathbf{z}(k), \mathbf{u}(k)) + \gamma(k) \end{aligned} \tag{24}$$

$$\begin{aligned} \hat{\mathbf{y}}(k) &= \mathbf{\Psi}_{net}(\hat{\mathbf{x}}(k), \mathbf{u}(k), \theta_\Psi(k)) + \nu(k) \\ &\equiv \mathbf{H}(\mathbf{z}(k), \mathbf{u}(k)] + \nu(k) \end{aligned} \tag{25}$$

where $\beta(k)$ denotes a vector of fictitious white noise, and $\gamma(k) = [\zeta(k)\ \beta(k)]^T$. Based on the above representation, the covariance matrix

$\mathbf{Q}(k)$ can be defined as:

$$\mathbf{Q}(k) = \begin{bmatrix} \mathbf{Q}_x(k) & 0 \\ 0 & \mathbf{Q}_\theta(k) \end{bmatrix} \tag{26}$$

where $\mathbf{Q}_x(k) = E[\zeta(k)\ \zeta(k)^T]$ and $\mathbf{Q}_\theta(k) = E[\theta(k)\ \theta(k)^T]$. The above equations can now be linearized about some nominal $\bar{\mathbf{z}}(k)$ and $\bar{\mathbf{y}}(k)$ as:

$$\begin{aligned} \delta\mathbf{z}(k+1) &= \mathbf{z}(k+1) - \bar{\mathbf{z}}(k+1) \\ &= \mathbf{F}(\mathbf{z}(k), \mathbf{u}(k)) + \mathbf{w}(k) - \mathbf{F}(\bar{\mathbf{z}}(k), \mathbf{u}(k)) \\ &= \mathbf{F}_0(k)\delta\mathbf{z}(k) + \mathbf{w}(k) \end{aligned} \tag{27}$$

$$\begin{aligned} \delta\mathbf{y}(k+1) &= \hat{\mathbf{y}}(k+1) - \bar{\mathbf{y}}(k+1) \\ &= \mathbf{H}(\mathbf{z}(k), \mathbf{u}(k)) + \nu(k) - \mathbf{H}(\bar{\mathbf{z}}(k), \mathbf{u}(k)) \\ &= \mathbf{H}_0(k)\delta\mathbf{y}(k) + \nu(k) \end{aligned} \tag{28}$$

where

$$\mathbf{F}_0(k) = \frac{\partial \mathbf{F}}{\partial \mathbf{z}}\bigg|_{\bar{\mathbf{z}}(k),\mathbf{u}(k)} = \begin{bmatrix} \partial\mathbf{F}/\partial\mathbf{x} & \partial\mathbf{F}/\partial\theta \\ \partial\theta/\partial\mathbf{x} & \partial\theta/\partial\theta \end{bmatrix} = \begin{bmatrix} \partial\mathbf{F}/\partial\mathbf{x} & \partial\mathbf{F}/\partial\theta \\ 0 & \mathbf{I} \end{bmatrix} \tag{29}$$

and

$$\mathbf{H}_0(k) = \frac{\partial \mathbf{H}}{\partial \mathbf{z}}\bigg|_{\bar{\mathbf{z}}(k),\mathbf{u}(k)} = \begin{bmatrix} \partial\mathbf{H}/\partial\mathbf{x} & \partial\mathbf{H}/\partial\theta \end{bmatrix} \tag{30}$$

If the *a priori* and *posteriori* estimates of the variable $\mathbf{z}$ at time k are denoted by $\mathbf{z}(k|k-1)$ and $\mathbf{z}(k|k)$, respectively, and the *a priori* and *posteriori* state covariance estimates denoted by $\mathbf{P}(k|k-1)$ and $\mathbf{P}(k|k)$, then the EKF algorithm at time k is composed of the following steps:

1. Compute the linearized dynamics $\mathbf{F}_0(k-1)$ and $\mathbf{H}_0(k-1)$ by linearizing $\mathbf{F}$ and $\mathbf{H}$ about the previous *posteriori* estimate $\mathbf{z}(k-1|k-1)$;

2. Compute the *a priori* state estimate:

$$\mathbf{z}(k|k-1) = \mathbf{F}(\mathbf{z}(k-1|k-1), \mathbf{u}(k-1))\ ;$$

3. Compute the *a priori* state noise covariance estimate:

$$\mathbf{P}(k|k-1) = \mathbf{F}_0(k-1)\mathbf{P}(k-1|k-1)\mathbf{F}_0^T(k-1) + \mathbf{Q}(k)\ ;$$

4. Compute the Kalman gain matrix $\mathbf{K}(k)$ as:

$$\mathbf{K}(k) = \mathbf{P}(k|k-1)\mathbf{H}_0^T(k-1)[\mathbf{H}_0(k-1)\mathbf{P}(k|k-1)\mathbf{H}_0^T(k-1)+\mathbf{R}]^{-1};$$

5. Compute the *posteriori* state estimate by using the new observation $\mathbf{y}(k)$:

$$\mathbf{z}(k|k) = \mathbf{z}(k|k-1) + \mathbf{K}(k)(y(k) - \mathbf{H}(\mathbf{z}(k|k-1), \mathbf{u}(k))) \;;$$

6. Update the state noise covariance:

$$\mathbf{P}(k|k) = (\mathbf{I} - \mathbf{K}(k)\mathbf{H}_0(k-1))\mathbf{P}(k|k-1)$$

In the above algorithm, the initial gain matrix $\mathbf{P}(0)$ reflects the level of confidence in the initial parameters. As such, it is set to a high value for highly nonlinear systems which are not closely approximated by the linearized model. As learning progresses, the gain matrix decreases in value, and the learning rate is controlled more by the level of noise reflected in $\mathbf{Q}$ and $\mathbf{R}$. A large $\mathbf{R}$ is indicative of little confidence in the measurement values, so learning is performed more slowly, whereas a large $\mathbf{Q}$ is indicative of smaller confidence in the parameter values, causing learning to be performed more aggressively. As such, the overall rate of convergence in EKF-based training is controlled by the relative values of $\mathbf{Q}$ and $\mathbf{R}$.

4 Performance Evaluation in Modeling

The effectiveness of MBRNN has been demonstrated for several examples. The first example is taken from the literature [10] so as to facilitate a comparison between MBRNN and other neural networks in terms of modeling effectiveness and training effort.

Example 1:

$$y(k+1) = f[y(k), y(k-1)] + u(k) \tag{31}$$

where

$$f[y(k), y(k-1)] = \frac{y(k)y(k-1)[y(k)+2.5]}{1+y^2(k)+y^2(k-1)} \tag{32}$$

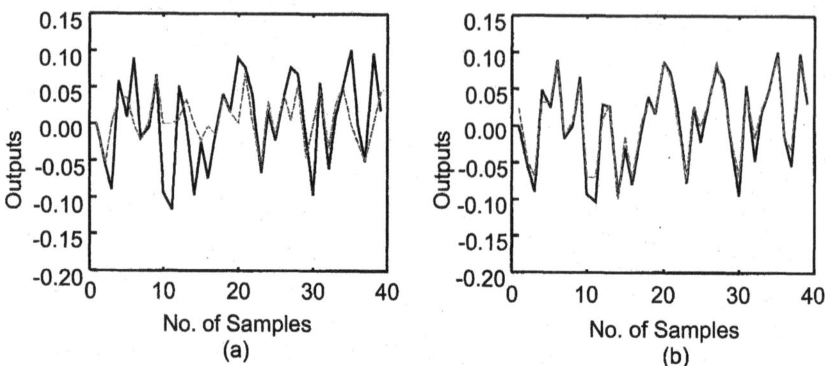

Figure 5. Outputs of the plant and MBRNN before training (a), and after training by EKF (b), for Example 1.

This example represents a single-input single-output plant, with a non-linear autoregressive part. The linearized state-space form of this model about the operating point ($x_1 = 0,\ x_2 = 0$) was obtained as:

$$\left\{ \begin{array}{c} x_1(k+1) \\ x_2(k+1) \end{array} \right\} = \left[\begin{array}{cc} 0 & 1 \\ 0 & 0 \end{array} \right] \left\{ \begin{array}{c} x_1(k) \\ x_2(k) \end{array} \right\} + \left\{ \begin{array}{c} 0 \\ 1 \end{array} \right\} u \tag{33}$$

$$y(k) = [\ 0 \quad 1\ ] \left\{ \begin{array}{c} x_1(k) \\ x_2(k) \end{array} \right\} \tag{34}$$

The MBRNN was structured according to the above state-space model and then trained by EKF using random excitation with values between -0.6 and 0.6. The initial structure of MBRNN for this example was quite similar to that of Figure 1, except that this MBRNN had one output and did not need to include nodes associated with d_1 and d_2. One epoch of training was used which consisted of 600 sample points. The trained MBRNN was then tested on data generated with random inputs from a seed different from that which generated the training data. The values of $\hat{y}$ and y for the test session before and after training are shown in Figure 5. The results indicate that the output of MBRNN is much closer to the plant output after training, despite the relatively short training session used for MBRNN. These results are similar to those obtained by a feedforward network that was trained with 100,000 sample points [10]. The considerably more efficient training of MBRNN is due to its fixed structure based on the linearized model of the plant.

Example 2:

$$\left\{\begin{array}{c} x_1(k+1) \\ x_2(k+1) \\ x_3(k+1) \end{array}\right\} =$$

$$\left[\begin{array}{ccc} -0.3(x_1(k)+\sin^2(x_1(k))) & 0 & 0 \\ 2.9x_1(k) & -0.62x_2(k) & -2.3x_3(k) \\ 0 & 2.3x_2(k) & 0 \end{array}\right] + \left\{\begin{array}{c} u \\ 0 \\ 0 \end{array}\right\} \tag{35}$$

$$y(k) = \left[\begin{array}{ccc} 1 & 1 & 0 \\ 1 & -3 & 1 \end{array}\right] \left\{\begin{array}{c} x_1(k) \\ x_2(k) \\ x_3(k) \end{array}\right\} + \left[\begin{array}{c} 0 \\ 1 \end{array}\right] u \tag{36}$$

The above model represents a single-input multiple-output system, with nonlinear state equations. The linearized state-space model of this plant about the operating point ($x_1 = 0,\ x_2 = 0,\ x_3 = 0$) was obtained as:

$$\left\{\begin{array}{c} x_1(k+1) \\ x_2(k+1) \\ x_3(k+1) \end{array}\right\} = \left[\begin{array}{ccc} -0.3 & 0 & 0 \\ 2.9 & -0.62 & -2.3 \\ 0 & 2.3 & 0 \end{array}\right] \left\{\begin{array}{c} x_1(k) \\ x_2(k) \\ x_3(k) \end{array}\right\} + \left\{\begin{array}{c} 1 \\ 0 \\ 0 \end{array}\right\} u \tag{37}$$

$$y(k) = \left[\begin{array}{ccc} 1 & 1 & 0 \\ 1 & -3 & 1 \end{array}\right] \left\{\begin{array}{c} x_1(k) \\ x_2(k) \\ x_3(k) \end{array}\right\} + \left[\begin{array}{c} 0 \\ 1 \end{array}\right] u \tag{38}$$

The MBRNN was structured according to the above state-space model and then trained by dynamic BP without a regularization parameter. The training session consisted of 1500 sample points generated with random excitation inputs with values between -6.0 and 6.0. One epoch of training was used. The trained MBRNN was then tested on data generated with random inputs from a seed different from that which generated the training data. The values of $\hat{y}_1$ and y_1 for the test session before and after training are shown in Figure 6. The results indicate a potential pitfall associated with dynamic BP as applied to MBRNN. The reason for the poor results in this application is entrapment of the system in a limit cy-

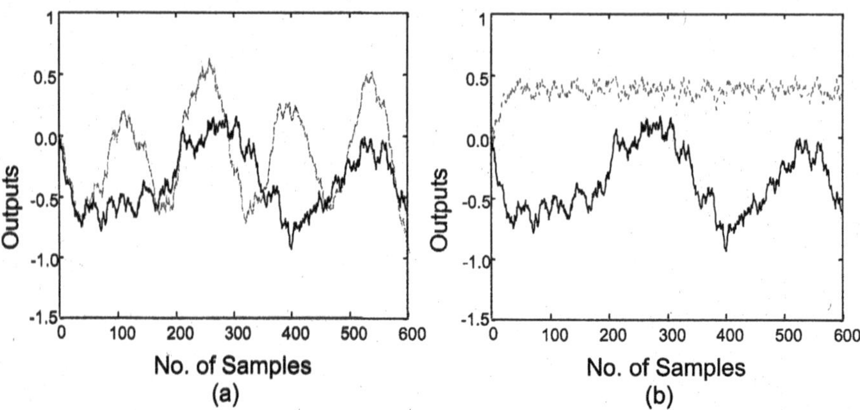

Figure 6. Outputs of the plant and MBRNN before training (a) and after training by dynamic BP without a regularization parameter (b) for Example 2.

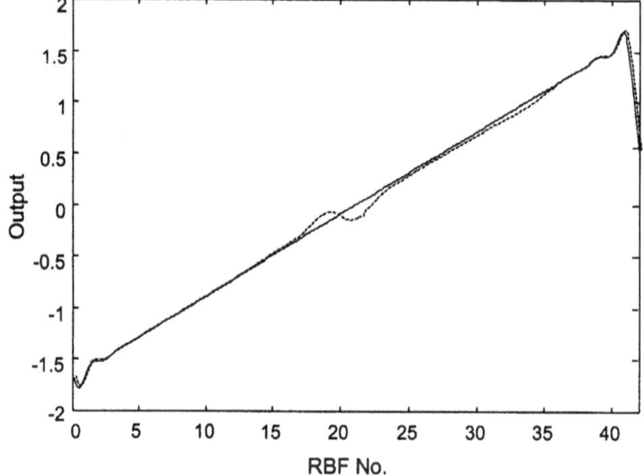

Figure 7. The modified activation function of the a_{22} component causing the limit cycle problem.

cle at $x_1^* = 0.475$ $x_2^* = -0.003$ $x_3^* = -0.0751$[1], which is caused by the shape of the activation function shown for one of the nodes in Figure 7. Similar results to those in Figure 6(b) can be obtained by introducing small excitation values for u to $\mathbf{\Phi}_{net}(\mathbf{x}^*, u)$.

The MBRNN was next trained by EKF using the same training data. The

[1]These points which are the equilibrium points of $\mathbf{x}^* = \mathbf{\Phi}_{net}(\mathbf{x}^*\ 0)$, represent the coordinates of a stable limit cycle. The stability of this limit cycle is verified by the eigenvalues of the Jacobian being inside the unit cycle.

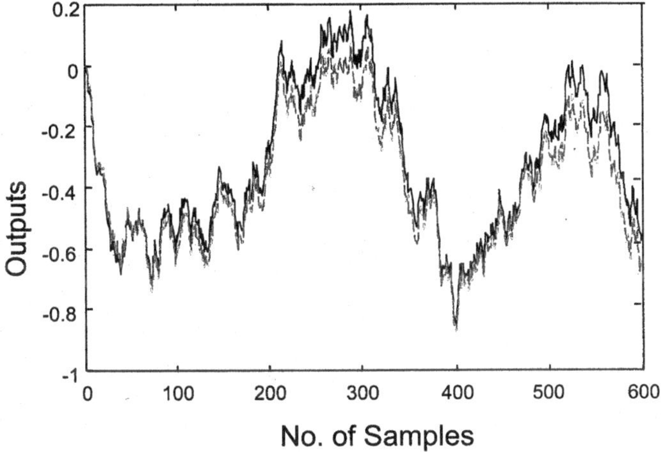

Figure 8. Output 1 of the plant and MBRNN after training by the extended Kalman filter for Example 2.

values of $\hat{y}_1$ and y_1 from this MBRNN are shown in Figure 8, indicating a much better representation by MBRNN.

Example 3:

$$\begin{bmatrix} (m_1+m_2)a_1^2 + m_2a_2^2 + 2m_2a_1a_2\cos\theta_2 & m_2a_2^2 + m_2a_1a_2\cos\theta_2 \\ m_2a_2^2 + m_2a_1a_2\cos\theta_2 & m_2a_2^2 \end{bmatrix} \begin{bmatrix} \ddot{\theta}_1 \\ \ddot{\theta}_2 \end{bmatrix} + \\ + \begin{bmatrix} -m_2a_1a_2(2\dot{\theta}_1\dot{\theta}_2 + \dot{\theta}_2^2)\sin\theta_2 \\ m_2a_1a_2\dot{\theta}_1^2\sin\theta_2 \end{bmatrix} + \\ + \begin{bmatrix} (m_1+m_2)ga_1\cos\theta_1 + m_2ga_2\cos(\theta_1+\theta_2) \\ m_2ga_2\cos(\theta_1+\theta_2) \end{bmatrix} = \begin{bmatrix} \tau_1 \\ \tau_2 \end{bmatrix} \tag{39}$$

The above model represents the dynamics of a two-link plannar elbow robot arm [24], where θ_1 and θ_2 represent the angular positions of the two arms, m_1 and m_2 denote their masses, and τ_1 and τ_2 represent the torques exerted on the arms. If we define the position vector $\mathbf{q}$ as $\mathbf{q} = [\theta_1\ \theta_2]^T$ and the generalized force vector τ as $\tau = [\tau_1\ \tau_2]^T$, then the above state-space equation can be written as

$$M(\mathbf{q})\ddot{\mathbf{q}} + V(\mathbf{q}, \dot{\mathbf{q}}) + G(\mathbf{q}) = \tau \tag{40}$$

where $M(\mathbf{q})$ denotes the inertia matrix, $V(\mathbf{q}, \dot{\mathbf{q}})$ represents the Coriolis/centripetal vector, and $G(\mathbf{q})$ denotes the gravity vector.

The linear state-space form of the above model about $\mathbf{q} = [0\ 0]^T$, $\dot{\mathbf{q}} = [0\ 0]^T$ was obtained as

$$\begin{Bmatrix} x_1(k+1) \\ x_2(k+1) \\ x_3(k+1) \\ x_4(k+1) \end{Bmatrix} = \begin{bmatrix} 1.0 & 0.0 & 0.01 & 0.0 \\ 0.0 & 1.0 & 0.0 & 0.01 \\ 0.0 & 0.0 & 1.0 & 0.0 \\ 0.0 & 0.0 & 0.0 & 1.0 \end{bmatrix} \begin{Bmatrix} x_1(k) \\ x_2(k) \\ x_3(k) \\ x_4(k) \end{Bmatrix} + \begin{bmatrix} 0.0001 & -0.0002 \\ -0.0002 & 0.0004 \\ 0.02 & -0.04 \\ -0.04 & 0.085 \end{bmatrix} \begin{Bmatrix} \tau_1 \\ \tau_2 \end{Bmatrix}$$

$$\begin{Bmatrix} y_1(k) \\ y_2(k) \\ y_3(k) \\ y_4(k) \end{Bmatrix} = \begin{bmatrix} 1.0 & 0.0 & 0.0 & 0.0 \\ 0.0 & 1.0 & 0.0 & 0.0 \\ 0.0 & 0.0 & 1.0 & 0.0 \\ 0.0 & 0.0 & 0.0 & 1.0 \end{bmatrix} \begin{Bmatrix} x_1(k) \\ x_2(k) \\ x_3(k) \\ x_4(k) \end{Bmatrix}$$

where $\mathbf{x}^T = [\mathbf{q}\ \dot{\mathbf{q}}]$. The MBRNN was structured according to the above state-space model and then trained by EKF. The training session consisted of 5500 sample points generated by random excitation inputs with values between -1.0 through 1.0 and -0.5 through 0.5 for two inputs, respectively. One epoch of training was used. The trained MBRNN was then tested on data generated with random inputs from a seed different from that which generated the training data. The values of $\hat{y}$ and y before and after training are shown in Figures 9 and 10, respectively. The results indicate that the outputs of the trained MBRNN are quite close to the plant outputs, again despite the relatively short training session used by MBRNN.

5 Application in Fault Diagnosis

Fault diagnosis is important for safety-critical and intelligent control systems. The correct detection or prediction of faults will avoid system shutdowns or catastrophes which may involve human lives and material damage.

Fault Detection and Isolation (FDI) solutions have been developed within various disciplines. For systems with analytical models, Model-Based FDI offers a system theoretic approach, where the model is used to obtain

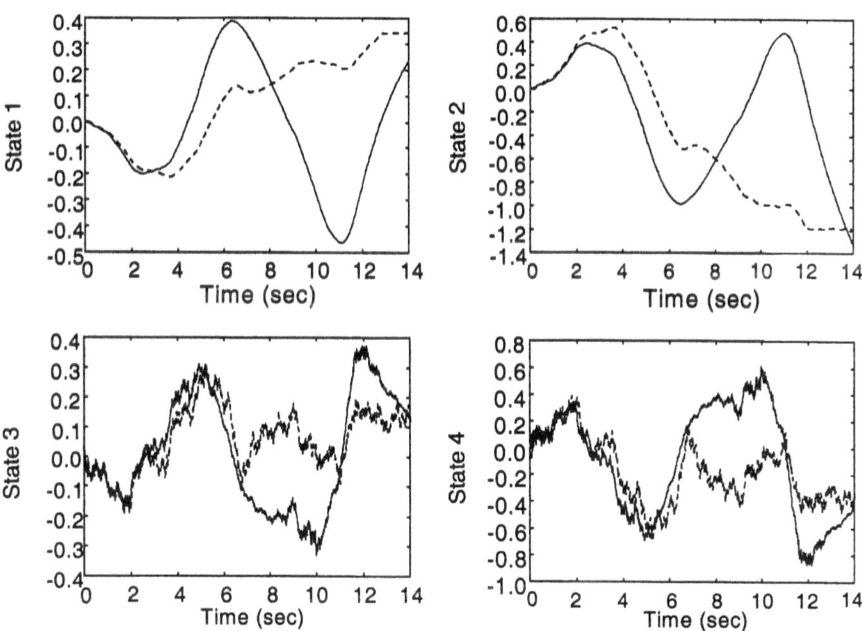

Figure 9. Four states of the plant and MBRNN before training for Example 3.

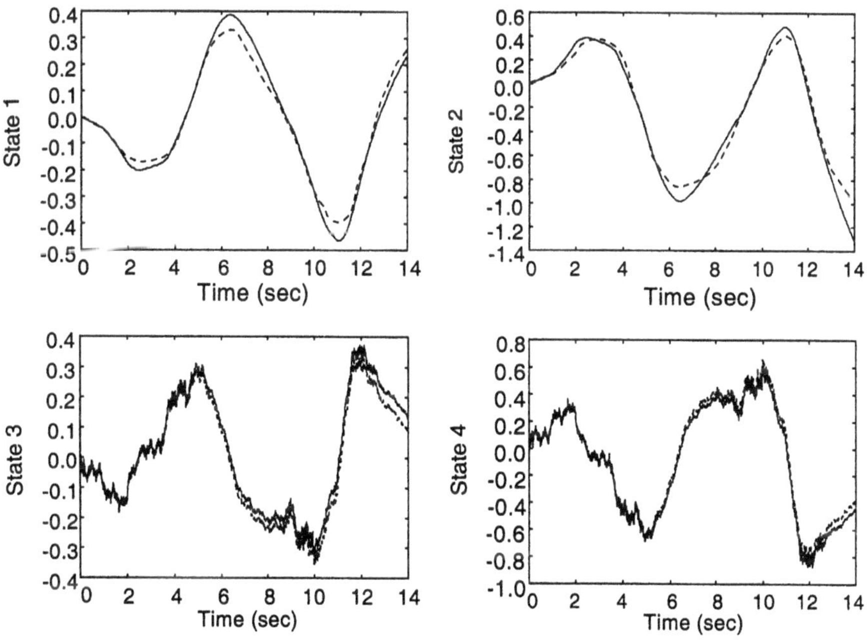

Figure 10. Four states of the plant and MBRNN after training for Example 3.

residuals which represent the difference between the measurements and their modeled values [25]. For cases where the residuals do not provide an adequate basis for fault diagnosis, Statistical FDI can be used to complement the analysis [26]. In a more abstract framework, Knowledge-Based FDI methods rely on the causal knowledge of the system when complexity precludes analytical modeling [27]. In contrast to the above approaches, Neural Network-Based FDI mostly ignores the knowledge of the process and provides an empirical solution by defining the fault signatures based on measurement-fault data. Although neural networks have been developed that can incorporate the knowledge of the process in their formulation [28], they are mostly used in a 'black box' format and rely solely on training to define the fault signatures [29].

The utility of the MBRNN is demonstrated in application to the IFAC Benchmark Problem [30]. This benchmark problem represents the nonlinear model of an electro-mechanical position governor used in speed control of large diesel engines. The governor consists of a brushless DC motor that connects to a rod through an epicyclic gear and arm. Two faults are considered (simulated) for this value: (1) a position sensor fault, and (2) an actuator fault. The main source of uncertainty is the load torque, which represents an unknown input.

5.1 The Benchmark Problem

The industrial actuator benchmark was based on a test facility built by the researchers at Aalborg University [30]. The equipment simulates the actuator part of a speed governor for large diesel engines. The governor is a device that controls the shaft rotational speed in a diesel engine. It regulates the amount of fuel loaded into each cylinder by controlling the position of a common control rod - equivalent to the throttle in an automobile. The rod can be moved by an actuator motor, which is part of the governor. The current and velocity of the motor are controlled by a power drive made in analog and transistor switch mode technology. The position of the rod is controlled by a micro-processor based digital controller. The system is thus a combination of continuous and discrete-time components. A nonlinear model of this actuator has been made available in Simulink^{TM} format, and its linear model, which is the basis for the model-based solutions, is defined as:

$$\begin{aligned} \mathbf{x}(k+1) &= \mathbf{\Phi}\mathbf{x}(k) + \mathbf{\Gamma}\mathbf{u}(k) + \mathbf{E}_1\mathbf{u}_d(k) + \mathbf{F}_1\mathbf{f}_a(k) \\ \mathbf{y}(k) &= \mathbf{C}\mathbf{x}(k) + \mathbf{E}_2\mathbf{u}_d(k) + \mathbf{F}_2\mathbf{f}_s(k) \end{aligned}$$

$$\mathbf{\Phi} = \begin{bmatrix} 0.51 & -0.36 & 0 \\ 0.63 & -9.09 \times 10^{-2} & 0 \\ 5.41 \times 10^{-5} & 3.94 \times 10^{-5} & 1 \end{bmatrix}$$

$$\mathbf{\Gamma} = \begin{bmatrix} 0.38 \\ 1.06 \\ 7.06 \times 10^{-5} \end{bmatrix}, \ \mathbf{F}_1 = \begin{bmatrix} -0.49 \\ 0.63 \\ 5.41 \times 10^{-5} \end{bmatrix}$$

$$\mathbf{C} = \begin{bmatrix} 0 & 1 & 0 \\ 0 & 0 & 0.98 \end{bmatrix}, \ \mathbf{F}_2 = \begin{bmatrix} 0 \\ 0.98 \end{bmatrix}$$

where u_d represents the unknown torque disturbance, f_a denotes the actuator fault, and f_s represents the sensor fault. Two possible faults can be simulated for the industrial actuator:

1. A temporary feedback element fault caused by loss of contact of the feedback wiper due to wear and dust. The fault is intermittent, and lasts for 0.2 seconds.

2. A component fault caused by malfunctioning of the end-stop switch. This can be caused by a broken wire or a defect in the switch element due to mechanical vibration, resulting in the power drive delivering only positive current.

Both of the above faults are multiplicative in nature, but they are represented as additive faults because most FDI methods are suitable for additive faults. The particular difficulty in FDI of the benchmark is that the load torque acts as an unknown disturbance input signal, which has a similar effect as the actuator fault. This can be noted from the coefficient vector $\mathbf{E} = [-1.21 * 10^{-2},\ 1.55 * 10^{-2},\ 1.33 * 10^{-6}]$ of the disturbance d being approximately linearly aligned with the fault weighting vector $\mathbf{F}_a = [-0.493,\ 0.635,\ 5.42 * 10^{-5}]$ of the actuator fault f_a. That is, the angle between these two vectors is so small that it is very difficult to differentiate between the disturbance and actuator fault.

Briefly, as a solution to this problem, Bogh [31] used model-based and statistical FDI to design a bank of observers to differentiate between faults and unknown inputs through multiple-hypothesis testing. It was shown that statistical testing was needed to improve the detectability of faults. In a similar approach, Grainger et al. [32] proposed a set of sequential probability ratio tests of the innovations from a bank of Kalman filters to detect the change in the dynamics of the system. Hofling and coworkers [33] treated the detection of sensor fault and actuator fault separately. They designed a simple observer-based residual generator with adaptive threshold to detect the sensor fault, and used signal-processing to detect the actuator fault. In a frequency domain approach, Garcia et al. [34] used H_∞-based optimization to design observers with residuals that are robust to unknown inputs (noises) and sensitive to the faults. Using the Extended Kalman Filter (EKF) as a parameter estimator, Walker and Huang [35] proposed to detect the faults through estimation of the position sensor bias and the actuator bias. This work showed that the EKF, designed according to a linear model, could detect the fault accurately when the system was excited by small inputs, but the magnitude of the sensor fault residuals were affected by the actuator fault for large inputs. Eigen-Structure Assignment (ESA) was also used to design residual generator observers that produced residuals de-coupled from disturbance inputs [36]. This method was successful in detecting faults in presence of small inputs and disturbances, but it was unable to detect the actuator fault for large input signals.

5.2 Traditional Neural Network Application

An overview of neural networks (NNs) FDI application of is presented in [29]. In most applications, the NNs have a black box format, so they require for training measurement data from normal operation of the plant as well as during fault occurrences. For example, a dynamic plant described by the nonlinear ARMA model:

$$\begin{aligned}\mathbf{y}(k) &= F(\mathbf{y}(k-1), \mathbf{y}(k-2), \cdots, \mathbf{y}(k-n_y),\\ &\quad \mathbf{u}(k), \mathbf{u}(k-1), \cdots, \mathbf{u}(k-n_u),\\ &\quad \mathbf{d}(k), \cdots, \mathbf{d}(k-n_d), \mathbf{f}(k), \cdots, \mathbf{f}(k-n_f))\end{aligned}$$

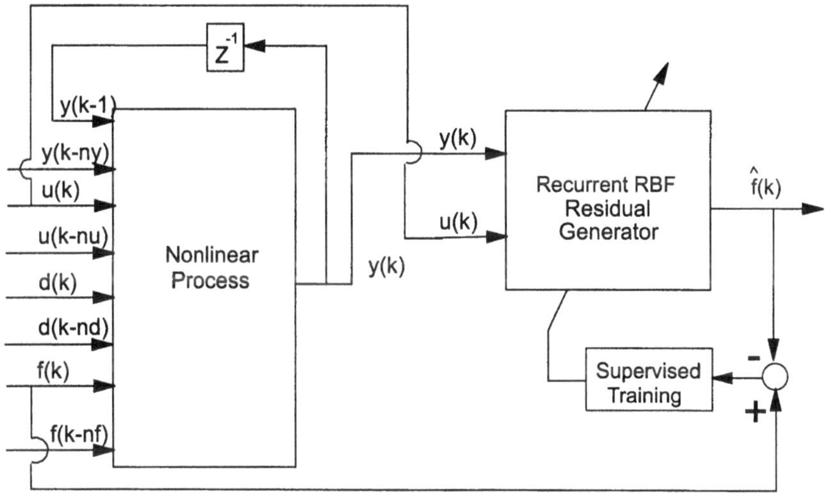

Figure 11. Application of recurrent neural networks in fault diagnosis of nonlinear plants (Scenario 1).

can be modeled by a recurrent NN using as inputs the present values of the plant inputs and outputs to generate as output an estimate of the fault. In the above model, $\mathbf{d}$ represents disturbance to the plant, and $\mathbf{f}$ denotes the sensor fault, actuator fault, or component fault. Using recurrent NNs, one scenario for residual generation is as shown in Figure 11, where the NN provides a nonlinear mapping from the measurement space $(Y,\ U)$ to fault space (F). The nonlinear mapping demand from the NN can be relaxed in cases where a linear model of the plant is available. In such cases, the difference Δy between the measured output and the output of the linear model can be used as the input to the NN (see Figure 12). In this second scenario, the NN is required to only represent the local difference between the linear model and the plant, so the demand for training is reduced considerably.

Both scenarios (Figures 11 and 12) were applied to the benchmark problem. The recurrent neural network used in this application was the RBF network proposed by Obradovic [7] (see Figure 13), where the number of RBFs are increased on-line during training so as to capture the dynamics of the plants. For the benchmark application, two RBF networks were trained in parallel, one to estimate the sensor fault and the other to detect the actuator fault. The number of RBFs in the single layer of each net-

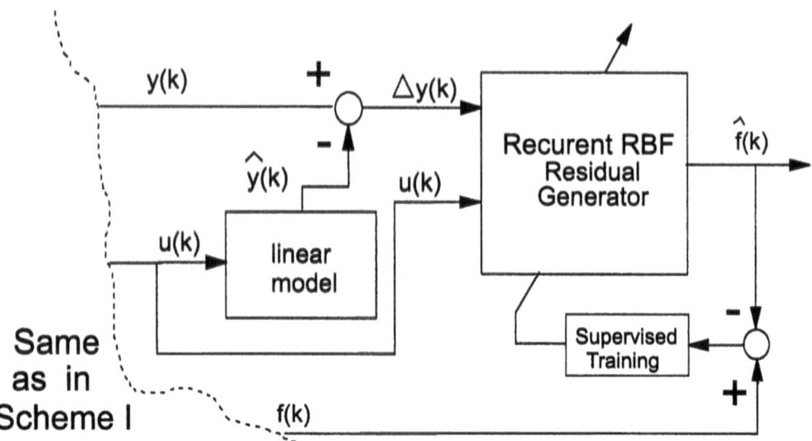

Figure 12. Application of recurrent neural networks in fault diagnosis of non-linear plants (Scenario 2).

work were respectively 215 and 200, that were determined based on 5000 sample points obtained from pseudo-random excitation of the nonlinear benchmark model. For details of the training algorithm, which is based on EKF, the reader can refer to [7]. The results from the first scenario are included in Figure 14, and those from the second scenario are shown in Figure 15. The results indicate that with the first scenario neither of the faults (actuator fault and sensor fault) could be identified with large input signals. The second scenario was successful in isolating the sensor fault, but it too had difficulty identifying the actuator fault. The relative success of the second scenario arises from the incorporation of the output of the linear model, which reduces the demand for mapping by the NN.

5.3 Result from Application of MBRNN

The MBRNN was applied to the benchmark problem by formatting it according to the Eigen-Structure Assignment (ESA) observer of Jorgensen et al. [36]. The motivation here is to investigate the possibility of extending the ESA observer to beyond the restrictions of linearity. The format of this observer as designed by Jorgensen et al. has the form [36]:

$$\hat{\mathbf{x}}(k+1) = \mathbf{\Phi}\hat{\mathbf{x}}(k) + \mathbf{\Gamma}\mathbf{u}(k) + \mathbf{K}(\mathbf{y}(k) - \mathbf{C}\hat{\mathbf{x}}(k)) \tag{41}$$

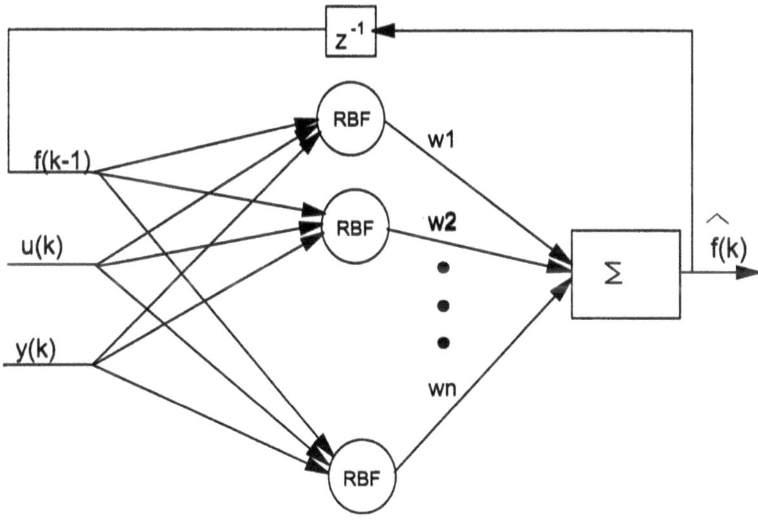

Figure 13. The configuration of the recurrent RBF network used in residual generation. The topology of this network is adapted during training by increasing the number of RBFs.

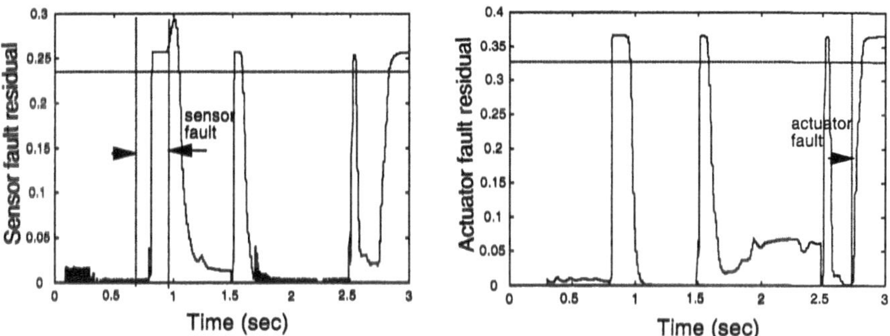

Figure 14. Residuals obtained from application of a recurrent neural network (Scenario 1).

where $\hat{\mathbf{x}}$ represents the estimated states. From this observer, the vectors of state and output estimation errors, $\mathbf{e}_x$ and $\mathbf{e}_y$ can be obtained as:

$$\begin{aligned}
\mathbf{e}_x(k+1) &= \mathbf{x}(k+1) - \hat{\mathbf{x}}(k+1) \\
\mathbf{e}_x(k+1) &= \mathbf{G}\mathbf{e}_x(K) + (\mathbf{E}_1 - \mathbf{K}\mathbf{E}_2)\mathbf{u}_d(k) + \\
&\quad \mathbf{F}_1\mathbf{f}_a(k) - \mathbf{K}\mathbf{F}_2\mathbf{f}_s(k) \qquad (42) \\
\mathbf{e}_y(k) &= \mathbf{y}(k) - \mathbf{C}\hat{\mathbf{x}}(k) \\
&= \mathbf{C}\mathbf{e}_x(k) + \mathbf{E}_2\mathbf{u}_d(k) + \mathbf{F}_2\mathbf{f}_s(k) \qquad (43)
\end{aligned}$$

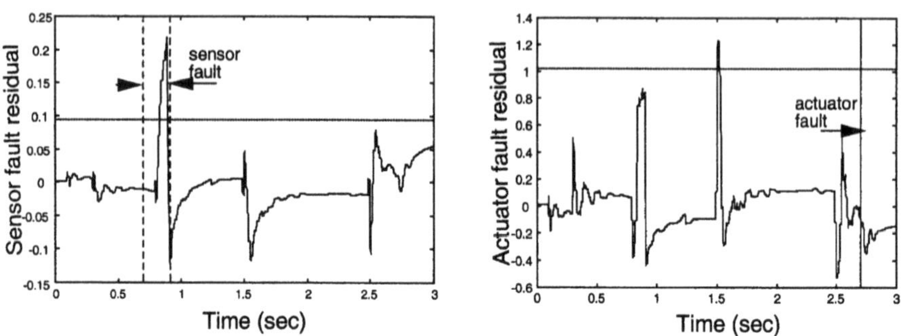

Figure 15. Residuals obtained from application of a recurrent neural network (Scenario 2).

where $\mathbf{G} = \mathbf{\Phi} - \mathbf{KC}$. To realize a fault detection and isolation scheme, a weighting matrix $\mathbf{H}$ is required to pre-multiply $\mathbf{e}_y$ to obtain

$$\mathbf{r}(k) = \mathbf{He}_y(k) = \mathbf{HCe}_x(k) + \mathbf{HE}_2\mathbf{u}_d(k) + \mathbf{HF}_2\mathbf{f}_s(k) \quad (44)$$

Briefly, the basic challenge of the design is to define the $\mathbf{H}$ and $\mathbf{C}$ matrices so that all the rows of $\mathbf{HC}$ are equal to the left eigenvectors of $\mathbf{G}$ (left eigen-structure assignment), or the columns of $\mathbf{F}_1$ and $\mathbf{KF}_2$ are equal to the right eigenvectors of $\mathbf{G}$ (right eigen-structure assignment) [37]. For the benchmark problem, the $\mathbf{K}$ and $\mathbf{H}$ were defined as [36]

$$\mathbf{K} = \begin{bmatrix} 0.515 & -0.195e-6 \\ 0.814 & -0.335e-6 \\ 0.799 & 1.038 \end{bmatrix}$$

$$\mathbf{H} = \mathbf{H}_1 + z^{-1}\mathbf{H}_2 = \begin{bmatrix} 0.978 & 0 \\ 0 & 0 \end{bmatrix} + z^{-1} \begin{bmatrix} 1.008 & 0.328e-6 \\ 0 & 0 \end{bmatrix}$$

which led to the observer defined as

$$\begin{Bmatrix} \hat{\mathbf{x}}(k+1) \\ \hat{\mathbf{x}}(k) \end{Bmatrix} = \begin{bmatrix} \mathbf{\Phi} - \mathbf{KC} & 0 \\ I & 0 \end{bmatrix} \begin{Bmatrix} \hat{\mathbf{x}}(k) \\ \hat{\mathbf{x}}(k-1) \end{Bmatrix} + \begin{bmatrix} \mathbf{\Gamma} & \mathbf{K} \\ 0 & 0 \end{bmatrix} \begin{Bmatrix} \mathbf{u}(k) \\ \mathbf{y}(k) \end{Bmatrix} \quad (45)$$

$$\mathbf{r}(k) = \left[\ -\mathbf{H}_1\mathbf{C} \quad -\mathbf{H}_2\mathbf{C}\ \right] \left\{ \begin{array}{c} \hat{\mathbf{x}}(k) \\ \hat{\mathbf{x}}(k-1) \end{array} \right\} + \left[\ \mathbf{H}_1 \quad \mathbf{H}_2\ \right] \left\{ \begin{array}{c} \mathbf{y}(k) \\ \mathbf{y}(k-1) \end{array} \right\} \tag{46}$$

The above observer was used to formulate the MBRNN, so that it can be subsequently trained to adapt to the nonlinearities of the plant. For training, the output during normal conditions, and with disturbance and various faults were generated by pseudo-random excitation of the nonlinear benchmark model. About 1000 sample points were used for training. The sensor fault was easy to detect, as was demonstrated by most linear methods. Therefore, only the detection of the actuator fault was attempted here.

The residuals provided by the MBRNN before and after training are shown in Figure 16. Before training, the output of MBRNN is identical to that of the linear observer by Jorgensen et al [36]. The results indicate that the residual violates the threshold at several instances during normal operation which would cause false alarms. After training of the MBRNN, however, the residual values during normal operation are attenuated to indicate more clearly the presence of the actuator fault.

6 Conclusion

A model-based recurrent neural network (MBRNN) is introduced which can be formulated according to the analytical knowledge of the plant. This network is defined to initially emulate a linearized state-space model of the plant. It can then be trained to accommodate the nonlinearities of the plant by modifying its activation functions, which are defined as contours of radial basis functions comprising each node. As such, the MBRNN has the structure of a modular network, where each module represents a node. Both dynamic backpropagation and the extended Kalman filter (EKF) can be used for training. Simulation results indicate that the EKF provides more satisfactory performance. The results also indicate that the MBRNN requires significantly less training than ordinary recurrent networks.

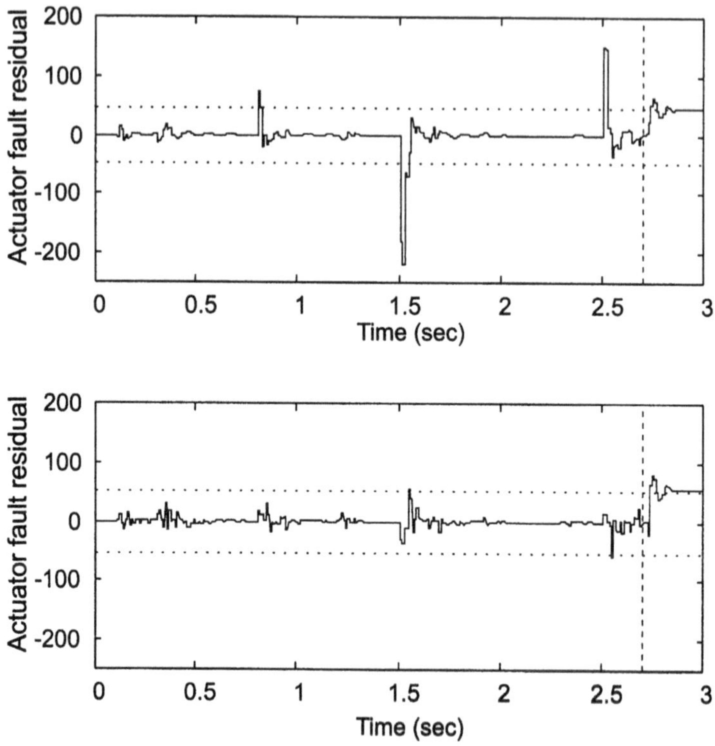

Figure 16. Top plot: the residuals obtained from the eigen-structure method (MBRNN before training); bottom plot: residuals after training MBRNN.

The MBRNN will have potential utility in control applications. A common drawback of most neuro-control schemes is the extensive training required to model the plant by the neural network. In these cases, training is needed for both establishing the topology of the network, as well as adjusting its connection weights. MBRNN not only provides a good initial structure for the plant model, but defines the connection weights of this neural network model according to the linearized model of the plant. As such, MBRNN provides a functional initial estimate for the plant model that can be used for control purposes from the beginning of operation and that can be subsequently improved over time with training.

The application of (MBRNN) is demonstrated in fault diagnosis as well. Since the topology and initial weights of the MBRNN are defined according to a state space model, it can be formulated according to any model-based FDI solution at first and subsequently trained to adapt to the nonlinearities of the plant. This approach is demonstrated for the IFAC Benchmark Problem, for which a variety of solutions exist. The results indicate that the MBRNN can improve these solutions considerably with little training.

Acknowledgement

This research is supported by the National Science Foundation (Grant No. CMS-9523087).

References

[1] Nerrand, O., Roussel-Ragot, P., Urbani, D., Personnaz, L., and Dreyfus, G. (1994), "Training recurrent neural networks: why and how? An illustration in dynamical process modeling," *IEEE Trans. on Neural Networks*, vol. 5, no. 2, pp. 178–184.

[2] Albus, J. (1975), "A new approach to manipulator control: the cerebellar model articulation controller," *ASME J. of Dynamic System, Measurement and Control*, vol. 97, pp. 220–227.

[3] Miller, W.T. (1989), "Real time application of neural networks for sensor-based control of robots with vision," *IEEE Trans. on Systems, Man, and Cybernetics*, vol. 19, pp. 825–831.

[4] Parlos, A.G., Chong, K.T., and Atiya, A.F. (1994), "Application of the recurrent multilayer perceptron in modeling complex process dynamics," *IEEE Trans. on Neural Networks*, vol. 5, no. 2, pp. 255–266.

[5] Srinivasan, A. and Batur, C. (1994), "Hopfield/art-1 neural network-based fault detection and isolation," *IEEE Trans. on Neural Networks*, vol. 5, no. 6, pp. 890–899.

[6] Srinivasan, B., Prasad, U.R., and Rao, N.J. (1994), "Back propagation through adjoints for the identification of nonlinear dynamic systems using recurrent neural models," *IEEE Trans. on Neural Networks*, vol. 5, no. 2, pp. 213–227.

[7] Obradovic, D. (1996), "On-line training of recurrent neural networks with continuous topology adaptation," *IEEE Trans. on Neural Networks*, vol. 7, pp. 222–228.

[8] Ku, C.C. and Lee, K.Y. (1995), "Diagonal recurrent neural networks for dynamic systems control," *IEEE Trans. on Neural Networks*, vol. 6, no. 1, pp. 144–156.

[9] Denoeux, T. and Lengelle, R. (1993), "Initializing back propagation networks with prototypes," *IEEE Trans. on Neural Networks*, vol. 6, pp. 351–363.

[10] Narendra, K.S. and Parthasarathy, K. (1990), "Identification and control of dynamical systems using neural networks," *IEEE Trans. on Neural Networks*, vol. 1, no. 1, pp. 4–27.

[11] Jang, J.S. and Sun, C.T. (1993), "Functional equivalence between radial basis function networks and fuzzy inference systems," *IEEE Trans. on Neural Networks*, vol. 4, pp. 156–159.

[12] Hunt, K.J., Haas, R., and Murray-Smith, R. (1996), "Extending the functional equivalence of radial basis function networks and fuzzy inference systems," *IEEE Trans. on Neural Networks*, vol. 7, pp. 776–781.

[13] Towell, G.G. and Shavlik, J.W. (1994), "Knowledge-based artificial neural networks," *Artificial Intelligence*, vol. 70, pp. 110–165.

[14] Omlin, C.W. and Giles, C.L. (1996), "Rule revision with recurrent neural networks," *IEEE Trans. on Knowledge and Data Engineering*, vol. 8, no. 1, pp. 183–197.

[15] Livstone, M.M., Farrell, J.A., and Baker, W.L. (1992), "A computationally efficient algorithm for training recurrrent connectionist networks," *ACC/WM2*, pp. 555–561.

[16] Hocking, R.R. (1976), "The analysis and selection of variables in linear regression," *Biometrics*, vol. 32, pp. 1–49.

[17] Hocking, R.R. (1983), "Developments in linear regression methodology," *Technometrics*, vol. 25, pp. 219–249.

[18] Orr, M.J.L. (1996), "Introduction to radial basis function networks," Tech. Rep., Centre for Cognitive Science, University of Edinburgh.

[19] Werbos, P.J. (1990), "Backpropagation through time: what it does and how to do it," *Proc. IEEE*, vol. 78, no. 10, pp. 1550–1560.

[20] Narendra, K.S. and Parthasarathy, K. (1991), "Gradient methods for the optimization of dynamical systems containing neural networks," *IEEE Trans. on Neural Networks*, vol. 2, no. 2, pp. 252–262.

[21] Gelb, A. (1974), *Applied Optimal Estimation*, Cambridge, MA: MIT Press.

[22] Rumelhart, D.E. and McClelland, J.L. (1986), *Parallel distributed processing: Explorations in microstructure of cognition*, Cambridge, MA: MIT Press.

[23] Hagan, M.T., Demuth, H.B., and Beale, M. (1996), *Neural Networks Design*, Boston: PWS Publishing Company.

[24] Lewis, F.L., Abdallah, C.T., and Dawson, D.M. (1993), *Control of Robot Manipulators*, Macmillan Publishing Company.

[25] Frank, P.M. (1990), "Fault diagnosis in dynamic systems using analytical and knowledge-based redundancy - a survey and some new results," *Automatica*, vol. 26, no. 2, pp. 459–474.

[26] Basseville, M. (1988), "Detecting changes in signals and systems - a survey," *Automatica*, vol. 24, no. 3, pp. 309–326.

[27] De Kleer, J. and Williams, B.C. (1987), "Diagnosing multiple faults," *Artificial Intelligence*, vol. 32, pp. 97–130.

[28] Jammu, V.B., Danai, K., and Lewicki, D.G. (1998), "Strucuture-based connectionist network for fault diagnosis of helicopter gearboxes," *ASME J. of Mechanical Design*, vol. 120, no. 1, pp. 100–105.

[29] Patton, R.J. and Chen, J. (1996), "Neural networks in fault diagnosis of nonlinear dynamic systems," *Engineering Simulation*, vol. 13, pp. 905–924.

[30] Blanke, M. and Patton, R.J. (1995), "Industrial actuator benchmark for fault detection and isolation," *Control Eng. Practice*, vol. 3, no. 12, pp. 1727–1730.

[31] Bogh, S. (1995), "Multiple hypothesis-testing approach to fdi for the industrial actuator benchmark," *Control Eng. Practice*, vol. 3, no. 12, pp. 1763–1768.

[32] Grainger, R.W., Holst, J., Isaksson, A.J., and Ninness, B.M. (1995), "A parametric statistical approach to fdi for the industrial actuator benchmark," *Control Eng. Practice*, vol. 3, no. 12, pp. 1757–1762.

[33] Hofling, T., Pfeufer, T., Deibert, R., and Isermann, R. (1995), "An observer and signal-processing approach to fdi for the industrial actuator benchmark test," *Control Eng. Practice*, vol. 3, no. 12, pp. 1741–1746.

[34] Garcia, E.A., Koppen-Seliger, B., and Frank, P.M. (1995), "A frequency domain approach to residual generation for the industrial actuator benchmark," *Control Eng. Practice*, vol. 3, pp. 1747–1750.

[35] Walker, B.K. and Huang, K.Y. (1995), "Fdi by extended kalman filter parameter estimation for an industrial actuator benchmark," *Control Eng. Practice*, vol. 3, no. 12, pp. 1769–1774.

[36] Jorgensen, R.B., Patton, R.J., and Chen, J. (1995), "An eigenstructure assignment approach to fdi for the industrial actuator benchmark test," *Control Eng. Practice*, vol. 3, no. 12, pp. 1751–1756.

[37] Patton, R.J. and Chen, J.A. (1991), "A review of parity space approaches to fault diagnosis," No. 1, (Baden-Baden), pp. 239–255.

Index

List of Contributors

K. Danai
Department of Mechanical and Industrial Engineering
University of Massachusetts
Amherst, Massachusetts
U.S.A.

J. Diederich
Machine Learning Research Centre
Faculty of Information Technology
Queensland University of Technology
Australia
joachim@fit.qut.edu.au

S.S. Fels
Department of Electrical and Computer Engineering
The University of British Columbia
Vancouver
Canada

C. Gan
(correspondence via Prof. K. Danai)
Department of Mechanical and Industrial Engineering
University of Massachusetts
Amherst, Massachusetts
U.S.A.

J. Ghosh
Department of Electrical and Computer Engineering
The University of Texas
Austin, TX 78712
U.S.A.

J.M. Hogan
Machine Learning Research Centre
Faculty of Information Technology
Queensland University of Technology
hogan@fit.qut.edu.au

A.J. Howell
School of Cognitive and Computing Sciences
University of Sussex, Falmer,
Brighton BN1 9QH
United Kingdom
jonh@cogs.susx.ac.uk

H.A. Kestler
Department of Neural Information Processing and
Department of Medicine II – Cardiology
University of Ulm
D-89069 Ulm
Germany

M. Lehtokangas
Signal Processing Laboratory
Tampere University of Technology
Tampere
Finland

A. Nag
Department of Electrical and Computer Engineering
The University of Texas
Austin, TX 78712
U.S.A.

M. Norris
Machine Learning Research Centre
Faculty of Information Technology
Queensland University of Technology
michaeln@fit.qut.edu.au

J. Saarinen
Signal Processing Laboratory
Tampere University of Technology
Tampere
Finland

A. Saastamoinen
Signal Processing Laboratory
Tampere University of Technology
Tampere
Finland

R. Salomon
Department of Information Technology
University of Zurich
Winterthurerstr. 190
8057 Zurich
salomon@ifi.unizh.ch

F. Schwenker
Department of Neural Information Processing and
Department of Medicine II – Cardiology
University of Ulm
D-89069 Ulm
Germany

K. Takahashi
ATR Media Integration & Communications Research Laboratories
Seika-cho, Soraku-gun
Kyoto 619-0288
Japan
kylyn@mic.atr.co.jp

A. Värri
Signal Processing Laboratory
Tampere University of Technology
Tampere
Finland

J. Weissmann
Department of Information Technology
University of Zurich
Winterthurerstr. 190
8057 Zurich
jody@ifi.unizh.ch